IN OUR HANDS

NATIVE PHOTOGRAPHY, 1890 TO NOW

EDITED BY

JILL AHLBERG YOHE JAIDA GREY EAGLE CASEY RILEY

Minneapolis Institute of Art

Yale | DISTRIBUTED BY YALE UNIVERSITY PRESS, NEW HAVEN AND LONDON

EXHIBITION CURATORS
Jill Ahlberg Yohe
Jaida Grey Eagle
Casey Riley

Minneapolis Institute of Art
October 22, 2023 - January 14, 2024

EDITOR
Jo Ann Reece

DESIGNER
Kevin Coochwytewa

FONTS
Apparat Font Family

DIGITAL IMAGE REPRODUCTIONS
David Anderson

IMAGE ACQUISITIONS AND PERMISSIONS
Joseph Doherty and Emily Rosenberg

INDEXER
David Luljak

PUBLISHING AND PRODUCTION MANAGEMENT
Jim Bindas, Books & Projects, LLC

LIBRARY OF CONGRESS CONTROL NUMBER
2023914712

ISBN
978-0-300-27216-1

This catalogue was published in conjunction with the exhibition "In Our Hands: Native Photography, 1890 to Now," organized by the Minneapolis Institute of Art.

2400 Third Avenue South
Minneapolis, MN 55404
artsmia.org

Inquiries should be addressed to:
Publications Manager
Minneapolis Institute of Art
2400 Third Avenue South
Minneapolis, MN 55404

Distributed by:
Yale University Press
302 Temple Street
P.O. Box 209040
New Haven, CT 06420-9040
yalebooks.com

Printed in Canada

In Our Hands: Native Photography, 1890 to Now is organized by the Minneapolis Institute of Art.

Lead Sponsors:

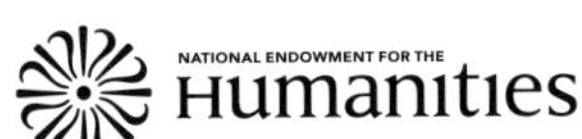

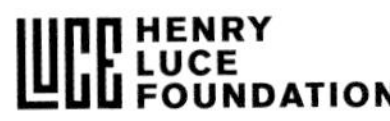

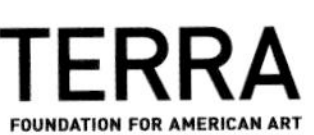

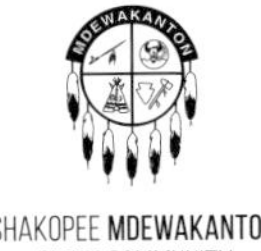

Major Sponsor:

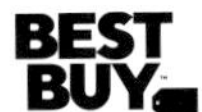

Generous Sponsors:

Lorraine R Hart

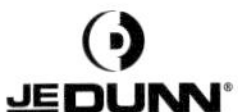

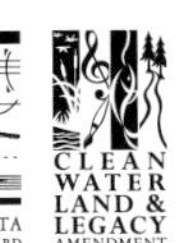

This activity is made possible by the voters of Minnesota through a Minnesota State Arts Board Operating Support grant, thanks to a legislative appropriation from the arts and cultural heritage fund.

Any views, findings, conclusions, or recommendations expressed in this exhibition do not necessarily represent those of the National Endowment for the Humanities.

Cover (top, from left):

B.A. (Benjamin Alfred) Haldane
Tsimshian, 1874-1941
Benjamin A. Haldane self-portrait in studio in Metlakatla, c. 1919-1920
Image courtesy of Ketchikan Museums: Photograph by Benjamin A. Haldane, 89.2.14.21

Ossie Michelin
Inuit, born 1983
Fracking protest, Elsipogtog, New Brunswick, 2013
Courtesy of the artist
© 2013 Ossie Michelin and APTN

Ryan RedCorn
Osage, born 1979
Celena White, 𐓷𐓘𐓻𐓘𐓻𐓟 𐓪𐓬𐓪 (Osage Cook), 2018
Sublimated fabric print
Courtesy of the artist
© Ryan RedCorn

Cover (bottom):

Sarah Sense
Chitimacha / Choctaw, born 1980
Custer and the Cowgirl with Her Gun, 2018
Woven archival inkjet prints on rice paper, pen and ink, wax, tape
Courtesy of Bruce Silverstein Gallery
© Sarah Sense

CONTENTS

DIRECTOR'S FOREWORD

IN OUR HANDS: NATIVE PHOTOGRAPHY, 1890 TO NOW is an exhibition centered upon Indigenous photographic knowledge and practice. Collaboratively organized by Jill Ahlberg Yohe, Associate Curator of Native American Art, guest curator and photojournalist Jaida Grey Eagle (Oglala Lakota), Casey Riley, Chair of Global Contemporary Art, and a Curatorial Council of fourteen advisors, *In Our Hands* heralds a new phase in the photographic representation of Native community, life, and experience. This broadly inclusive exhibition traces the intersecting histories of photography and diverse Indigenous cultures from the Rio Grande to the Arctic Circle, from the late nineteenth to the twenty-first centuries. Most importantly, it celebrates the legacies of First Nations, Métis, Inuit, and Native American photographers and their consequential impact upon the medium.

The work of Native photographers has long been recognized within Indigenous communities and scholarship. Still, many encyclopedic museums of art have only begun to recognize the extraordinary contributions of photographic artists from Native nations. Crucially, *In Our Hands* is rooted in Native knowledge and practice. Decisions for the project were grounded in Indigenous methodologies, the tenets of which include consensus, relationship building, mutual respect, and reciprocity. Native voices guided the project to its completion: from the formation of the checklist to the interpretive frameworks for the show, to the research and writing of the exhibition catalogue.

Mia has been a leader in co-creating exhibitions in partnership with Native artists, exemplified by the acclaimed exhibition *Hearts of Our People: Native Women Artists* (2019). Mia continues to develop long-term, mutually beneficial collaborations and relationships with Native artists, scholars, communities, and organizations.

Mia is grateful for the support of the Shakopee Mdewakanton Sioux Community (SMSC), whose extraordinary generosity to this project included the funding of three consecutive yearlong fellowships. We extend appreciation to our lead sponsors: the National Endowment for the Humanities, the Henry Luce Foundation, the Terra Foundation, and the Shakopee Mdewakanton Sioux Community. We also thank Lorraine R Hart, JE Dunn, and Best Buy for their generous support. This project is also made possible by the voters of Minnesota through a Minnesota State Arts Board Operating Support grant, thanks to a legislative appropriation from the arts and cultural heritage fund.

I am especially grateful to Jill Ahlberg Yohe, Jaida Grey Eagle, and Casey Riley for shepherding this project from its inception, along with the members of the two councils that were central to the creation of this important project. For their generous and insightful contributions to this project, I offer my sincere thanks to Curatorial Council members Rhéanne Chartrand, Mique'l Icesis Dangeli, Rosalie Favell, Tom Jones, Amy Lonetree, Shelley Niro, Veronica Passalacqua, Jami Powell, Jolene Rickard, Cara Romero, Hulleah J. Tsinhnahjinnie, Emily Voelker, Laura Wexler, and Will Wilson, and to Community Council members Alexandra Buffalohead, Sharon Day, Coral Gessner, Rafael Gonzalez, Heidi Inman, Delaney Keshena, Bazille Owen-Reese, Iyekiyapiwin Darlene St. Clair, and Maryam Marne Zafar. Together, they have created an essential exhibition for our time.

KATHERINE CRAWFORD LUBER, PhD
Nivin and Duncan MacMillan Director and President
Minneapolis Institute of Art

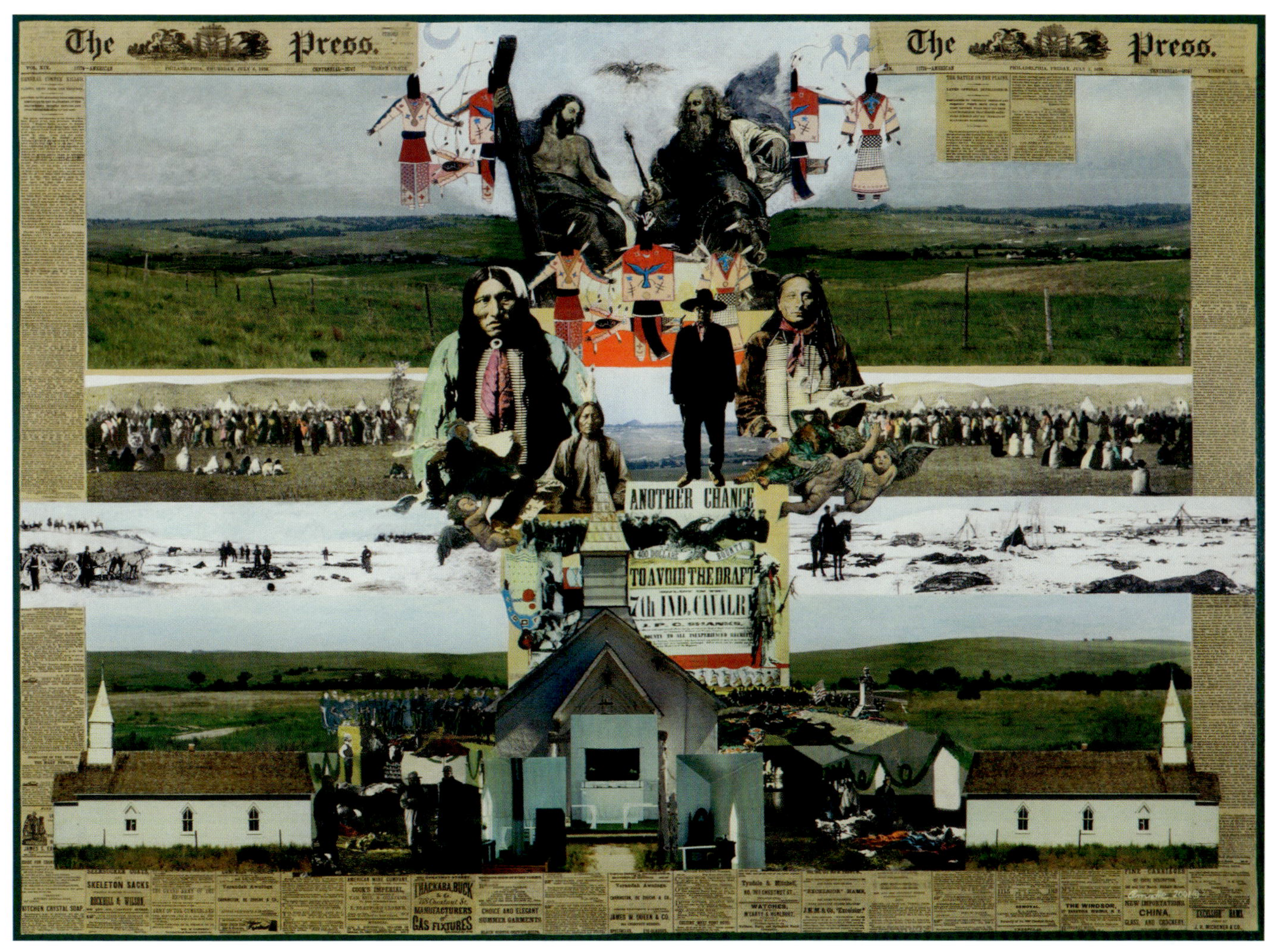

Arthur Amiotte (Wanblí Ta Hócoka Washté
or Good Eagle Center)
Oglala Lakota, born 1942
Wounded Knee III, 2001
Acrylic and collage on canvas
The David and Alfred Smart Museum of Art,
The University of Chicago;
Gift of Miranda and Robert Donnelley
Photograph © 2022 courtesy of The David
and Alfred Smart Museum of Art,
The University of Chicago

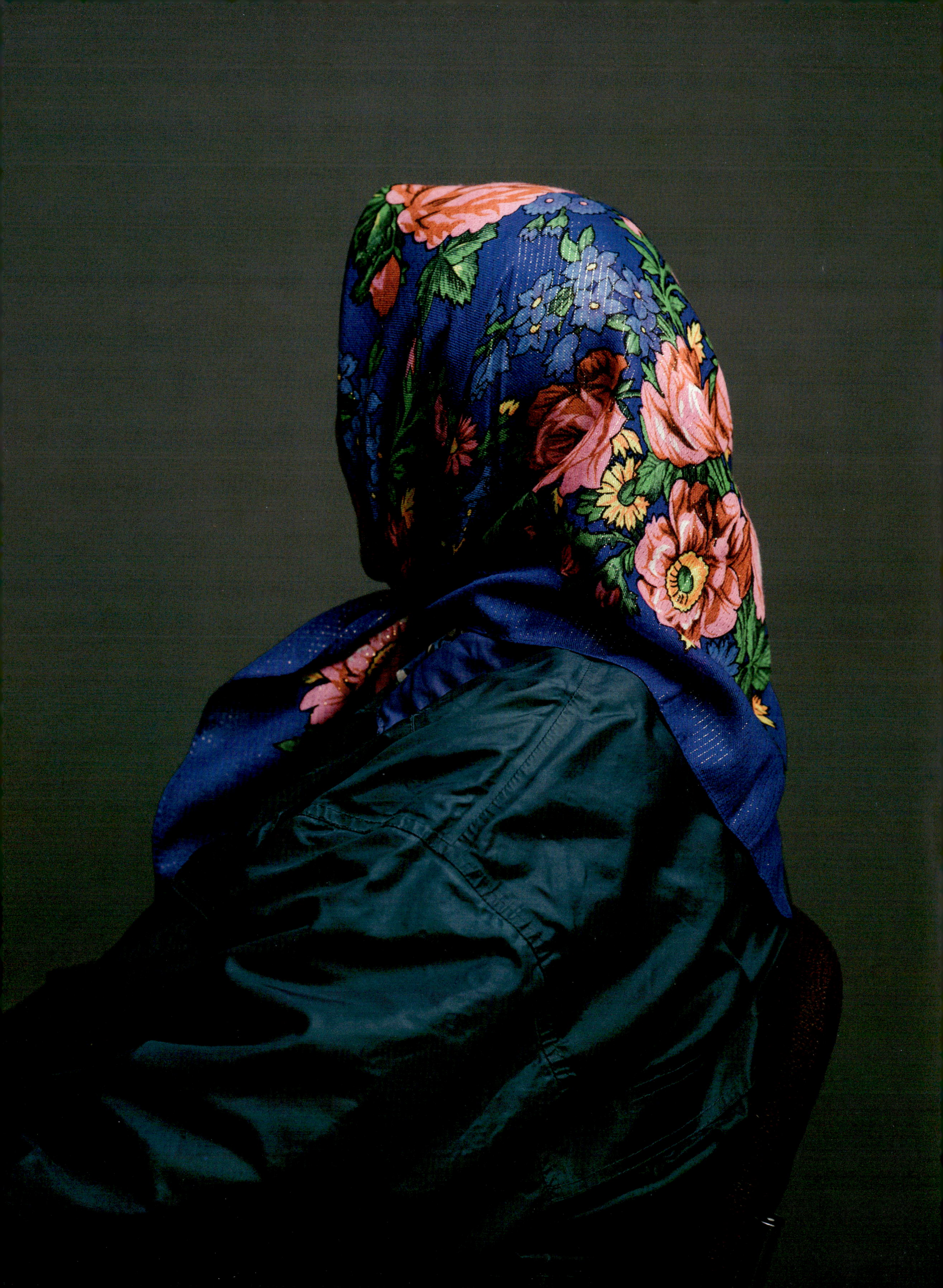

INTRODUCTION AND ACKNOWLEDGEMENTS

OUR PROJECT BEGAN IN THE SPRING OF 2020, when the Minneapolis Institute of Art—Mia—sent its staff home and closed its doors to the public in response to the COVID-19 crisis. One of us, Jaida, had worked a single day as the Shakopee Mdewakanton Fellow at Mia before the shutdown; another, Casey, had just over a year under her belt as Curator of Photography and New Media; our third, Jill, Associate Curator of Native American Art, was in the midst of overseeing the national tour of the acclaimed exhibition and publication, *Hearts of Our People: Native Women Artists (HOOP)*, which had opened at Mia in the summer of 2019. The latter's plans for collaboration with Jaida, a graduate of the Institute of American Indian Arts, noted photojournalist, and enrolled member of the Oglala Lakota nation, were effectively halted by our collective homebound assignment.

Physically separate but digitally connected, we began a conversation around Native photography that quickly engendered more questions than answers. If we were to collaborate on a project for Mia at this challenging moment in time, what might that entail? We were deeply excited by the idea of creating an exhibition sweeping in its historical scope, encompassing not only contemporary artists' practice but extending to the late nineteenth century. We shared a desire to be inclusive in our research and not to privilege certain types of photography over others; any photographs taken by Native people were of interest to us, from those taken with snapshot cameras to ones that were realized with state-of-the-art equipment. Most importantly, we wanted to make a meaningful contribution to the scholarship surrounding Native photographic history, and to illuminate the work of Native photographers in an encyclopedic museum of art—an acknowledgement that such institutions were only beginning to recognize their substantial legacy.

Pat Kane
Algonquin Anishinaabe, Timiskaming First Nation, born 1979
Maryann Mantla, Gameti, 2017
Digital print on wood-fibre veneer
Courtesy of the artist

Because we understood that our knowledge was still nascent, and because of Jill's partnership with Native artists and scholars, we knew that it was vital to consult those who had created and nurtured the field of Native photographic history for decades. Our initial conversations over Zoom, with the artist and Director of the C.N. Gorman Museum, Hulleah J. Tsinhnahjinnie, as well as the artist and Associate Professor of Art History and Visual Studies at Cornell University, Jolene Rickard, awakened us to the complexity and gravity of our assignment, and the necessity of respecting the labor of Native photographic knowledge-sharers and scholars, many of whom were excluded from mainstream institutions of art until the latest years of the 20th century. In short: it was important for us to recognize that any show mounted at Mia would be built upon the foundational scholarship and artistic legacies of the many Native people who preceded us. Our inquiry was not new; we were merely new to a discourse and a tradition that had been self-sustaining from the medium's inception, a parallel ecosystem of photographic knowledge, mutual assistance, collaboration and training, and historical record-keeping that our own training had largely overlooked.

With the help of Jill's relationships in Native art circles, we were able to connect with relevant artists, scholars, and knowledge-sharers who were willing to provide their insight and expertise to a broader project; they were stuck at home, too, and ready for deep engagement in our topic. With funding from the museum, we assembled a group of fourteen mostly Native artists and writers based in the United States and Canada and organized an online discussion in the fall of 2020. The wide-ranging discussion prompted by our questions yielded some important early tenets for the project: the contributions of senior artists were to be respected and upheld, even as the work of newer artists should be included; work by non-Native photographers—especially Edward Curtis—was not to appear on the checklist or to be used comparatively in any way; the voices of Native artists and scholars should be centered in the publication. Even after several hours of conversation, it was clear that we would need a great deal more time to discuss the scope and intentions for our project, and for members of the group to commit to such a collaboration. We met again a month later, and then again several months later; individual conversations with our Council members were ongoing and provided deeper insight still and helped to improve our thinking. Throughout these long Council meetings and individual consultations, we solidified the contours of what would become *In Our Hands: Native Photography, 1890 to Now:* a show created with, for, and by Native people, with a checklist of works selected by our Curatorial Council and a publication that illuminated their expertise.

This edited volume reflects the multivocal nature of our process. With essays by members of our Curatorial Council and reproductions of works by First Nations, Métis, Inuit, and Native American artists, as well as the work of photographers with deep connections to our region, this publication highlights the diversity of perspective encompassing our collaboration. From personal remembrances to scholarly analysis, our authors speak from direct experience and a shared feeling of responsibility to the communities that sustain them. We trust that their voices will remain with you long after reading their words, and hope that their knowledge will inspire your own inquiries into Native photographic history and practice, as well as Native life in the broadest possible sense.

All three editors of this volume wish to thank the many people and organizations who generously supported this project during the challenging years of the pandemic. First and foremost, our most humble thanks go to the Dakota people, as well as our Anishinaabe and Ho-Chunk neighbors. We are equally grateful to the Native artists, public institutions, and local organizations across the United States and Canada who so generously lent work from their collections to this exhibition and publication; without them, this project would not have been possible. We are indebted to the organizations that have committed their financial support to this project, including the National Endowment for the Humanities, the Henry Luce Foundation, the Terra Foundation for American Art, and the Shakopee Mdewakanton Sioux Community (SMSC), among others. Our special thanks to SMSC and Mia Board member Jessamyn Kerchner for her faith in and support of this project, and to Lorraine R Hart, JE Dunn, and Best Buy for so generously supporting this exhibition.

We offer our most heartfelt thanks to the Mia colleagues and contractors who worked tirelessly on this publication and exhibition over the last several years. No project this vast happens without the participation of the entire museum staff, our cherished colleagues and friends, and the following is an invariably incomplete catalog of these.

Our greatest thanks to the Mia leadership team, and especially to our Director, Katie Luber, and Deputy Director and Chief Curator, Matthew Welch, for their steadfast support of this project throughout these turbulent pandemic years. Chief Advancement Officer Julianne Amendola, Senior Advancement Officer Darcy Berus, and the rest of our talented colleagues in Advancement devoted countless hours to shepherding grant proposals through deadlines with patience, yielding early success in the funding of this project and sustaining its growth over several years despite broader economic challenges. Mia's Head Librarian, Janice Lurie, helped us to access resources for our research despite the roadblocks presented by the pandemic and continued to support our knowledge throughout this project. Virajita Singh, Mia's Chief Diversity and Inclusion Officer, and Celina Kane, Executive Assistant to the Deputy Director and Chief Curator, provided vital counsel in the latter stages of this exhibition and publication; we are indebted to them for their steady wisdom and enthusiasm for collaborative curatorial enterprise. Our Head of Exhibition Planning and Strategy, Jennifer Komar Olivarez, was instrumental to the budgeting and project management surrounding such a complicated endeavor. The entire Registration department at Mia worked literally night and day to facilitate complicated loan agreements, shipping and printing schedules, and more; heartfelt thanks to Brian Kraft, Kara Furman, Megan Dischinger, Maggie Davis, and Leslie Ory Llewellen for their excellent work on this project. Former Mia Content Strategist Alex Bortolot and Manager of Audience Research and Impact Alice Anderson, in collaboration with outside consultant Nicole Martin Rogers (White Earth Nation descent), provided vital insight and support in shaping the interpretive framework and content within this show for Mia's audiences, striving to create as accessible and inclusive an experience as possible for our visitors. The visionary talent of Mia's Exhibition Designer, Yaumu Huang, as well as the expertise of Mia's outstanding art crew led by Charles Capistrant, ensured a dynamic visual and material experience for visitors to the show. Our special gratitude goes to Sam Molstad and Sarah Evenson for spearheading the framing of the many prints within this show and ensuring their gorgeous display, and equally to Dan Dennehy and Josh Lynn for processing the many images necessary for this publication. In collaboration with Josephine Lampone, Head of Interactive Media Michael Dust and Media Production Lead Ryan Arlee brought the voices in this show to life, producing engaging interviews with Council members and each of us. Our exceptional colleagues in the Audience Division, including Molly Lax, Evan Gruenes, Anna Dilliard, Diane Richard, Jill Blumer, and Taylor Bye, worked cheerfully and on deadline to select a title as well as the visual identity for this project, organize programming, and craft a successful communications strategy for promoting the exhibition and publication. Heartfelt thanks as well to Bridget Gallagher-Larkin, Sheila McGuire, Debra Hegstrom, and Kara Zumbahlen for so capably managing the educational outreach for this project. For their careful management of the necessary and complex financial aspects of this project, as well as their research regarding audience impact, we thank members of Mia's finance team, especially Kris Davidson and Rachel Wolff. Enormous thanks are due to Rita Mehta and her team in the Mia store for their ongoing work with Native artists and businesses. Our sincere thanks to our curatorial colleagues in Global Contemporary Art and the Department of the Arts of the Americas, including Dennis Jon, Nicole Soukup, Leslie Ureña, Valéria Piccoli, and Robert Cozzolino, for their efforts to champion Native artists and support of each of us throughout this interdepartmental project. This publication reflects the brilliance of our publishing team, who met our elastic deadlines with creativity, good humor, and endless patience: hugest thanks to Jim Bindas of Books & Projects, graphic designer Kevin Coochwytewa of Lightning Kev, and copy editor Jo Ann Reece for making this book shine. Finally, we wish to thank Ethan Aro Jones of Big Al's for so beautifully printing many of the works in this show.

To the Mia colleagues, past and present, who worked most closely with us in the realization of this project, we owe the deepest gratitude. Joe Doherty, Emily Rosenberg, Justice Jensvold, Keisha Williams, Tobie Miller, Heather Everhart, Juan Lucero, and Nora Stewart: the depth of talent, insight, expertise, and wisdom each of you brought to this process made it possible. Your careful stewardship of the checklist, your facilitation at meetings, your patience in chasing down elusive sources and artists for permissions and contracts, your advocacy for and your insights into the necessities for this project were instrumental to realizing this project. For your care, respect, and unending professionalism: thank you.

To our friends and families, we offer the greatest possible thanks for your love and support as we have worked on this engrossing project. Jill offers her deepest thanks to her children, Lauren and Nathaniel, and her family, Amy, Andrew, Carla, Brook, Ashley, Steve, Marcia, Catherine, Dave, Ellen, the Owens family, Angela Leyva, the Willeto/Damon family and Chris Yohe and family; her loving, inspiring, patient, and brilliant friends, including Joan Levitt, Dakota Hoska, Adriana Greci Green, Nicole LaBouff, Celita Levinson, Jim and Patty Thunderhawk, Todd Bockley, and to all of her friends and family in the Native art community who have generously shared their wisdom, wit, and warmth. Jaida offers her greatest thanks to her partner Tyler Steffenhagen and their pup-pup Strider and Sica, Shy, Sky, and Link; her parents, Jeaneen Lonehill and Robert Grey Eagle; Jackie and Julian Steffenhagen and the Steffenhagen family; Laura Engebretson, Zach Van Harris, her brother Jesse Grey Eagle and his family Rita, Icamna, and Chante; her sister Caitlyn Bird, Barbara Ann Wynn, and the Bird family; her little sister Rose Whipple and big sister Holyelk Lafferty; Bernie Lafferty and the Lafferty family; her IAIA family, Delaney Keshena, Greg Ballenger, Shelley Patrick, Brian Walker III; Mikayla Patton; Teresa, Jayden, Theo, and Jacob Day; her McLaughlin and Lonehill family; Brad Heck and Willow O'Feral and Ruben; Vanessa Casillas, Little Bear and Oreo; Nina, Nolan, and the Berglund Family; Jarrette Werk; Wanja Kuria; Molina and Brian Parker; Dave, Kelsey, Autumn, Jax and Summer Clark; Ty, Jalen, and Robin Dixon; Peyton Lonehill; Eryn Wise; Maida Branch; Hannah Smith; Maggie Thompson; her fierce mentors Ben Brody and Nina Robinson; Kilii Yuyan; Mukhtar Ibrahim and the forever supportive *Sahan Journal* family; Report for America; Indigenous Photographs; Women Photographs and 400 Years Project. Casey offers her heartfelt thanks to the friends who sustained her throughout the last several years, especially Agnes Gund, Elizabeth Easton, Caitlin Palmer, Emma Payne, Christa Clarke, Katherine Brinson, Lisa Çakmak, Ainsley M. Cameron, Julie Crooks, Laura De Becker, Janet Dees, Daisy Desrosiers, Maria C. Gaztambide, Emily Liebert, Legacy Russell, Gabriela Urtiaga, Ann O'Leary, Caroline Berz, Mary Peck, Camilla Shannon, Anjuli Lebowitz, Erin Nolan, Corey Keller, Liz Siegel, Sophie Hackett, Sarah Meister, Sarah Kennel, Kate Herlihy, Christina Nielsen, Leslie Hammons, Kate Carmody, Aidan O'Connor, Henriette Huldisch, and Pujan Gandhi; enduring love and gratitude as well to her dear family members, Rob, Ronan, Mimi, Finn, Aloura, Jasper, and Di. Together we are grateful for the many people who have inspired us to embark upon such a collaboration, and to one another for seeing this monumental project to completion.

Finally, and most crucially, we wish to thank the members of both our Curatorial and Community Councils for all that they have given to this process: Rhéanne Chartrand, Mique'l Icesis Dangeli, Rosalie Favell, Tom Jones, Amy Lonetree, Shelley Niro, Veronica Passalacqua, Jami Powell, Jolene Rickard, Cara Romero, Hulleah J. Tsinhnahjinnie, Emily Voelker, Laura Wexler, and Will Wilson; Alexandra Buffalohead, Sharon Day, Coral Gessner, Rafael Gonzalez, Heidi Inman, Delaney Keshena, Bazille Owen-Reese, Iyekiyapiwin Darlene St. Clair, and Maryam Marne Zafar. The tenacity, generosity, intellectual rigor, and support of our Council members—as well as their advice when we went astray—have strengthened our thinking and refined the goals of this project toward better ends. Their knowledge and advocacy are at the heart of this project, and all three of us have done our best to translate that expertise into a public-facing historical experience. Crucially, we recognized early on that our contribution to the field would be an imperfect one, meant to stimulate further inquiries and efforts that would invariably improve upon our own. This book is dedicated to our Council members, with respect and gratitude for their guidance, patience, and care.

JILL AHLBERG YOHE

JAIDA GREY EAGLE

CASEY RILEY

Aggeok Pitseolak
Inuit, 1906-1977
Peter Pitseolak with 2222 camera, c. 1947
Inkjet print
Courtesy of the Canadian Museum of History
2000-188, CD2000-219-015

Pages 16-17:
Zig Jackson (Rising Buffalo)
Sahnish (Arikara), Minitari (Hidatsa), Numakiki (Mandan), born 1957
China Basin District, 1997
from Entering Zig's Indian Reservation series
Gelatin silver print
Courtesy of the artist
© Zig

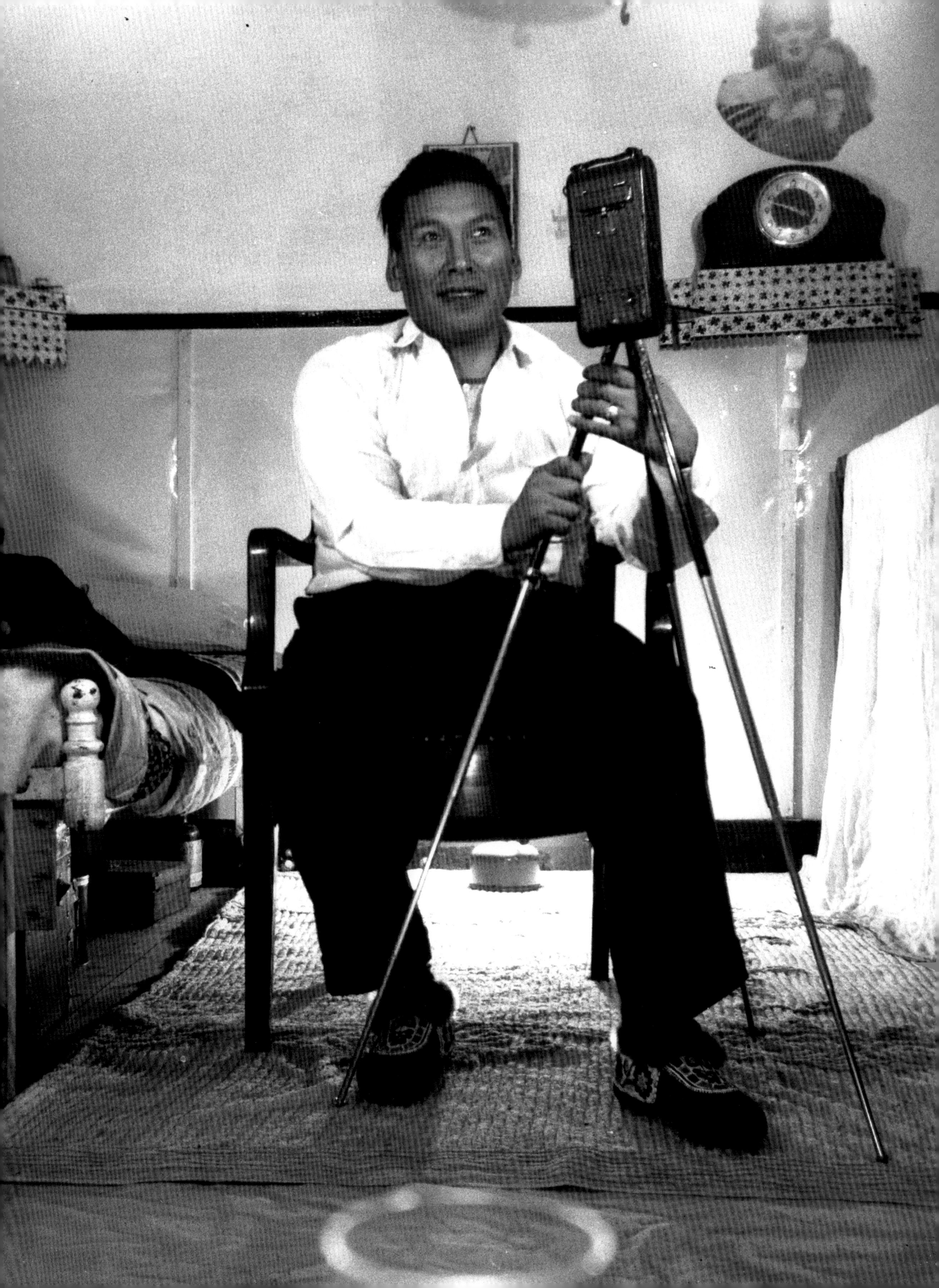

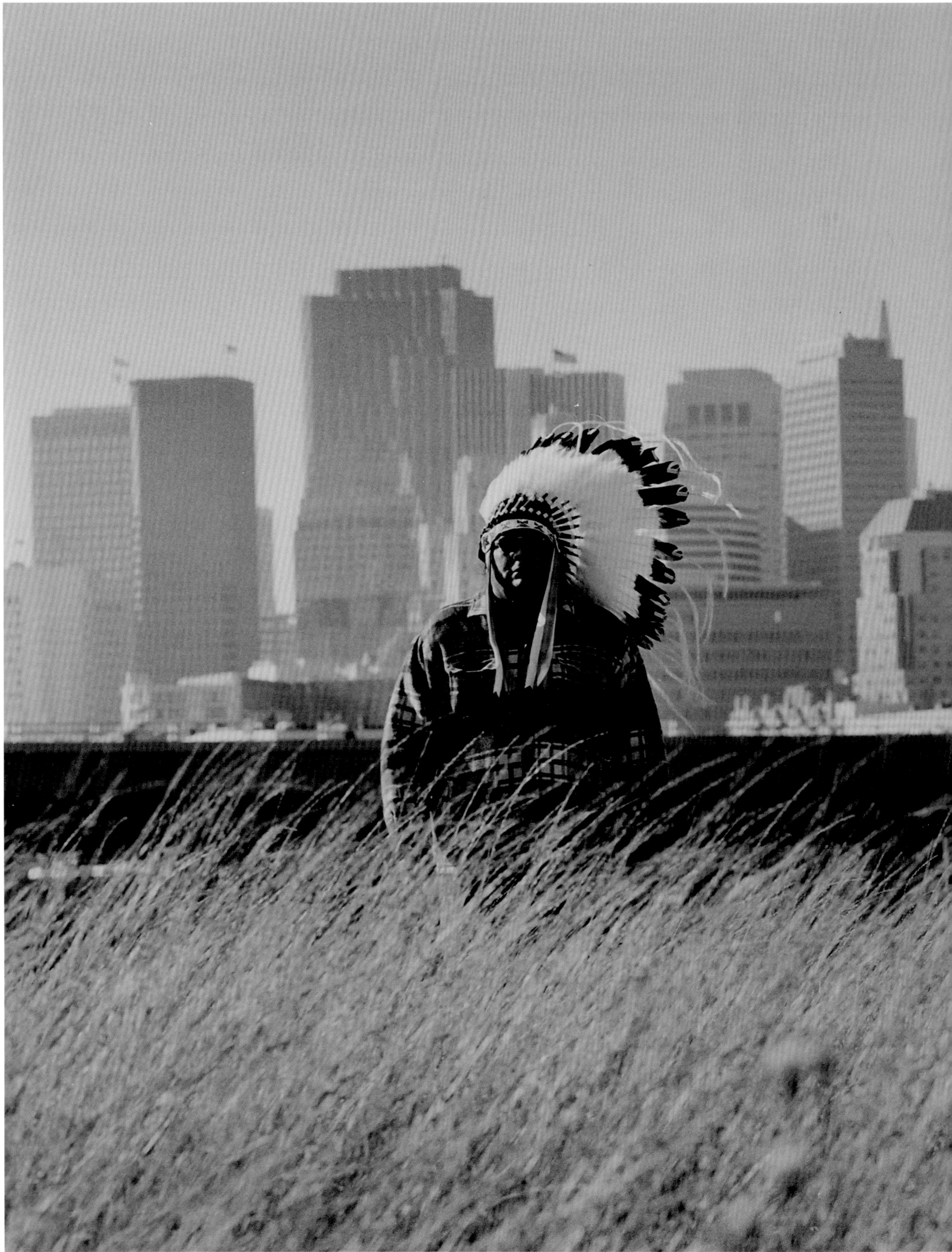

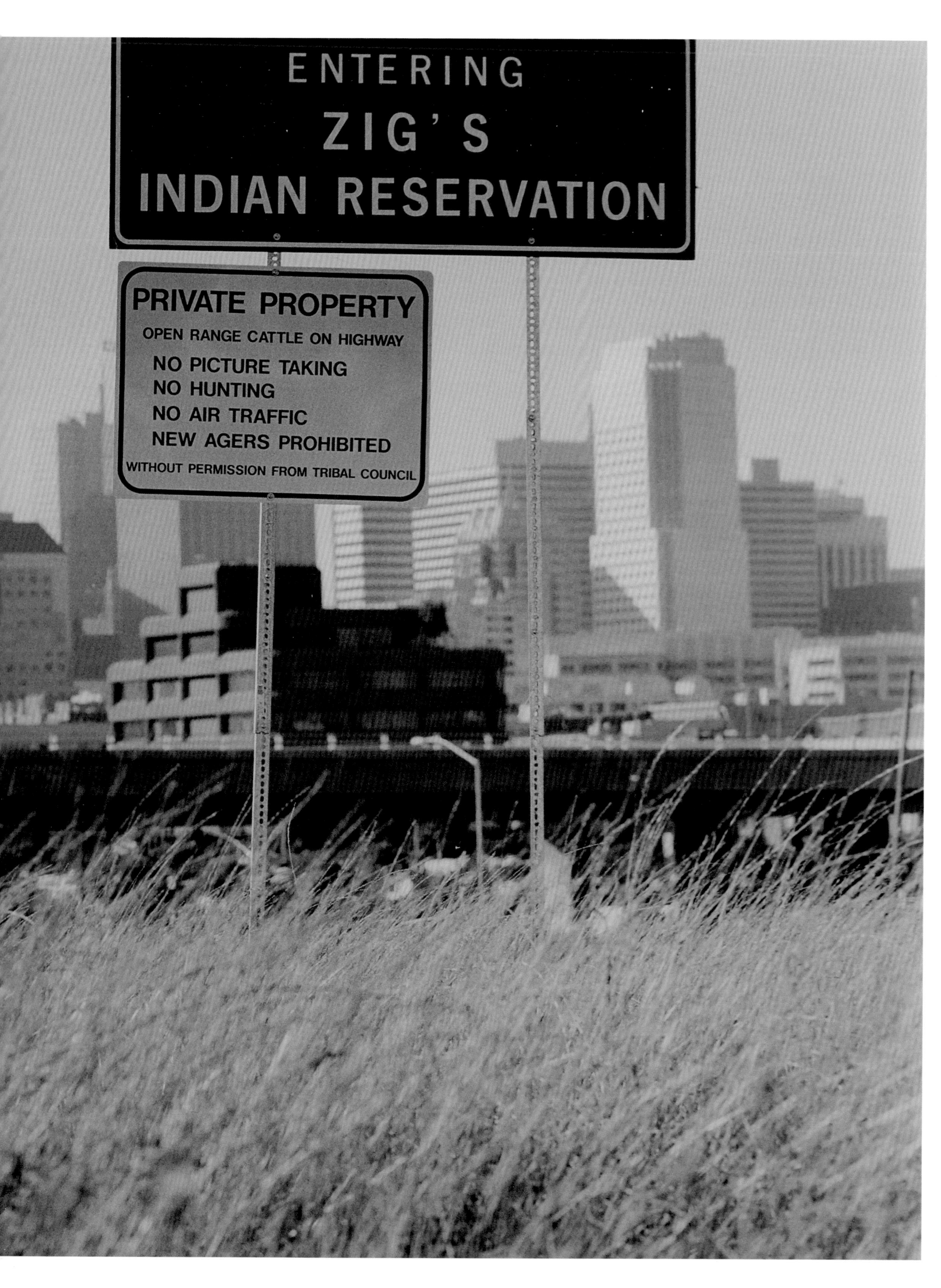
ENTERING
ZIG'S
INDIAN RESERVATION
PRIVATE PROPERTY
OPEN RANGE CATTLE ON HIGHWAY
NO PICTURE TAKING
NO HUNTING
NO AIR TRAFFIC
NEW AGERS PROHIBITED
WITHOUT PERMISSION FROM TRIBAL COUNCIL

CURATORIAL COUNCIL MEMBERS

BIOGRAPHIES

Rhéanne Chartrand* (Métis) is the Curator of Indigenous Art at McMaster Museum of Art. She holds a master's degree in museum studies from the University of Toronto. A Métis curator/creative producer based in Hamilton and Toronto, Chartrand has curated interdisciplinary and multidisciplinary exhibitions, showcases, and festivals for the City of Toronto, Art Gallery of Mississauga, the Aboriginal Pavilion at the Toronto 2015 Pan Am Games, and the National Museum of the American Indian in Washington, DC. Her curatorial work focuses upon the praxis of survivance, Indigenous epistemes, relational aesthetics, and representational politics. Chartrand organized the 2018 exhibition *"#nofilterneeded: Shining light on the Native Indian/Inuit Photographers' Association, 1985–1992,"* which illuminated the organization's key role as an advocate for Indigenous photographers across Turtle Island (North America) and its importance to the history of Indigenous art in Hamilton and the surrounding region.

Mique'l Icesis Dangeli* (Tsimshian Nation of Metlakatla, Alaska), Assistant Professor, School of Creative Arts, University of the Fraser Valley. Dr. Dangeli belongs to the La<u>x</u> sgiik (Eagle Clan) and carries the Tsimshian name Sm Łoodm 'Nüüsm and Tlingit name Táakw Shaawát. She served her community for eight years as the Director of the Duncan Cottage Museum, where she worked closely with the staff at the Alaska State Museum. For the past 12 years she has also worked for the Annette Island Service Unit in Metlakatla as the Curator of their Healing Art Collection. Dr. Dangeli's PhD is in art history from the University of British Columbia; she also holds an MA degree in art history from the University of British Columbia and a BA degree in art history from the University of Washington.

Rosalie Favell* (Metis) is a photo-based artist, born in Winnipeg, Manitoba. Drawing inspiration from her family history and Metis (Cree/English) heritage, she uses a variety of sources, from family albums to popular culture, to present a complex self-portrait of her experiences as a contemporary aboriginal woman. To date, Favell's work has explored the relation of photography to issues of identity. Over the course of her long career, Favell's work has appeared in exhibitions in Canada, the US, and in other countries, and numerous institutions have acquired her artwork. A graduate of Ryerson Polytechnic Institute, Favell holds a Master of Fine Arts degree from the University of New Mexico and a PhD (ABD) from Carleton University in Cultural Mediations.

Tom Jones* (Ho-Chunk) is an artist, curator, writer, and educator. He graduated with a Bachelor of Fine Arts in Painting from the University of Wisconsin-Madison, a Master of Fine Arts in Photography and a Master of Arts in Museum Studies from Columbia College in Chicago, Illinois. He is currently Professor of Photography, University of Wisconsin-Madison.

Jones's artwork is a commentary on the identity, experience, and perception of American Indian communities. For the past 25 years he has worked on an ongoing photographic essay on his tribe, the Ho-Chunk Nation of Wisconsin. His current work *Strong Unrelenting Spirits* are portraits of tribal members, which incorporates beadwork directly onto the photographs.

Jones co-authored the book *People of the Big Voice: Photographs of Ho-Chunk Families by Charles Van Schaick, 1879-1942.* He is the co-curator for the exhibition and contributing author to the book, *For a Love of His People: The Photography of Horace Poolaw* for the National Museum of the American Indian. His current book project is dedicated to Ho-Chunk baskets and their makers.

His artwork is in forty public collections, most notably: the National Museum of the American Indian, Polaroid Corporation, Sprint Corporation, the Nerman Museum of Contemporary Art, the Minneapolis Institute of Art, the Museum of Contemporary Native Arts, the Museum of Contemporary Photography, and Microsoft.

Amy Lonetree* (Ho-Chunk) is an enrolled citizen of the Ho-Chunk Nation and a Professor of History at the University of California, Santa Cruz. She received her PhD in Ethnic Studies from the University of California, Berkeley. Her scholarly research focuses on Native American history, public history, visual studies, and museum studies, and she has received fellowships in support of this work from the School for Advanced Research, the Newberry Library, the Georgia O'Keeffe Museum Research Center, the Bard Graduate Center, the Institute of American Cultures at UCLA, and the University of California, Berkeley Chancellor's Postdoctoral Fellowship Program. Her publications include: *Decolonizing Museums: Representing Native America in National and Tribal Museums* (University of North Carolina Press, 2012); a co-edited book with Amanda J. Cobb, *The National Museum of the American Indian: Critical Conversations*

(University of Nebraska Press, 2008); and a co-authored volume, *People of the Big Voice: Photographs of Ho-Chunk Families by Charles Van Schaick, 1879-1942* (Wisconsin Historical Society Press, 2011). Her articles have appeared in *The Public Historian*, the *American Indian Quarterly*, the *American Indian Culture and Research Journal*, and the *Journal of American History*. Cobb is currently working on two new book projects. The first is a visual history of the Ho-Chunk Nation that explores family history, tourism, settler colonialism, and Ho-Chunk survivance through an examination of two exceptional collections of studio portraits and tourist images of Ho-Chunk people taken between 1879–1960. The second research project is a history of Indigenous child removal in the United States.

Shelley Niro* (Mohawk) is a multi-disciplinary artist and a member of the Six Nations Reserve, Turtle Clan, Bay of Quinte Mohawk. Niro attended a graphic arts course for a while at Durham College in Oshawa, concentrating on photography, drawing, and art history. Years later, Niro went to Ontario College of Art in Toronto and graduated with honors. In 2019, she was given an honorary doctorate from the Ontario College of Arts and Design University. Niro was the inaugural recipient of the Aboriginal Arts Award presented through the Ontario Arts Council in 2012. In 2017, Niro received the Governor General's Award for The Arts from Canada Council, the Scotiabank Photography Award, and the Hnatsyshyn Foundation Reveal Award. She became an honorary elder in the Indigenous Curatorial Collective. In 2019, Niro was the Laureate of the Paul de Hueck and Norman Walford Career Achievement Award for Photography. Niro has recently completed production on her film, *CAFE DAUGHTER*, which has received support from Telefilm Canada, the Indigenous Screen Office, Ontario Creates and The Northern Ontario Film Office. Niro's visual works on canvas, paper, and film tackle the misconceptions or stereotypical portrayals of Native women.

Recent Niro exhibitions: *Shelley Niro: 500 Year Itch*, NMAI, Washington, DC, and New York; *A Good, Long Look* at the Art Gallery of Southwestern Manitoba; Dunlop Art Gallery, Regina, Saskatchewan; *Shelley Niro: women, land, river* at the Art Gallery of Peterborough. *Something Cold and Hard Like Winter*: The Robert Langen Art Gallery, Wilfred Laurier University, Waterloo, Ontario, Kitchener and Greater New York: at PS1 MOMA, New York, and *Boundless*: Art Gallery of Windsor, Windsor Ontario.

Veronica Passalacqua* is the Executive Director of the C.N. Gorman Museum at the University of California, Davis. As a writer, curator, and scholar of Native North American art her research emphasis and curatorial practices are based upon collaboration with contemporary Indigenous artists. Her doctoral thesis in museum studies from Oxford University examines lens-based artworks by contemporary Native American artists.

Jami Powell (Osage) is the Hood Museum of Art's Associate Director of Curatorial Affairs and first curator of Native American art. Powell, a citizen of the Osage Nation, has a PhD in anthropology from the University of North Carolina at Chapel Hill. Prior to working at the Hood, she was a faculty lecturer in the American Studies Program at Tufts University. She has focused her research on American Indian expressive forms through an interdisciplinary lens.

Jolene Rickard (Tuscarora) is a curator, photographer, and associate professor and the Director of the American Indian Program at Cornell University. She was born a member of the Turtle Clan in the Tuscarora Nation of Iroquois peoples. She earned her BFA at Rochester Institute of Technology. In 1991 she received her master's degree at Buffalo State and completed her PhD in American Studies with a Native component in 1996 at SUNY Buffalo. Rickard was one of a select group of curators who helped to design the permanent exhibitions at the National Museum of the American Indian in Washington, DC, which opened in 2004. Her installations and photographs revolve around Native American issues.

Cara Romero* (Chemehuevi) is a contemporary fine art photographer. An enrolled citizen of the Chemehuevi Indian Tribe, Romero was raised between contrasting settings: the rural Chemehuevi reservation in Mojave Desert, CA, and the urban sprawl of Houston, TX. Romero's identity informs her photography, a blend of fine art and editorial photography, shaped by years of study and a visceral approach to representing Indigenous and non-Indigenous cultural memory, collective history, and lived experiences from a Native American female perspective. As an undergraduate at the University of Houston, Romero pursued a degree in cultural anthropology. Since 1998, Romero's expansive oeuvre has been informed by formal training in film, digital, fine art, and commercial photography.

Hulleah J. Tsinhnahjinnie (Seminole/Muscogee/Diné) born into the Bear Clan of the Taskigi Nation, born for Tsi'naajinii of the Diné Nation, adopted into the Eagle House of Metlakatla, and adopted into the Killer Whale Fin House of Klukwan. Tsinhnahjinnie's education includes the Institute of American Indian Arts (Santa Fe, NM), California College of Arts and Crafts (Oakland, CA), and the University of California Irvine. During her residency in the Bay Area (1978–1998), she worked with several Native American organizations, the San Francisco Indian Center, Intertribal Friendship House, and Gay American Indians. In 2004, Tsinhnahjinnie was appointed as Director of the C.N. Gorman Museum and Professor within the Native American Studies Department at the University of California Davis. Tsinhnahjinnie is known nationally and internationally as a photographer and multimedia artist creating portraiture and social commentary art works. Tsinhnahjinnie's photographs respond to the perpetuating stereotypes of Native Americans caused by ubiquitous early Western photography of Native people fixed in a historical past. Tsinhnahjinnie's work is held in several collections, including NMAI, MoMA, The Eiteljorg Museum, and the Fred Jones Jr Museum of Art.

Emily Voelker* is an assistant professor of art history at the University of North Carolina, Greensboro. Voelker is a historian of nineteenth-century art and the history of photography, whose work centers on transatlantic exhibition culture, Indigenous representation, and changing meanings and uses of the archive over time. She holds a PhD from Boston University (2017), an MA from Tufts University (2008), and a BA from Emory University (2006). She has taught at Boston University and Vassar College and is the former Estrellita & Yousuf Karsh Assistant Curator of Photographs at the Museum of Fine Arts, Boston. Her current book project, "Circulating Pictures/Contested Geographies: Photography, Native American Sovereignty and the French Atlantic Imaginary," examines photographs of Northern Plains sitters either sent to, or made at, Paris exhibitions in the closing decades of the nineteenth century.

Laura Wexler* is professor of American Studies, professor of Women's, Gender, and Sexuality Studies, and Co-Chair of the Women's Faculty Forum at Yale University. Wexler studies the social life of photographs, interrogating the power of photography's place at the intersections of gender, race, sexuality, class, and nationalism, as configured within and across the visual cultures of the United States. She is Principal Investigator of the Photogrammar Project, which has received NEH and ACLS support to make a web-based interactive research system for visualizing the 180,000 American photographs created by the Farm Security Administration and Office of War Information between 1935–1945. Wexler is currently working on a monograph entitled *Photography After Freedom*, examining US photography's production of gender, race, time and crisis after Reconstruction.

Will Wilson* (Citizen of the Navajo Nation) is a Santa Fe–based photographer and Associate Professor of Photography at UT Austin. Wilson is a photographer who spent his formative years living in the Navajo Nation. Born in San Francisco in 1969, Wilson studied photography at the University of New Mexico and Oberlin College. In 2007, Wilson won the Native American Fine Art Fellowship from the Eiteljorg Museum, and in 2010 he was awarded a prestigious grant from the Joan Mitchell Foundation. Wilson has held visiting professorships at the Institute of American Indian Arts (1999–2000), Oberlin College (2000–01), and the University of Arizona (2006–08).

** Denotes an author contributing to the publication.*

PART I

ALWAYS PRESENT

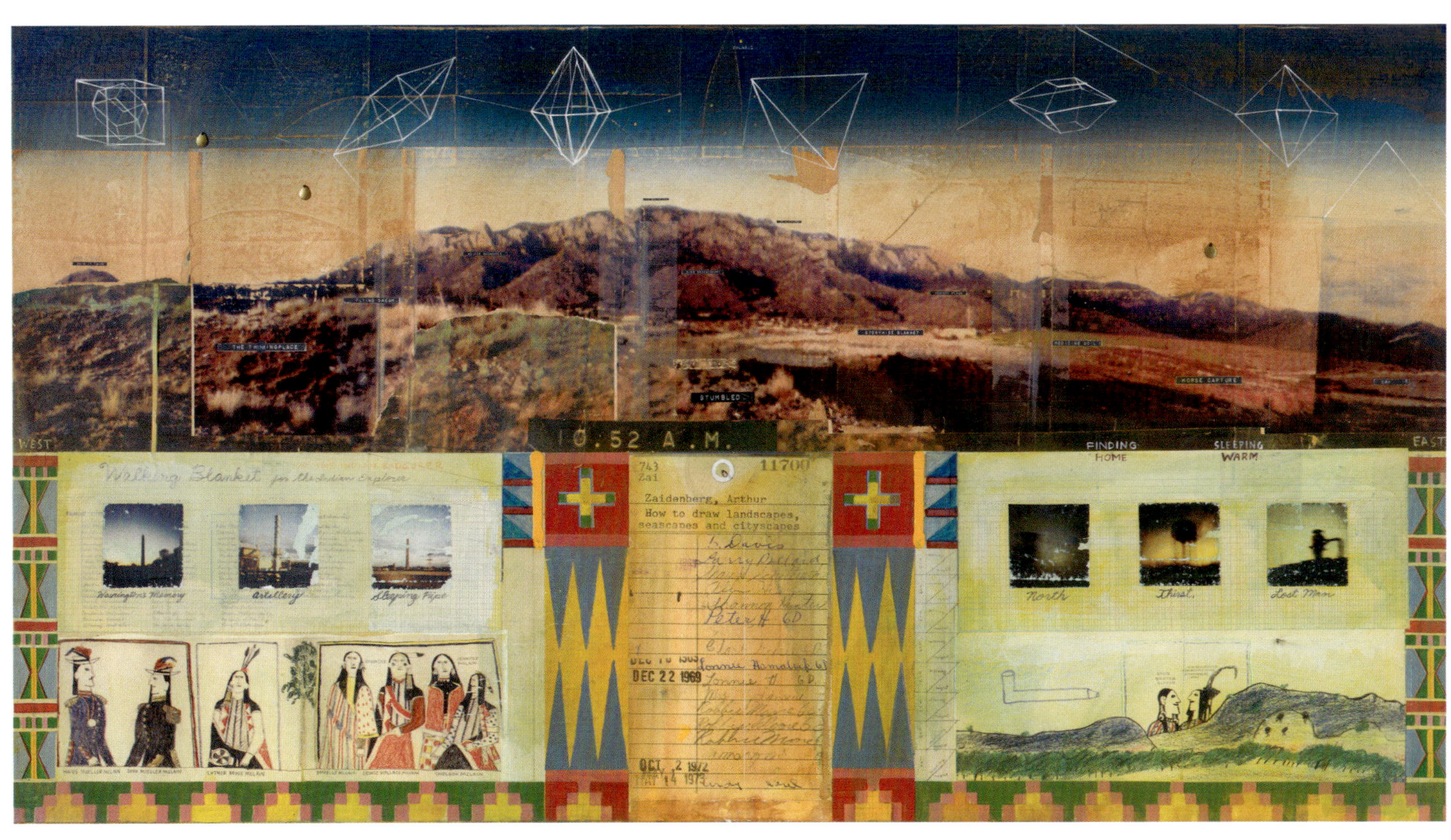

Kimowan Metchewais (Kimowan McLain)
Cree [Cold Lake First Nations], 1963-2011
Sandias, 2012
Canvas, photograph/photographs, paper, ink, acrylic paint, adhesive tape
National Museum of the American Indian
Bequest of the artist, 2012, 26/9429

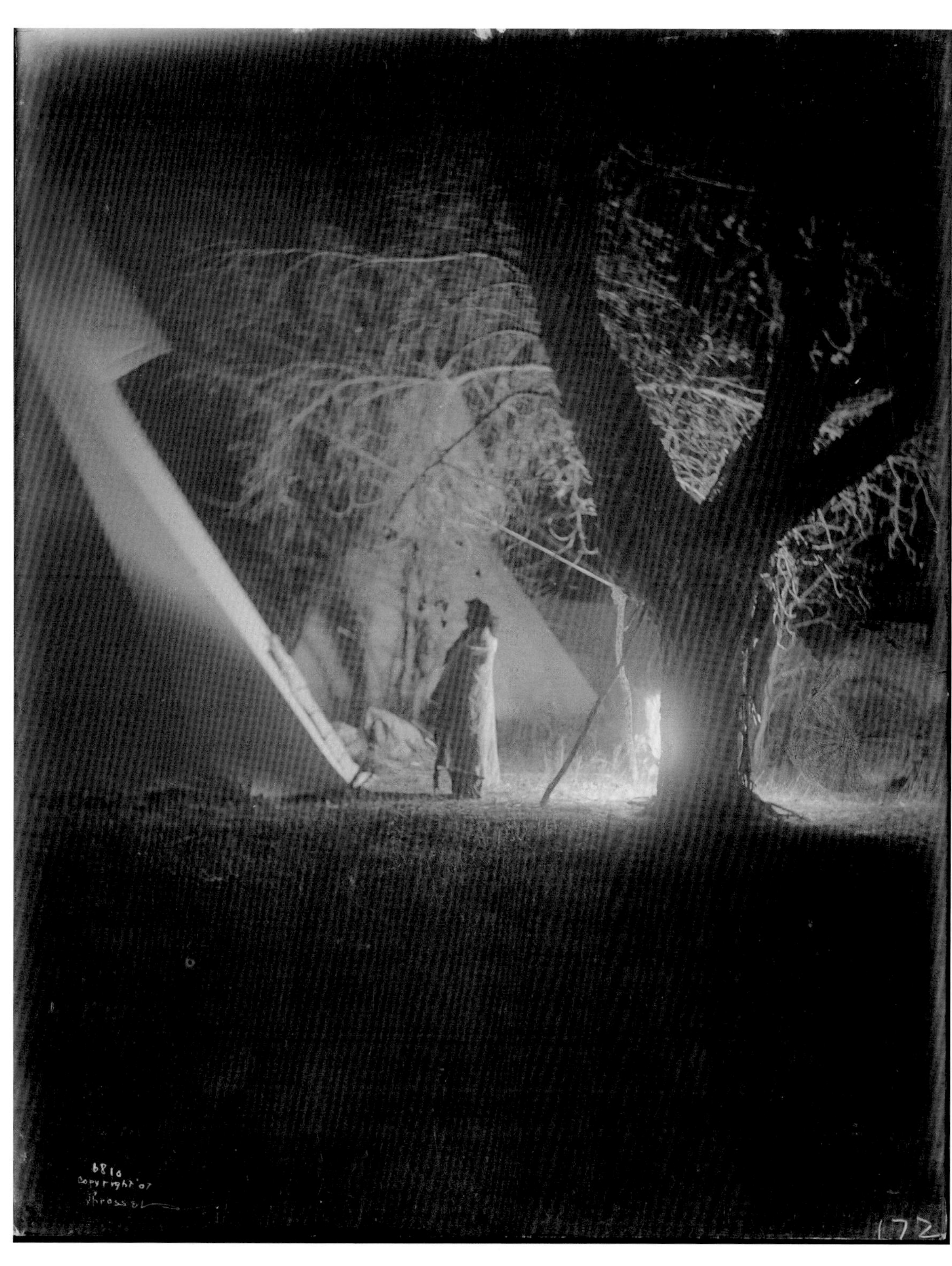

Richard Throssel
Nehiyawak (Cree) / Adopted Apsáalooke,
1882–1933
Camp fire no. 2, 1902-33
Richard Throssel collection, #2394,
Courtesy of the American Heritage Center,
University of Wyoming

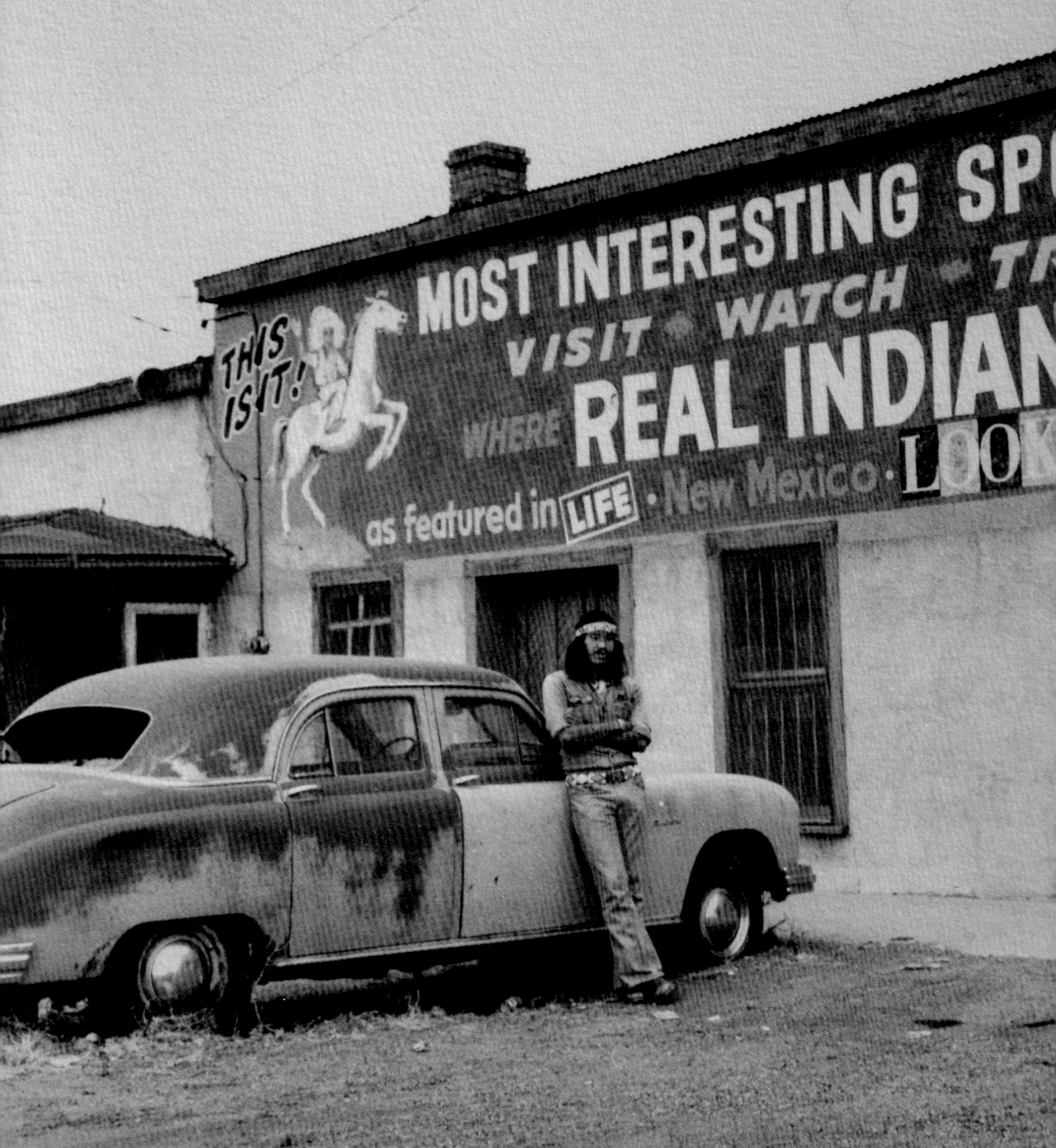
THIS IS IT!
MOST INTERESTING SP
VISIT WATCH
WHERE REAL INDIAN
as featured in LIFE · New Mexico · LOOK

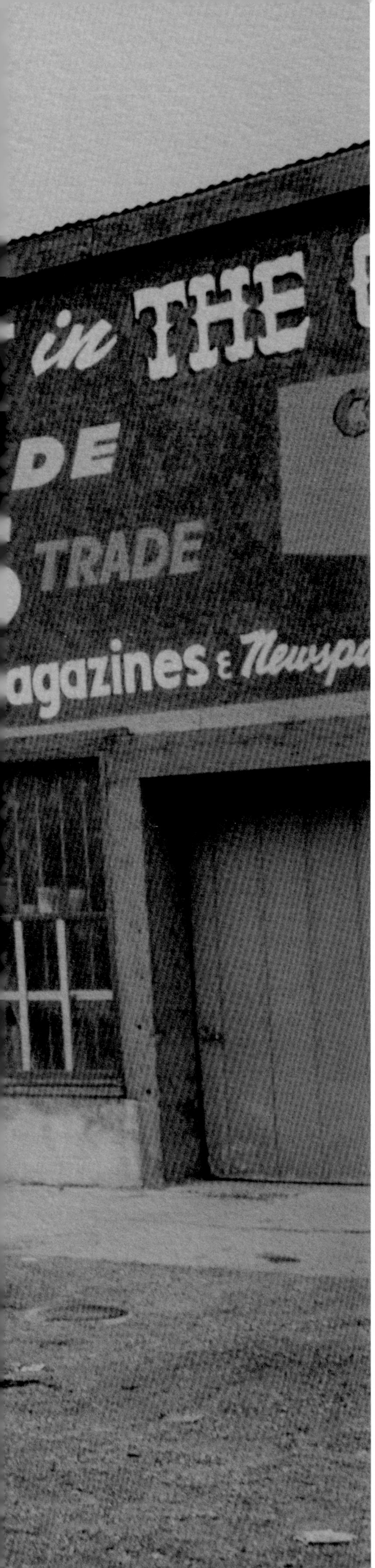

Larry McNeil
Dakl'aweidi K'eet Gooshi H'it, Killer Whale
Fin House Tlingit / Nisga'a, born 1955
Real Indians, 1977 (printed 2017)
Gelatin silver print
Courtesy of the artist
© Larry McNeil

Pages 30-31:
Camille Seaman
Shinnecock / African American, born 1969
Iceberg in Blood Red Sea, Lemaire Channel,
Antarctica, 29 December 2016, 2016
Archival inkjet print
Courtesy the Artist
© Camille Seaman

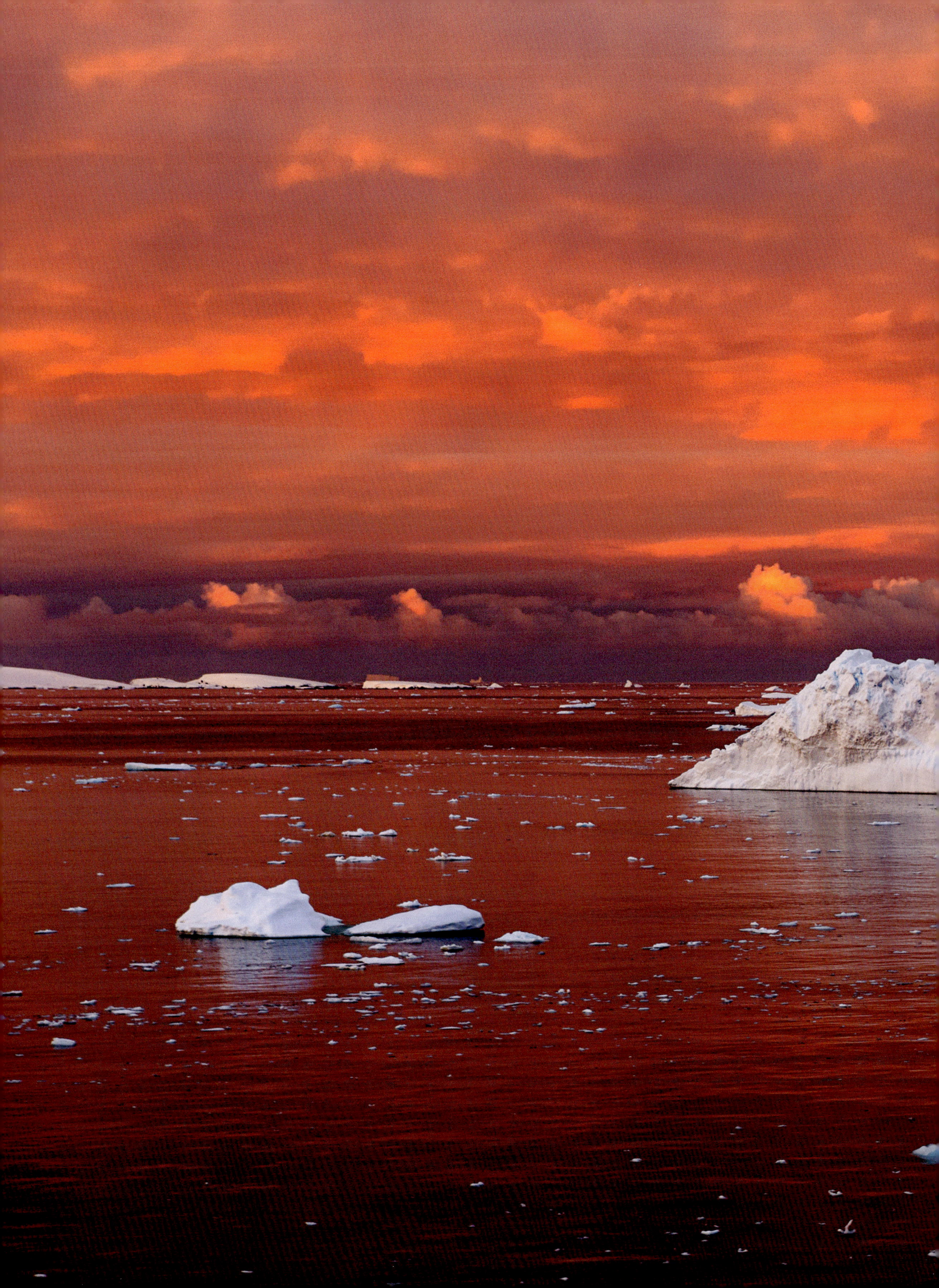

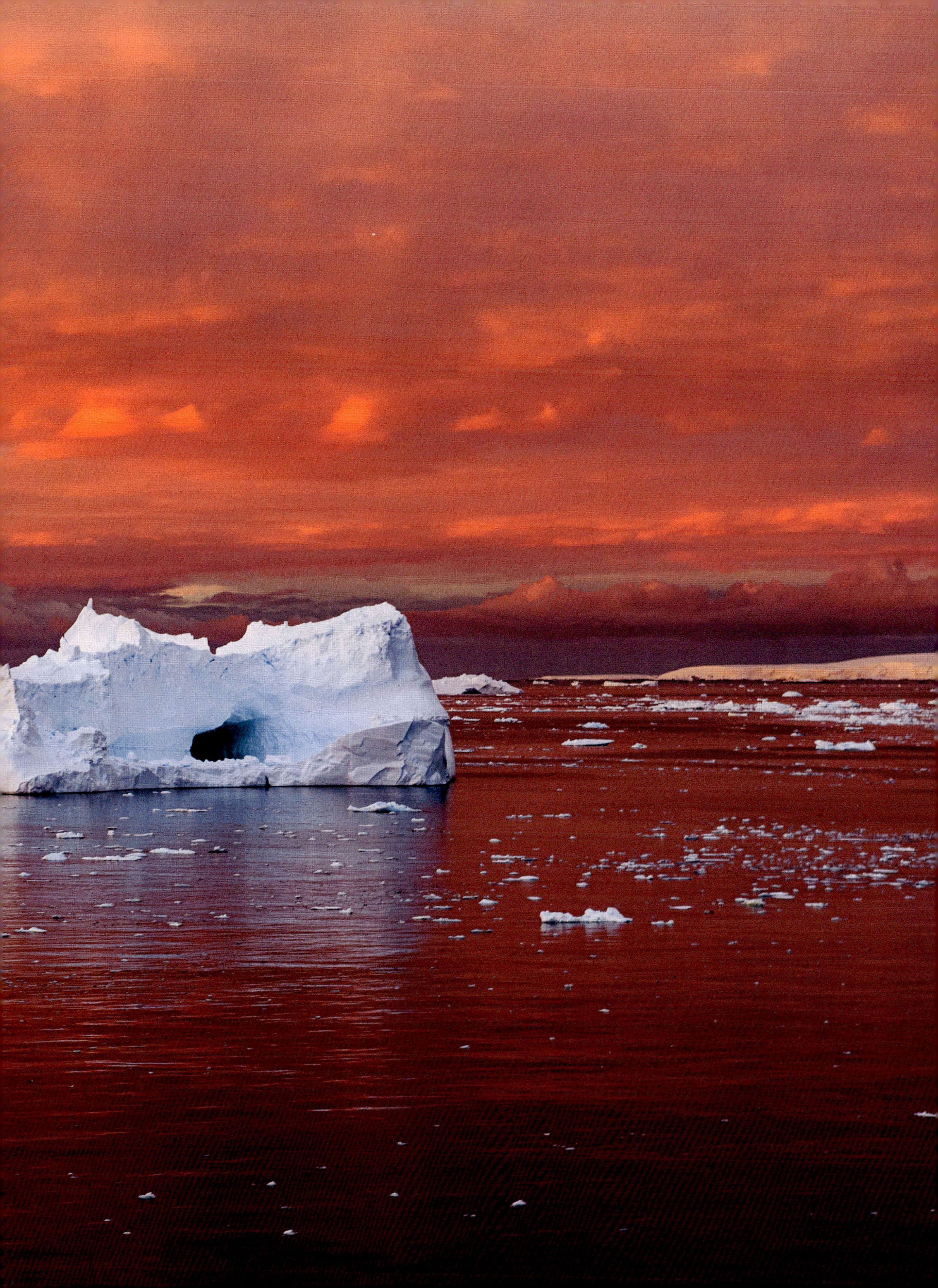

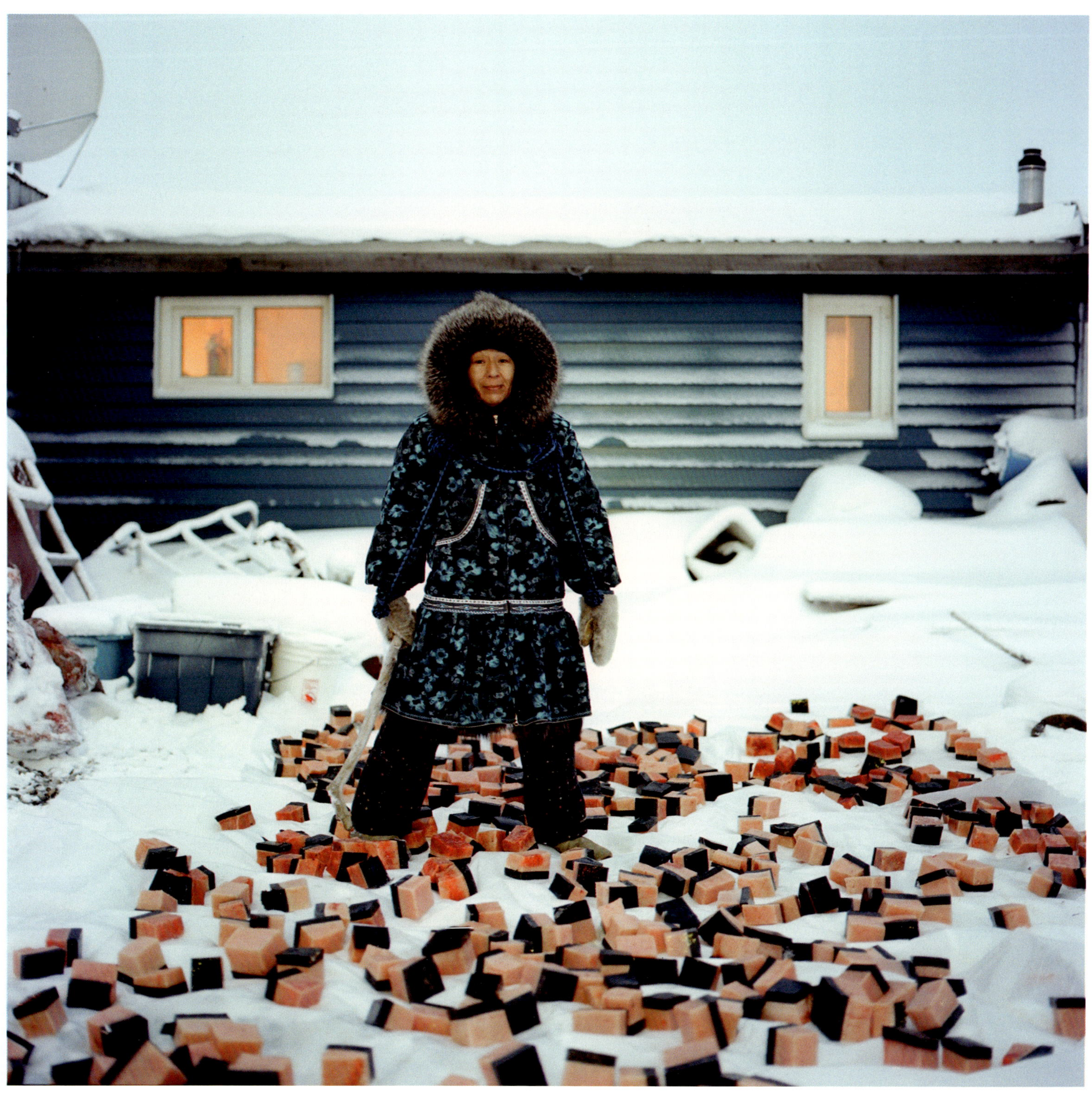

Brian Adams
Iñupiaq, born 1985
Marie Rexford of Kaktovik, Alaska
preparing maktak for the villages
Thanksgiving Day feast, 2015
from I am Inuit series
Chromogenic print (medium format film)
Courtesy the artist
© Brian Adams

Richard Throssel
Nehiyawak (Cree) /
Adopted Apsáalooke, 1882–1933
Baby Stuart (An Indian Girl with Dog), 1902-33
Inkjet print
Richard Throssel collection, #2394,
Courtesy of the American Heritage Center,
University of Wyoming

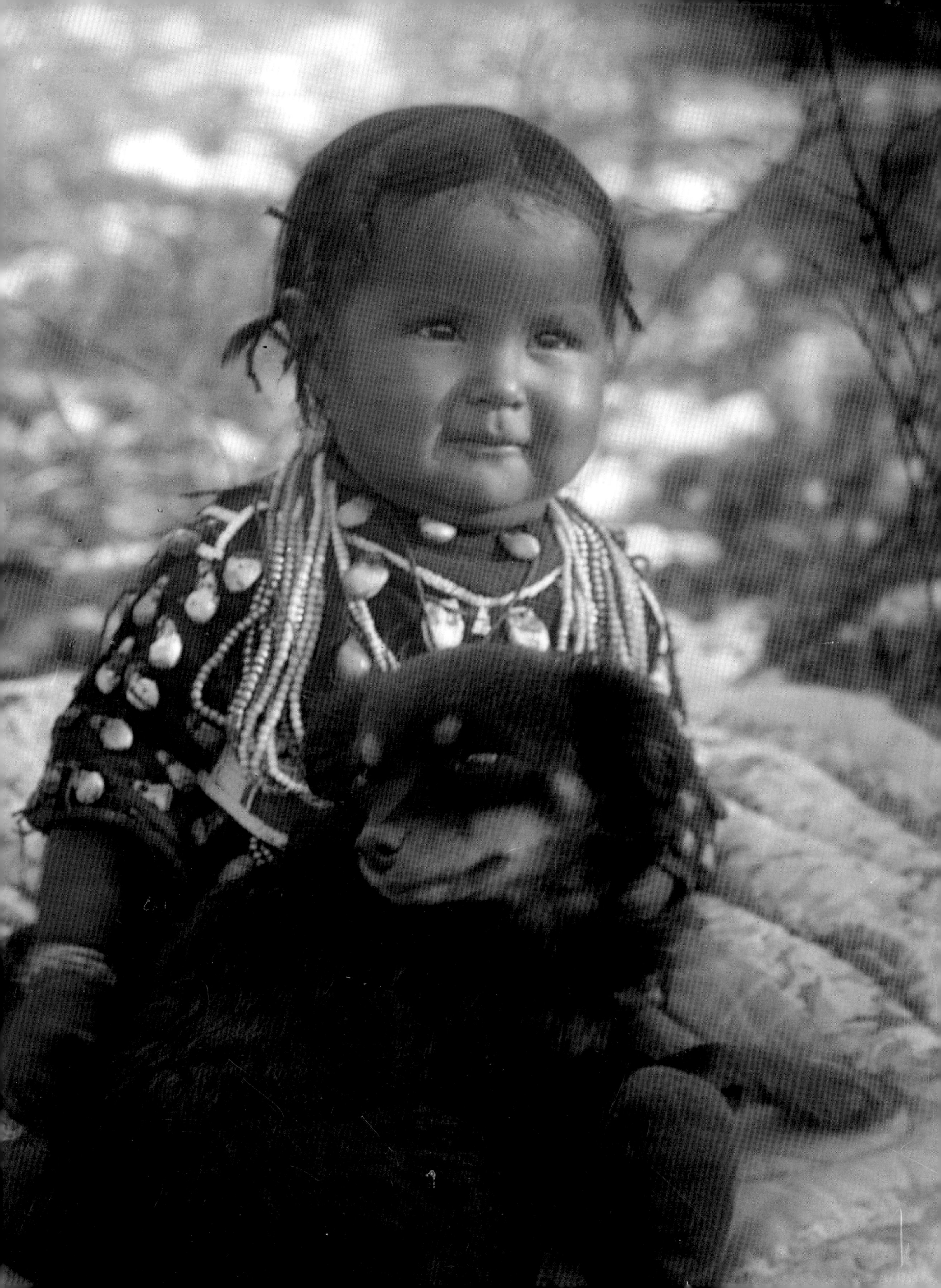

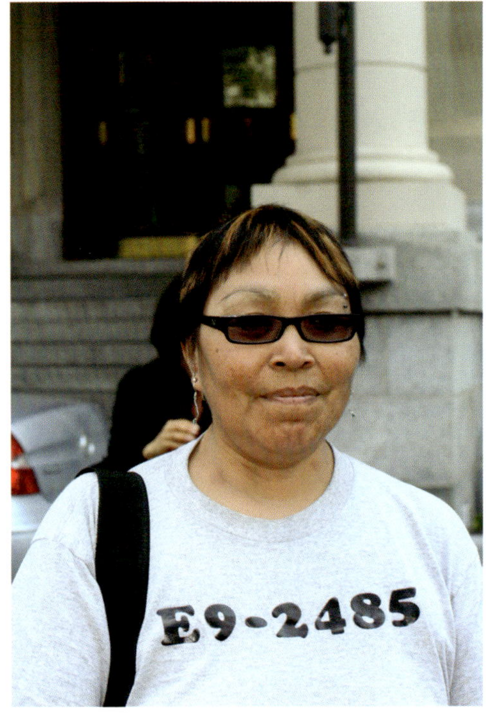

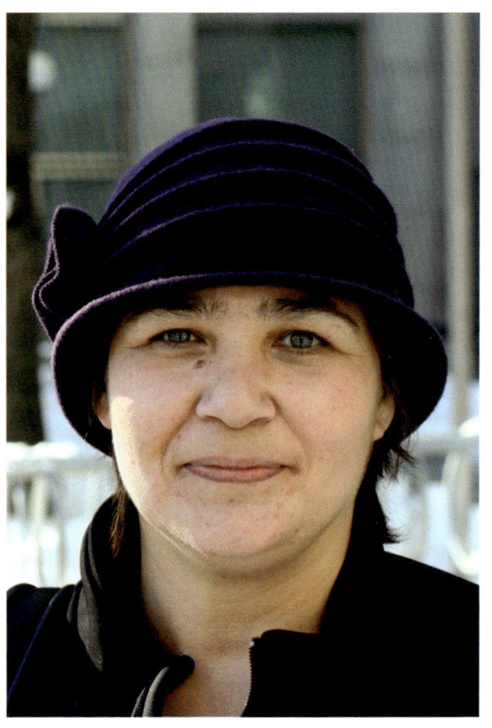

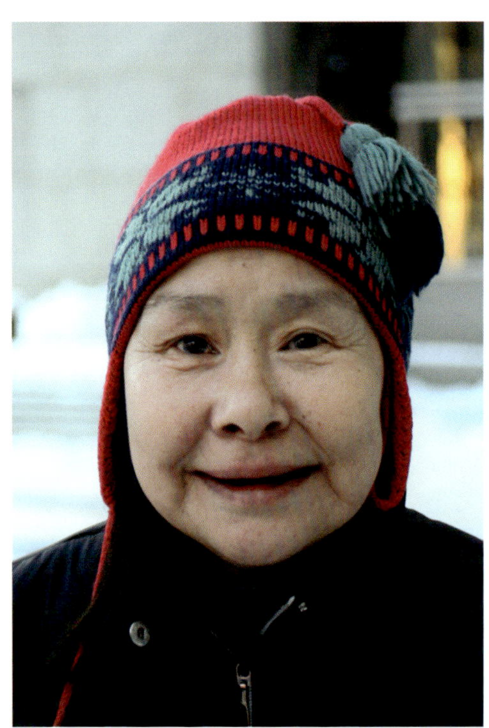

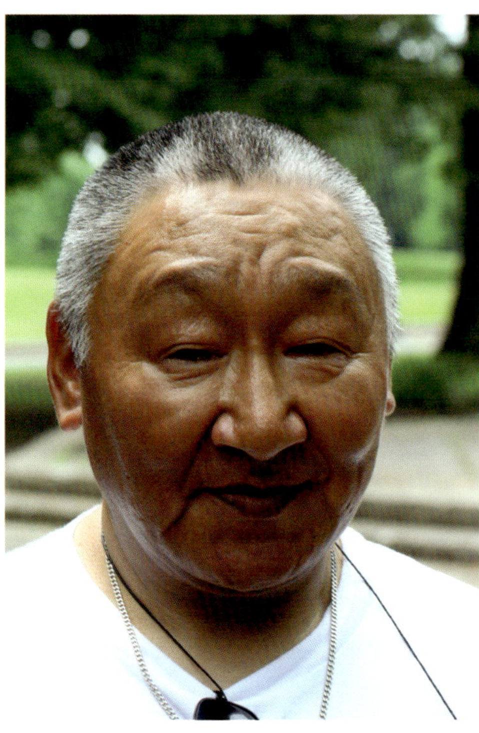

Barry Pottle
Inuit, born 1961
Clockwise from top left:
[Dora], 2009-2011
[Rosemary], 2009-2011
[Leeteea], 2009-2011
[Mathewsie], 2009-2011
from Awareness Project series
Chromogenic print
Courtesy of the Art Gallery of Hamilton,
Purchase, Permanent Collection Fund, 2016

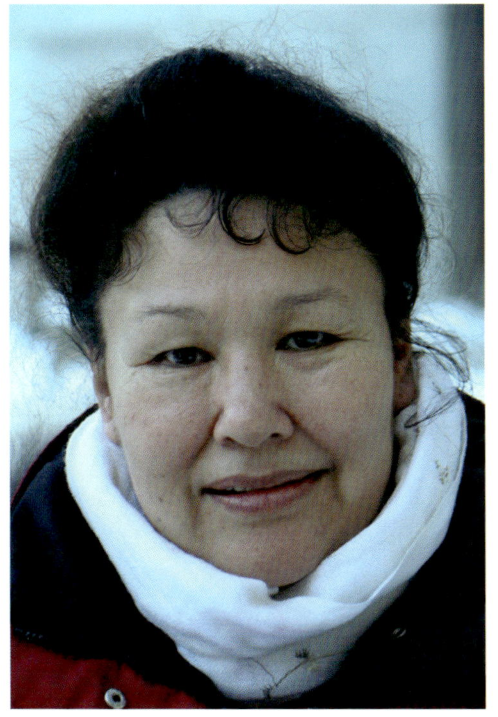

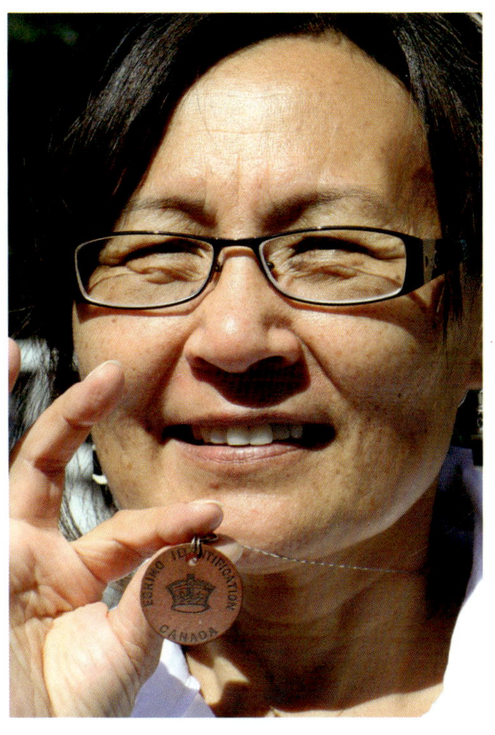

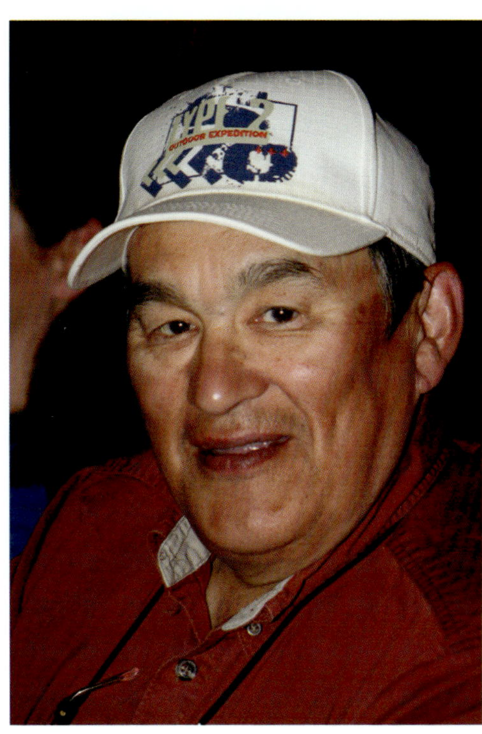

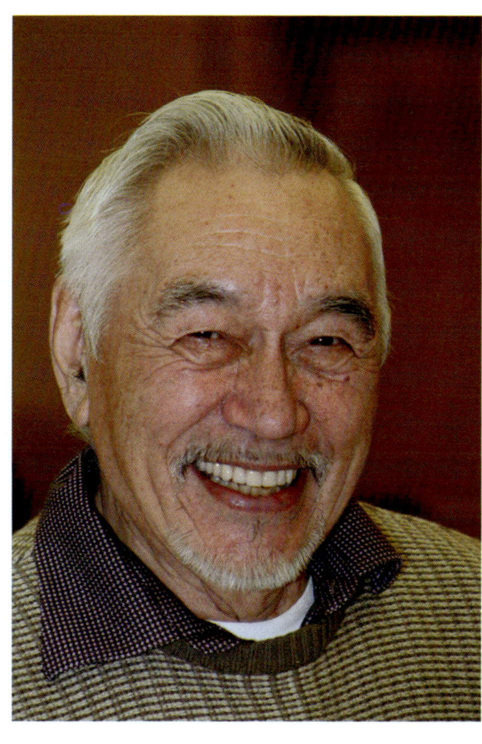

Barry Pottle
Inuit, born 1961
Clockwise from top left:
[Reepa], 2009-2011
[Leena], 2009-2011
[Willie], 2009-2011
[Albert], 2009-2011
from Awareness Project series
Chromogenic print
Courtesy of the Art Gallery of Hamilton,
Purchase, Permanent Collection Fund, 2016
© Barry Pottle

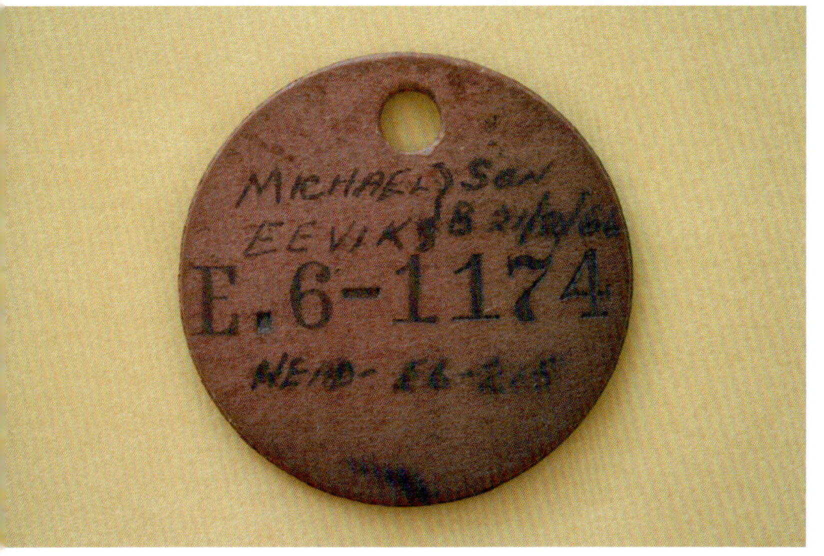

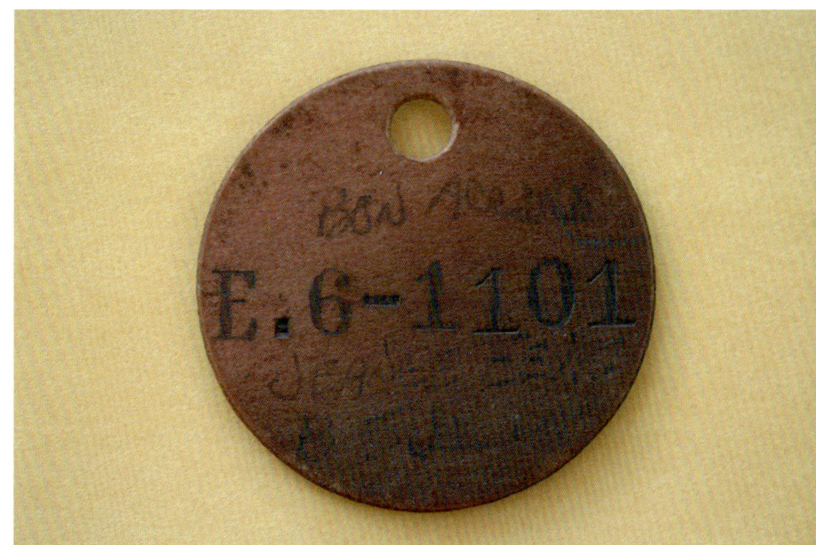

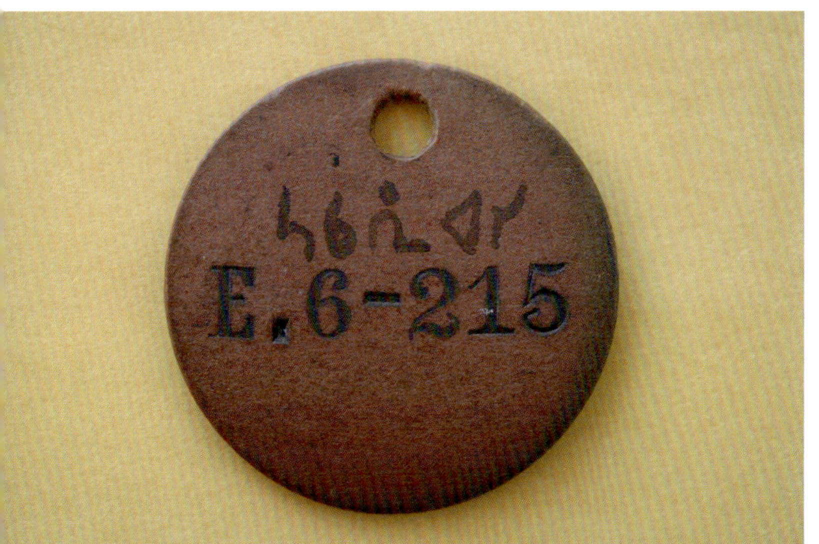

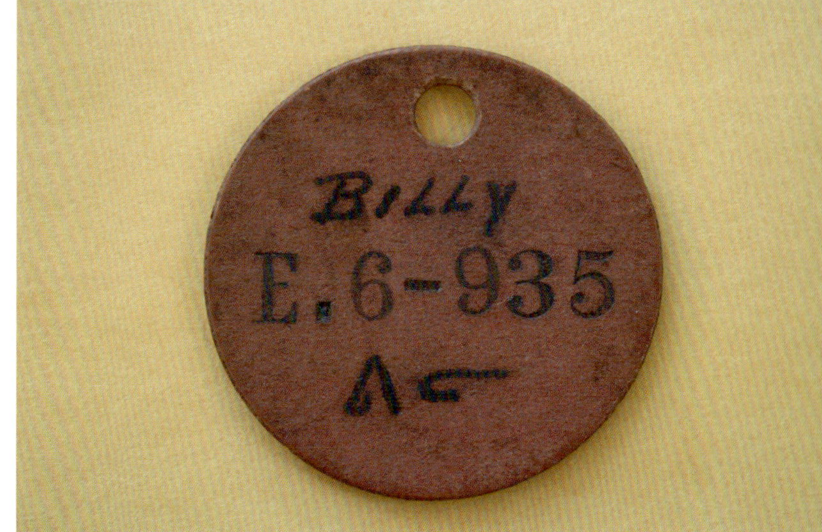

Barry Pottle
Inuit, born 1961
From top, left to right:
[E.6-1174], 2009-2011
[E.6-1101], 2009-2011
[E.6-658], 2009-2011
[E.6-1326], 2009-2011
[E.6-215], 2009-2011
[E.6-935], 2009-2011
[E.6-205], 2009-2011
[E.6-1445], 2009-2011
from Awareness Project series
Chromogenic print
Courtesy of the Art Gallery of Hamilton,
Purchase, Permanent Collection Fund, 2016
© Barry Pottle

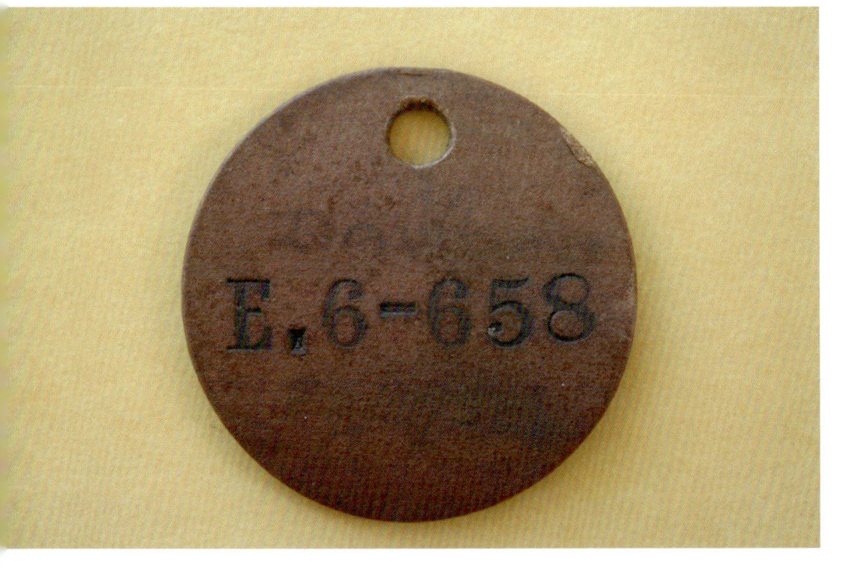
E.6-658
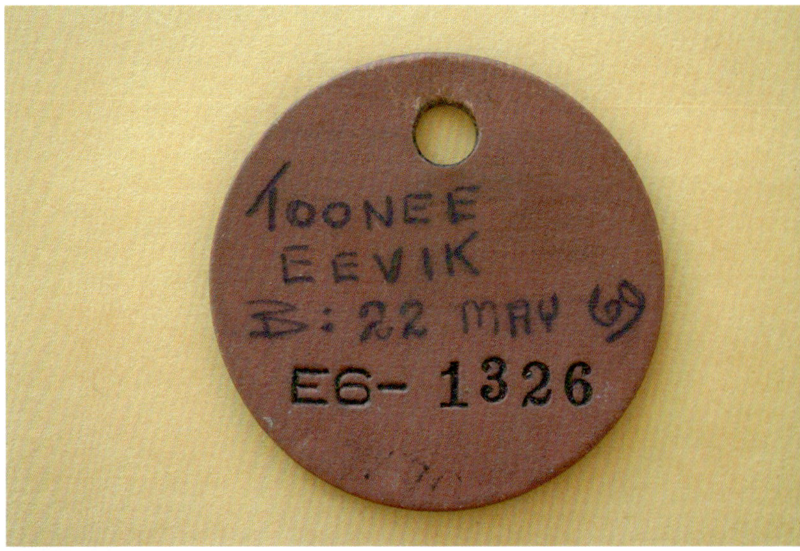
TOONEE
EEVIK
B: 22 MAY 69
E6- 1326
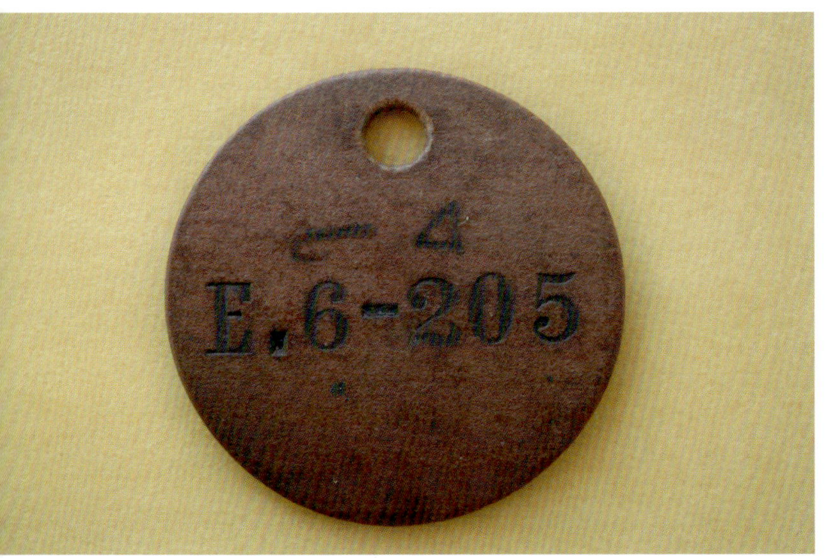
E.6-205
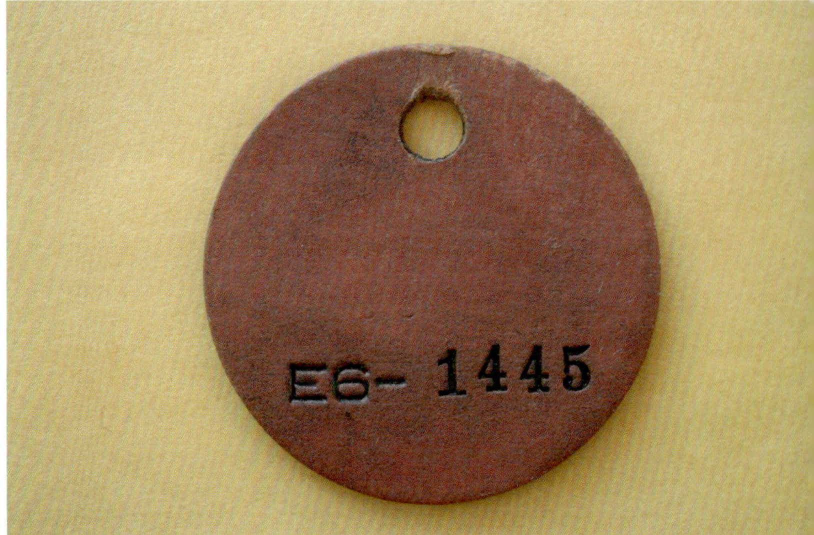
E6- 1445

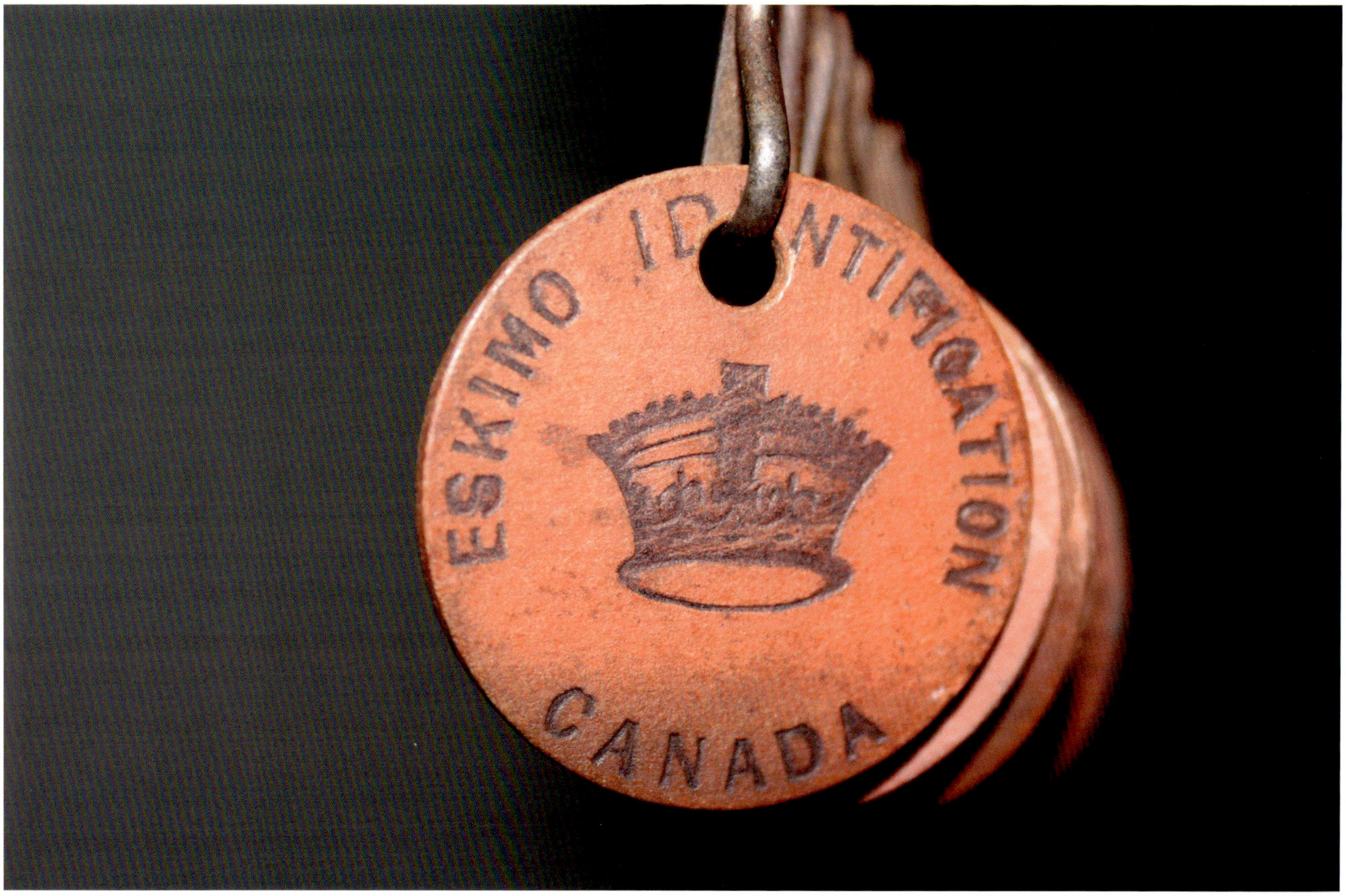

ESKIMO IDENTIFICATION
CANADA
BILLY 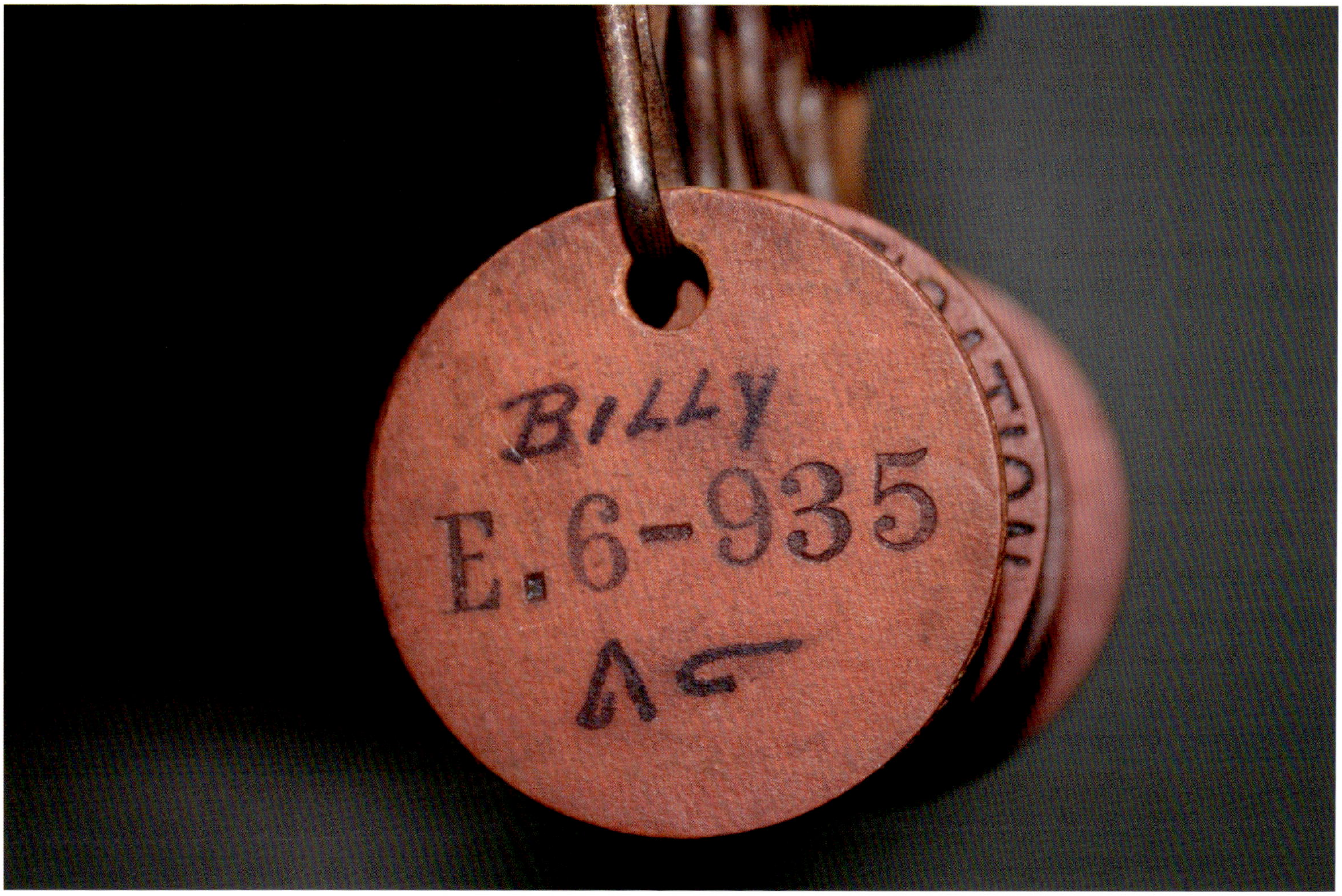
E.6-935

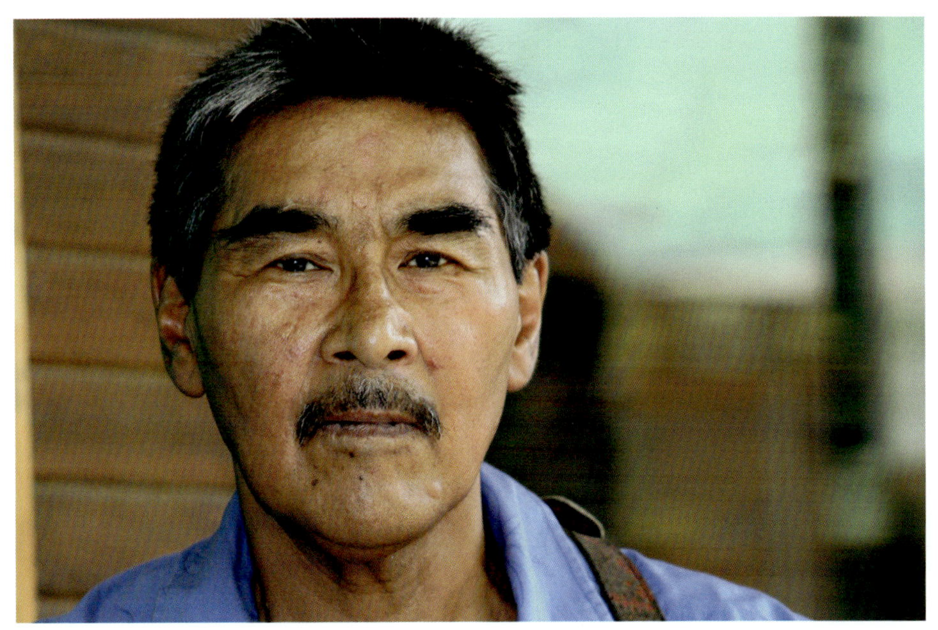

Barry Pottle
Inuit, born 1961
[David], 2009-2011
from Awareness Project series
Chromogenic print
Courtesy of the Art Gallery of Hamilton,
Purchase, Permanent Collection Fund, 2016

Page 38:
Barry Pottle
Inuit, born 1961
[untitled], 2009-2011
[untitled], 2009-2011
from Awareness Project series
Chromogenic print
Courtesy of the Art Gallery of Hamilton,
Purchase, Permanent Collection Fund, 2016

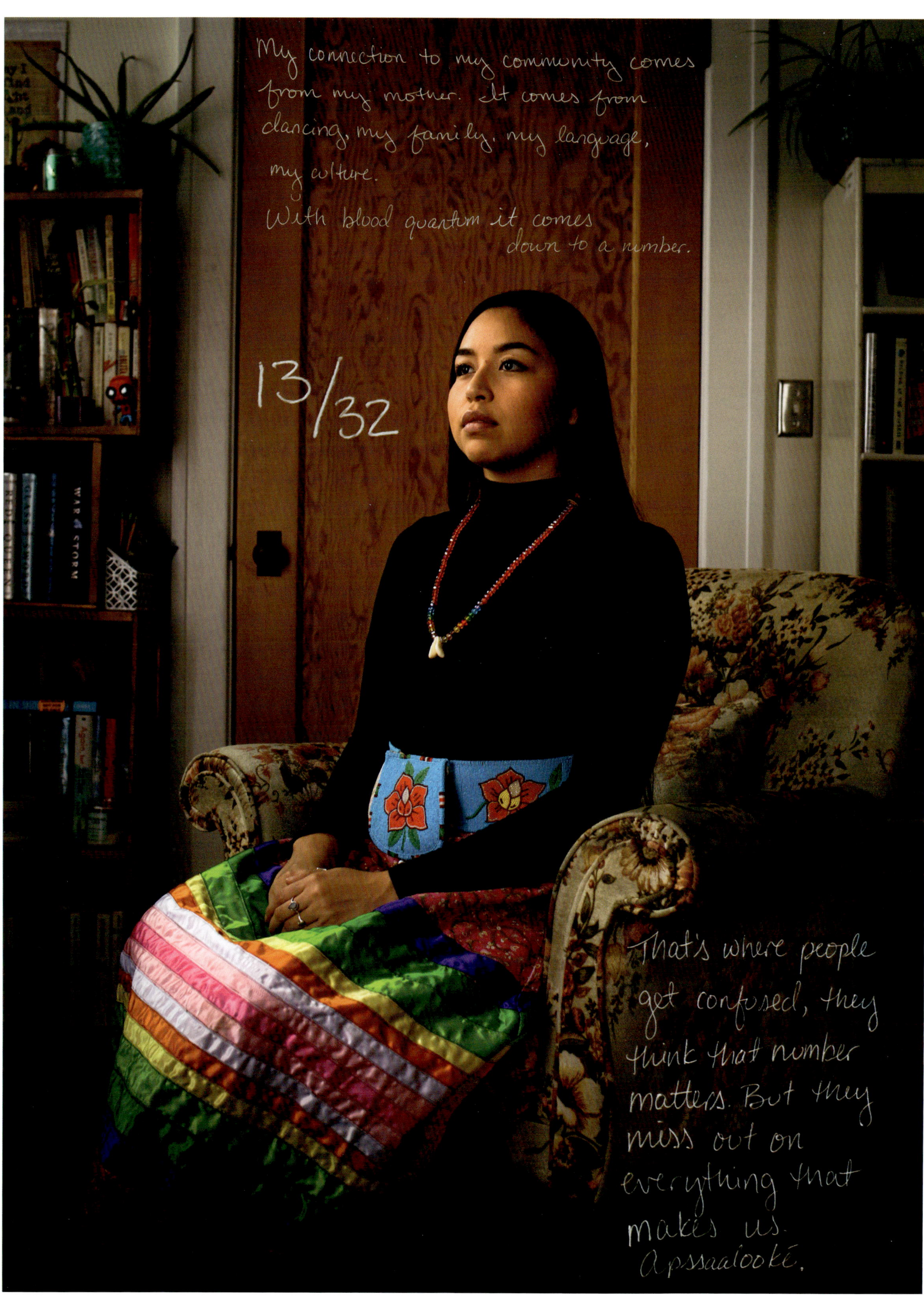

My connection to my community comes
from my mother. It comes from
dancing, my family, my language,
my culture.
With blood quantum it comes
down to a number.
13/32
That's where people
get confused, they
think that number
matters. But they
miss out on
everything that
makes us.
Apsáalooke.
WAR STORM

TO THE FUTURE

BY JAIDA GREY EAGLE

GROWING UP, I NEVER KNEW THERE WERE SO MANY INDIGENOUS PHOTOGRAPHERS out there, past and present. I barely ever heard my teachers talk about Indigenous people in general; in fact, they would often brush over the brutal past of colonization. I always remember the eye contact they would make with me when they would declare a white man "discovered" America but that there were Indigenous people here and nod towards me, this shy little kid whose presence made them acknowledge an entire people. Their definition of history and time never really made sense to me as I was told differently at home. Being a Native person, you learn from a young age of the two worlds you have to live in and navigate, and both of those worlds are declaring they are the truth of what happened to your people.

Luckily, I found photography at a young age. I was and am forever fascinated by the ability to stop time. When the world feels like too much or even too little, I can take a small piece of it and hold on. I often think of what drives me as an Indigenous woman and so much of what that is, is survival. I only speak English because my family adapted to it in boarding schools, in order to survive. I live in a city far from my reservation because of opportunities to expand who I am in all ways. I cultivate artistic practices that help bring our epistemologies into the current moment, because I believe in them wholeheartedly. I take photographs for the future so that they will know we survived and we're still here creating, living, loving, and breathing. I was so often talked out of pursuing photography. I have probably been told "no" far more than I have been told "yes" in this world; however, you just need to keep going. To have an artistic practice that feels so powerful can often be scary but it's also empowering. I believe I pursued photography because it has that ability. It can both terrify me but also empower me.

When I joined the team at Mia to co-curate this project, I had just finished my degree at the Institute of American Indian Arts. I had been immersed in the world of Indigenous art

Tailyr Irvine
Confederated Salish and Kootenai, born 1993
Reservation Mathematics, 2019
Inkjet print
Courtesy of the artist
© Tailyr Irvine

in Santa Fe, New Mexico, and wherever I could find similar surroundings, is where I wanted to be. While I was in Santa Fe, I took a course that introduced me to so many Indigenous photographers of the not so distant past, and I was also accepted into the collective "Indigenous Photograph." Through both of these outlets, I have been introduced to many of the works featured in this publication and exhibition.

I started at Mia through the Mdewakanton Fellowship but have stayed on throughout the years as a co-curator. Coming off the success of *Hearts of Our People*, our project began to come to fruition. It was important to bring the cumulative timetable of Indigenous photographers into this exhibition, as I truly believe that it is important for the legacy of all photographers to know this history, and it is the history of the land you are more than likely standing upon. This history, and the stories told by the photographers are an incredible testament to the original people of this land. Learning about all our pasts is important to our collective growth as a people.

I often think back to what it must have been like for Indigenous photographers to be doing this work 100 years ago and if they were thinking of the impact they would have on future Native photographers. I think of them often and their ability to send their worldviews into the future, the way they document their communities and how they see the world is still with us, and it deeply resonates and will continue to do so. Currently a new era of Indigenous photographers is being cultivated. I sleep so easily knowing this work is in good hands. It is all thanks to those that came before us and it's for those that will come after us. I hope that because of our collective journeys the next Indigenous youth that says they want to be a photographer is believed wholeheartedly by their family, community, and us. It is a beautiful life, and we will be waiting for you with open arms and hearts.

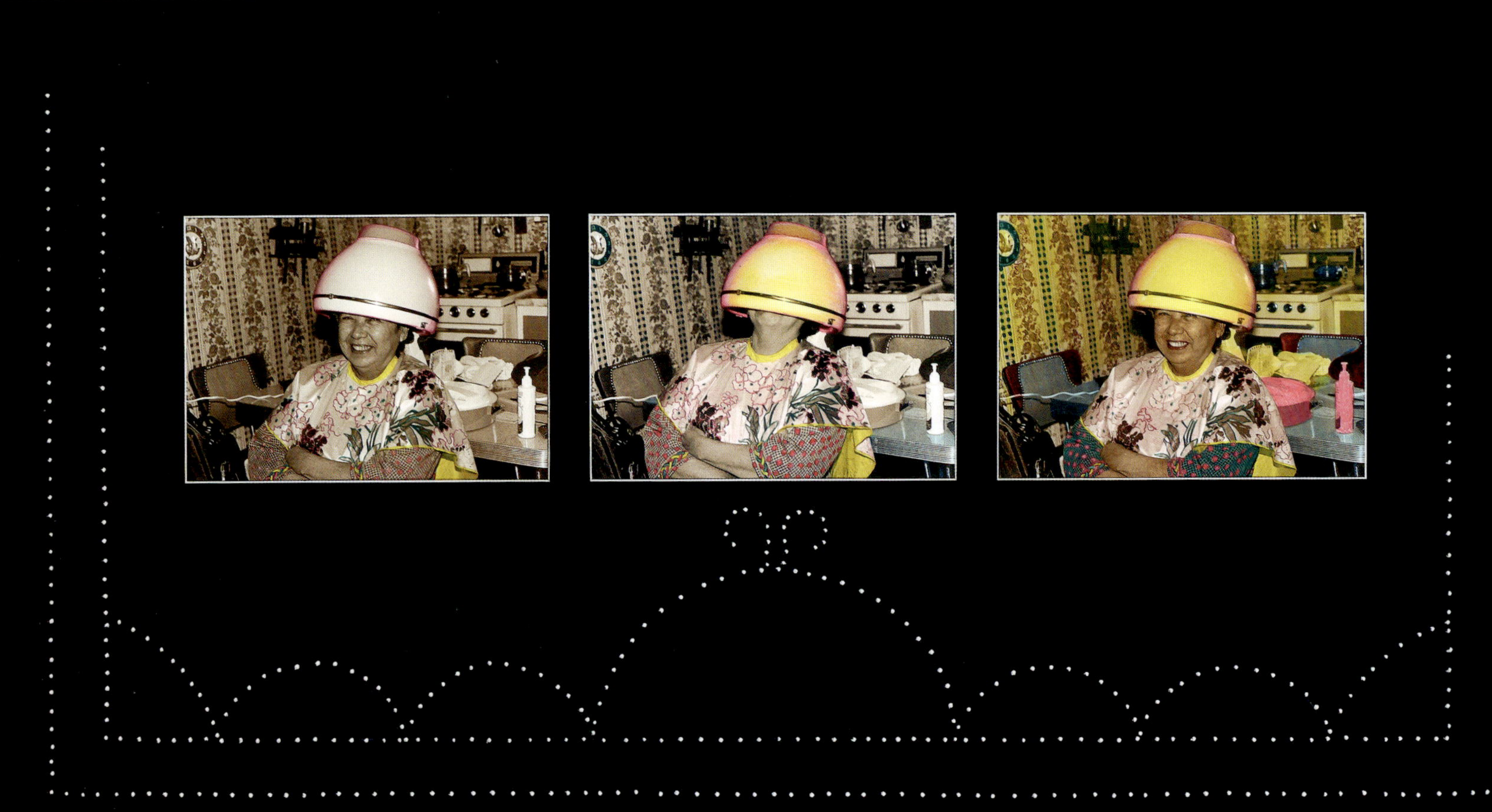

Plate and Fig. 1
Shelley Niro
Bay of Quinte Mohawk, Six Nations
Turtle clan, born 1954
The Iroquois is a Highly Developed
Matriarchal Society, 1991
Hand-colored gelatin silver prints
Courtesy of the artist

REMATRIATING PHOTOGRAPHY

BY VERONICA PASSALACQUA

SHELLEY NIRO'S ICONIC WORK, *The Iroquois is a Highly Developed Matriarchal Society* (1991), features her mother, Mrs. Doxtater, sitting in the kitchen of Niro's sister, Beverly, as the willing participant in her sister's hair-stylist training. Niro vibrantly hand tints the three photographs to differentiate the first and last images, and she creates movement by mounting them close together in a linear fashion amidst a scene filled with familiarity and laughter. In the surrounding matt board, Niro encompasses the work with hand drilled designs of the sky-dome and celestial trees, reflecting Haudenosaunee beadwork.

Niro invokes double entendre in the title, associating humor and irony to the steadfast anthropological statement while simultaneously creating her own visual narrative within the intimate scene. She places her mother, the family matriarch, at the center surrounded by the artist and her sister outside the frame but present. In this work, Niro recognizes her matrilineal society, but strives to show the flexibility to "loosen it up a bit too".[1] Niro discusses her titling further:

"'The Iroquois is a highly developed matriarchal society' is a statement usually used by anthropologists when describing the Iroquois. This description is not used just for the Iroquois but for other Indigenous groups around the world. I know the fundamental meaning but what is the intention of this meaning when used by the anthropologists, archaeologists, and historians. Were they recording what they saw when they first came into contact with this kind of communal living? Was it their way of taking power away from the masculine presence in these otherwise organized communities? Did the women run things? I grew up knowing this line by memory. It was confusing to be living in an historically important part of the country, nodding our heads to this description of my community but at the same time accepting violence against women as normal living conditions. Something has changed from then and now. We have to make things as they should be."[2]

Niro's visual interrogation of the conceptional and physical impacts to matrilineage, in relation to this work, was ahead of its time. The questions she poses remain salient and perhaps even more significant today with the ongoing violence against women and the calls for true reparations, to make things better. The Sogorea Te' Land Trust in the San Francisco Bay Area, founded by Corrina Gould and Johnella La Rose, promotes and articulates a concept known as rematriation. As part of the land trust led by urban Indigenous women, rematriation is the practice of restoring people to their rightful place, "to heal and transform the legacies of colonization, genocide and patriarchy and to do the work our ancestors and future generations are calling us to do."[3]

Images of Indigenous peoples by colonizers and outsiders through government agendas, propaganda, research, and cultural exoticism is foundational to the multiple histories of the medium of photography. Though Gould and La Rose utilize rematriation to address land claims, it is useful to consider the terminology in relationship to photography. Native photographers and the canon of Native photography have the ability to restore people to their rightful place. It has the capacity and power to be healing and transformative, and address legacies of colonization.

As Native photography has been established and furthered by Indigenous artists, curators, and authors (the majority of whom are women), it can and should be considered a sovereign space. When contemporary Native photography started emerging in exhibitions in the early 1980s, very little was known of earlier generations of Indigenous photographers. Native artists and authors undertook the arduous research of early photographers from within public and private archives, local histories, and tribal communities. Identifying early Native photographers was further complicated in that many archival images do not specify the photographer, with captions limited to place names and the sitter, if any at all. With continuing research, the number of early Native photographers continues to grow and be recognized, solidifying the history and foundations of the canon.

"No longer is the camera held by an outsider looking in, instead the camera is held with brown hands opening familiar worlds. We document ourselves with a humanizing eye, we create new visions with ease, and we can turn the camera and show how we see you."—Hulleah J. Tsinhnahjinnie.[4]

Contemporary Native photography emerged at a nexus of histories with a clear political voice, foremost articulating Indigenous resistance and survival. Alongside exhibitions, by the early 1990s, main-stream photographic publications, *Aperture* (1995), *Exposure* (1993), and *The*

Journal of Photography of New England (1993), had dedicated full issues to Native photography, and included space for Native artists and authors to present and frame artwork and the field from a Native perspective.[5] Visual sovereignty expressed ownership, mediation, and articulation of the artworks and the field.

Photographic artists utilized and inverted the reifying power of photography to rematriate the narratives and photographic political practices that had functioned so effectively against Indigenous peoples in the past. From the outset, Native photography confronted complex political histories from the past and present, often directly through photographic content or indirectly, by existence and continuance.

Many of Hulleah Tsinhnahjinnie's works include archival images layered through hand and digital collage. *"When Did Dreams of White Buffalo Turn to Dreams of White Women?"* (1990) and *We'wha, The Beloved* (2008) are two examples of this technique. At the base of her creative process, Tsinhnahjinnie writes:

"There exists a deep passion within my being to gather dreams and visions. Visions that have survived the vulgarities of war, flowing through thick rivers of ancestral blood, currents of thoughts that have transmitted through lowered voices surrounded by protective night skies. Dreams, visions and thoughts that are safely wrapped in stubborn Indigenous persistence prepared for a long journey. When constructing dreams and visions, I find that collages work well. The cutting, pasting, and choosing is followed by another favorite of digital construction, ultimately rendering the vision seamlessly."[6]

The dream and vision she creates in *"When Did Dreams of White Buffalo Turn to Dreams of White Women?"* is complexly layered through hand collage of silver-gelatin prints, postcard images, Xerox copies, and book pages. At the center is her friend, Carol, dressed in fine Nez Perce beadwork and regalia, as Tsinhnahjinnie's view of beauty. Holding a corn husk bag and eagle fan, she sits in a mid-century home, surrounded by rich works of beaded bags, moccasins, corn husk cap, and blankets. Behind her is an archival image from the American Ethnology collection of a nineteenth century Native man, representative of the vast government collections. At his shoulder is a white woman's face in the classic Hollywood portraiture style of idealized western beauty. For the artist, these two images together "portray the schizophrenic ideology of the United States."[7]

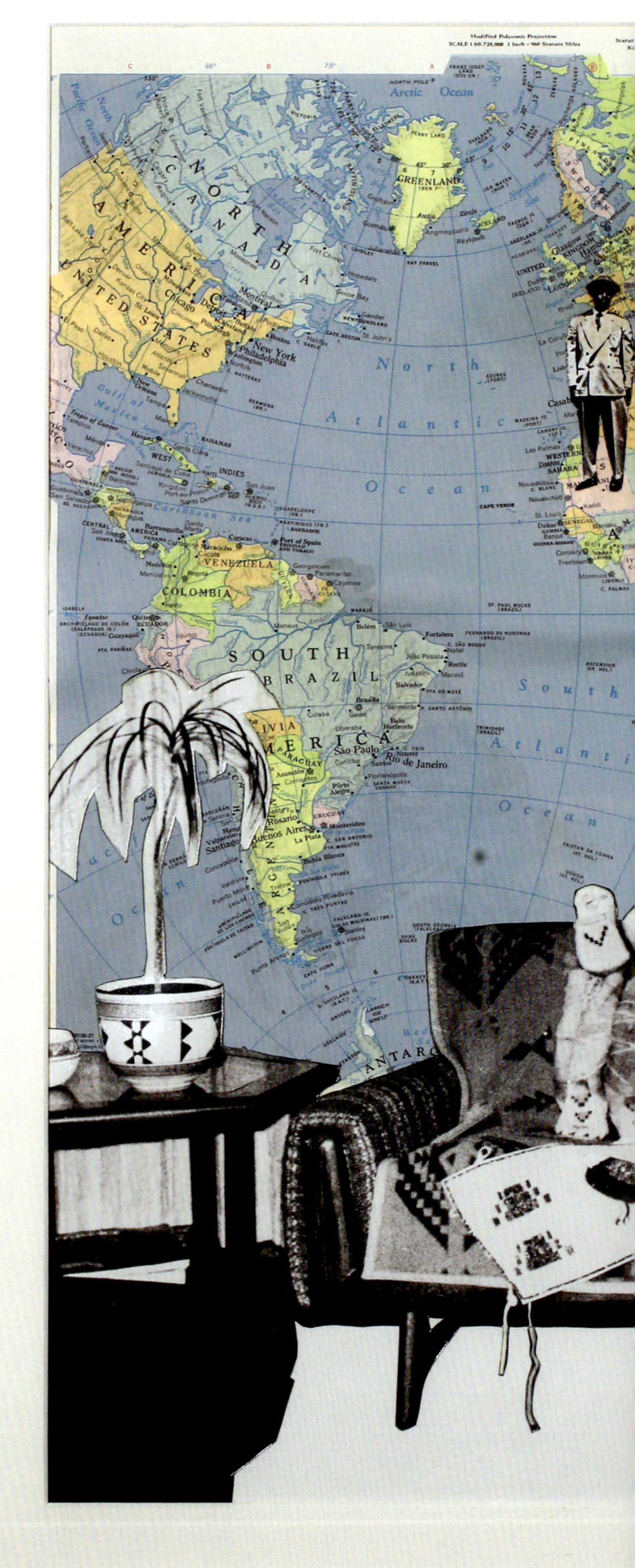

Hulleah J. Tsinhnahjinnie
Diné (Navajo) / Seminole / Muscogee (Creek), born 1954
When Did Dreams of White Buffalo Turn to Dreams of White Women?, 1990
Photo collage
Minneapolis Institute of Art, Gift of funds from Nancy and Rolf Engh 2022.44

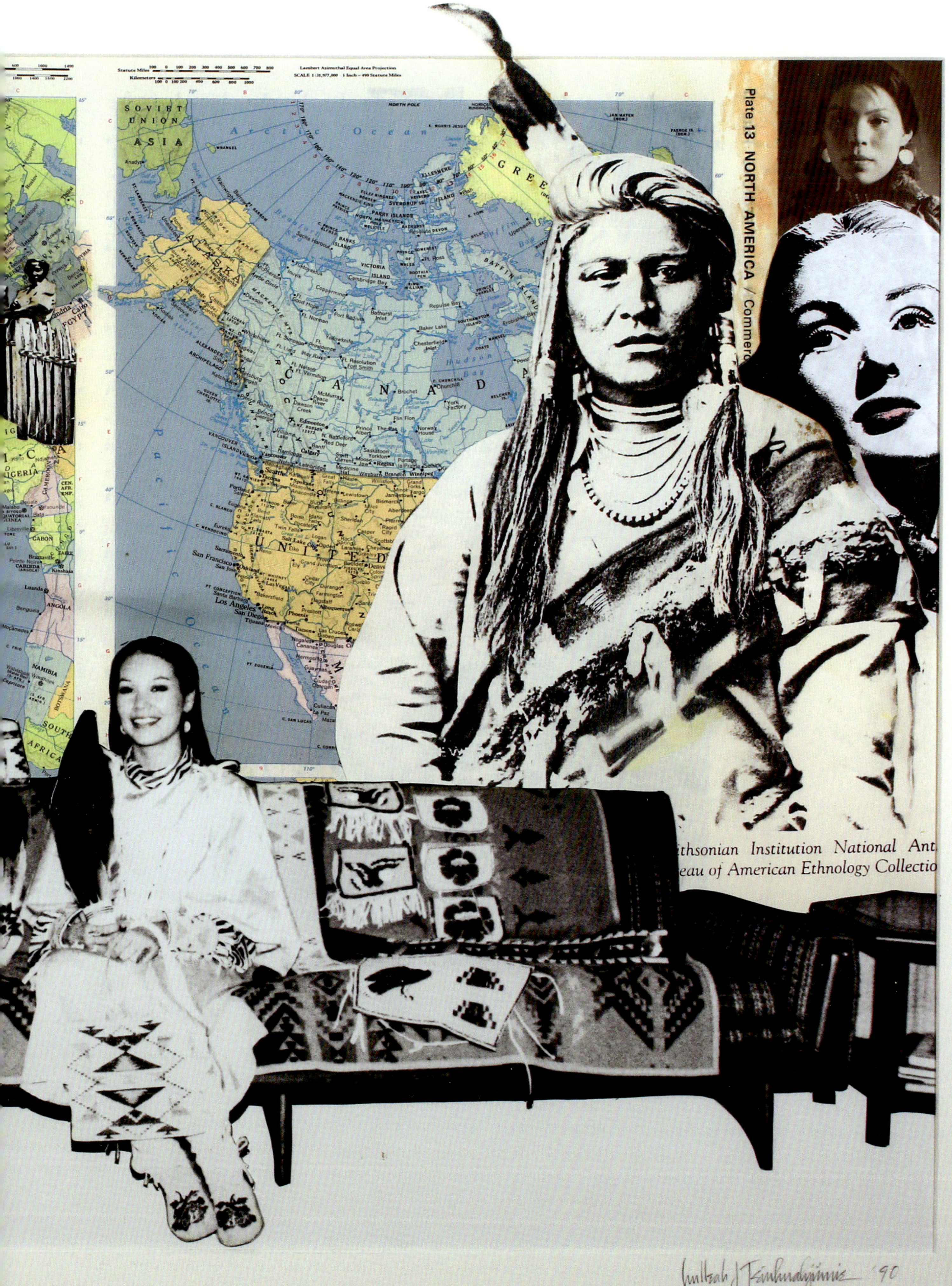
Plate 13 NORTH AMERICA / Commerc
ithsonian Institution National Ant
eau of American Ethnology Collectio
SOVIET UNION ASIA
ALASKA
CANADA
UNITED
Los Angeles
San Francisco
'90

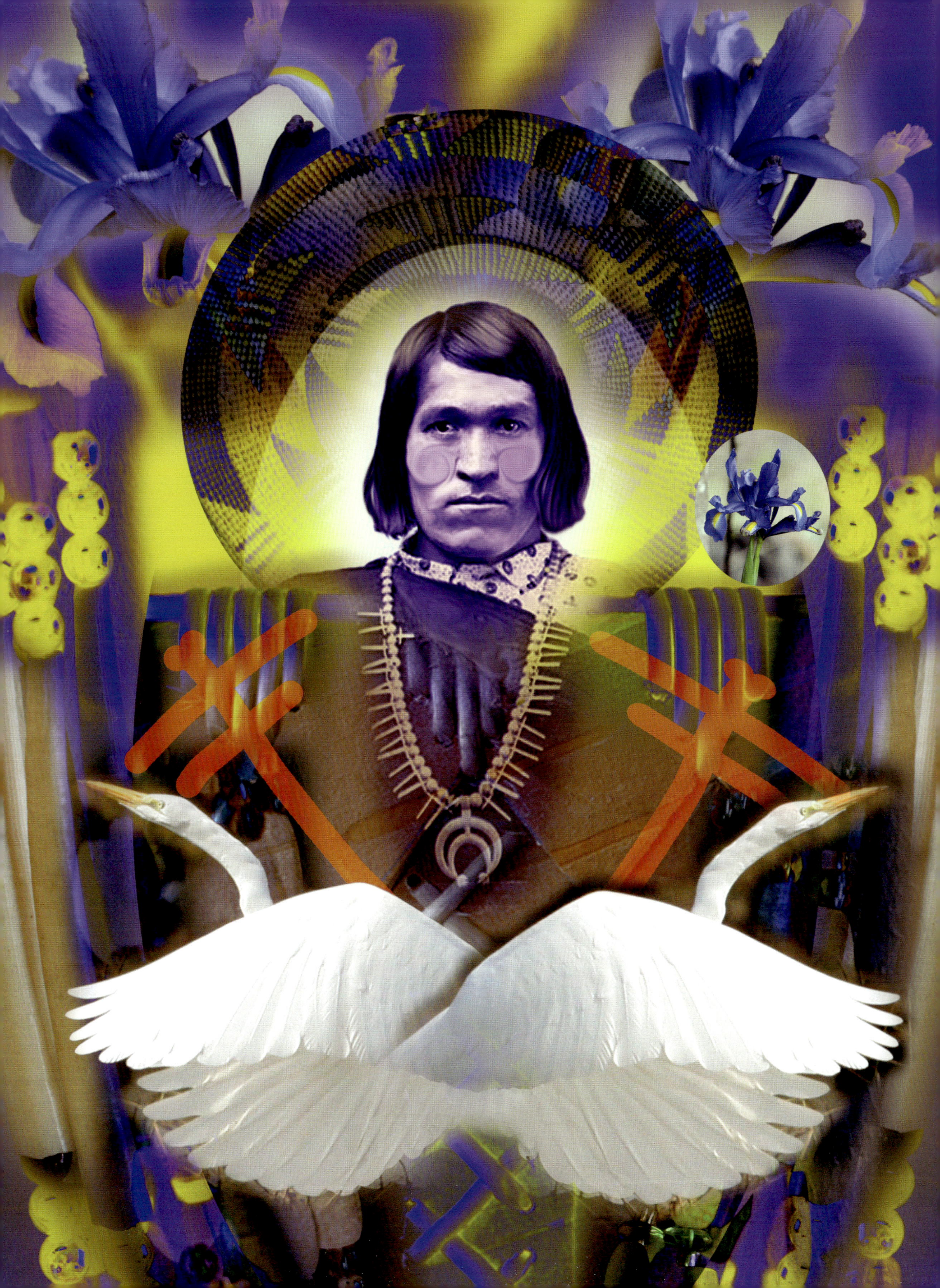

Tsinhnahjinnie's visual response and vision of beauty includes her portrait of Idelia, rendered into a soft "comfortable" sepia tone in the background.[8] Wall-papering the room is an atlas map of the world, reflecting shared Indigenous experiences of global colonization and displacement. Also layered into this piece is time itself with a sense of witnessing, as the artist takes the viewer first to the foreground and main subject, with a sense of familiarity that leads the viewer beyond the sofa, and on to interpret the complexities of colonialism and change around the world over time.

The shift to digital collage in the work, *We'wha, The Beloved* (2008) allows for the seamless layering the artist mentions earlier with smooth blending and blurring between each of the layers. At the center of the piece is the photographic portrait of We'wha by John K. Hillers from between 1884–1897. We'wha (1849–1896) was known as a two-spirit person, spiritual leader, and cultural ambassador for the Zuni nation. When Tsinahnahjinnie acquired the historical cabinet card, she created her own visual reinterpretation and remembrance of We'wha that is lushly surrounded by purple irises, regalia, and basketry in a halo form. Egrets allow We'wha to fly and travel, with the agility and warrior fierceness of two red dragonflies.

Fig. 2. John Hillers (German, 1843–1925), We-wha, 1884–1897. Albumen silver print, (Bureau of American Ethnology Collec.on).

These photographic works are embedded in a range of political discourses and experiences that extend to encompass the canon of Native photography. Tsinhnahjinnie and Niro, alongside other lens-based women artists in the field, rematriate the imagery of colonial histories into new narratives surrounded and supported by Indigenous knowledge, experiences, and perspective.

The images are meant to convey love, beauty, friends, and family in relationship with the photographic artist. Interpretation is complex, but it is unquestionable that authority and ownership—visual sovereignty—lies with the artist.

Plate and Fig. 3
Hulleah J. Tsinhnahjinnie
Diné (Navajo) / Seminole / Muscogee (Creek), born 1954
We'wha, The Beloved, 2012
Courtesy the Artist

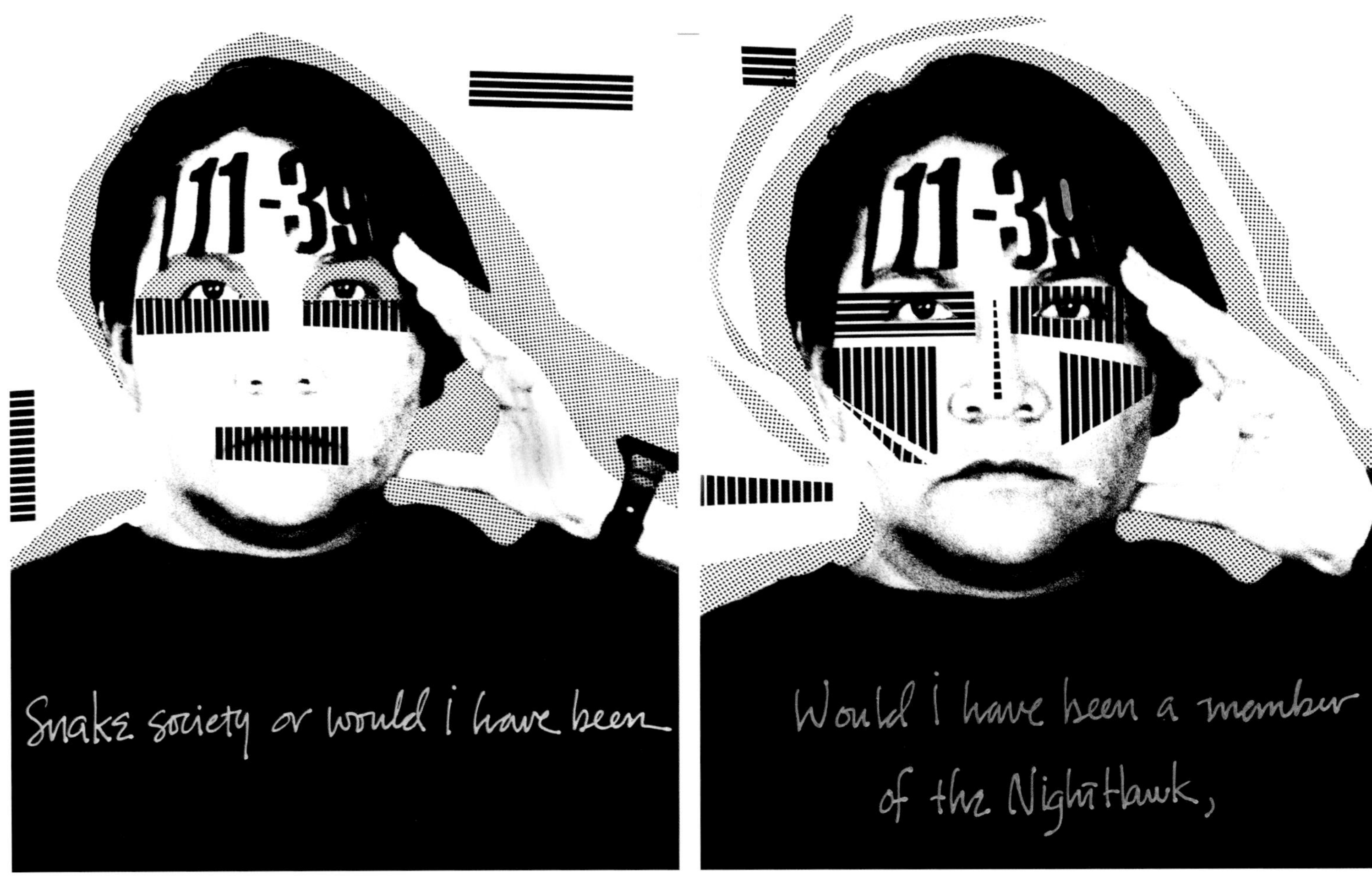

In 1996, Jolene Rickard advocated for "a separate but permeous space" where Native artists create art that "reflects the synthesis of their multiple experiences while still being centered within Indigenous world views." Such a space, according to Rickard, "privileges Indigenous cultural tenets; oral tradition, spiritual beliefs, aesthetic and political histories as the most important consideration in cultural analysis."[9]

The depth of the canon of Native photography is limitless. The growth and expansion of the field encompasses early Native photographers from across the continent as early as the medium itself, depicting and documenting images seen through the viewfinder. The launch of exhibitions and publications in the 1980–90s brought the canon to public realms and recognition, addressing past and present experiences. Digital and new technologies widen the canon

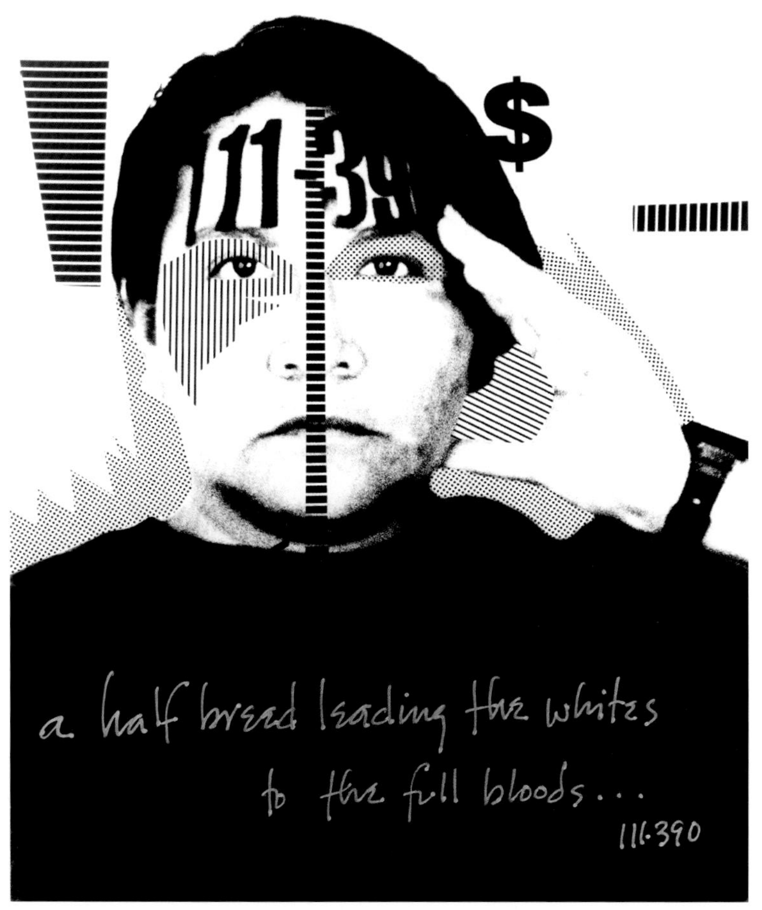

Hulleah J. Tsinhnahjinnie
Diné (Navajo) / Seminole / Muscogee (Creek), born 1954
Would I Have Been A Member of the Nighthawk Snake Society or Would I Have Been a Half Breed Leading the Whites to the Full-Bloods?, 1991
Courtesy of the artist
© 2023 Hulleah J. Tsinhnahjinnie

further, enabling accessibility in creating works, as well as circulation, exhibitions, and publishing platforms. The canon of Native photography encompasses a rich history of generations of artists exploring and pushing the boundaries of the medium, creating and engaging with narratives across time that include the past, present, and looks ahead to multiple futures and the multiverse.

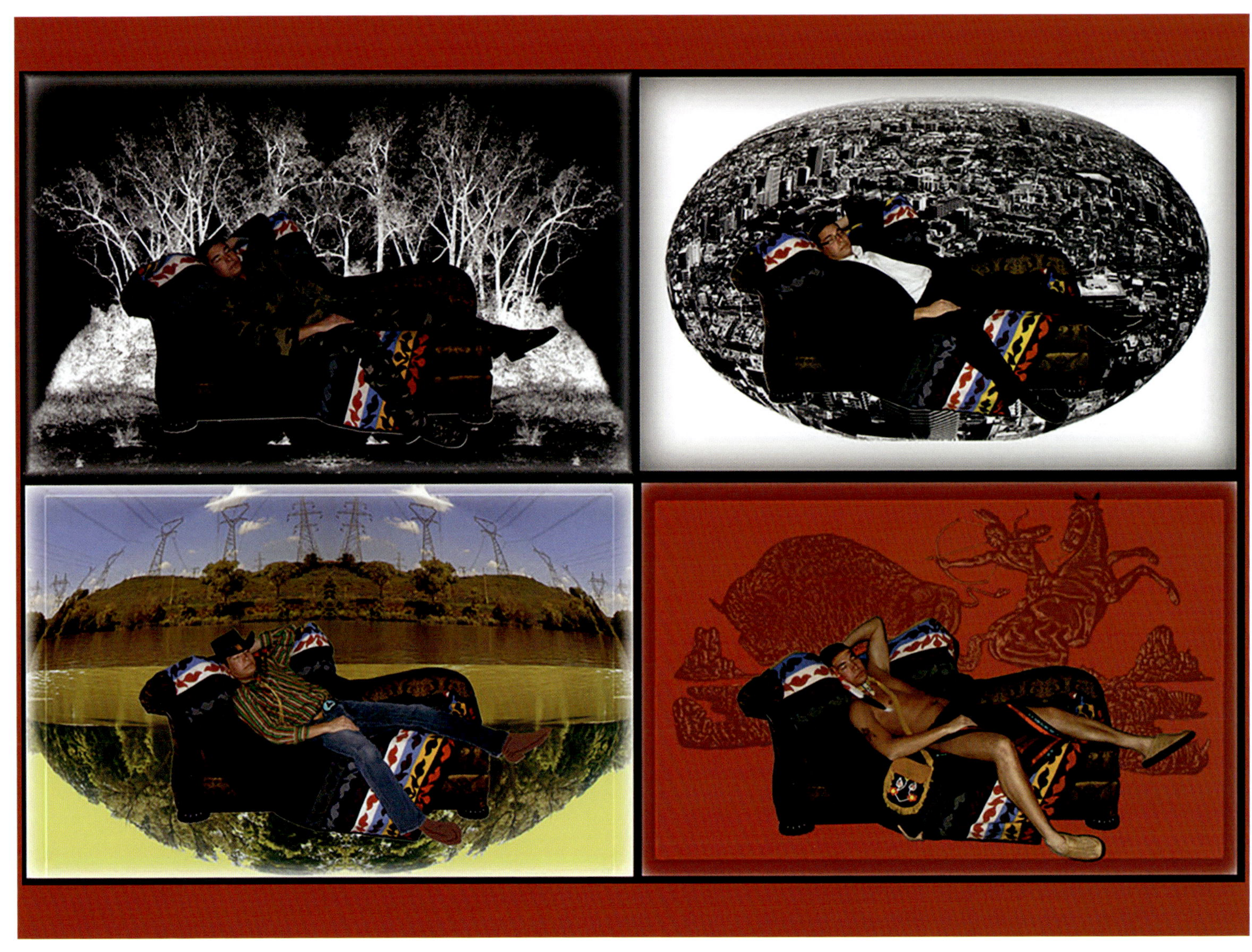

Shelley Niro
Bay of Quinte Mohawk,
Six Nations Turtle clan, born 1954
Four Directions of Warrior, 2012
from Sleeping Warrior series
Digital photograph
Gift of funds from Nancy
and Rolf Engh 2022.43.1

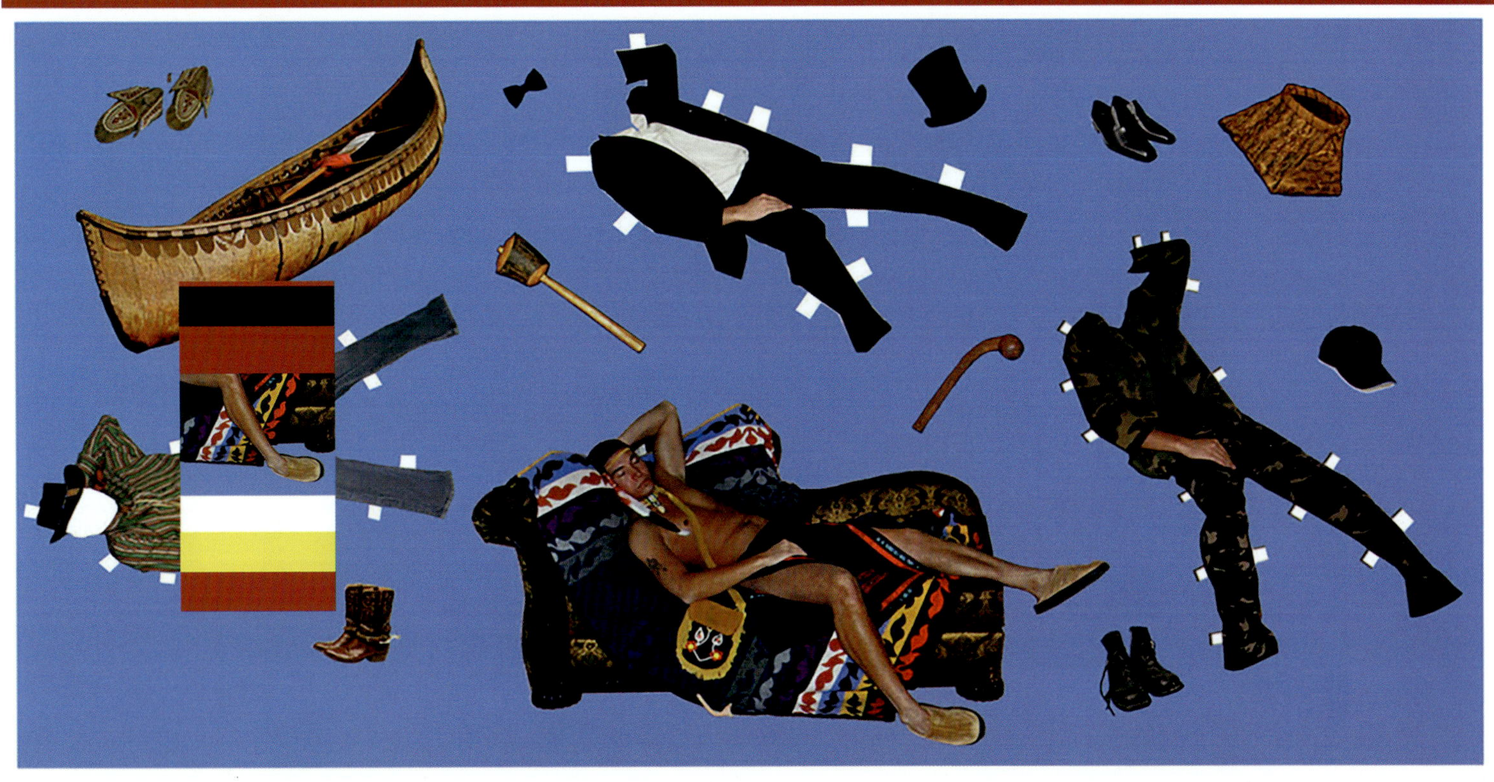

Shelley Niro
Bay of Quinte Mohawk,
Six Nations Turtle clan, born 1954
Dressing Warrior, 2012
from Sleeping Warrior series
Digital photograph
Gift of funds from Nancy
and Rolf Engh 2022.43.4

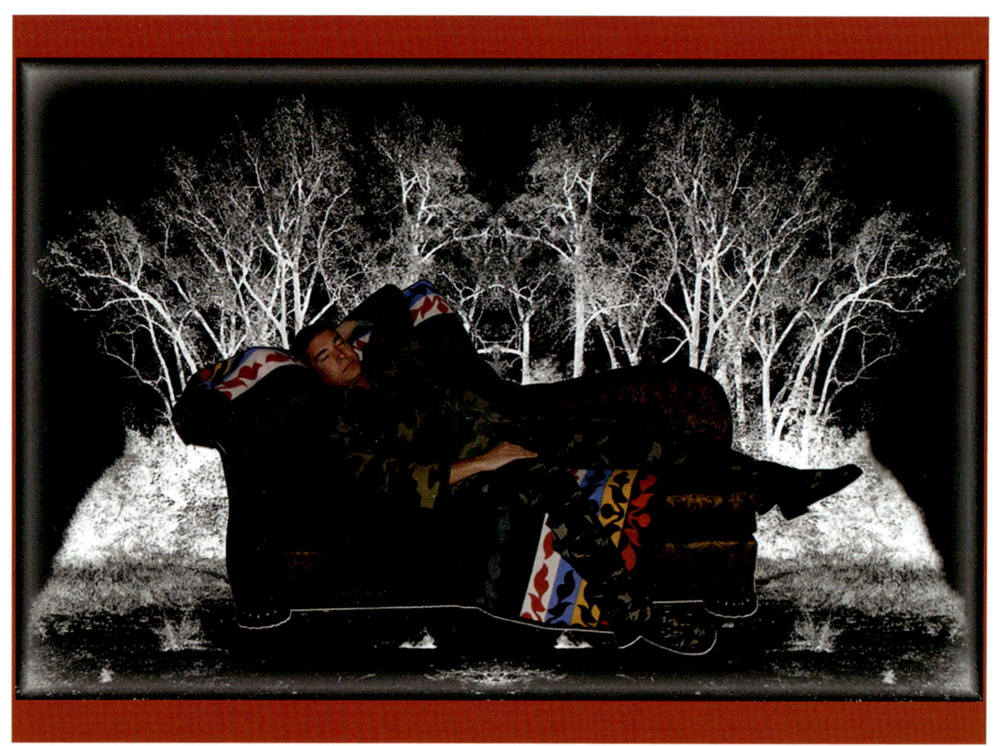

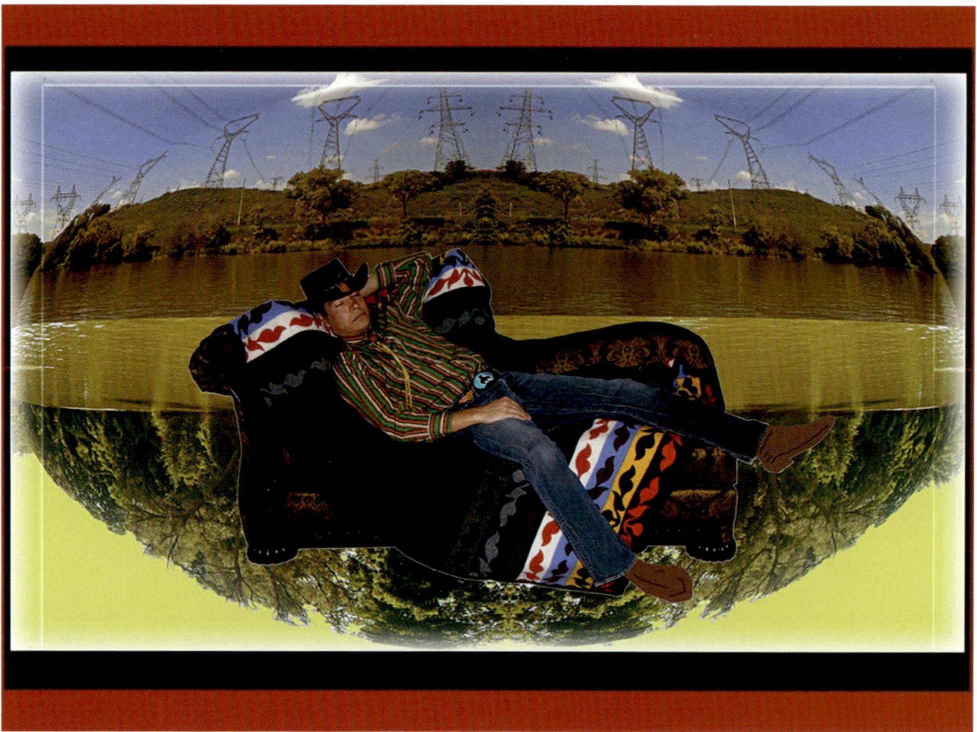

Shelley Niro
Bay of Quinte Mohawk,
Six Nations Turtle clan, born 1954
Dreaming of Fighting No More, 2012
from Sleeping Warrior series
Digital photograph
Gift of funds from Nancy
and Rolf Engh 2022.43.2

Shelley Niro
Bay of Quinte Mohawk,
Six Nations Turtle clan, born 1954
Dreams of Pastures and Power, 2014
from Sleeping Warrior series
Digital photograph
Gift of funds from Nancy
and Rolf Engh 2022.43.5

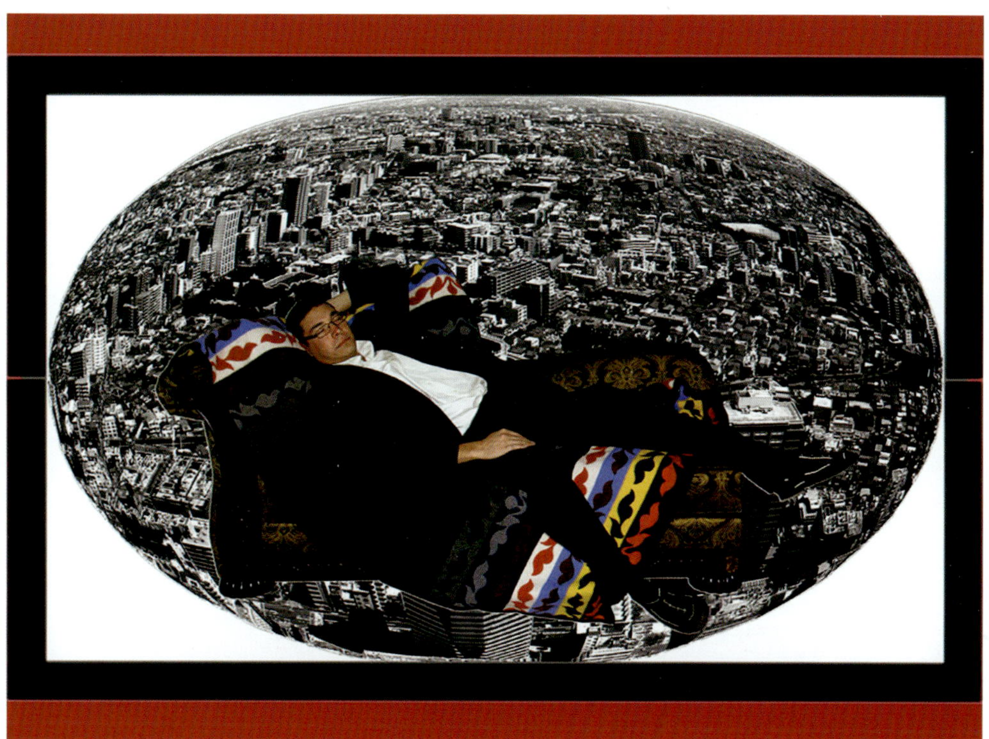

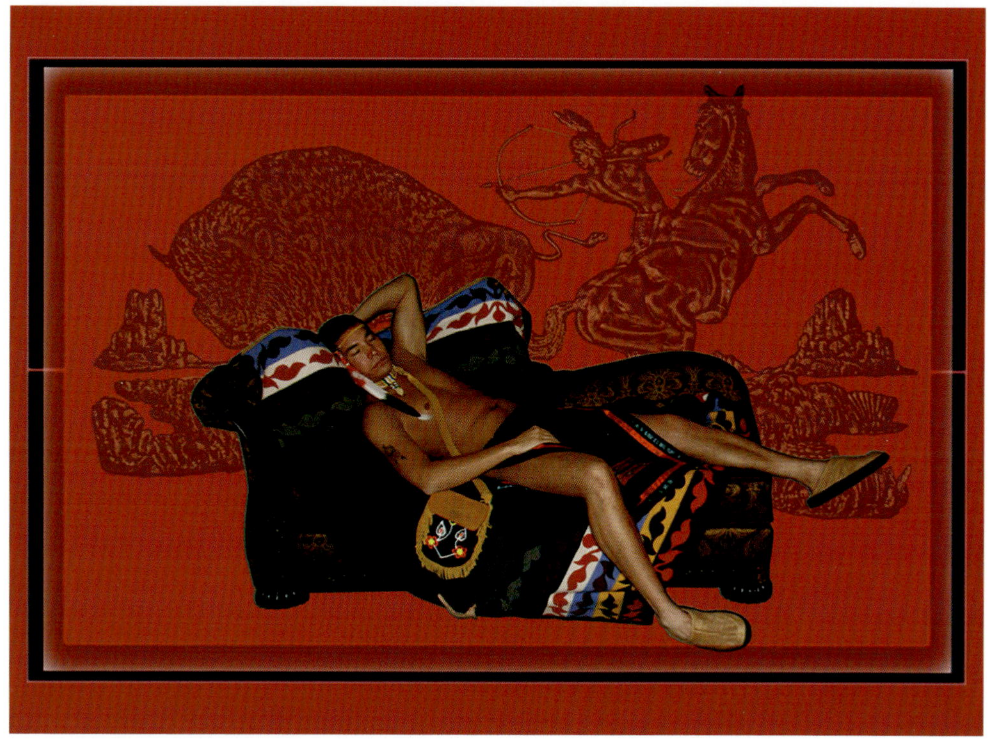

Shelley Niro
Bay of Quinte Mohawk,
Six Nations Turtle clan, born 1954
Dreaming of Life in the Sky, 2012
from Sleeping Warrior series
Digital photograph
Gift of funds from Nancy
and Rolf Engh 2022.43.3

Shelley Niro
Bay of Quinte Mohawk,
Six Nations Turtle clan, born 1954
Dreams of Hunting, 2014
from Sleeping Warrior series
Digital photograph
Gift of funds from Nancy
and Rolf Engh 2022.43.6

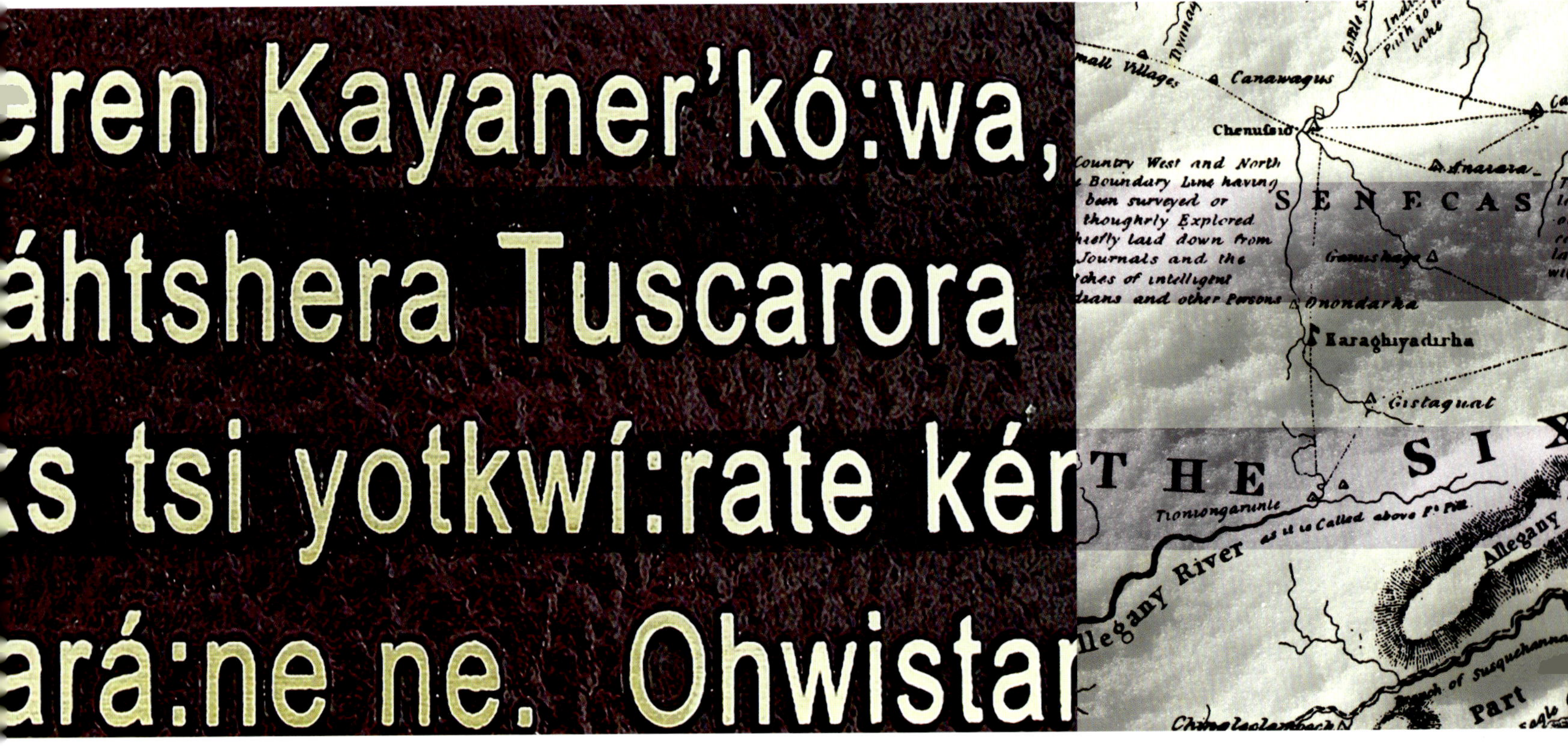

Jolene Rickard
Tuscarora Nation, Turtle Clan, born 1956
Lines of Power, 2023
Inkjet print
Courtesy of the artist

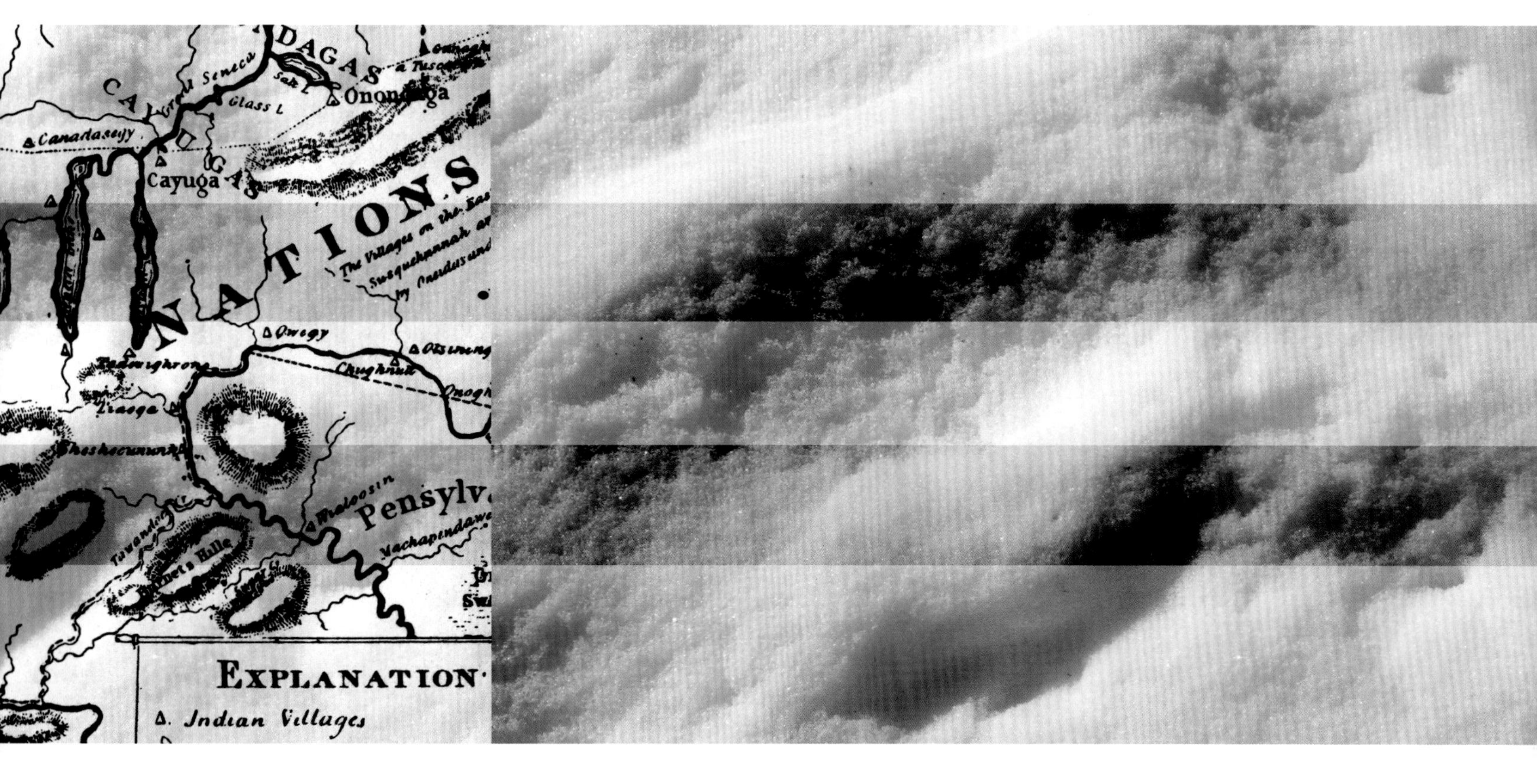

Cayuga
NATIONS
Glass L
Owegy
Chughnut
EXPLANATION
Indian Villages

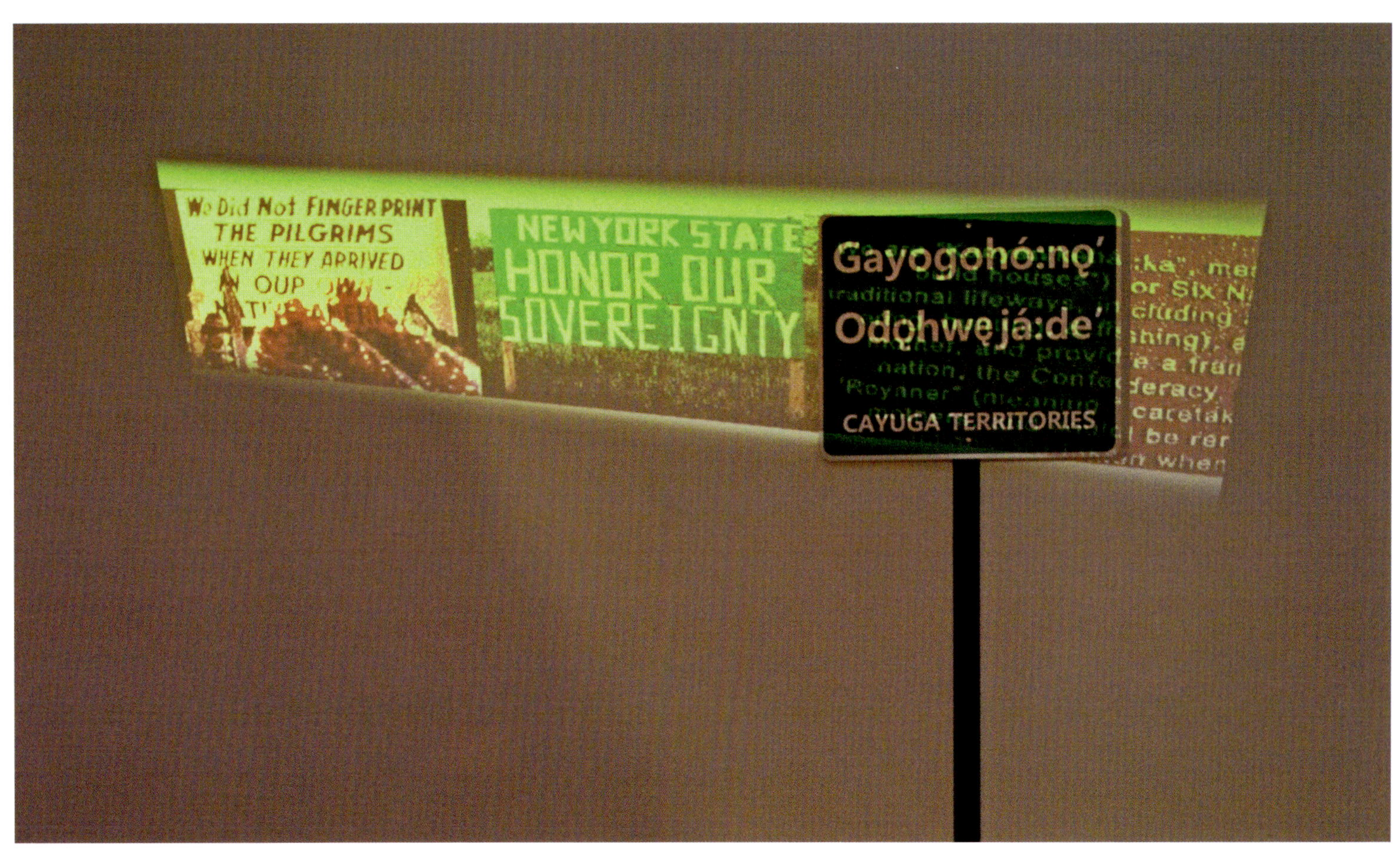

Jolene Rickard
Tuscarora Nation, Turtle Clan, born 1956
Fight For The Line, 2012
Single channel video projection onto
Painted metal
Courtesy of the artist

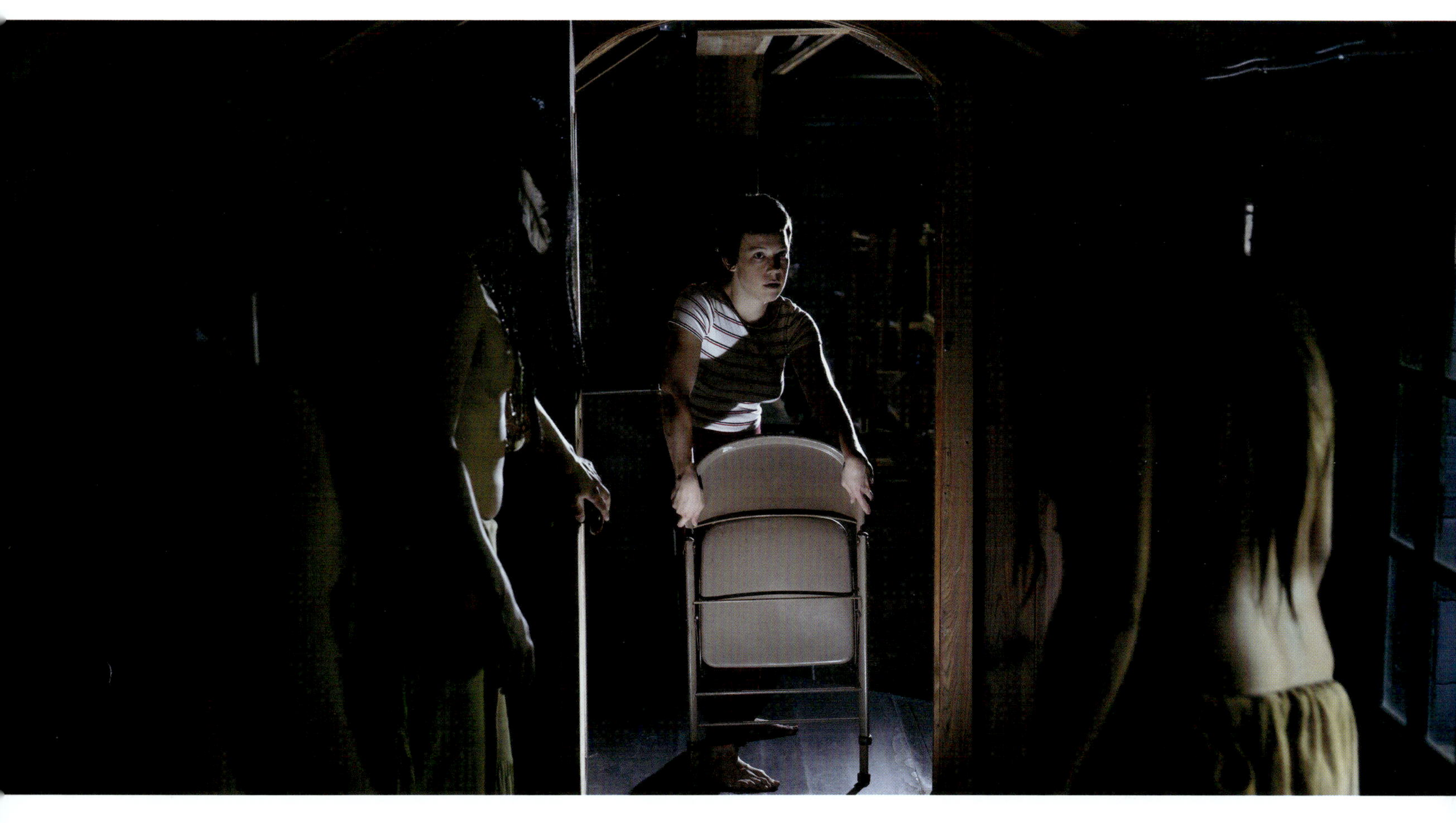

Jeremy Dennis
Shinnecock Indian Nation, born 1990
Door Prop, 2018
from Rise series
Archival inkjet print on matte paper
Courtesy of the artist

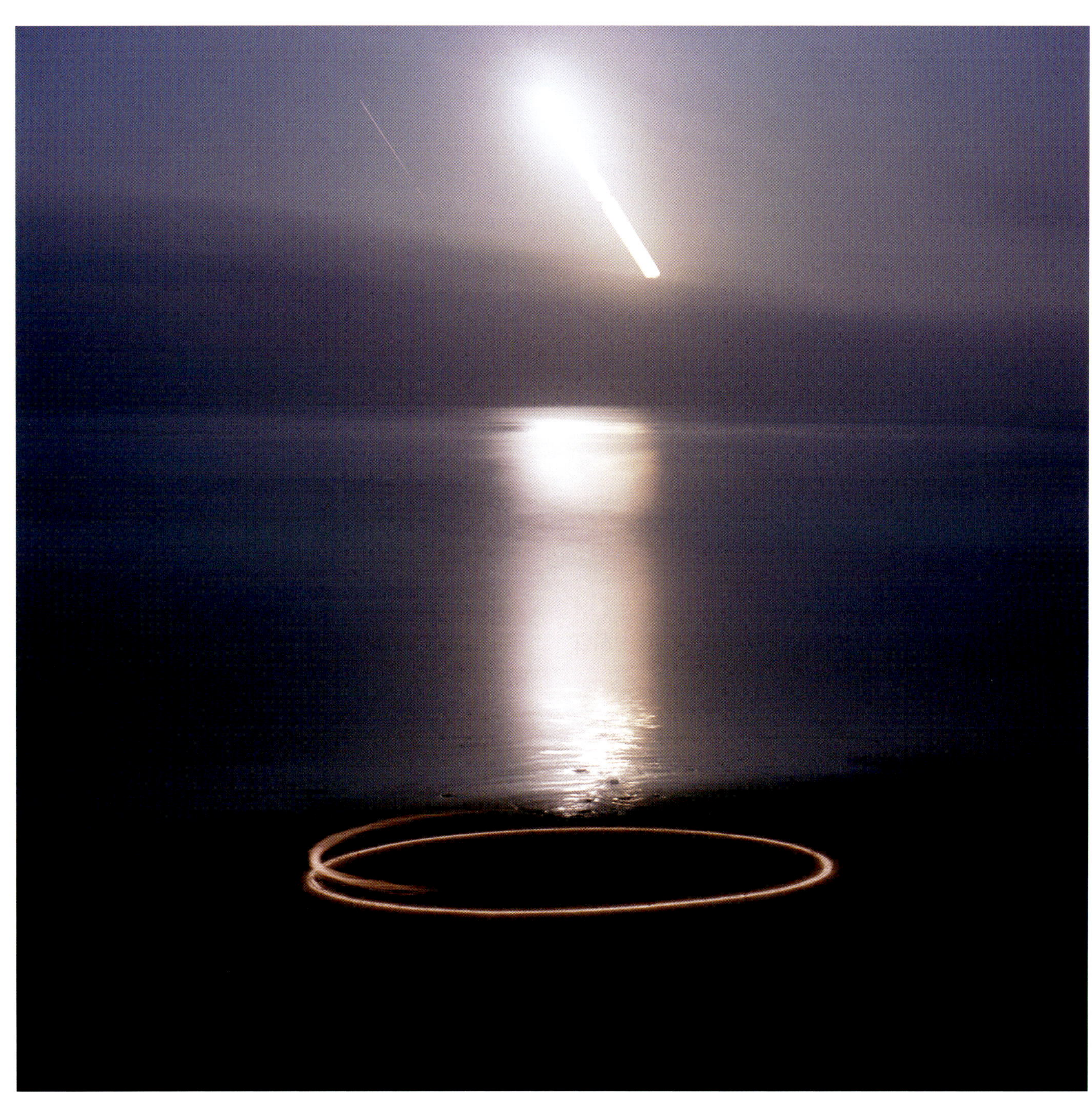

Lewis deSoto
Cahuilla, born 1954
Ellipse/Tide, Encinitas, California, 1982-87
Inkjet print, printed 2021
Courtesy of the Museum of Modern Art,
gift of the artist, 399.2021.1

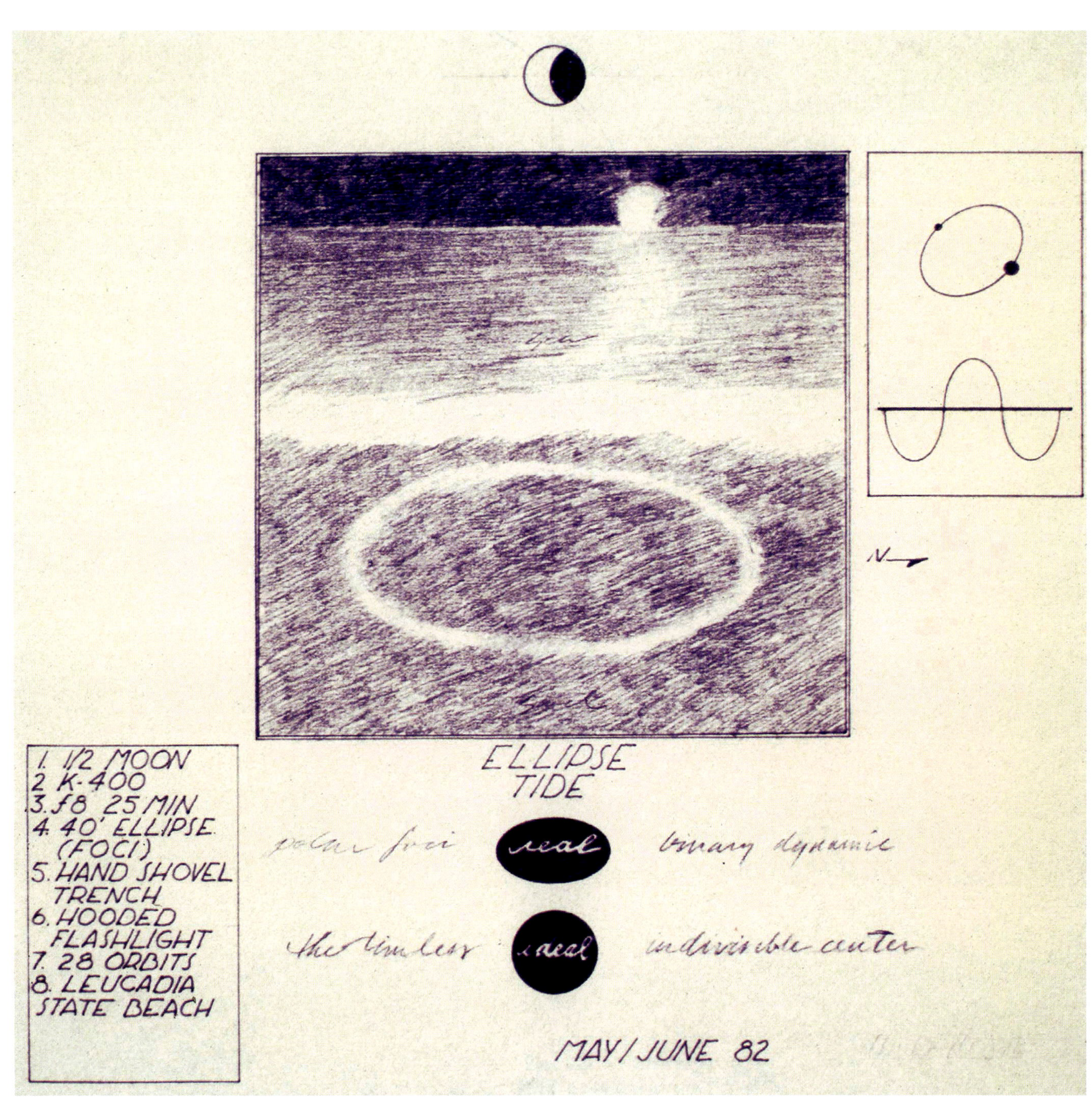

Lewis deSoto
Cahuilla, born 1954
Ellipse/Tide, Encinitas, California, 1982
Inkjet print of the original diazo print, printed 2021
Courtesy of the Museum of Modern Art, gift of the artist, 399.2021.2

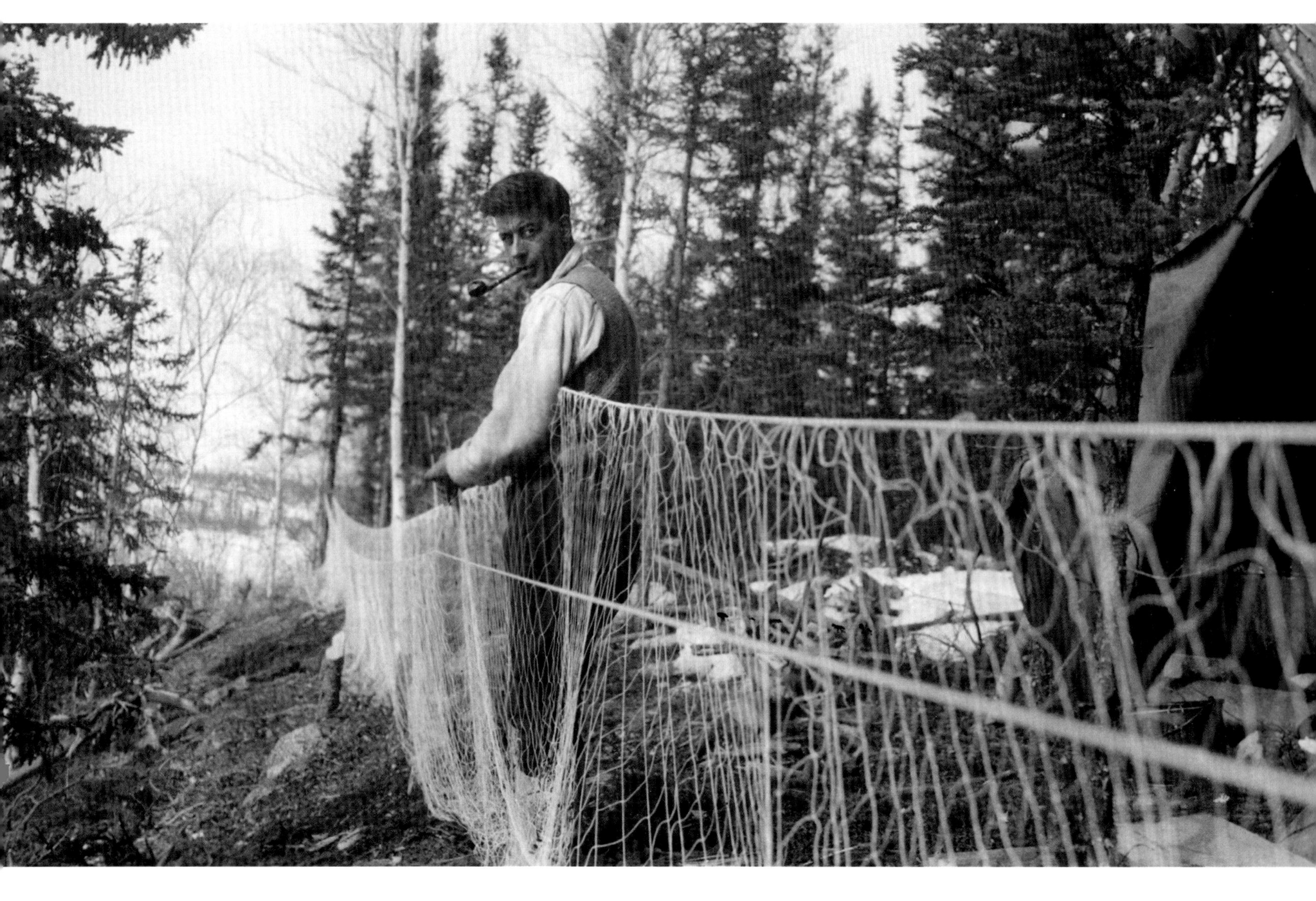

James (Jim) Patrick Brady
Métis, 1908-1967 (disappeared, presumed deceased)
Malcolm Norris hanging nets, 1934
Courtesy of Glenbow Archives, PA-2218-94

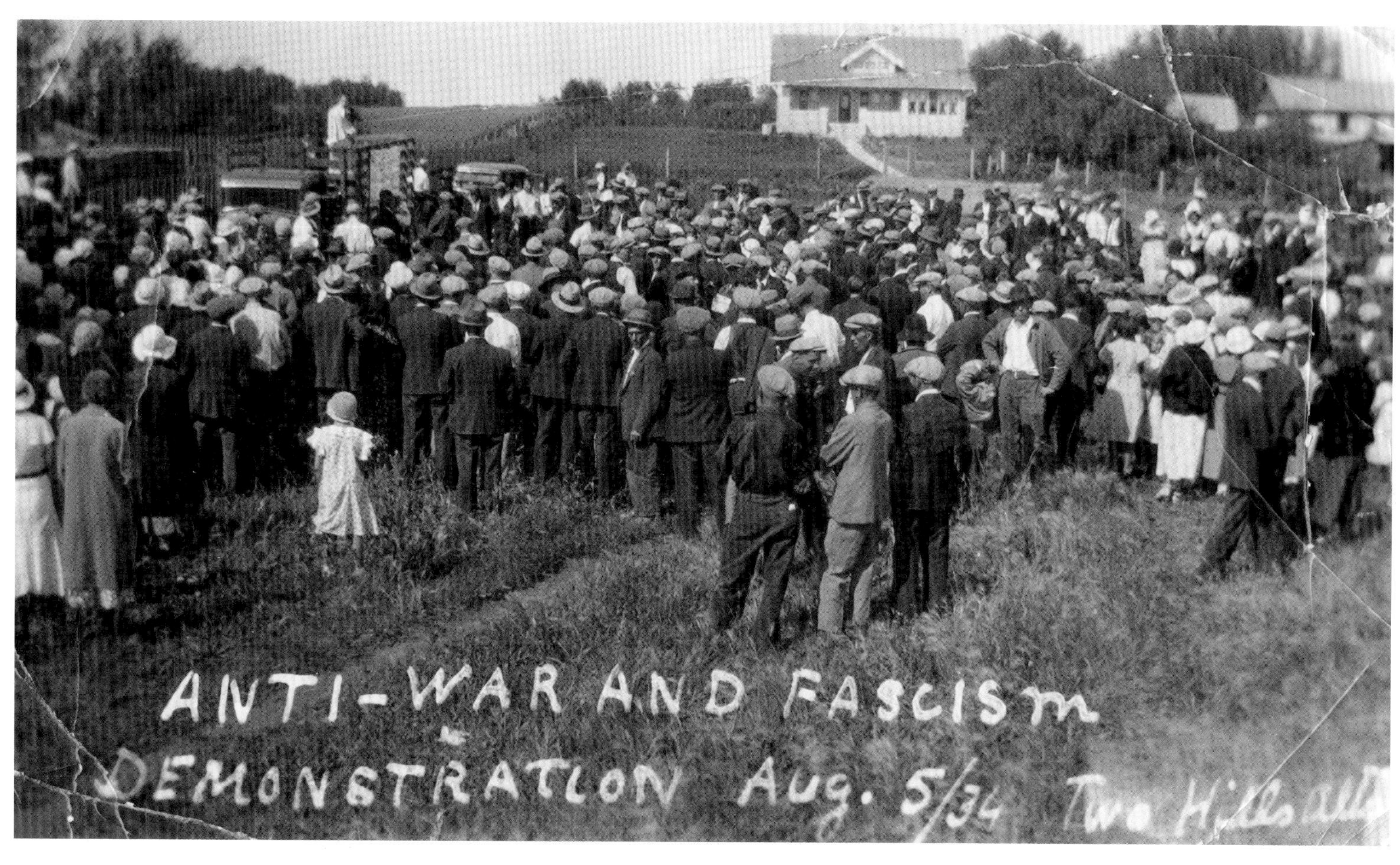

James (Jim) Patrick Brady
Métis, 1908 1967 (disappeared,
presumed deceased)
Anti War and Fascism Demonstrations,
5th August, 1934, 1934
Courtesy of Glenbow Archives, PA-2218-107

Pages 66-67:
Bently Spang
Northern Cheyenne, born 1960
War Shirt #1, 1998
from *Modern War* series
Mixed media
Collection of Sandra P. Spang
Photo by Joshua Ferdinand and courtesy of
The Nelson-Atkins Museum of Art
© 1998 Bently Spang

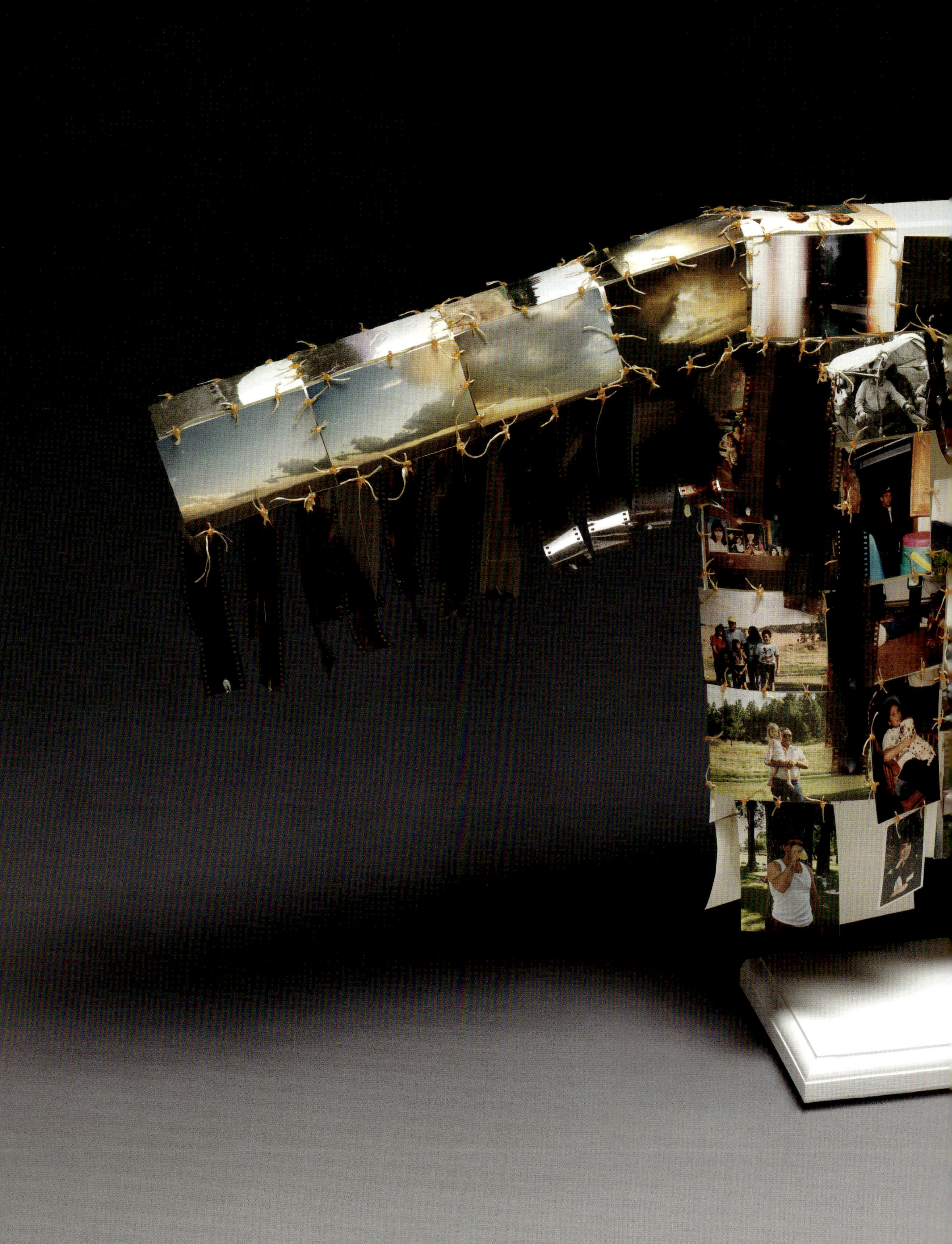

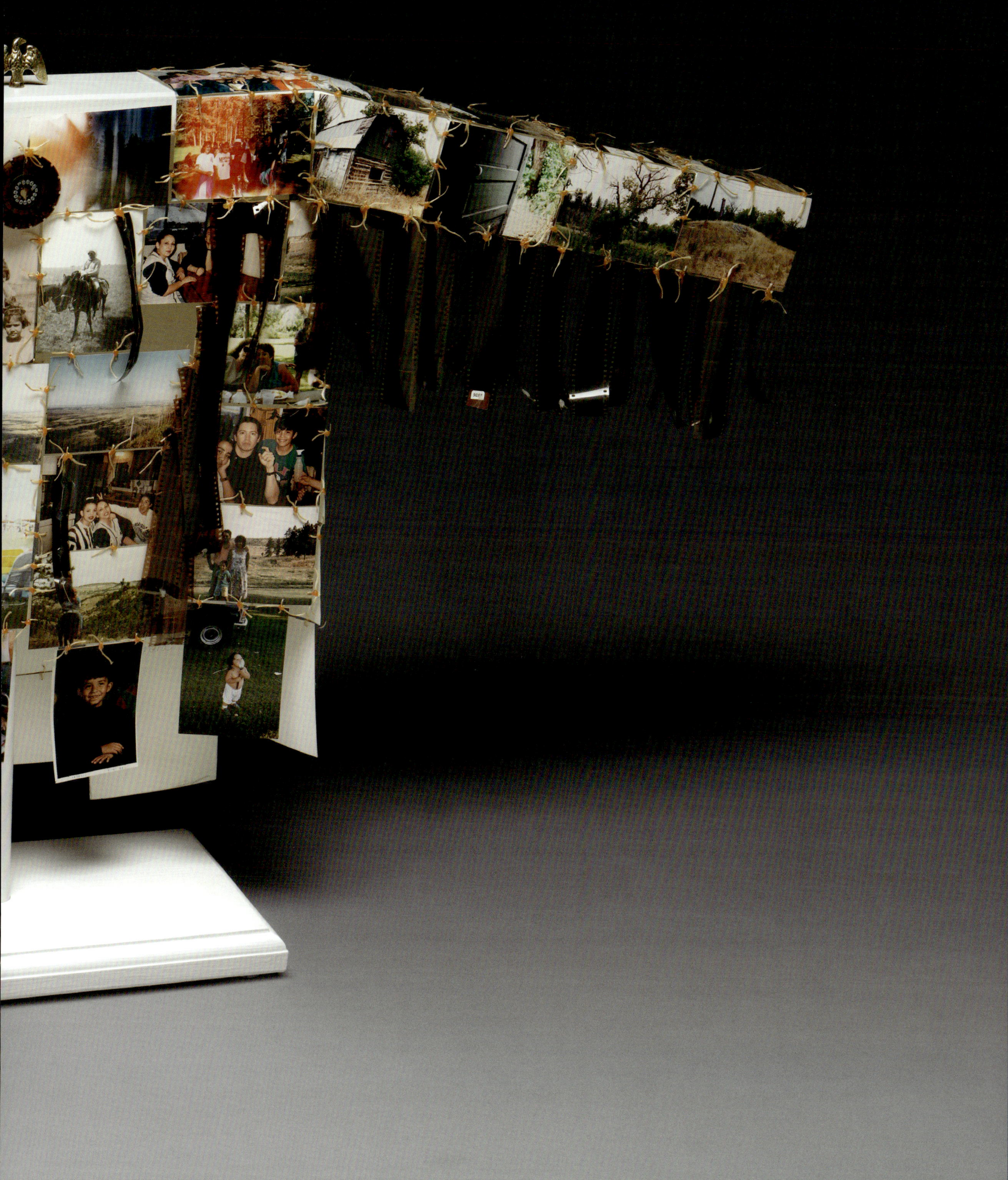

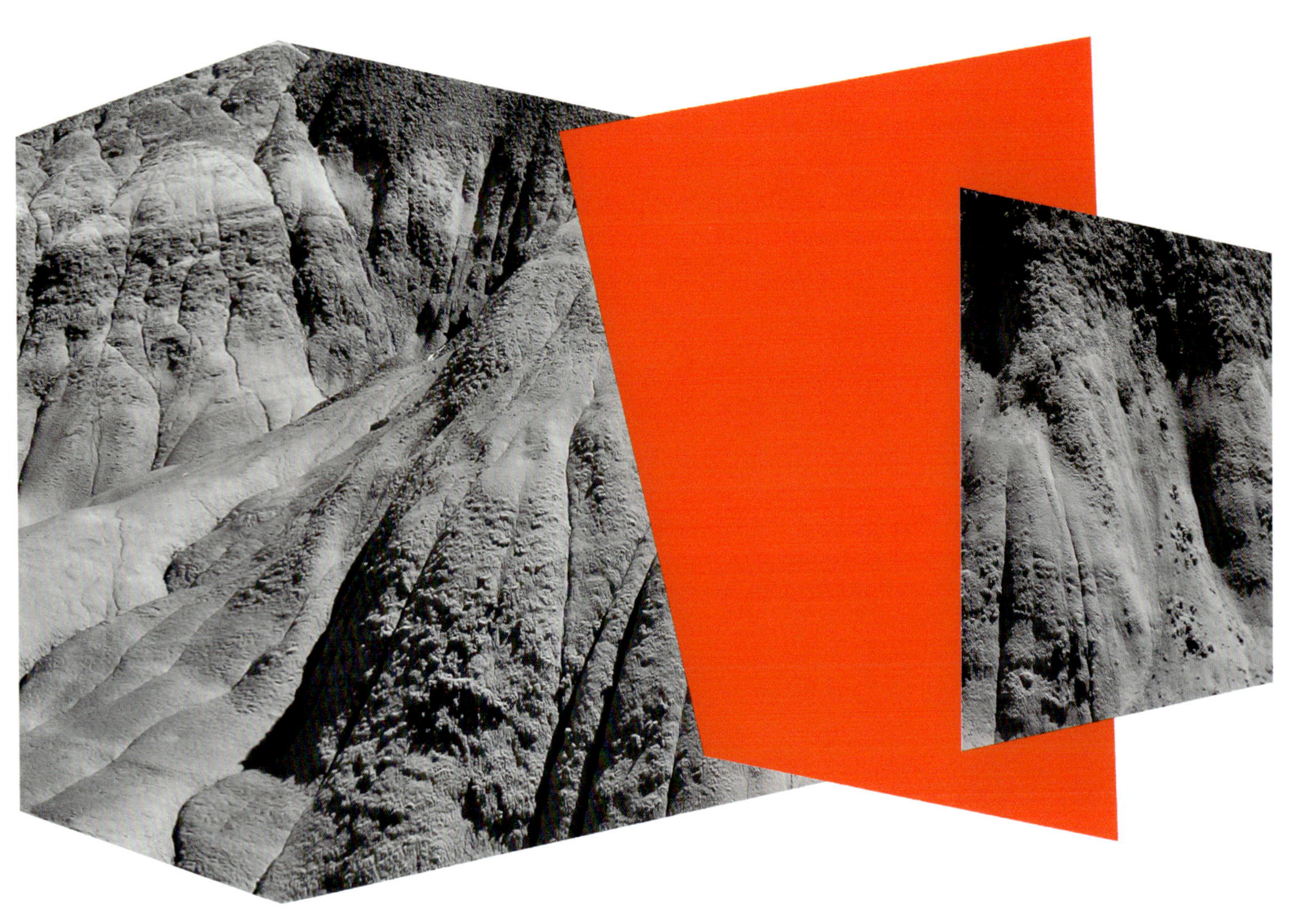

Michael Namingha
Tewa / Hopi, born 1977
Black Place #1, 2019
from Black Place II series
Digital C-Print face-mounted to shaped plexiglass
Courtesy of the artist

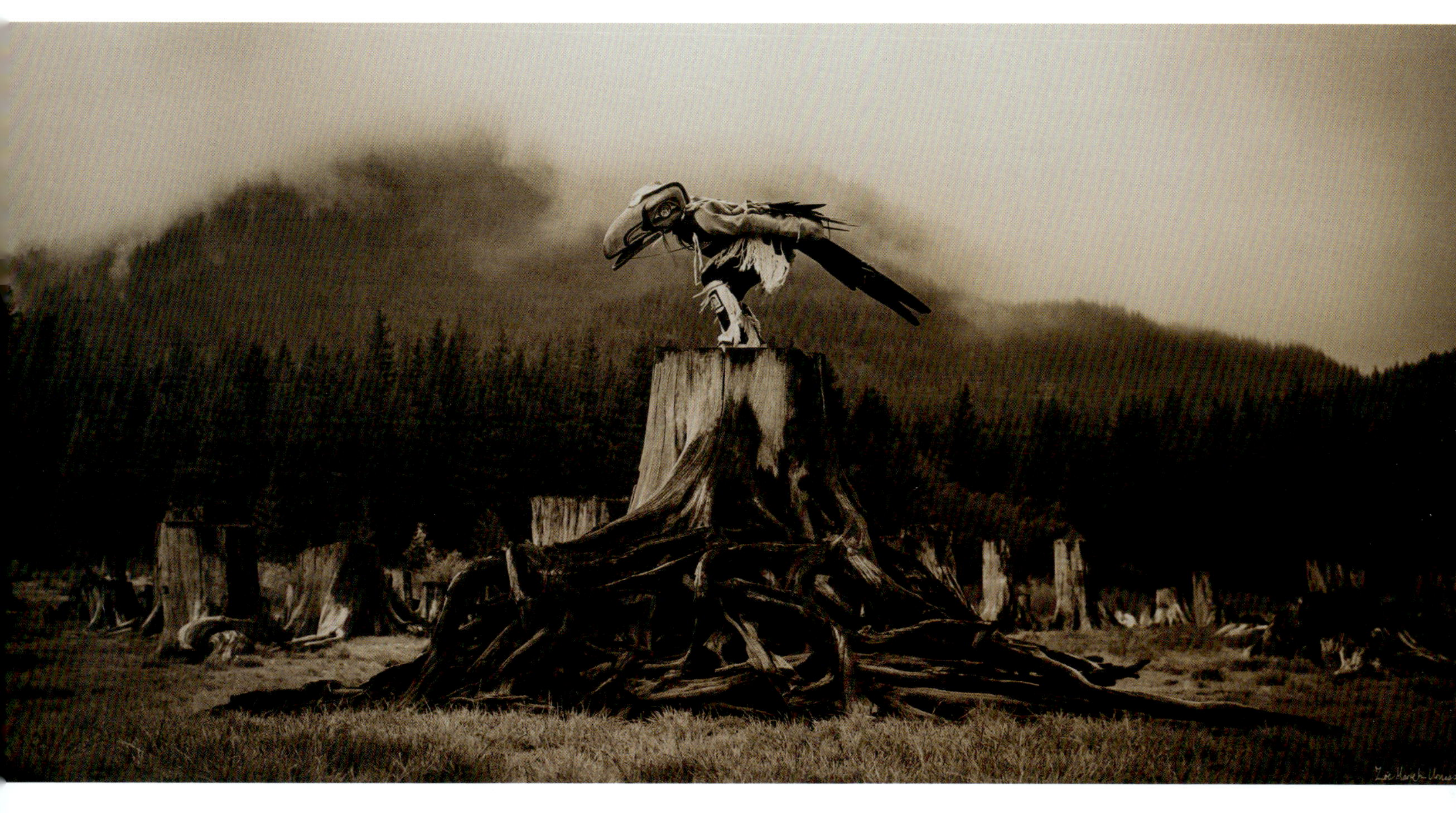

Zoë Marieh Urness
Tlingit, born 1984
Raven Tells His Story in the Fog, not dated
Light exposed print mounted on Aluminum Dibond
Courtesy of the Tacoma Art Museum, 2020.5,
Gift of the Aloha Club

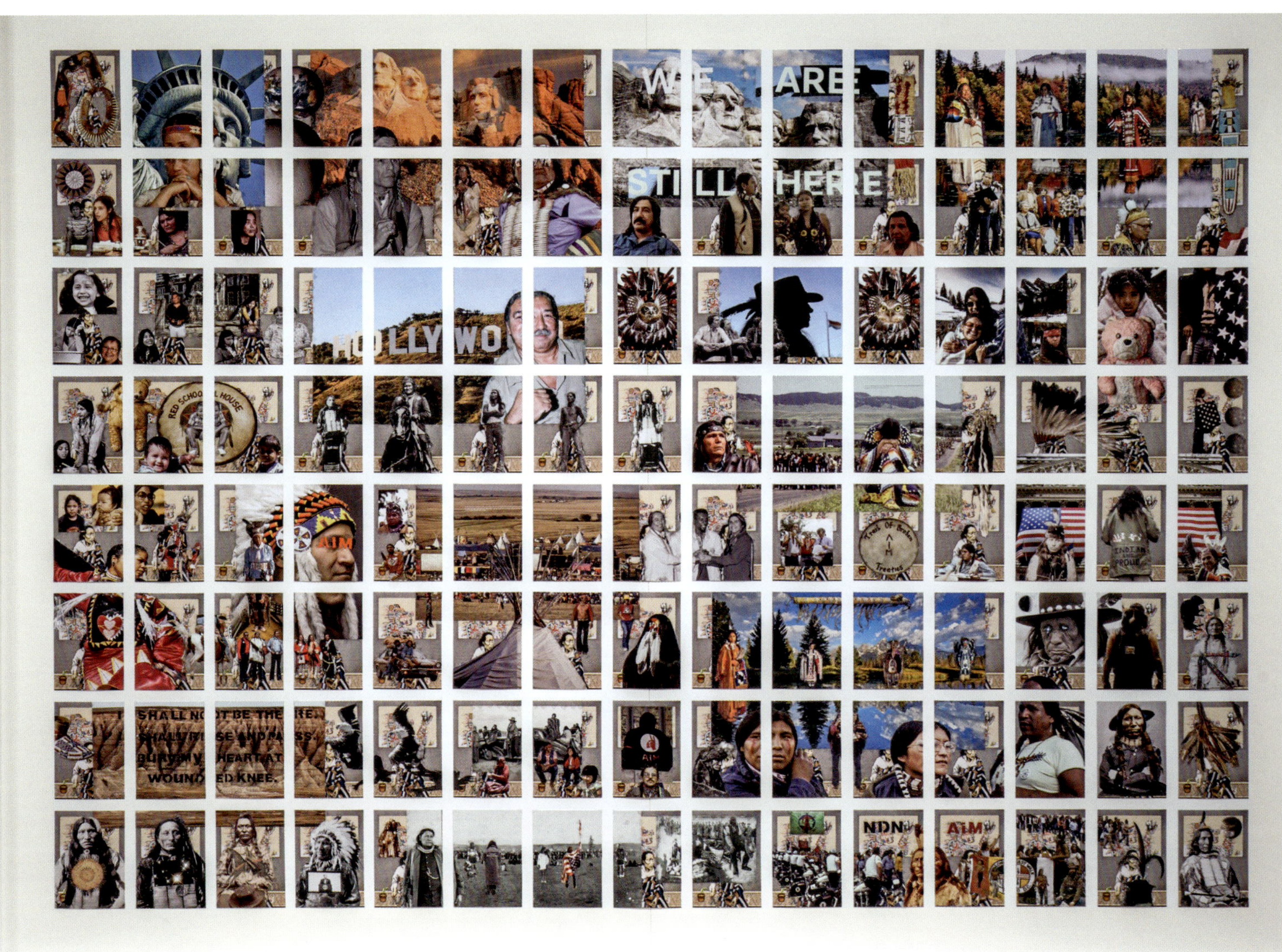

Frank Big Bear
White Earth Nation, born 1953
We Are Still Here, 2014
Collage on found paper
Collection Nerman Museum of Contemporary Art,
Overland Park, Kansas, 2014.37
Photo: EG Schempf

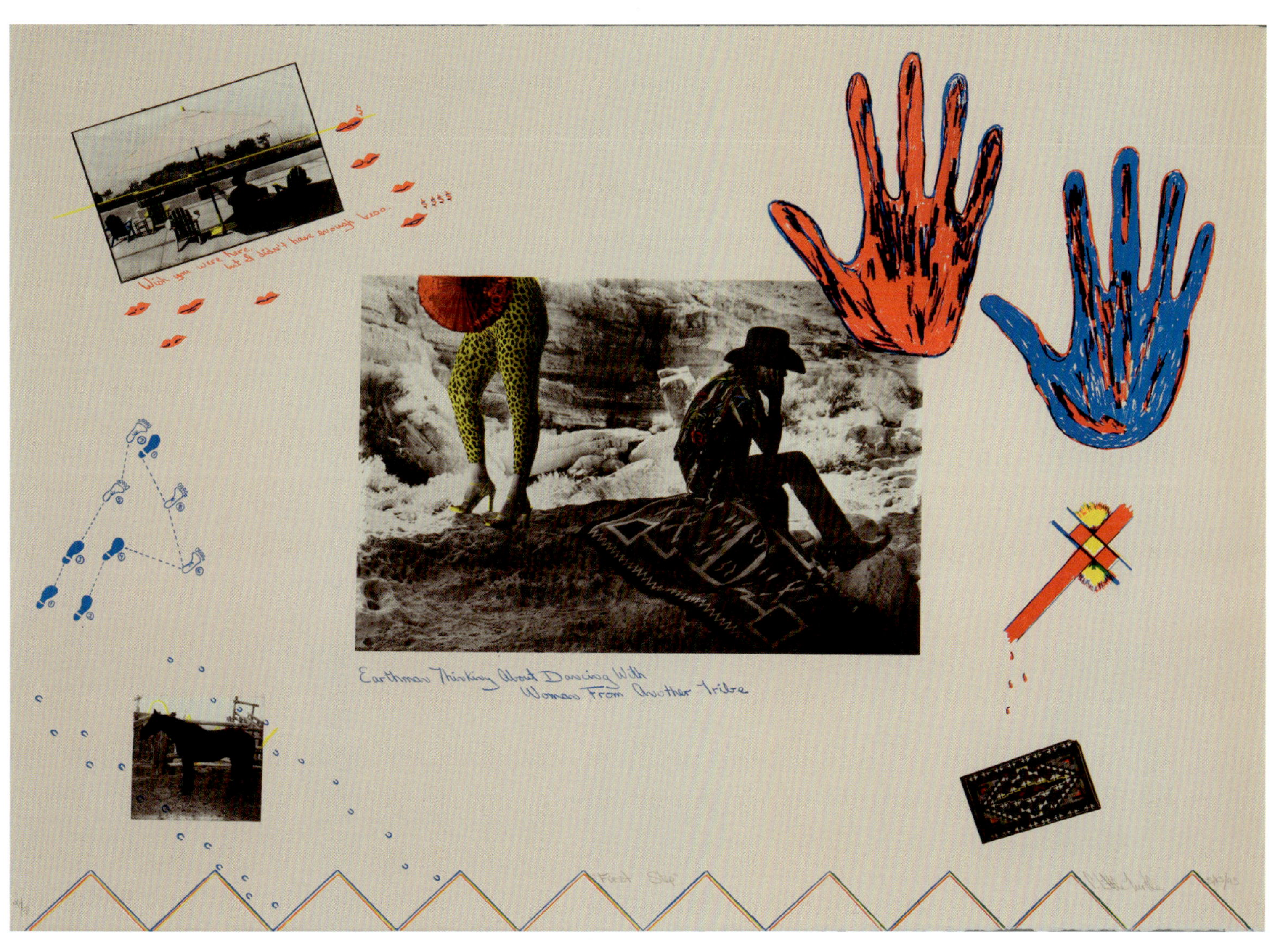

Carmelita Little Turtle
Apache / Tarahumara, 1952- 2016
First Step, 1995
Offset Lithograph
Courtesy of Arizona State University,
Gift of the Brandywine Workshop and Archives,
Philadelphia, Pennsylvania

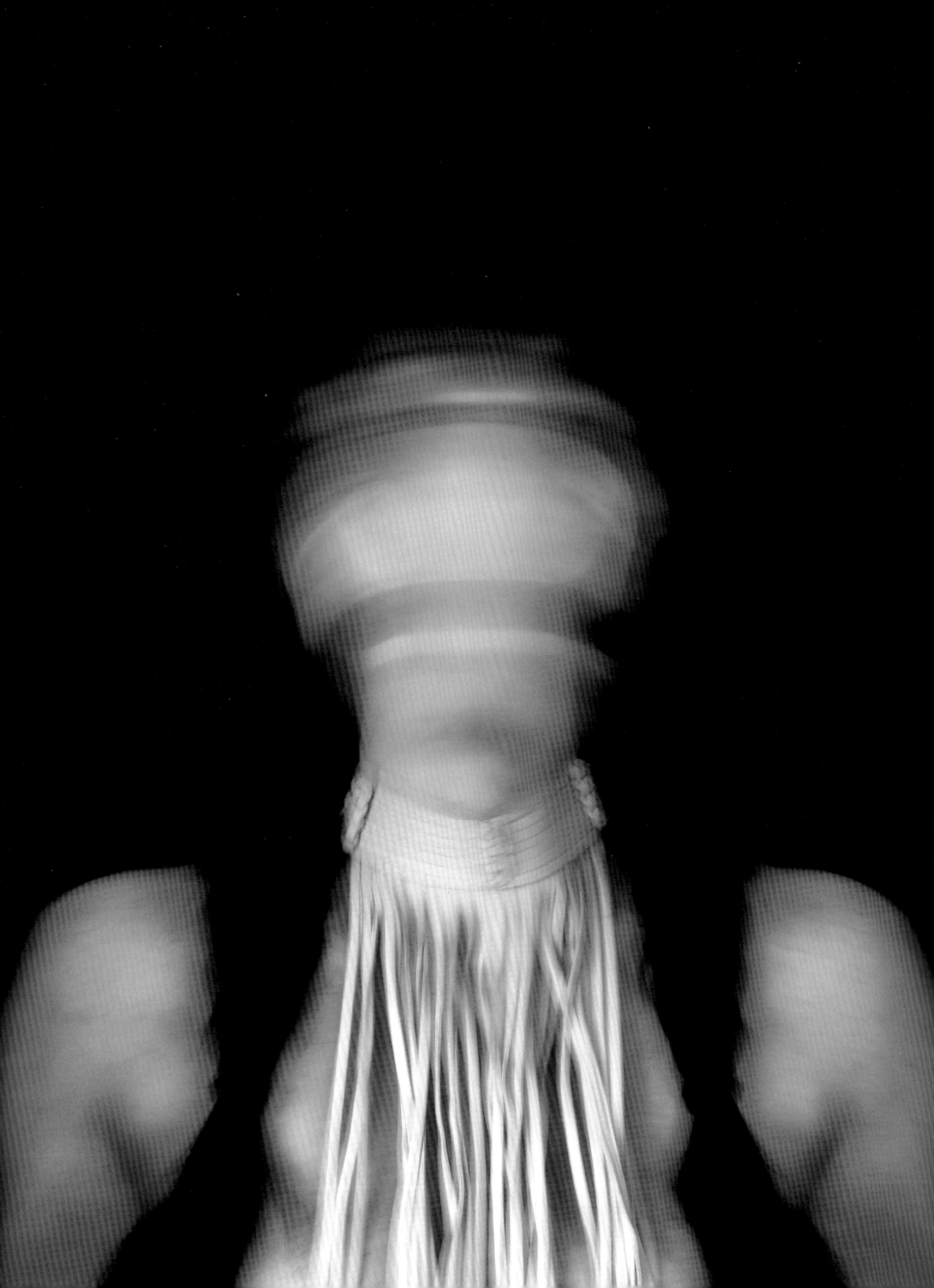

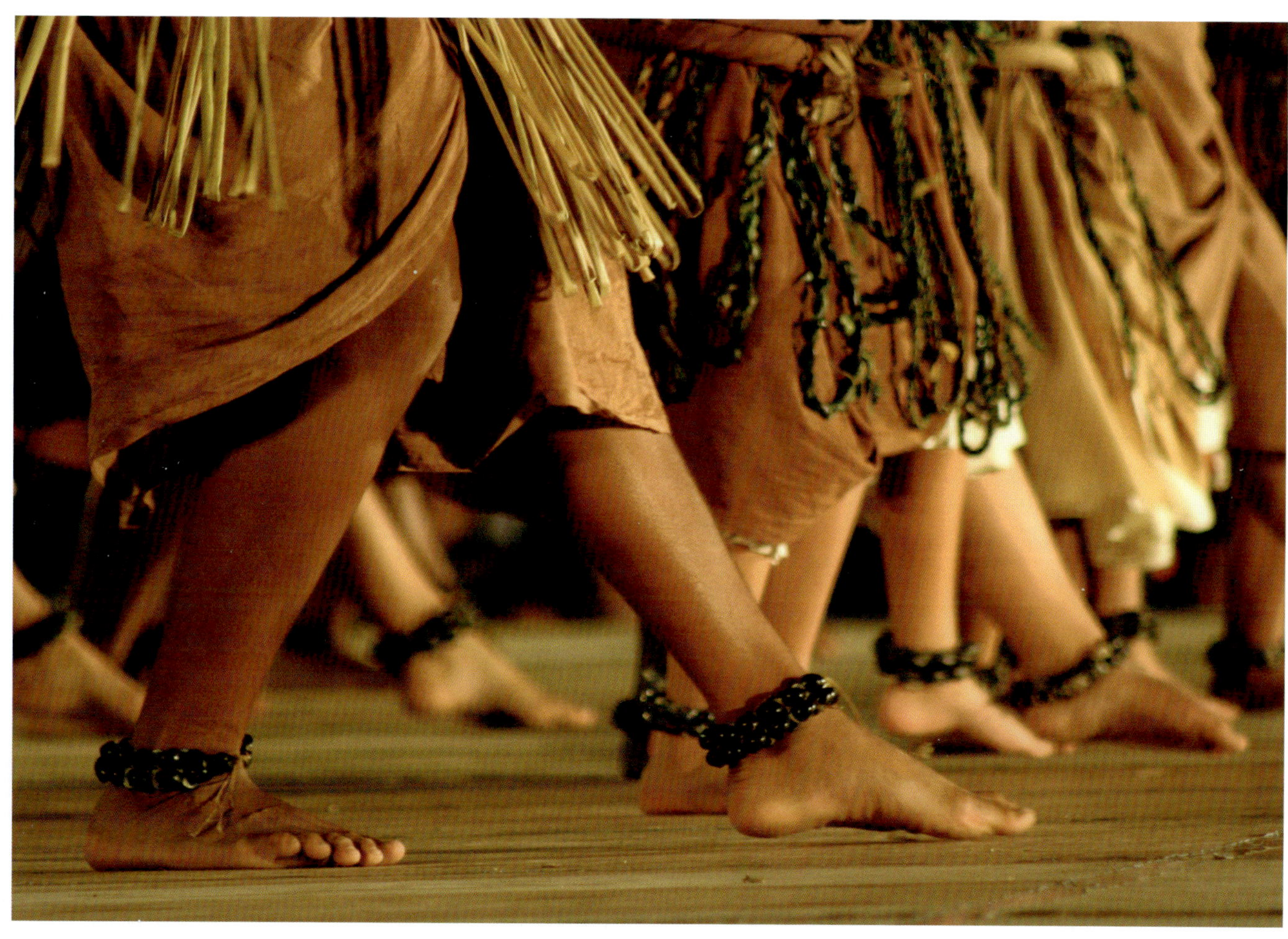

Lehuanani C. Waipa Ah Nee
Kānaka Maoli, born 1981
Na Kanikupe'e I ke kai (The Sound of the Kupe'e When it Falls into the Ocean), 2008
Digital photograph
Courtesy of the C.N. Gorman Museum
2022.20.10.28

Donna Garcia
Muscogee, born 1976
Muscogee, 2018
from Indian Land For Sale series
Archival inkjet print on rag paper
Courtesy of the artist

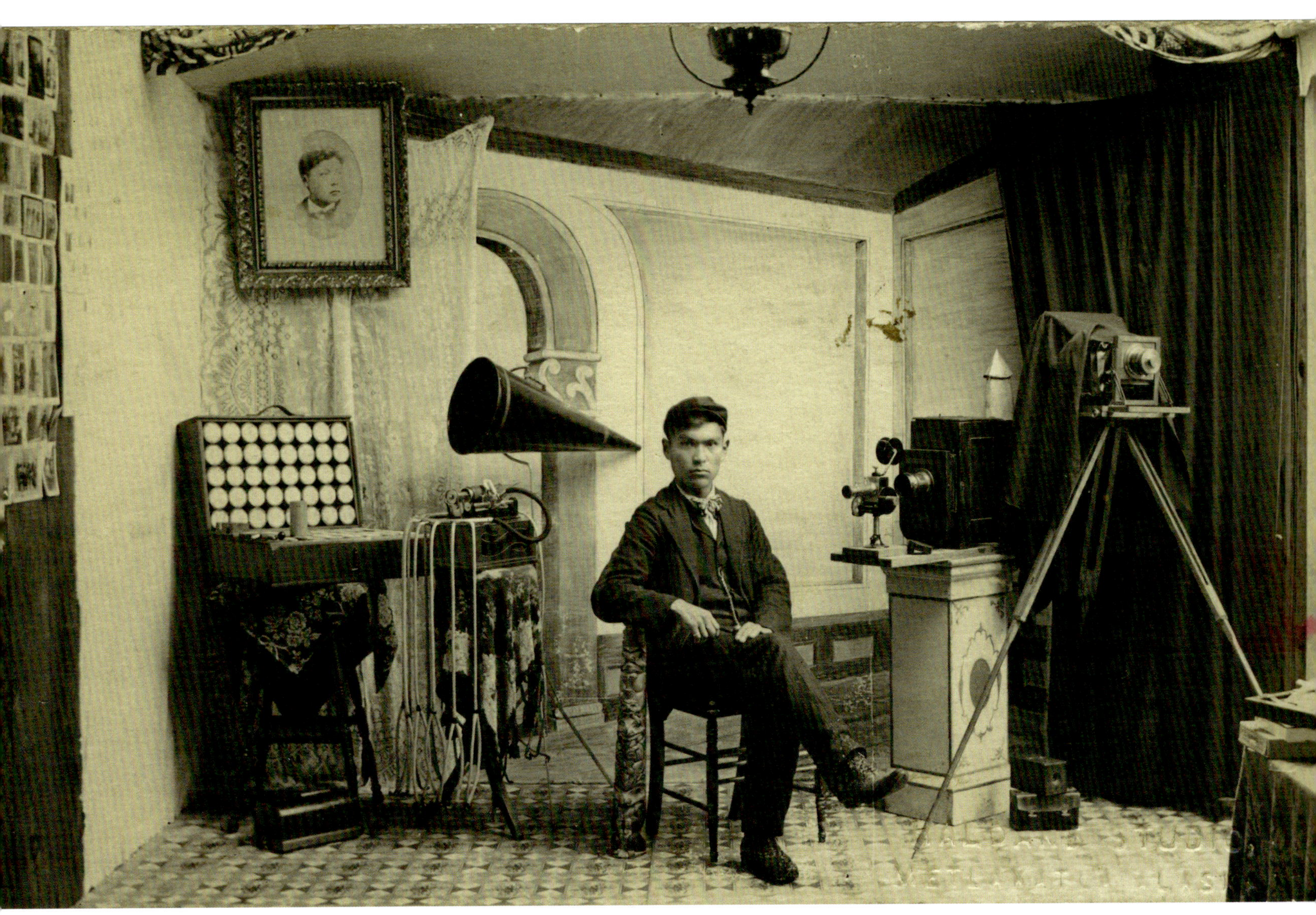

Plate and Fig. 2
B.A. (Benjamin Alfred) Haldane
Tsimshian, 1874–1941
Benjamin A. Haldane self-portrait
in studio in Metlakatla, c. 1919–1920
Image courtesy of Ketchikan Museums:
Photograph by Benjamin A. Haldane,
89.2.14.21

B.A. HALDANE

INSPIRING RESURGENCE THROUGH IMAGES OF RESISTANCE

BY MIQUE'L ICESIS DANGELI

GROWING UP IN METLAKATLA, ALASKA, I first learned about B.A. (Benjamin Alfred) Haldane's photography from my Gram Corrine Reeve (Tsimshian, b. 1924–2006). It was the summer of 2004, and I was visiting with her about a beautiful photograph taken of her as a little girl. She was about four years old in the photo, holding a bouquet of flowers as big as she was. Viewing this image as her granddaughter, I saw my Gram standing in front of the steps of the home where she was raised, where she then raised ten children of her own—my mother being the oldest—and where in that moment she and I sat visiting at the kitchen table. To my surprise, she began describing the experience of having the photograph taken and her recollection of the photographer. She said, "Oh ... I remember that picture, B.A. took it for my Mom!"[10] Commenting on B.A., she stated, "Everyone knew him, he was always taking pictures, and he was a real good musician too."[11] I adore this photo not only because of my close relationship with my Gram, and our family's home, but also because in it she is wearing tiny gold bracelets engraved with our *La̱xsgyiik* (eagle clan) crest (see pgs. 76 and 77). Seeing the bracelets that I heard so much about from her was a visual affirmation for me of my great-great-grandparents' efforts to maintain and instill our clan identity into their grandchildren during one of the most intense times of our cultural oppression. Their resilience is the reason for the survival of my family's clan identity today. This photograph was the first of many images taken by B.A. that correlates with our *adaawx* (oral history) as further evidence of the subversive means through which our cultural practices continued in our community despite assimilation efforts led by the lay missionary William Duncan.[12] At the heart of B.A.'s photography practice was his tremendous love for his people, strong relationships with neighboring tribes, and unwavering resistance to the colonial regime they lived under.

A proud Tsimshian from the Laxgyibuu (wolf clan) of the Ginadoyks (people of the swift water tribe), B.A. Haldane (b. 1874-1941) was born to Matthew and Ada Haldane in Metlakatla, British Columbia. He was thirteen years old when, in 1887, he participated in the mass movement of

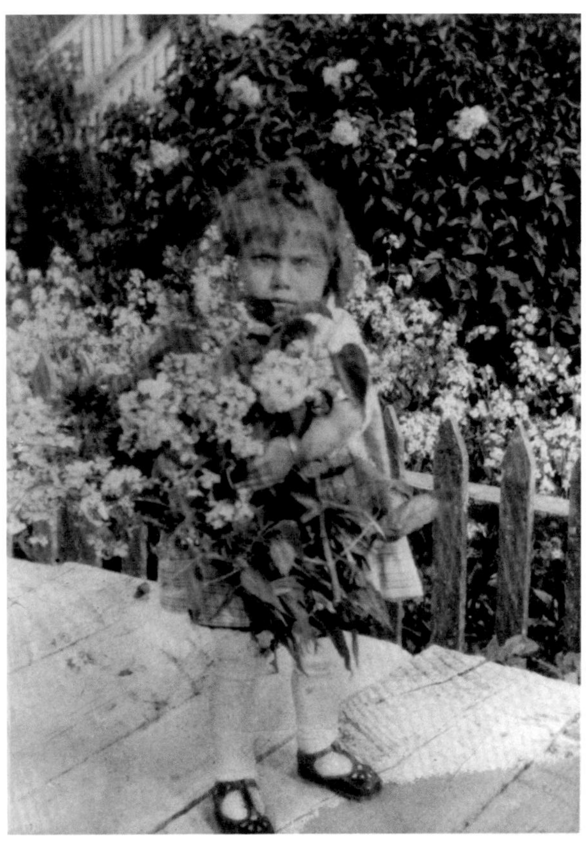

Fig. 1a My Gram, Corrine (neé Lang) Reeve (four years old), standing on the boardwalk in front of her house in Metlakatla, Alaska, ca. 1929. Photo by B.A. Haldane. (Courtesy of Author).

823 Tsimshian people who, accompanied by Duncan, established our community of Metlakatla, Alaska, in their quest for government-sanctioned land rights.[13] Two years later, B.A.'s formal schooling was cut short when, after he had completed the third-grade reading material, Duncan expelled him, stating, "There was nothing more for him to learn."[14] He did not allow Duncan's attempt to cut off his access to greater opportunities to discourage him from continuing his education independently. Working in the salmon cannery from age sixteen to nineteen, B.A. purchased a variety of books and "studied every day of the year."[15] An avid reader with a remarkable aptitude for learning, B.A. taught himself photography from these resources.[16] Around 1890, when he was sixteen years old, B.A. began his career as a photographer by taking individual and family portraits in Metlakatla using family homes or linens as backdrops. Nine years later, he established a business as a "Scenic and Portrait Photo-Grapher" by opening a Victorian-style portrait studio in Metlakatla with the standard props, backdrops, and floor décor of the time.[17] While visiting Metlakatla in 1903, George G. T. Davis made note of B.A.'s strong work ethic and dedication to this photographic practice: "The village photographer, Benjamin A. Haldane, does not hesitate to work in the cannery when it is running and looks after his picture-making and developing after or before work. Mr. Haldane is a versatile and talented young man. In addition to being an excellent photographer, he is the leader of the village band, and plays the pipe organ in church."[18]

In a self-portrait made around 1900, B.A. represents his career, both as a photographer and musician, and declares his Tsimshian identity (see pg. 74). Placing himself at the center of the composition, B.A. is flanked by his photography equipment on his left, including a large camera, a lantern, and a Kodak Brownie camera on the floor. On his right are objects relating to his teaching and love for music including a megaphone, a gramophone with five sets of earphones, and an open case of cylinders. Although B.A. had a variety of props that he could use to hold himself up, he chose to attach visually to his body a model totem pole with his

Laxgyibuu (Wolf Clan) crest represented by the bottom figure. In this image, B.A. confidently positions himself as physically and metaphorically supported by our cultural values and beliefs and looks directly to the viewer to assert its importance. In ways that are very similar to the photo he took of my Gram, this detail—which may seem small to most viewers—resonates deeply and powerfully with Tsimshian viewers, especially those of us who have dedicated our lives to the cultural resurgence that grew out the resistance of B.A.'s generation. These early efforts to continue our people's ancient ways of being and knowing despite Duncan's Declaration, which outlawed them, were observed by anthropologist Viola Garfield in 1922 when she was a teacher in Metlakatla.[19] She states:

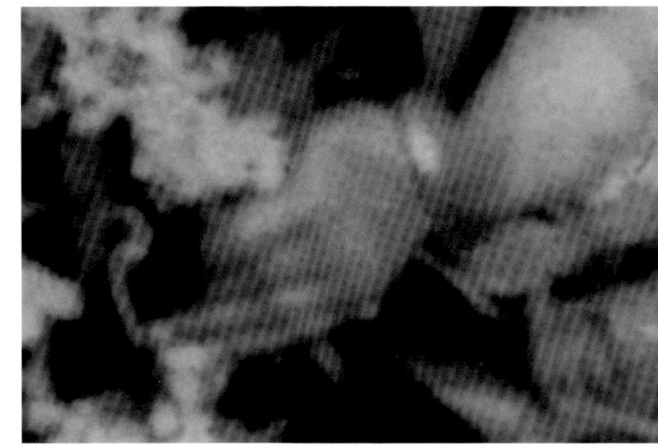

Fig. 1b Detail of Gram's bracelet. (Courtesy of Author).

> Many teachers and village heads leave the village without realizing any of the current aboriginal belief, thought, and practices possessed by the people. They do not know of the night ceremonies with weeping and feasting for the dead, nor of the clan affiliations which color many village activities, especially those of the church.[20]

Garfield's awareness of the complex and subversive ways that our people continued to practice our culture then led her to return to our community in the 1930s to conduct fieldwork for her master's thesis on Tsimshian marriage customs. During that time, she worked closely with Tsimshian carver Sm'oogyit Neesh Loot (Chief Sidney Campbell) of the Gisbutwada (Killer Whale Clan) of the Ginadoyks (people of the swift water tribe).[21] Sm'oogyit Neesh Loot (ca. 1849–1934) was born at Lax Kw'allams (Fort Simpson, BC).[22] He was a leader in the movement to establish our community in 1887. Sm'oogyit Neesh Loot was known for his vast knowledge of Tsimshian songs, dances, and *adaawx* (oral history) and was one of the few documented members of the *Gitsontk.*[23] As an exclusive society of powerful carvers, the Gitsontk made objects that were used in the dancing and initiation ceremonies of secret societies formed around the concept of *Halaayt,* a complex set of beliefs and practices concerning the supernatural and its powers. B.A. documented the continuation of Sm'oogyit Neesh Loot's Gitsontk practices with a group of men from our community, most of whom were also elected tribal council members, with whom he shared these teachings. The remote location in which B.A. took this photograph, compared to B.A.'s photograph of a family in regalia (plate and

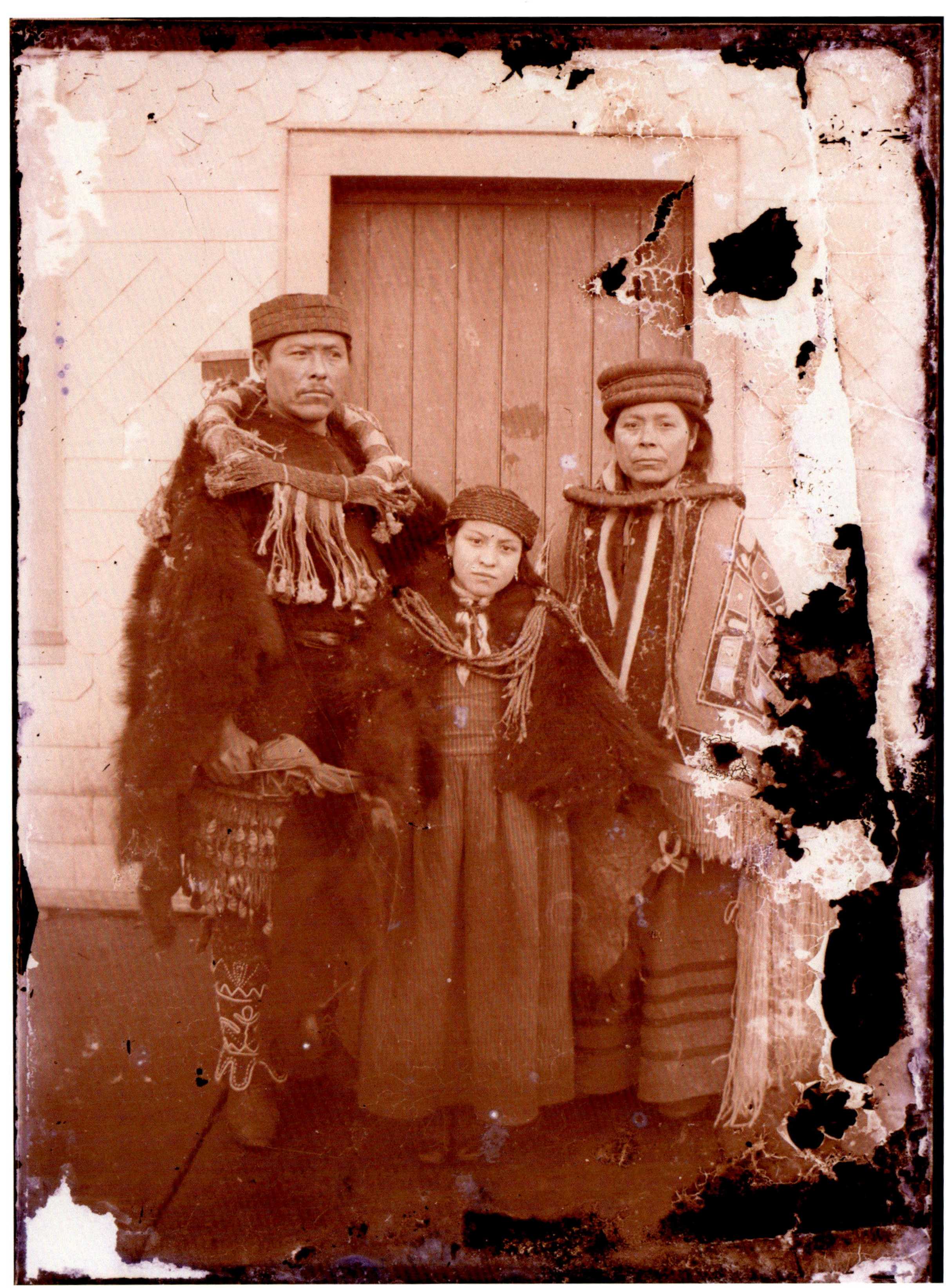

Plate and Fig. 4
B.A. (Benjamin Alfred) Haldane
Tsimshian, 1874-1941
Family in Regalia, c. 1899-1910
Image courtesy of Ketchikan Museums:
Photograph by Benjamin A. Haldane, 2018.2.30.54

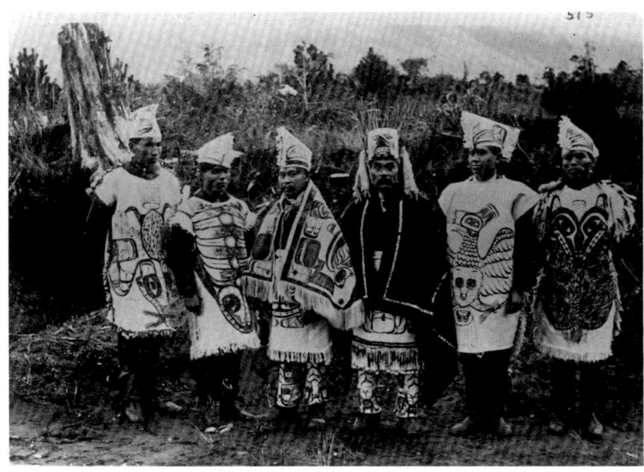

Fig. 3. Sm'oogyit Neesh Loot (Sidney Campbell) is identified as the fourth man from the left in a note signed "M. W. Minthorn, 1926," on the back of a badly damaged print in the archives of the Duncan Cottage Museum. On a photocopy of this image found in his records, Metlakatla Historian Ira Booth (1912–1996) confirmed Minthron's identification. Booth also listed the name of rest of the men: (left to right) Paul Mather, Joel Baines, Bob Nelson, Sidney Campbell, Henry Booth, and Walter Calvert. Image from glass plate negative, William Duncan Memorial Church Archives, Metlakatla, Alaska. (Courtesy of the author).

figure 4) demonstrates their efforts to remove themselves from the public, which is the protocol of the Gitsontk during their ceremonies. In the 1909 book, *The Apostle of Alaska: The Story of William Duncan of Metlakahtla* by John Archtander, is another image of Sm'oogyit Neesh Loot wearing the same apron, leggings, and *aamhalaayt* (Chief's headdress), but with a painted robe instead of the *gwishnapala* (button robe),[24] in regalia taken around 1880 in British Columbia. This confirms that Sm'oogyit Neesh Loot brought his regalia over from British Columbia and continued to use it in our community once again defying Duncan's authority.[25]

The family portrait in regalia was likely not taken in Alaska. Their woven cedar bark headbands and neck rings, as well as the *gwishalaayt* (also known as Chilkat blanket) worn by the mother, indicates that this photo may have been taken during B.A.'s many journeys to the Nass River valley to teach music in Nisga'a villages. B.A. played the piano, pipe organ, cornet, trombone, and violin, as well as composing both orchestral music and translating Tsimshian songs to sheet music.[26] From the time he was a young adult until late in his life, B.A. held the positions of band and choir director of the Metlakatla Christian Church in addition to teaching music in other First Nations communities and organizing several brass bands.[27] In 1899, B.A. worked to support his family by teaching music there for an entire winter.[28] As a teacher of music, B.A. was often called Professor Haldane.[29] The composition of this family portrait is consistent with that of his early family portraits in Metlakatla where, prior to the establishment of his portrait studio, he used family homes as backdrops.[30] This image is produced by one of 163 glass plate negatives that were salvaged from the fire of our local waste facility in 2004.[31] Along their edges, these burned and broken negatives carry the scars of our near loss of this rich archive of B.A.'s photography. A large part of my research is dedicated to locating prints made from these negatives before they were damaged. I have been particularly successful in doing so at the National Archive–Pacific Alaska Region in Anchorage.

Over his forty-year career, B.A. produced a diverse body of work. His photographs ranged from formal portraits of Indigenous people, families, bands, choirs, and sports teams to images of historical events in their communities throughout southeast Alaska and northern British Columbia, including cultural ceremonies that at the time were outlawed by the Potlatch Ban in Canada.[32] This family portrait may have been taken just before such a ceremony. By 1905, colonial authorities viewed photographs taken at potlatches as concrete evidence of illegal activities.[33] In a 1907 court case, a group of Kwakwaka'wakw people were even fully prosecuted as violators of the Potlatch Ban using photographs taken years earlier as evidence.[34] Thus this image could have put B.A. and the family in this photograph at risk of prosecution under the Indian Act.

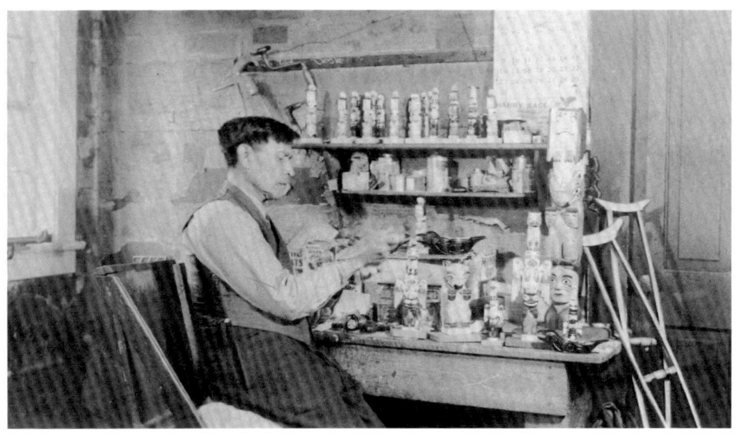

Plate and Fig. 5
B.A. (Benjamin Alfred) Haldane
Tsimshian, 1874-1941
Tsimshian man named Eli Tait sits at workbench with wood carvings, Northwest Coast of North America, c. 1923
Courtesy of University of Washington Libraries.
Special Collections Division, NA3537

Through recovery of B.A.'s images and their histories, we have been able to rebuild our own archive. It has been an emotional experience for us because we continue to be subjected to the archive built by Duncan and supporters of his work, which was used to create and widely circulate a colonial narrative depicting our conversion to Christianity as a complete rejection of our Tsimshian identity and cultural practices.[35] Within the last fifty years, there has been a great resurgence of potlatching, totem pole raising, dancing, and other Tsimshian traditions in Metlakatla. This shifting ground has brought up many unresolved issues concerning the effects of colonialism on our community. The reclamation of B.A.'s photography has us thinking through the many early artists from our community, like Sm'oogyit Neesh Loot and others, who B.A. documented through his photography and how their contribution to our cultural resurgence go back much further in our community's history. This includes Tsimshian carver Eli Tait (1872–1949), considered to have originated the popular model totem pole, *Good Luck Totem*.[36] Contemporaries in age and artistic practice, Eli was just two years older than B.A. Both made the voyage between Metlakatla, BC, and Alaska as children and attended Duncan's school together. In B.A.'s 1923 photograph of Eli carving at his work bench, he is surrounded by model totem poles that he carved to sell to curio shops in nearby Ketchikan, Alaska, (plate and fig. 5). This is also where B.A. sold postcard prints of his photographs.[37] His grandson Francis Haldane provided me with a photo of B.A. with his camera taken around this same time (fig. 6). I bring these images together as both Eli and B.A. are shown with the tools they used to provide for their families through their artform, while perpetuating our people's cultural knowledge—a way of being that is continued by many artists from our community today. One artist, in particular, that I would like to dedicate this essay to is B.A's. grandson, carver, and culture bearer Wayne Hewson (1952–2022), who we are devastated to have lost in August 2022. Over thirty of Wayne's totem poles, ranging in size from six-feet to thirty can be found at the Alaska Rainforest Sanctuary in Ketchikan. On February 28th, 2006, I presented many of the images I've discussed here to B.A.'s family after receiving their permission to research and write about his work.[38] In response to my presentation, Wayne stated:

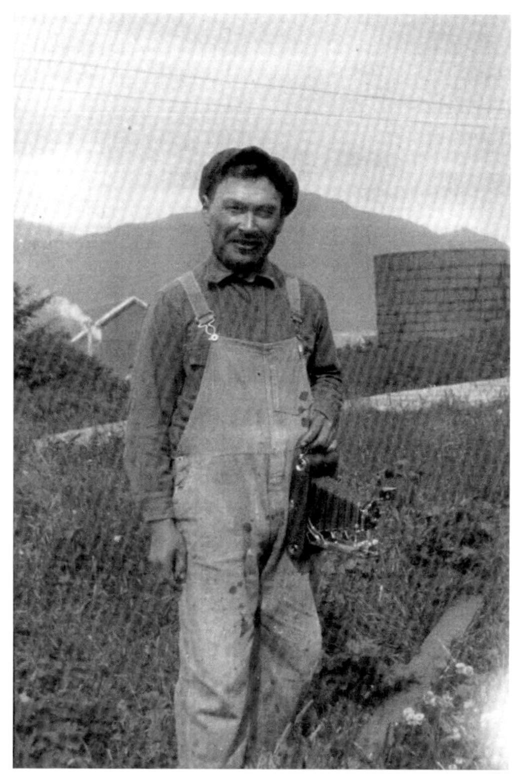

Fig. 6 Benjamin Alfred (B.A.) Haldane with his camera in Metlakatla, Alaska, ca. 1920. (Image Courtesy of his grandson Francis Haldane).

> It made me proud of the fact that my grandfather helped record history, not just ours but all the people he traveled to, and that he continued to attend potlatches. In our family, the descendants of Haldane women, we were always told by our mothers that we are from the Killer Whale Clan of the *Git Laan* and to be proud of who we are. These photographs show that our people were proud and that we didn't give up our culture.[39]

Wayne has eloquently summarized the overall objective of my work on B.A.'s photography. After viewing B.A.'s images and learning of the findings of my research, he reflected upon the clan and tribal lineage that his mother, grandmother, and aunts made integral to the identities of their children. Through this process, he acknowledged how these foundational cultural teachings have continued to be passed down despite intense assimilation efforts. By coming into a deeper and more complex understanding of our community's history through B.A.'s photography, many of our people, like Wayne, have furthered strengthen our cultural resurgence by recognizing that "we did not give up our culture." Our cultural resurgence is a continuation of the resistance of many generations of our people including B.A., Sm'oogyit Neesh Loot, Eli Tait, and many others.

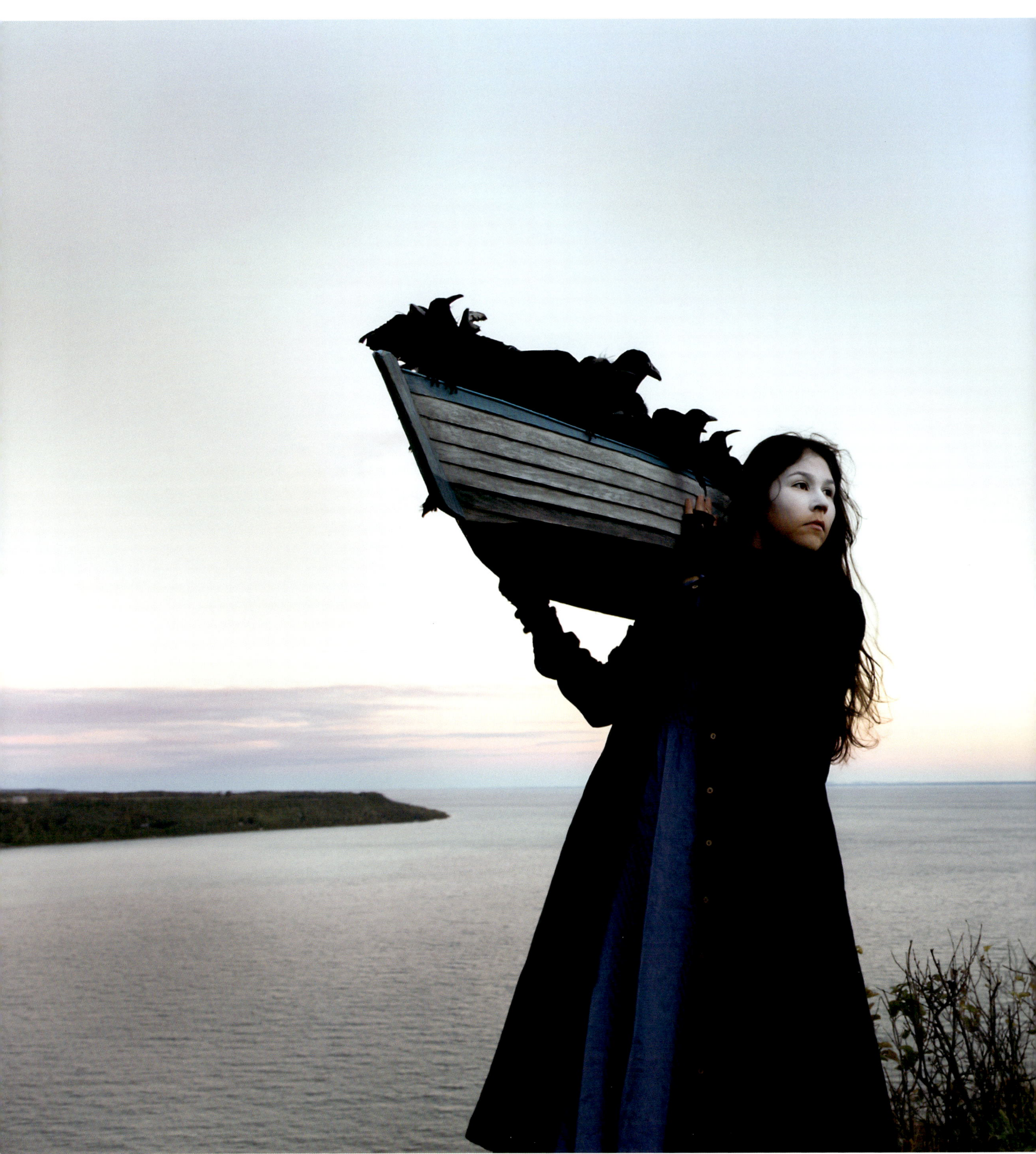

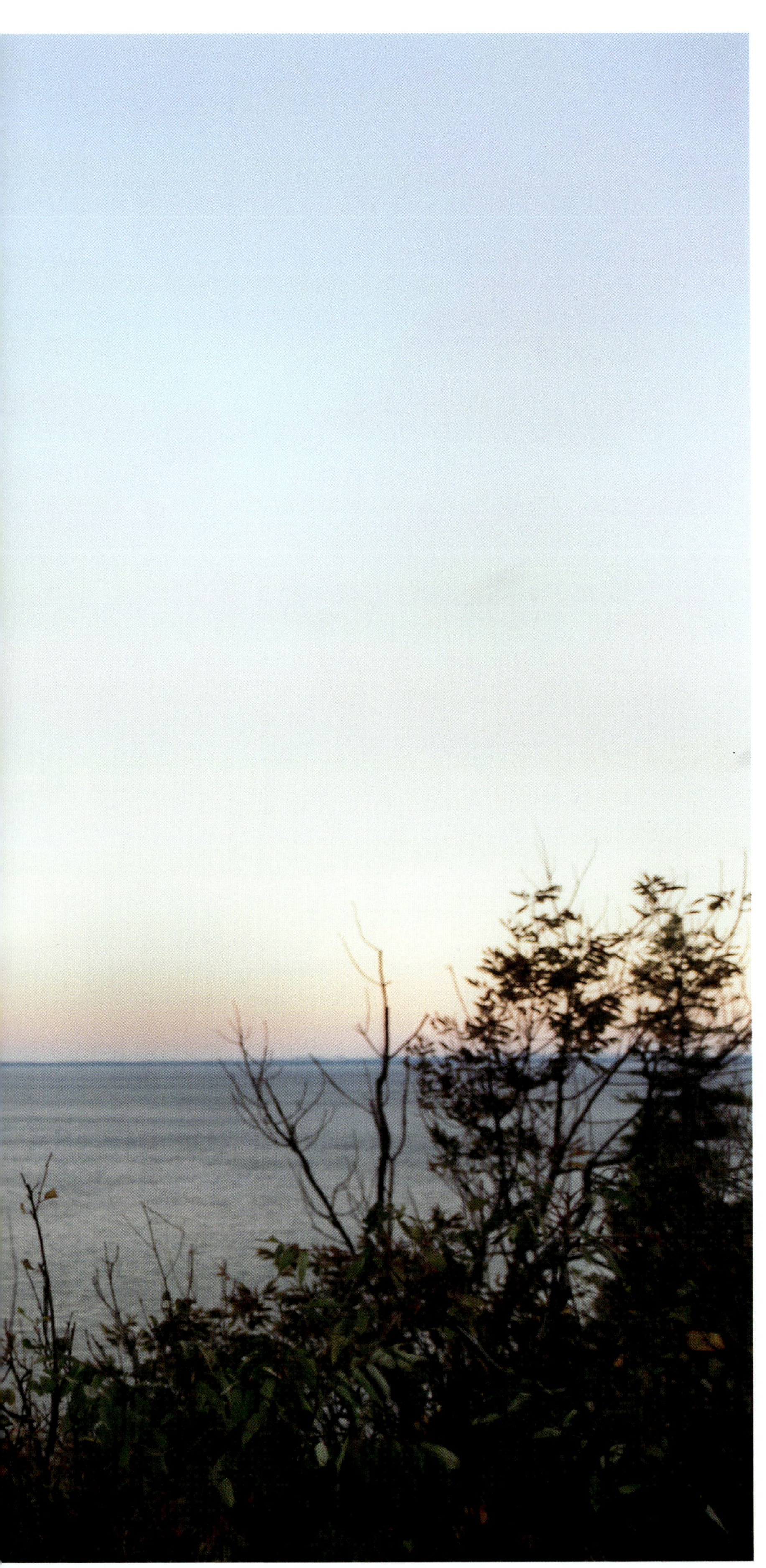

Meryl McMaster
Nêhiyaw (Plains Cree) / English / Dutch, born 1988
On The Edge of This Immensity, 2019
Digital chromogenic print
Courtesy of the artist

Pages 84-85:
Katherine Takpannie
Inuit, born 1989
Our Women and Girls Are Sacred #1, 2016
Archival pigment print on Baryta paper
Courtesy of the Olga Korper Gallery Inc.

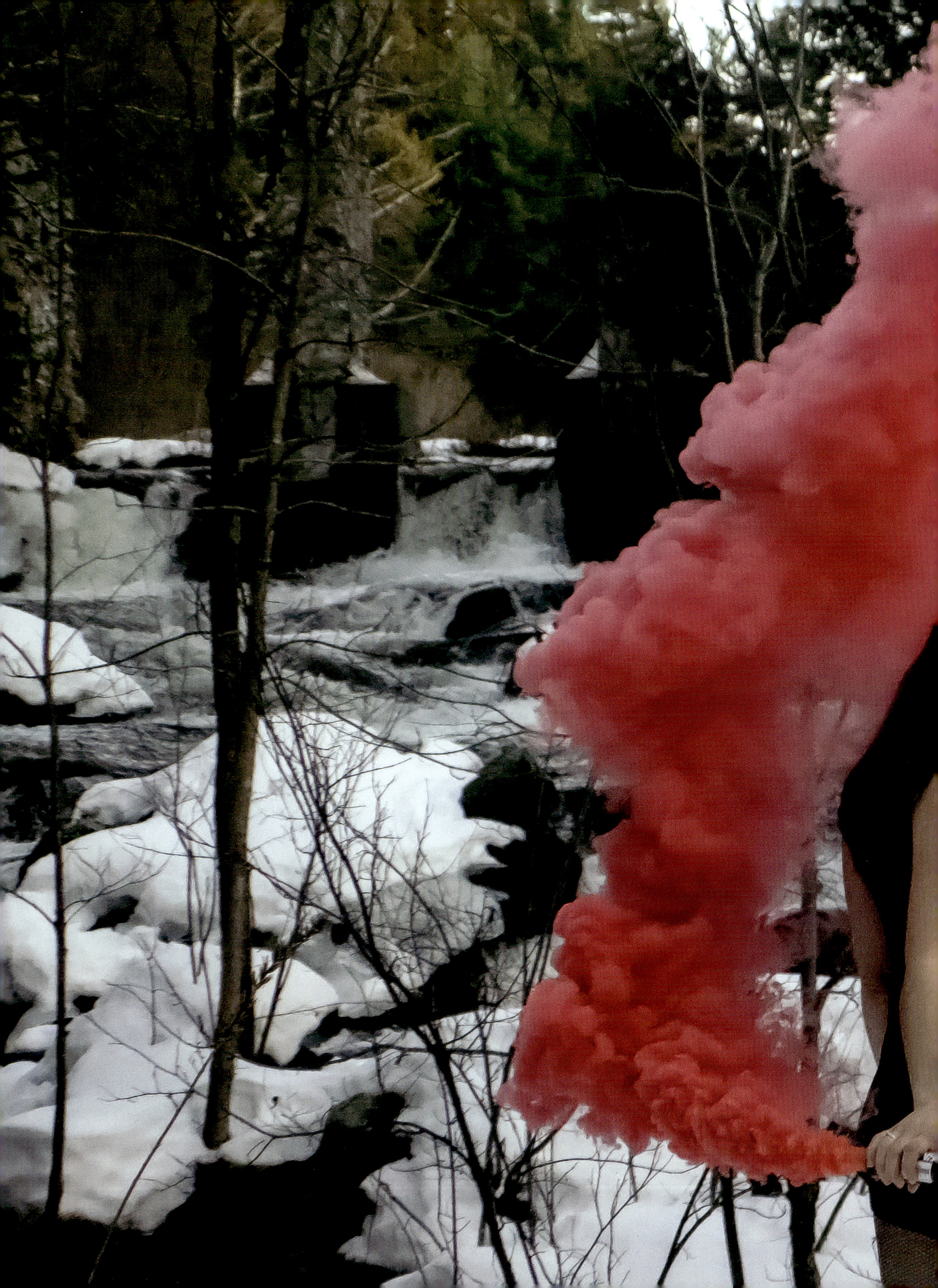

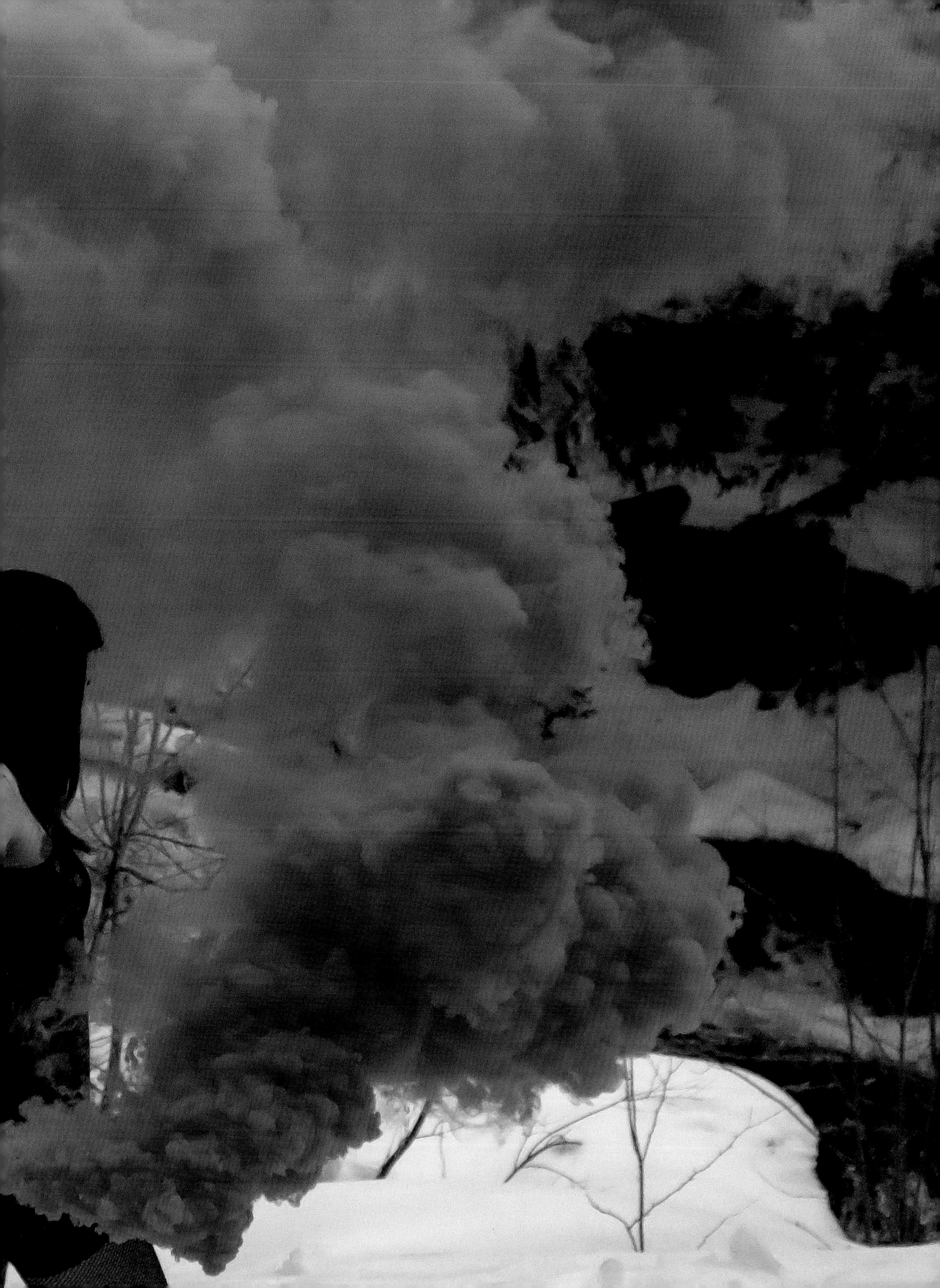

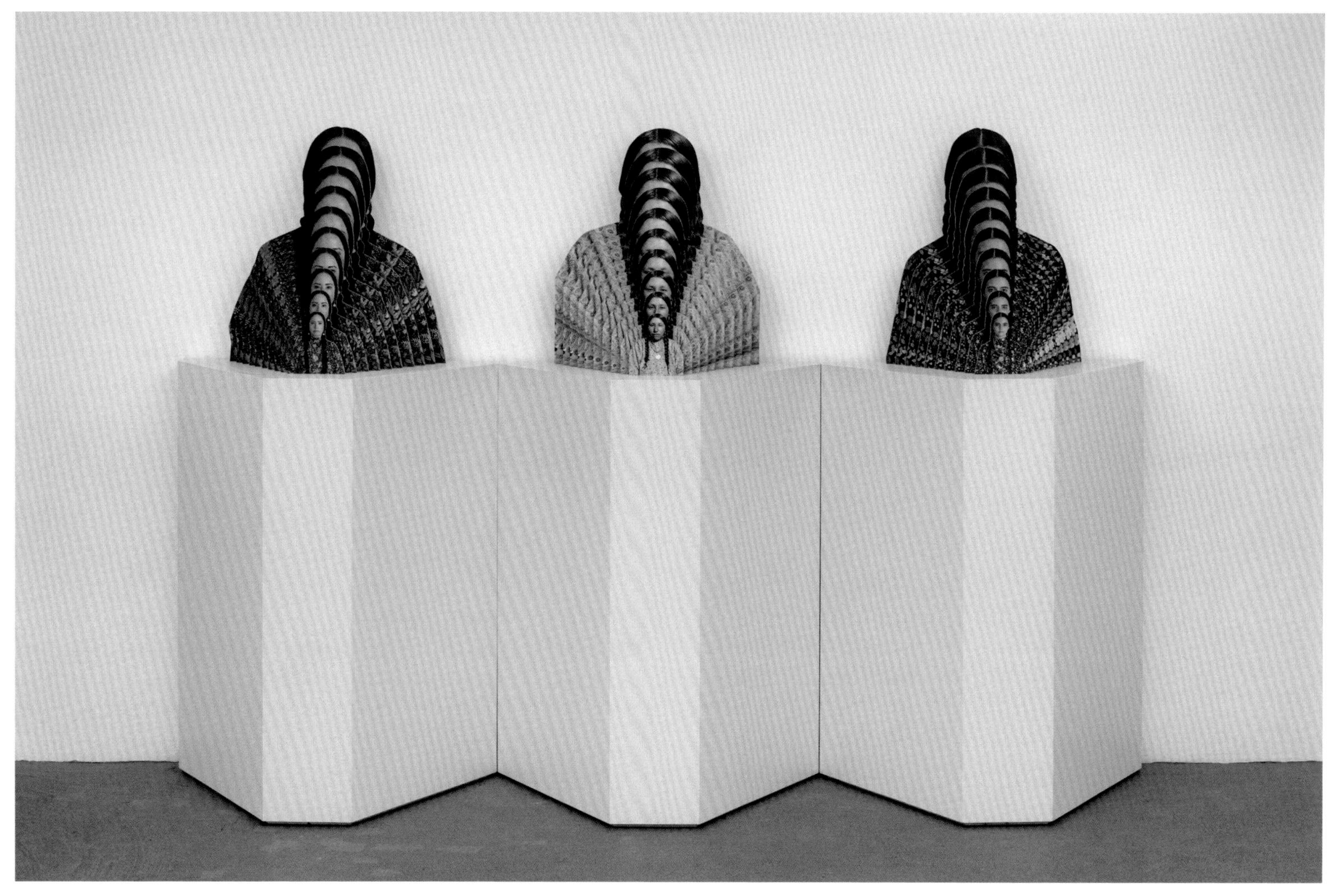

Wendy Red Star
Apsáalooke, born 1981
Amnía (Echo), 2021
Archival ink on paper, board
San Antonio Museum of Art, Purchased with The Brown Foundation Contemporary Art Acquisition Fund, 2022.7.a-c.
Photography by Nicholas Knight, courtesy of Sargent's Daughters, New York, New York.
© Wendy Red Star

Alejandra Rubio
Yavapai-Apache Nation, born 1981
Native Rider Steele, 2019
from Rodeos series
Digital print
Courtesy of the artist
© 2022 Alejandra Rubio

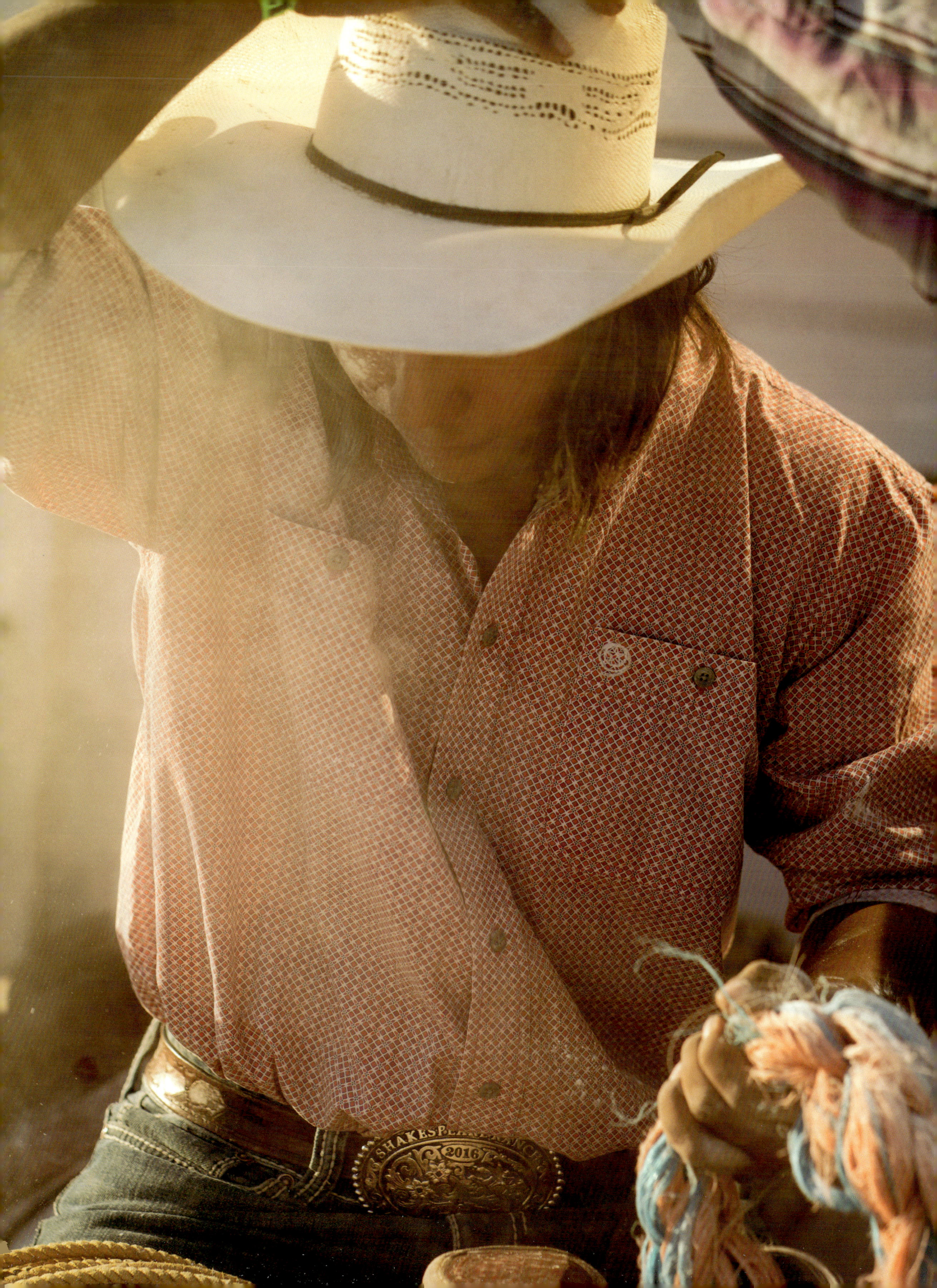
2016

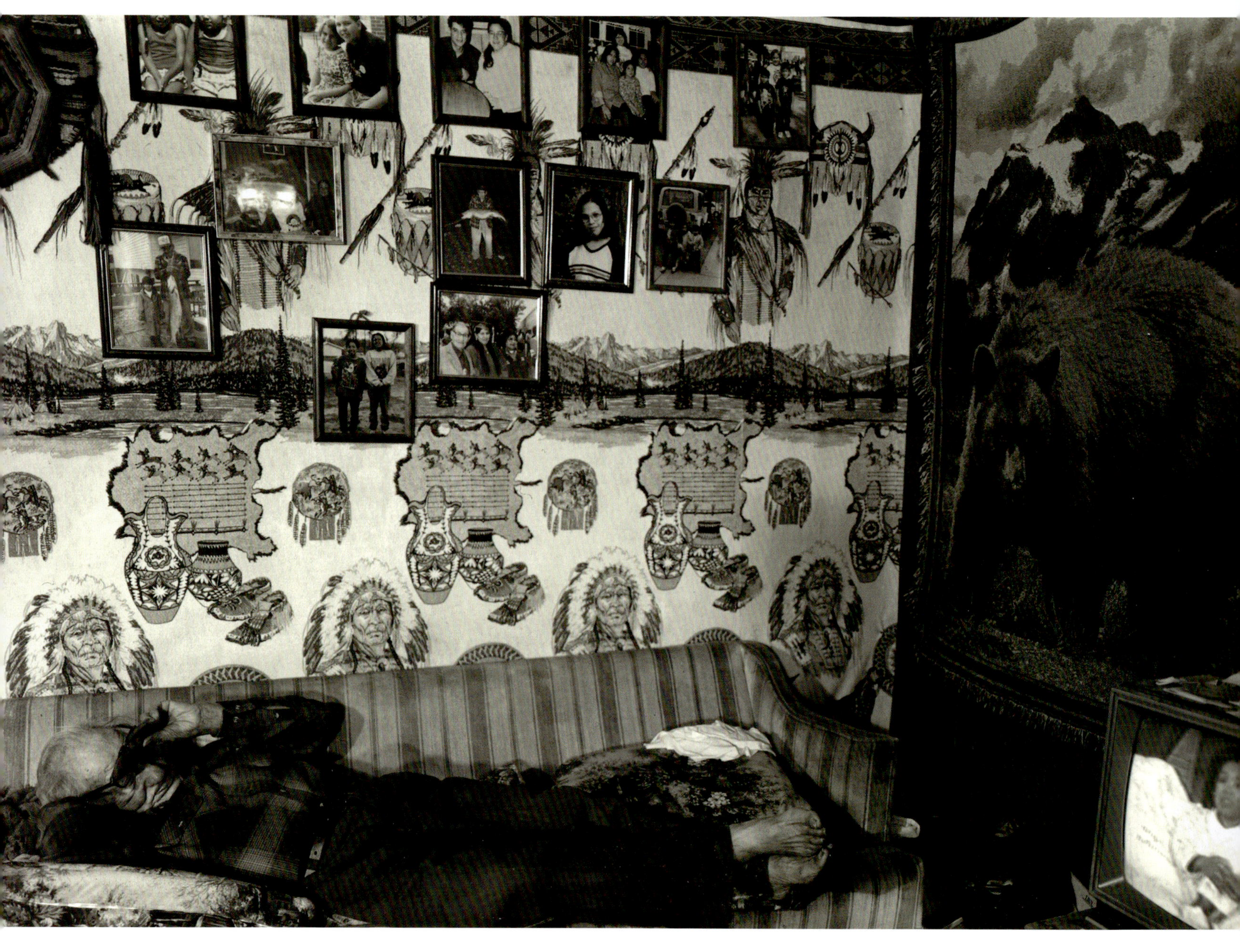

Tom Jones
Ho-Chunk, born 1964
Choka Watching Oprah, 1998
Gelatin silver print
Courtesy of the artist

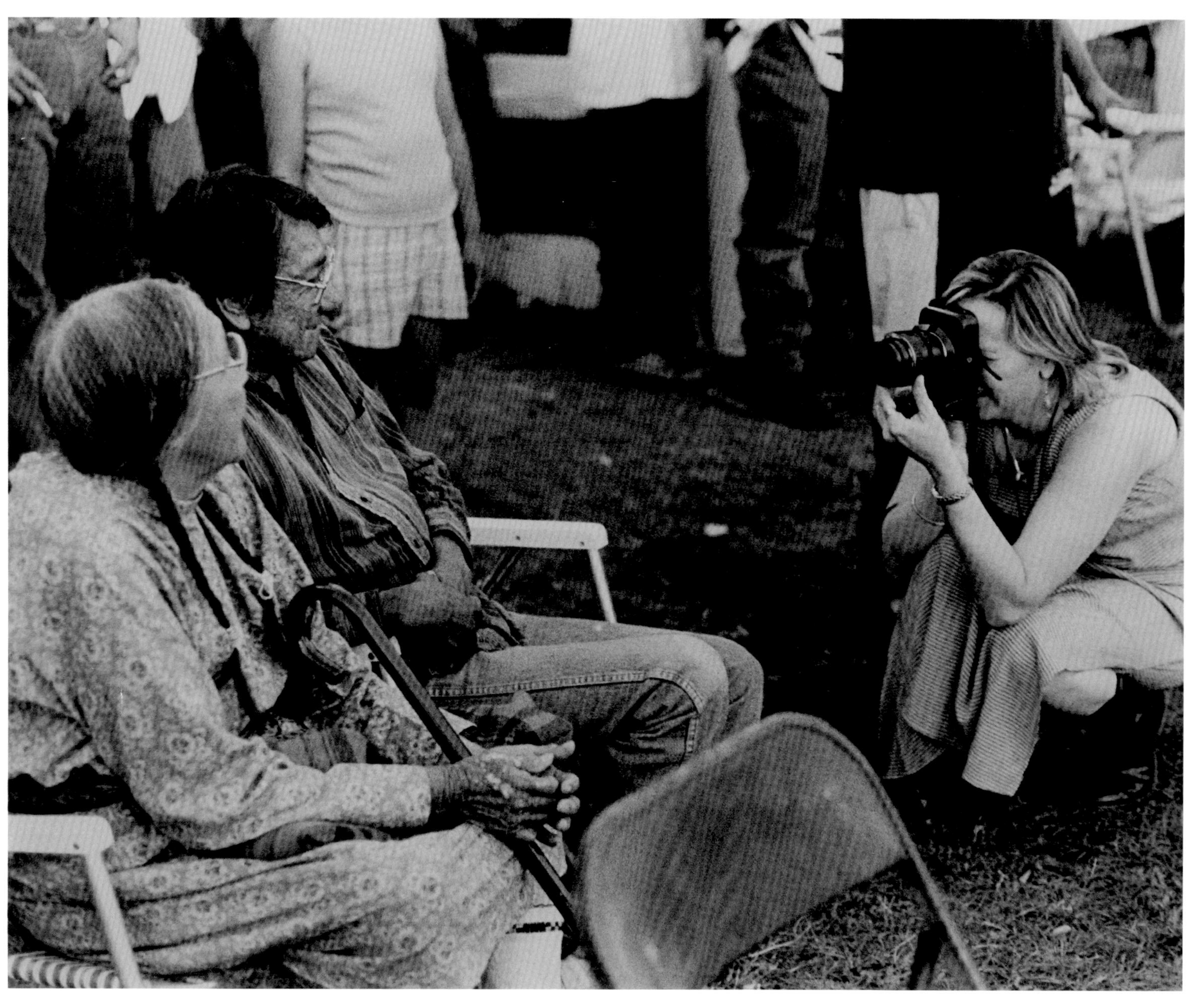

Zig Jackson (Rising Buffalo)
Sahnish (Arikara), Minitari (Hidatsa), Numakiki (Mandan), born 1957
Indian Photographing Tourist Photographing Indians, Crow Agency, Montana, 1991
Gelatin silver print
Purchase with the Madeleine Pinsof Plonsker (Class of 1962) Fund, Mount Holyoke College Art Museum, South Hadley, Massachusetts 2018.8.3

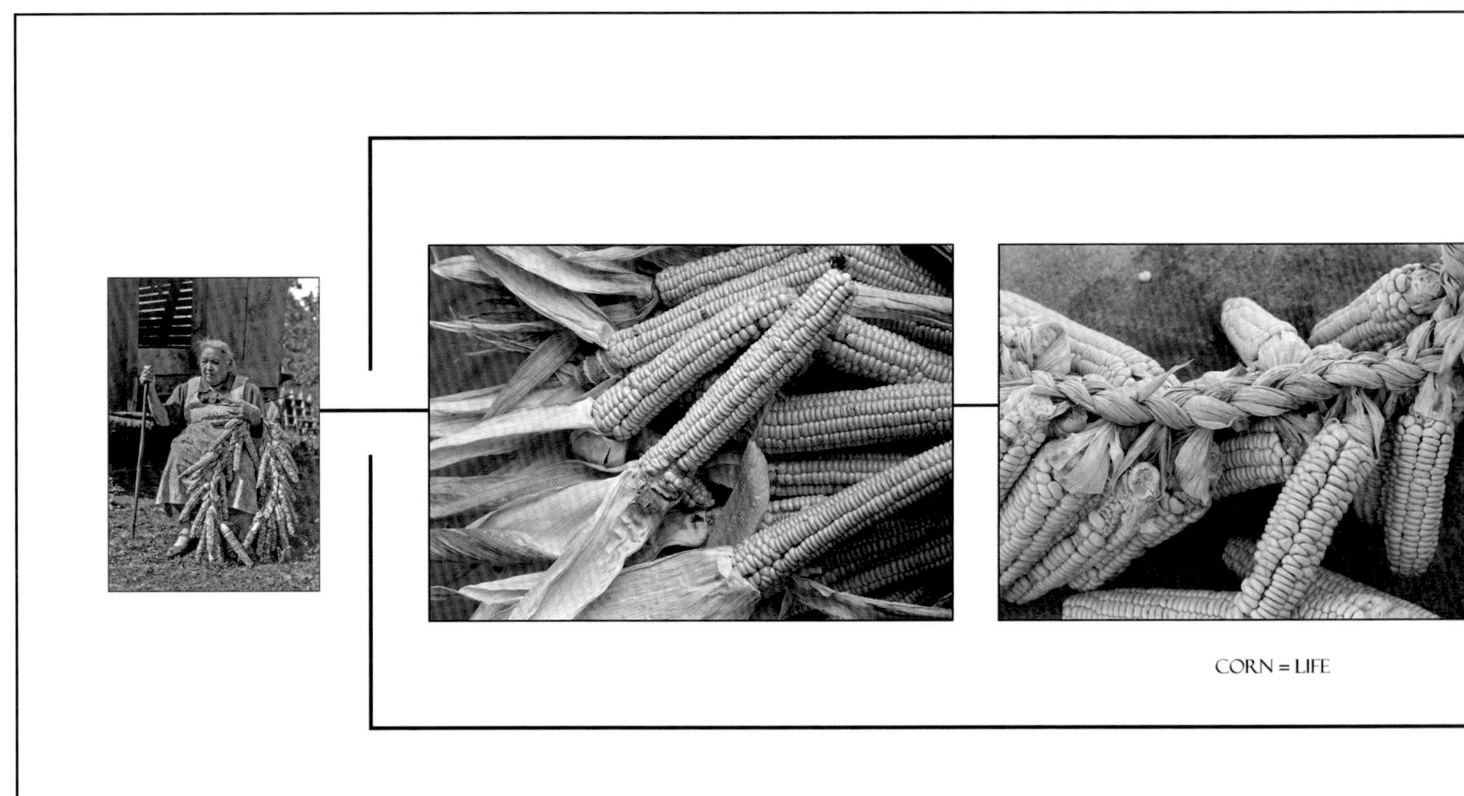

CORN = LIFE

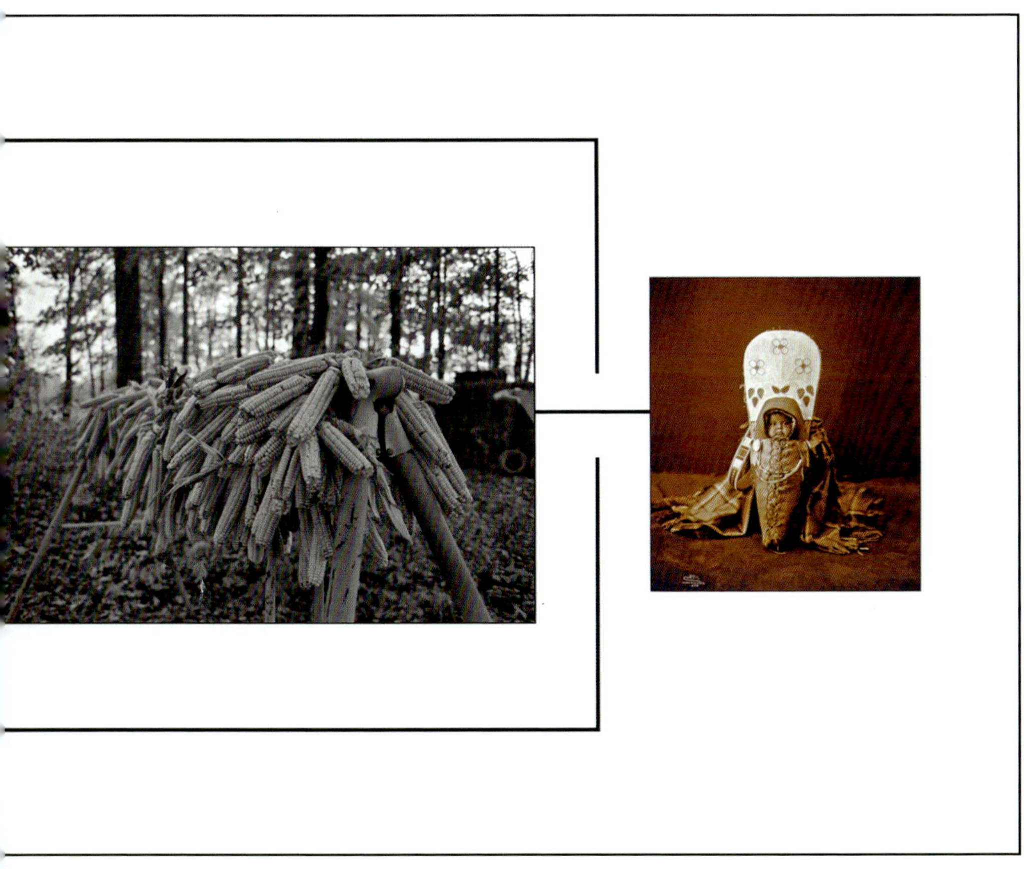

Jeffrey M. Thomas
Urban-Iroquois / Onondaga, born 1956
Corn = Life, 2021
Archival pigment print
Courtesy of the artist
© Jeffrey M. Thomas

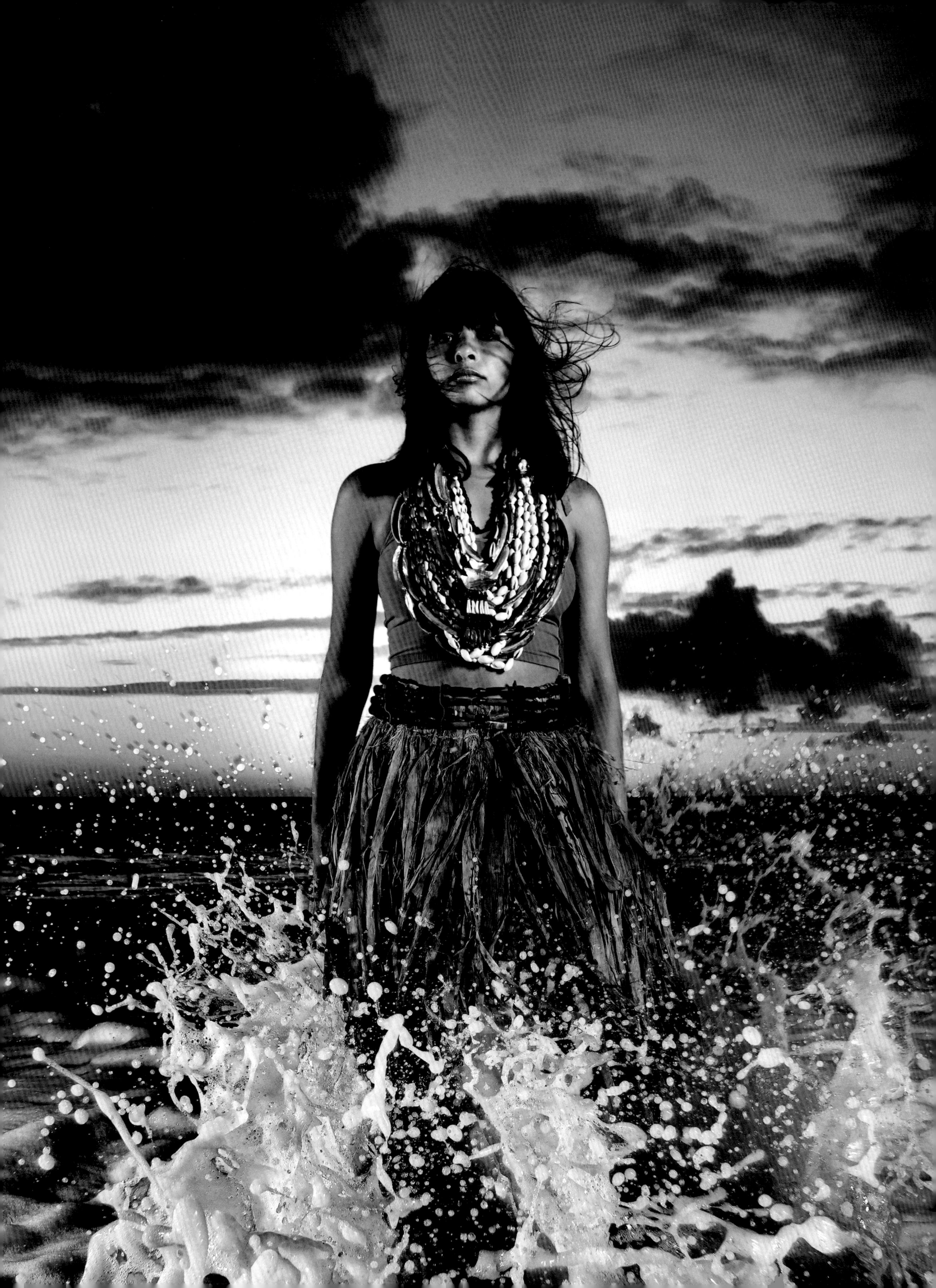

FROM WEAPON TO GIFT

MY JOURNEY AS AN INDIGENOUS PHOTOGRAPHER

BY CARA ROMERO

I OFTEN THINK OF MY FAMILY PHOTOGRAPHS: my great grandmother riding a paint in downtown Las Vegas when there were just two casinos; my great uncles boxing portraits that show him wearing silk shorts, his boxing gloves, and a Paiute headdress; old cars on dusty roads with cowboys and girls with dahlias in their hair. Beautiful, sentimental memories on film that capture humans with pretty brown skin and sparkling eyes. These images were erased from everywhere but our own homes.

To the outside world, "real" Indians looked like they did in the pages of *National Geographic*, or a Curtis coffee table book. Looking at false depictions of your own culture is exhausting, and frustrating, and confusing. The images were labeled like zoo animals, "'Chemehuevi boy with top knot." Taken by white men, these images defined us as mythic and bygone, and contributed to our erasure.

My first cameras were the disposable kind. When I stepped into a darkroom in college, I had never used a sophisticated camera with a lens, shutter speeds, and f-stops. I had to shyly borrow one from a friend to take the class. Most of the other students had experience in high school darkrooms, or with family. It was a feeling of not belonging that I knew all too well.

Photography is expensive. From paper, to film, to darkroom access, or digital workflow; the cost associated with the medium is a barrier to rez kids. Cost keeps kids from marginalized communities from telling their own photographic stories. Yet, we are rich with content, rich with stories, rich with ways of knowing.

When I stumbled into Professor Bill Thomas's black-and-white photography class at the University of Houston, my whole life changed. It was the 1990s when avenues of Native studies were relegated to anthropology, archeology, and history. Up until that point, I had only imagined myself rewriting textbooks or becoming a professor.

Cara Romero
Chemehuevi, born 1977
Hermosa, 2021
Archival HD pigment print on
Canson Baryta Prestidge paper
Minneapolis Institute of Art, Gift of funds
from Eric and Celita Levinson 2021.81

Within a year, a scholarship I received to attend the Institute of American Indian Arts granted me access to the education and funds I needed to pursue photography. That school is so pivotal for so many kids from the rez, like it was for me. It helped me overcome a financial disadvantage and introduced me to the only program in the world that focuses on work that is relevant to us as Indigenous people.

Getting to see the work of Zig Jackson, Shelley Niro, and Hulleah J. Tsinhnahjinnie; getting to meet Lee Marmon, and study the creative process of Laura Gilpin inspired me to see that it IS actually possible for a Native person to become a great photographer. In his class, Thomas emphasized content over technical ability; and I immediately understood that photography is power.

I had a lot to say, about everything, all at once.

But the odds were stacked against me, and I almost quit many times. I am a woman. Photography is a nontraditional medium. It's exploitative by nature and has been used against our community. But I loved it. My work has always come from a place of love, it was a thing between me and the Creator.

Along the way, tribal elders encouraged me. So many of them are gone, but when I look back at those uncertain years, I think of the small (but huge) affirmations from them. My grandmother framed my weird New York City street photography and hung it in her home on the rez. My uncle David forced his girls to get up before sunrise and pose for me while I was in school. People trusted me to document ceremonies, knowing I would never break that trust.

When I first set out to pursue photography, there wasn't any reference of Native people doing that work. When I started taking pictures, I was emulating the works of these non-Native photographers, like Edward Curtis, creating these sepia toned images devoid of modern context. I had this moment of existential reflection; I thought "this is odd, why am I doing this?" There was a lot to unpack.

I was interested in our beauty as Native Americans, what I saw in those shoebox photos I grew up with. I was interested in our diverse identities, and the multitude of stories we have as contemporary Indigenous people. Moving into fine art was a continuation of this story.

When I was a young woman, probably eighteen years old, I went to a bookstore and found *Love Medicine* by Louise Erdrich, I read it from front to back twice. That's when I found magical realism; I really resonated with what she was doing creatively. Now, twenty years later, I incorporate magical realism into my pieces. I feel it allows people to come to peace with their own spirituality and story. That is one of my favorite things about art; letting people feel what's already inside of them.

My journey to the work I make has been very intuitive, it comes from my heart. I don't think about everything I do before I do it. I find myself trusting in the process, and looking back and thinking, "okay, this is what happened for me." Like being a mother, and how that played into my creative process. It led me to staging these theatrical images.

During the mundane activities of motherhood—washing dishes, or folding laundry—I would wander off into my own imagination and think about contemporary Native issues, letting it all come together in my mind's eye. Then I would clear my calendar for a weekend and stage a shoot.

The universe opened up for me, and I used all the gifts I had acquired up to that point.

When my work was well received in the Native community it was a confirmation. It allowed me to see that I had found my voice, and this is the kind of work I wanted to be making.

As Native people, I feel like we live in a parallel universe. My grandmother used to tell me that Native people didn't really know that there was a Great Depression because they were living in a different way, so separate from the rest of Americans. I think that's still true today, our private communities exist in a parallel universe.

We often hear these overused expressions of walking in two worlds. It really interests me to think about how I can visually express that. It makes me fall in love with the medium of photography even more.

I think we still have a long way to go as far as navigating the industrial art complex of being seen by and interacting with non-Native people and non-Native institutions. They need to adjust to our ways of being to ensure the presence of inclusivity, and the creativity that comes from marginalized communities.

I look back now and see that I was not an outlier, but an innovator.

It's only very recently that museums have shown interest in collecting BIPOC work. I was recently interviewed by the Museum of Modern Art, and they asked why I still do Indian Market in Santa Fe, and it really affected me. They asked the question like Indian Market was beneath me. When I was a kid, Indian Market was *it*. There was nothing bigger than being at this summit of Indian art.

All of these things are kind of happening at the same time; museums are putting a moratorium on buying only "white men" artwork, having this deep reckoning with Native Americans, the Asian diaspora, and Black artists being American artists. They're scrambling to balance their inclusion. And suddenly, we've arrived. With not only a very strong voice, but one that's been here, unnoticed, for a very long time.

We have this wealth of content, and thousands and thousands of stories to be told. I find it a very exciting time, and one I never imagined would come, but here it is.

Art has this power to disarm people. I think it's so important to see artistic pursuit as being as important as intellectual pursuit. To study basket weaving, for example, and become a basket weaver is to become a cultural bearer, and that is highly intellectual. It's deeply connected to the health of our Indigenous ecosystem, and of all the unseen things they don't teach in academia.

As Native people, we have to work with allowing our young people to follow alternative, artistic pursuits to be able to save our culture. Sometimes, we internalize oppression and think some things aren't worthwhile pursuits. Saving art practices and traditional ecological knowledge is the most worthwhile.

Art is truly magic. I am so thankful to understand that.

Something that I find unique to being an Indigenous artist is that we are always bringing the past with us. Culture is not a pond sitting over there, stagnant. It is a flowing river going around the boulders of boarding schools, and technological advances, and extraction of resources, and we are really moving all together.

You can be a purveyor of our culture and a contemporary artist at the same time. There are things we don't depict, taboos. Things that are too culturally private. We have deep respect for our arts that have been around for thousands of years, the ones that are interconnected with landscape, and kinship, and community.

When we look forward, and into Indigenous Futurisms, it's always going to be wrapped up in taking the past with us. We are always going to exist together in this river we're floating down.

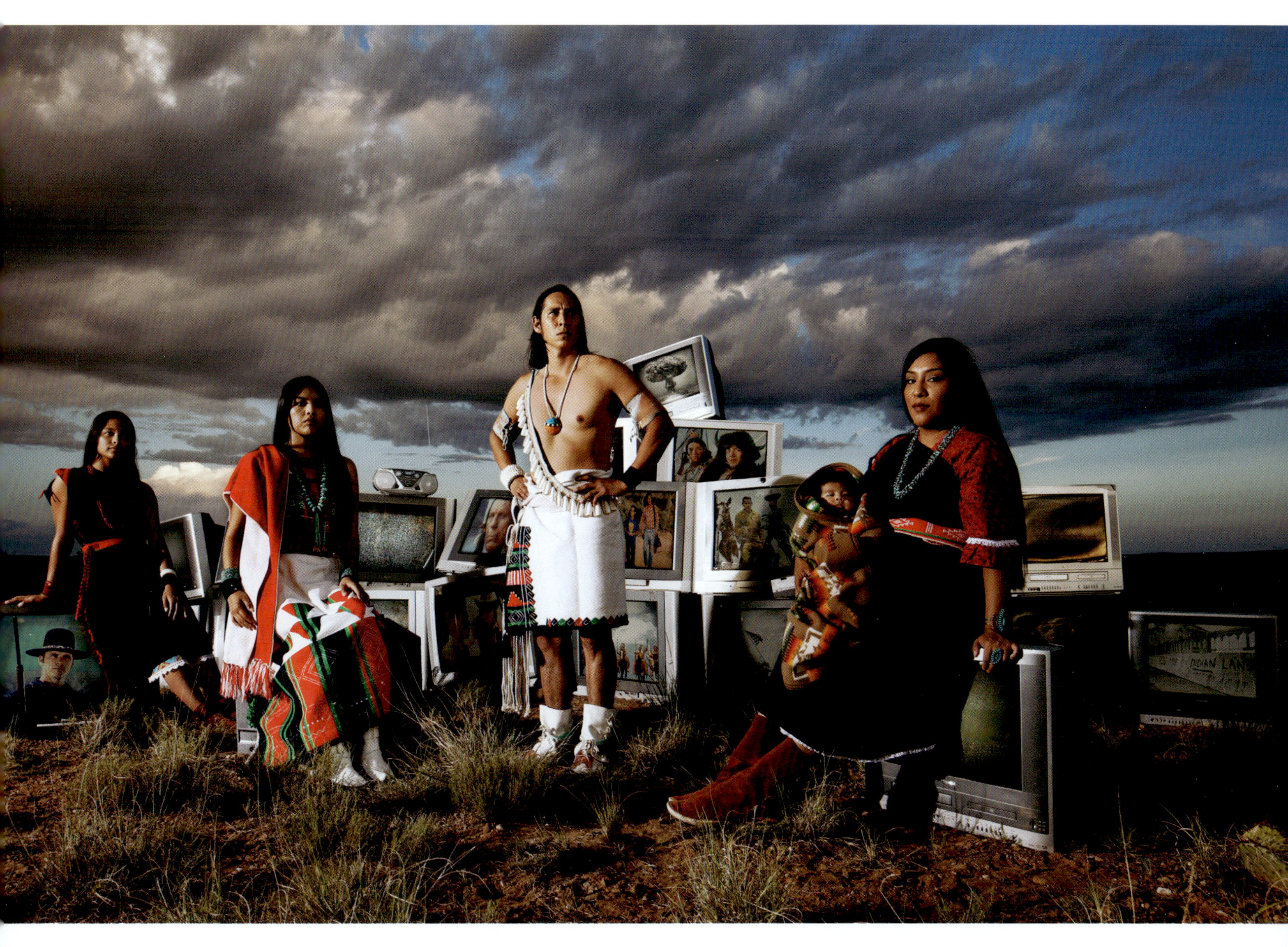

Cara Romero
Chemehuevi, born 1977
TV Indians, 2017
Archival inkjet print
Courtesy of the artist
© Cara Romero

PART II

ALWAYS LEADERS

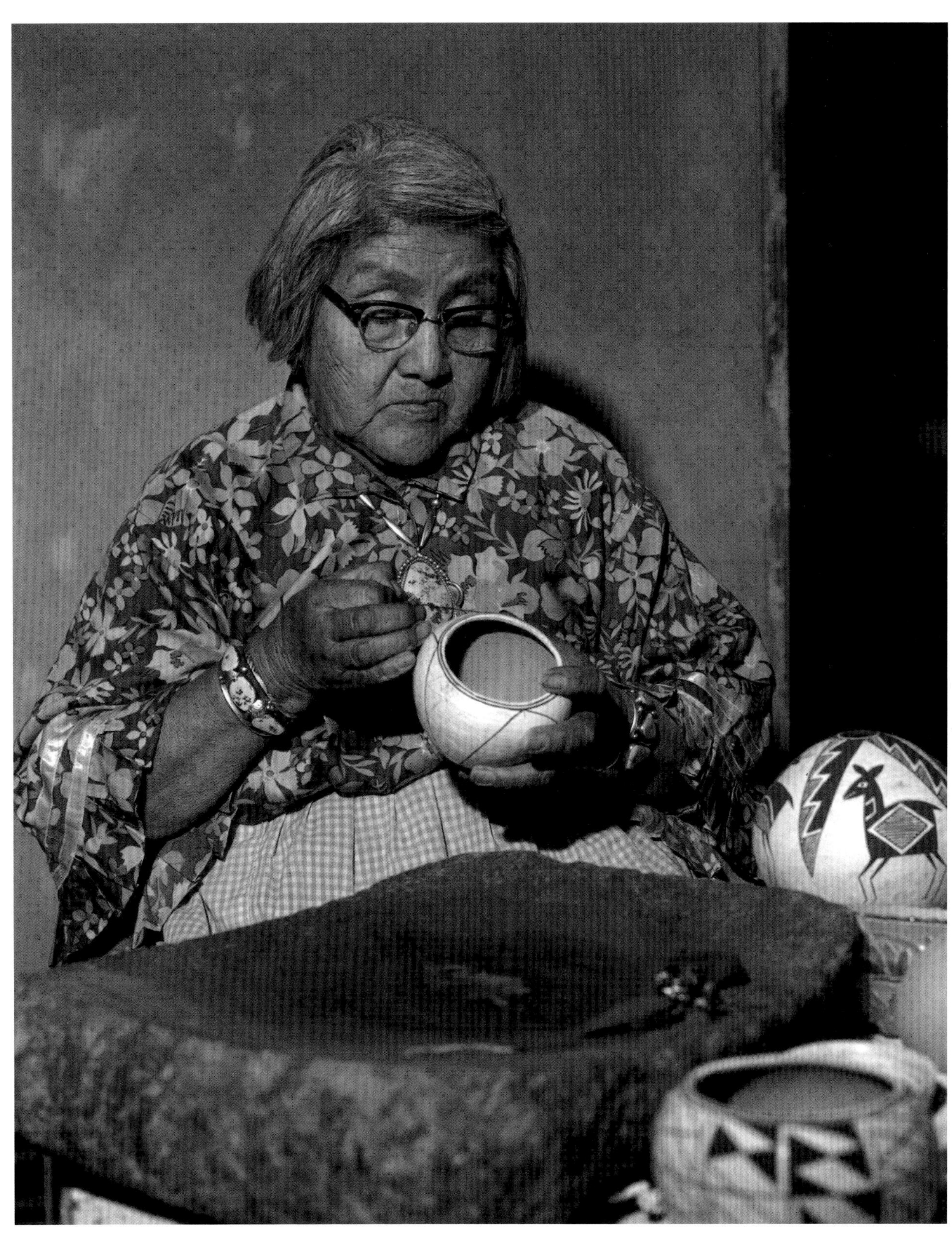

Lee Marmon
Laguna Pueblo, 1925–2021
Portrait of Lucy Lewis, potter from Acoma, painting on a pot, 1960
Courtesy of University of New Mexico Center for Southwest Research and the Indian Pueblo Cultural Center

Ryan RedCorn
Osage, born 1979
Celena White, 𐓏𐓘𐓻𐓘𐓻𐓟 𐓪𐓡𐓪́ (Osage Cook), 2018
Sublimated fabric print
Courtesy of the artist

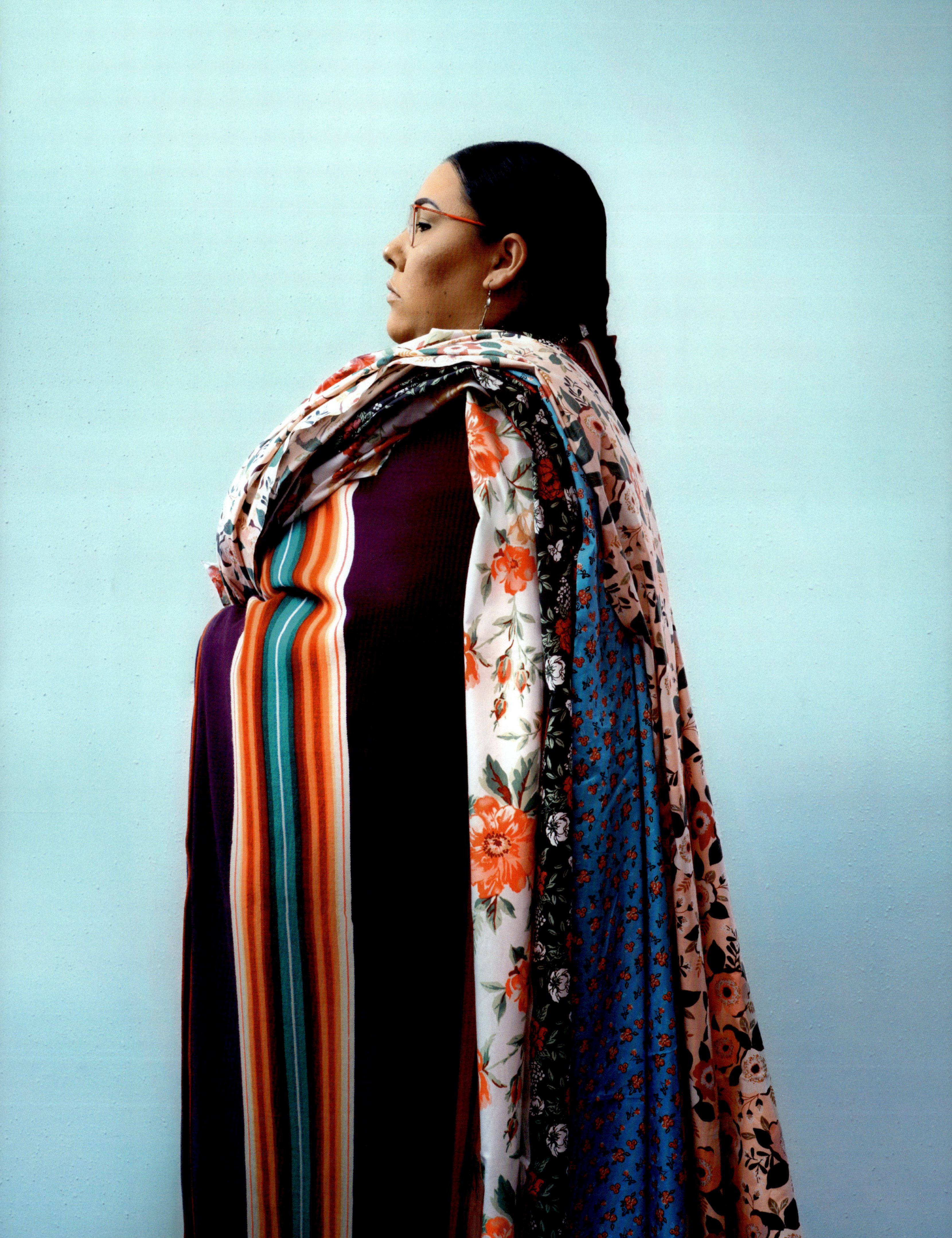

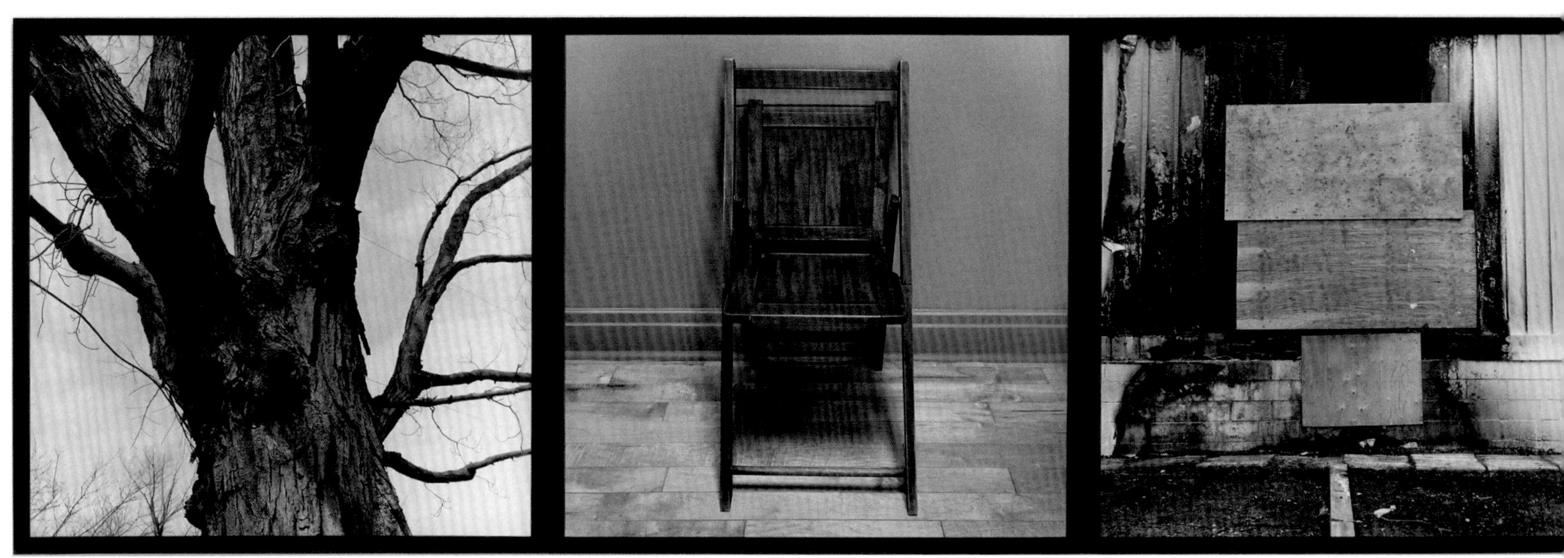

Greg Staats
Kanien'kehá:ka (Mohawk), Six Nations
Hodinǫhsǫ:ni, born 1963
auto mnemonic six nations, 2005
Six gelatin silver prints mounted on aluminum
Courtesy of the National Gallery of Canada,
Ottawa, Photo: NGC

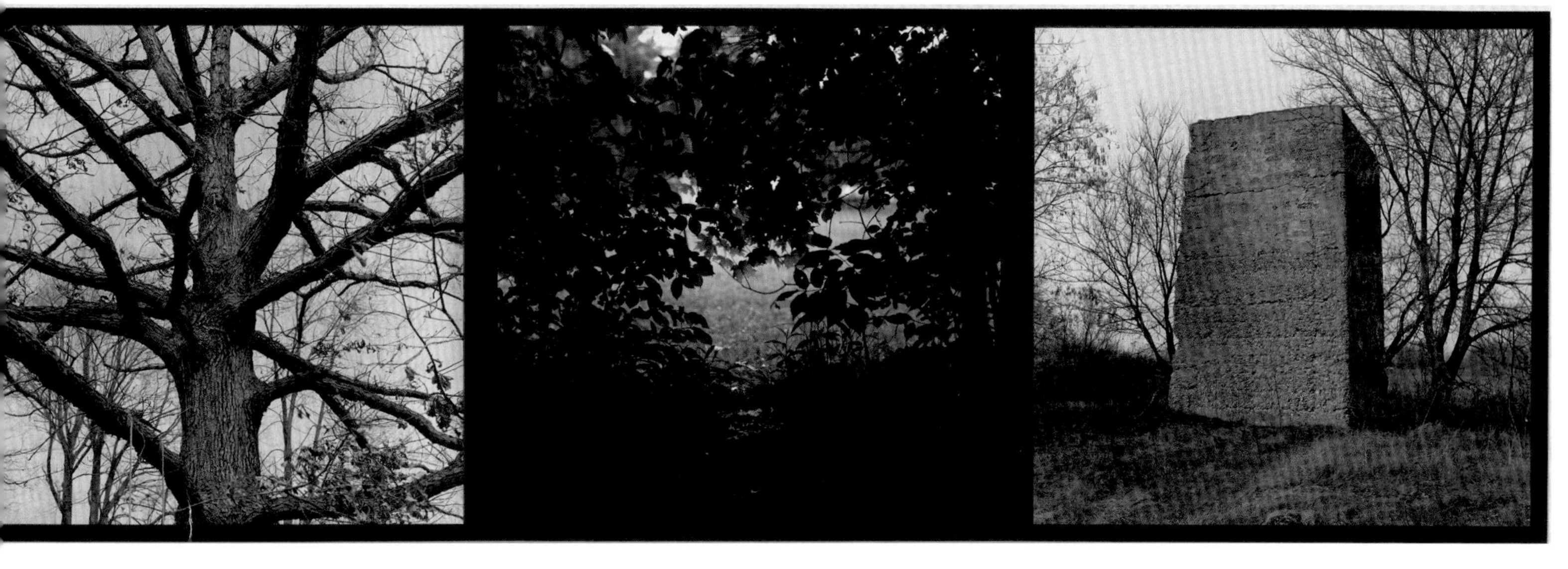

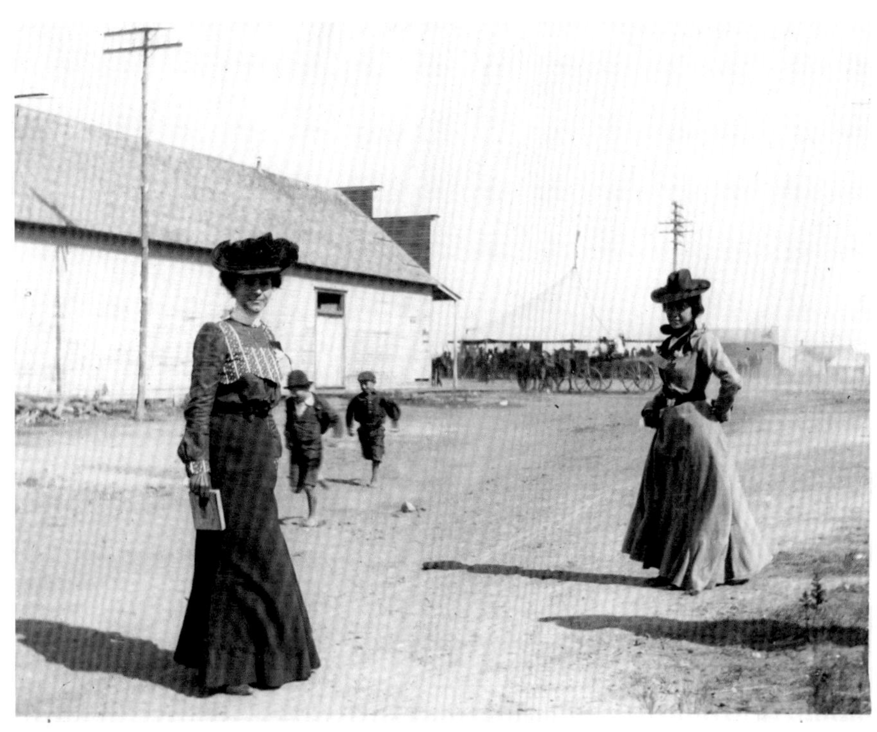

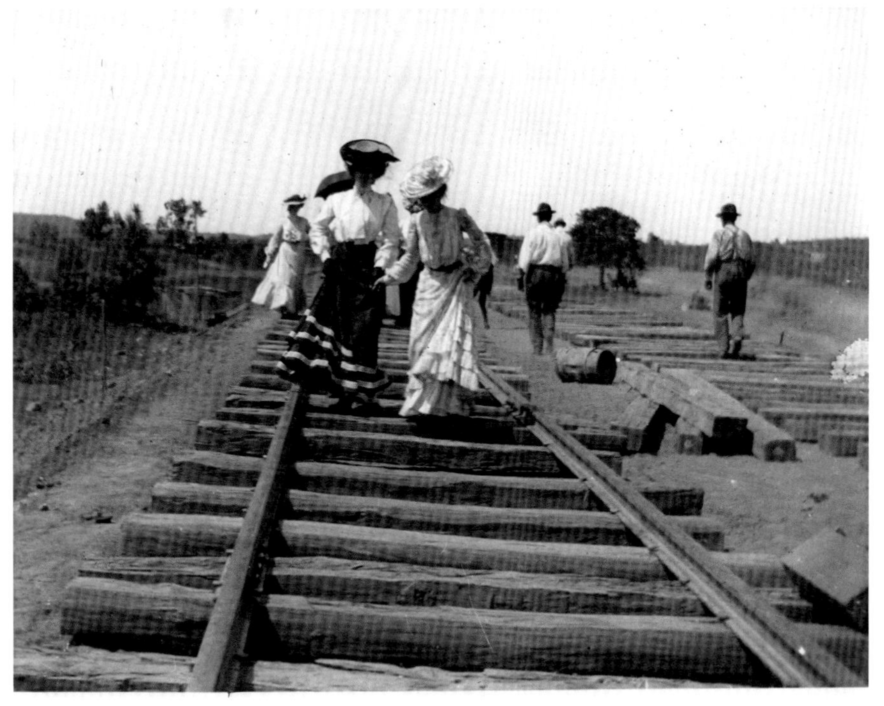

Jennie Ross Cobb
Cherokee, 1881–1959
Cherokee Female Seminary, c. 1900-1902
Courtesy of the Oklahoma Historical Society,
Jennie Ross Cobb Collection, 20661.12

Jennie Ross Cobb
Cherokee, 1881–1959
Ozark & Cherokee Central Railroad, 1902
Courtesy of the Oklahoma Historical Society,
Jennie Ross Cobb Collection, 20661.17

POST CARD

Dear Los Angeles,

This was typed on the ancestral homelands of the Tongva, Chumash and Kizh Indigenous peoples. The Tongva people are still fighting for federal recognition as a nation. This area is also now home to several other Indigenous diasporas who were removed from their homelands through policies of continued settle colonialism, which has made this land the current home of the largest Indigenous population of any city in the U.S.

Miigwech (thank you) for supporting this project!

You Are on Native Land
for Black Hills Legal Defense Fund
by Eve-Lauryn LaFountain & Postcards for John
Awesiinh (Wild Animals)

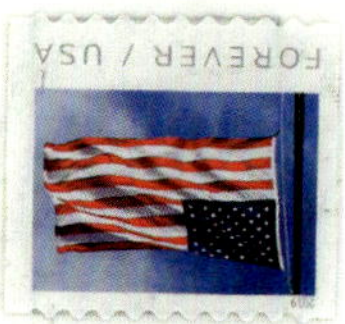

El Pueblo de Los Angeles
125 Paseo De La Plaza
Los Angeles, CA 90012

Photo
ILFORD MULTIGRADE IV RC PORTFOLIO

Eve-Lauryn LaFountain
Turtle Mountain Band of Chippewa / Jewish, born 1986
AWESIINH (WILD ANIMALS), 2020
from *You Are on Native Land*
16mm and 35mm film taped together with words etched into the film, contact printed on double weight Ilford multigrade pearl postcard paper
Courtesy of the artist
© 2020 Little Shell Studios

Dear Santa Fe,

POST CARD

This text was written in O'Ga P'Ogeh Owingeh or "White Shell Water Place." The Tewa people and their ancestors have been caretakers of this land and its waters for generations. On August 10, 1680 the Pueblo people drove the Spanish colonizers out of Santa Fe for 12 years, the only successful Native uprising against a colonizing power in the United States. Now the Santa Fe Indian Market, the largest Native art show in the world, happens every August on the same plaza, and Santa Fe continues to be a meeting place for Indigenous communities from near and far.

Miigwech (thank you) for supporting this project!

You Are on Native Land
for Black Hills Legal Defense Fund
by Eve-Lauryn LaFountain & Postcards for John
Niibidoon (Weave)

FOREVER / USA

Palace of the Governors
105 W Palace Avenue
Santa Fe, NM 87501

ILFORD MULTIGRADE IV RC PORTFOLIO

Eve-Lauryn LaFountain
Turtle Mountain Band of Chippewa / Jewish, born 1986
NIIBIDOON (WEAVE), 2020
from You Are on Native Land
16mm and 35mm film taped together with words etched into the film, contact printed on double weight Ilford multigrade pearl postcard paper
Courtesy of the artist

POST CARD

Dear Minneapolis,

You are receiving this postcard on Očhéthi Šakówiŋ and Wahpekute territory. The Dakota and Anishinaabe peoples have a long history in this area. Dakota cultural history begins at Bdóte, a sacred place where the Minnesota and Mississippi Rivers meet. On December 26, 1862 Abraham Lincoln ordered 38 Dakota men to be hanged in Makato in the largest mass execution in U.S. history. A century later the Indigenous population in the Twin Cities grew enormously as a result of the 1957 Indian Relocation Act. These new communities founded the American Indian Movement in Minneapolis in 1968.

Miigwech (thank you) for supporting this project!

You Are on Native Land
for Black Hills Legal Defense Fund
by Eve-Lauryn LaFountain & Postcards for John
Agindamaage (She Reads for People)

Minneapolis Institute of Art
2400 Third Avenue South
Minneapolis, MN 55404

Eve-Lauryn LaFountain
Turtle Mountain Band of Chippewa / Jewish, born 1986
AGINDAMAAGE (SHE READS FOR PEOPLE), 2020
from You Are on Native Land
16mm and 35mm film taped together with words etched into the film, contact printed on double weight Ilford multigrade pearl postcard paper
Courtesy of the artist
© 2020 Little Shell Studios

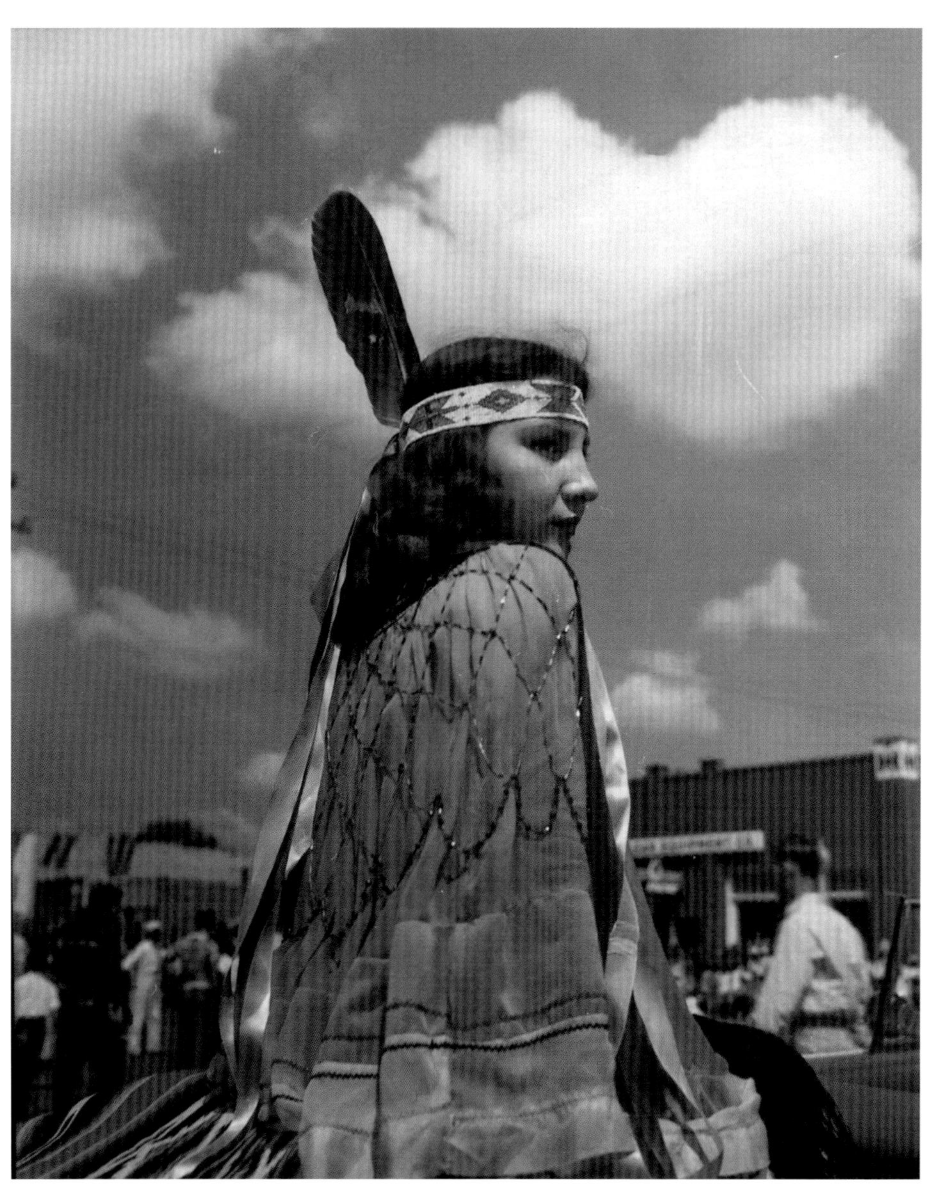

Horace Poolaw
Kiowa, 1906-1984
Eula Mae Narcomey Doonkeen (Seminole)
in the American Indian Exposition Parade, 1952
Courtesy of the Poolaw Family and the
University of Science and Arts of Oklahoma,
Chickasha, Horace Poolaw Collection, (45EXCW6)

A POOLAW PHOTO, PICTURES BY AN INDIAN

BY TOM JONES

KIOWA PHOTOGRAPHER HORACE POOLAW (1906–1984) was actively and passionately engaged in recording the intricacies of the modern daily life of American Indians in twentieth-century Oklahoma. The history of photography and its relationship to American Indians has been fraught with invasiveness and mistrust created by White photographers racing to document a "vanishing race." Poolaw had intrinsic insider knowledge, giving the viewer a unique vantage point and complex record of a community that was made up of multiple tribes living within Oklahoma. Through his camerawork, he situates and gives access to the many tribes represented within his photographs, which were the Arapaho, Caddo, Cheyenne, Delaware, Kiowa, Apache tribe of Oklahoma, Fort Sill Apache, Osage, Otoe, Pawnee, Ponca, Wichita, and Comanche. He actively made the point of being an insider by creating a rubber stamp that read, *A Poolaw Photo, Pictures by an Indian, Horace M. Poolaw, Anadarko, Okla.*

While I was in graduate school at Columbia College Chicago in 1998, I began to research other Native photographers and came upon the *Aperture* magazine issue, "Strong Hearts: Native American Visons and Voices." This is where I was first introduced to Horace Poolaw's work. At last, I had found a Native photographer who photographed his own community, as I was also doing. Approximately eight years later the universe aligned when I was invited by fellow faculty member Ada Deer to have lunch with Dr. Nancy Marie Mithlo, who was in the process of being hired as a faculty member in the Art History department at the University of Wisconsin-Madison where I still teach. We somehow got to the subject of Horace Poolaw and Nancy shared with me that she was related to him through marriage. Her aunt Elvina was married to Horace's youngest son Bryce Poolaw; then, Nancy told me that Poolaw's nearly 2,000 negatives were still in the family's possession. I learned that many of the negatives were nitrate negatives, and because of this they could spontaneously combust. This concerned me since all the negatives were housed together. I told her we needed to find a way to digitize the

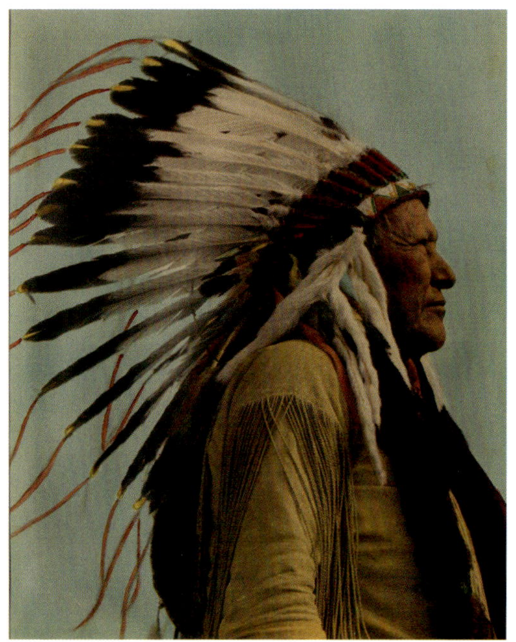

Fig. 1. George Poolaw (collection of the author).

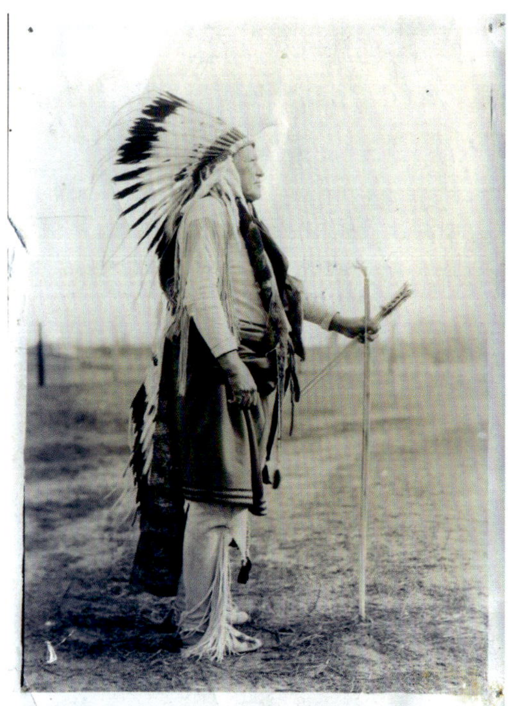

Fig. 2. George Poolaw. Photo by Poolaw, Anadarko, OK, (from the Oklahoma Historical Society 1971.041).

archive, in order to preserve the negatives. Poolaw's daughter Linda Poolaw has tirelessly advanced knowledge of her father's work, since her collaboration with Stanford University in 1989.[40] Out of that collaboration came a student curated exhibition in 1990 titled, *War Bonnets, Tin Lizzies, and Patent Leather Pumps: Kiowa Culture in Transition, 1925–1955*. I was excited at the possibility of expanding the access of this important archive for future researchers since many of these photographs had never been seen before.

In 2008, Mithlo and I took a group of UW-Madison students to the University of Science and Arts of Oklahoma (USAO) in Chickasaw, Oklahoma.[41] We conducted this field project over two consecutive summers, during which we scanned nearly 1,400 of his negatives and conducted interviews with community members. This was especially important in furthering an understanding of the scope of Poolaw's work. Because of the cost of photographic materials, many of Poolaw's negatives were never printed during his lifetime.

Our mission in digitizing the negatives was to support the Poolaw family in the preservation and circulation of this valuable photographic legacy. Once the research was completed, we proposed an exhibition to the National Museum of the American Indian (NMAI), which was accepted. This would never have advanced without the support of the late Fred Nawooksy, senior advisor at the NMAI. The museum generally does not accept shows curated by people outside of the institution, but through his advocacy the show was approved. The exhibition *For a Love of His People: The Photography of Horace Poolaw,* which opened at the NMAI New York in August 2014 and Washington, DC, in November 2016, also featured an accompanying book published through Yale University Press. *For a Love of His People* continued as a traveling exhibition onto the Eitlejorg Museum in Indianapolis, Indiana, in May 2019 and continues to be exhibited in other venues today. In Poolaw's own lifetime, he had only one exhibition, which took place at the Southern Plains Indian Museum in Anadarko, Oklahoma, in 1979. The visibility of Poolaw's work has now been opened up to new scholarship and has firmly placed him into the canon of Indigenous photography.

UNIVERSITY OF WISCONSIN-MADISON

While Poolaw was not able to make a living as a professional photographer, he consistently pursued his passion for photography throughout his lifetime. At the age of sixteen he learned the photographic trade while apprenticing with photographers George Long and John Coyle. During this time, he began documenting the daily life of his family and was hired on occasion by individuals within the community to document weddings, funerals, political functions, and community gatherings such as the Carterville Indian Fair (1924–1933) and the Medicine Lodge Indian Peace Treaty Pageant (beginning in 1927). In 1930, Poolaw began serving as the official photographer for the American Indian Exposition in Anadarko, Oklahoma. During the early 1940s he was an arts and crafts supervisor for the Civilian Conservation Corps–Indian Division housed within the US Interior Department. In 1943, Poolaw was recruited and trained by the US Army Air Forces to teach aerial photography at MacDill Field in Tampa, Florida, during World War II. He only stopped photographing in the 1970s when his eyesight declined due to diabetes.

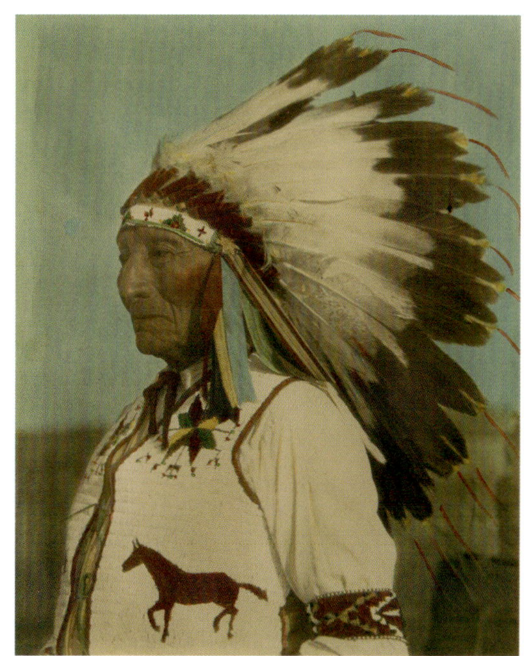

Fig. 3. Hand-colored photo of Heap of Bears (collection of the author).

There were only a handful of Native professional photographers in the early decades of the twentieth century, in part due to the high cost of its materials. This prohibitive cost often dictated Poolaw's style of shooting. He would slowly and meticulously compose his photographs, often only taking one or two pictures on 5 x 7 or 4 x 5 negative. One of Poolaw's earliest photographs of his father George Poolaw Pohd-Lonk (Old Wolf), circa 1930, is a tightly cropped hand-colored portrait (fig. 1). This regal portrait reflects a serene stillness emanating from the sitter, but simultaneously is visually activated by the multiple ermines and otter furs cascading from his war bonnet that frames his face. The photograph is further energized and movement is created through Poolaw's hand-coloring of the horse hair. He accentuates this effect by placing thick red lines over the horse hair that flows from the bonnet. Poolaw offers the viewer a truer experience of the individual through the act of hand coloring the black-and-white photograph. Though this added color alteration is a facsimile of the real photograph, it allows the viewer to experience the individual's skin tone and the softness of the buckskin.

The original uncropped negative of the elder Poolaw is a full-length portrait of him standing in an empty Oklahoma landscape in profile wearing a buckskin outfit with a blanket wrapped around his waist, while holding arrows and a bow in his left hand (fig. 2). Poolaw chose to crop it at the waist, highlighting his father's torso and face. When reading a photograph of American Indians, a complicated intersection of history, anthropology, and ethnographic rhetoric is placed on the image, blurring the boundaries between the documentary and artistic expression. Poolaw's portrait elevates the awe and beauty of the individual. His aesthetic choice of composing the individual from the waist up echoed so-called grand-manner portrait painting, utilized generally by wealthy aristocrats in prior centuries. By cropping the image and placing emphasis upon his upper body and facial features, Poolaw gives us a visual reverence and demonstrates the respect he had for his father. The entanglement of painting and photographic traditions illuminates Poolaw's democratic use of photography and showcases the people of his community with respect.

Similar framing and composition were incorporated in his portrait titled *Kiowa, Heap of Bears* (fig. 3, pg. 111). During this time period (ca. 1930s), Poolaw would often use a short depth of field on the individuals he photographed, offering the viewer only a blurred-out representation of the Oklahoma landscape. For him it was more important for the viewer to concentrate on the sitter, to celebrate and recognize them. Though it was rare for Poolaw to employ the use of cropping in the majority of his photographs, this photo was also cropped. In the original photo, Heap of Bears has his hands clasped on his stomach. In this version, Poolaw places the beaded horse on the edge of the frame, again activating the stillness of the sitter, in order to energize and create movement in the image. This particular vest worn by Heap of Bears must have been brought by Horace's brother, Bruce Poolaw, to the same photoshoot, because it was worn by other individuals, including Bruce Poolaw and Rainy Mountain Charley.

The majority of Poolaw's photographs were sold in the form of real photographic postcards. On rare occasions, he would sell larger prints on 8 x 10 inch or 11 x 14 inch paper, like the ones of George Poolaw and Heap of Bears. The text placed next to the image on these postcards was created with a stencil in the darkroom printing process. It read, "American Indian Exposition,

Anadarko, Oklahoma, Poolaw." In a later conversation, Linda Poolaw shared with me that her father would take members of the family to the railroad depot to sell the postcards to the tourists. Tellingly, they were also sold during the American Indian Exposition or other gatherings to Native and White attendees.

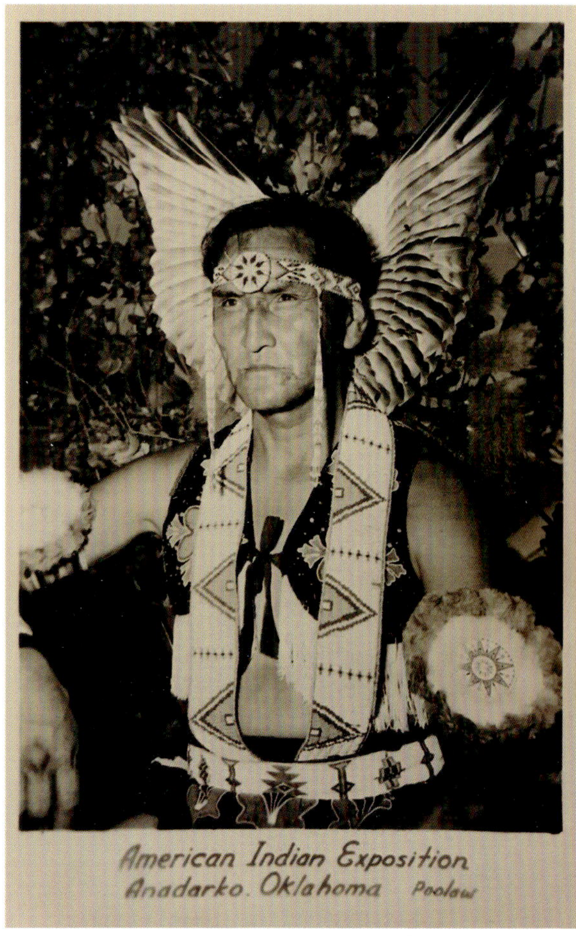

Fig. 4. Postcard of Jack Ho-Ke-Ah (aka Jack Hokeah) (Kiowa), 1946 (American Indian Exposition, Anadarko, Oklahoma, Poolaw).

Poolaw spent fifty years photographing in Oklahoma, creating a visual document of a place and its people. In doing so, he actually followed in the footsteps of his father, George Poolaw, also known as Kiowa George, who was a traditional calendar keeper for the tribe, and would record tribal history by drawing a visual document of the events that had happened each year on canvas or buckskin. Poolaw gives us a glimpse into a Native community positioned in an ever-changing world. In the 1970s, a White curator told him that no one would be interested in his photographs of everyday life, only the older pictures of his people in traditional dress positioned within the landscape. Instead of embracing a "vanishing race" mentality, Poolaw shared with the world a vibrant and resilient culture that actively participated in the advancing of new modern technologies alongside their White contemporaries. In creating "Pictures by an Indian," he documented and preserved the daily life of the American Indians in the twentieth century for future generations.

Culturally as a Ho-Chunk we are taught to help others. At a young age we are told to be observant and to be aware of when you can assist when it is needed. You should not have to be asked. Through the act of digitizing Horace Poolaw's archive, I wanted to help preserve his legacy and thank him for his important impact on my own growth as a photographer. While this is a service I have given to the field of photography, as my mother JoAnn Jones said, "You are doing this for all of Indian country."

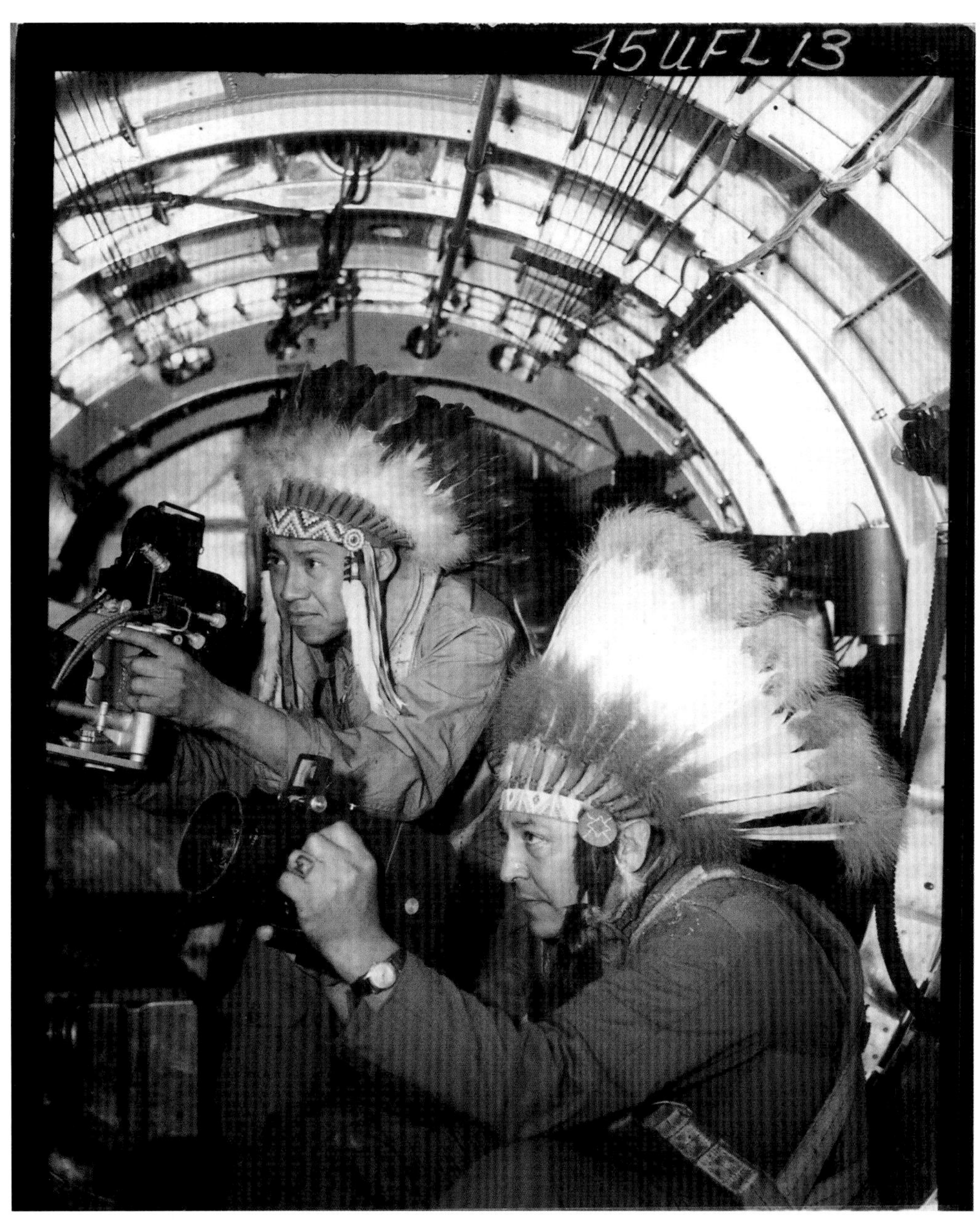

Horace Poolaw
Kiowa, 1906–1984
Horace Poolaw aerial photographer, and
Gus Palmer (Kiowa), side gunner inside a B-17
Flying Fortress, Tampa, Fla., c. 1944
Photographic print
Courtesy of the Poolaw Family and the
University of Science and Arts of Oklahoma,
Chickasha, Horace Poolaw Collection, (45UFL13)

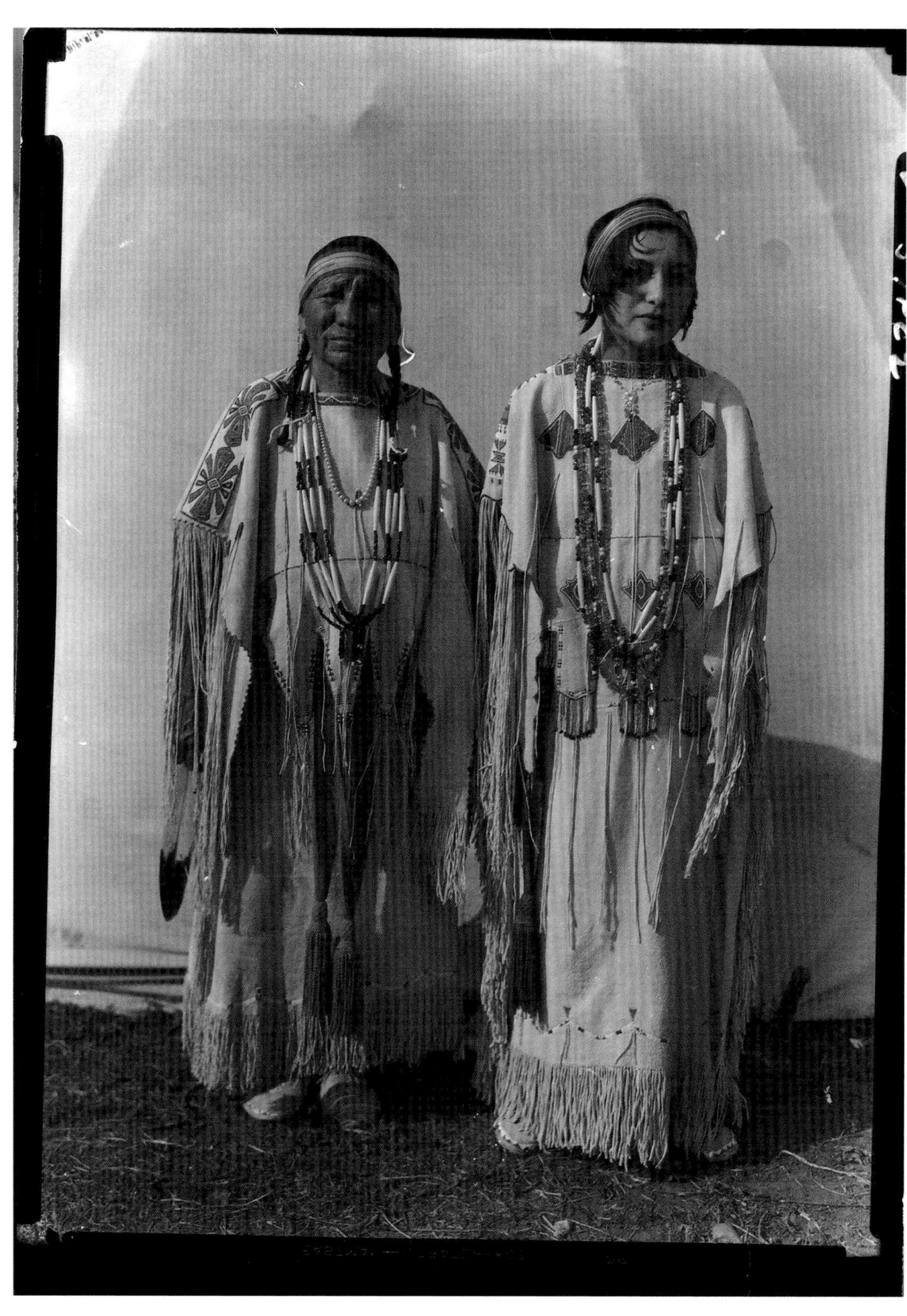

Horace Poolaw
Kiowa, 1906–1984
Sindy Libby Keahbone (Kiowa),
Hannah Keahbone (Kiowa), Oklahoma City, c. 1930
Courtesy of the Poolaw Family and the
University of Science and Arts of Oklahoma,
Chickasha, Horace Poolaw Collection, (57PC2)

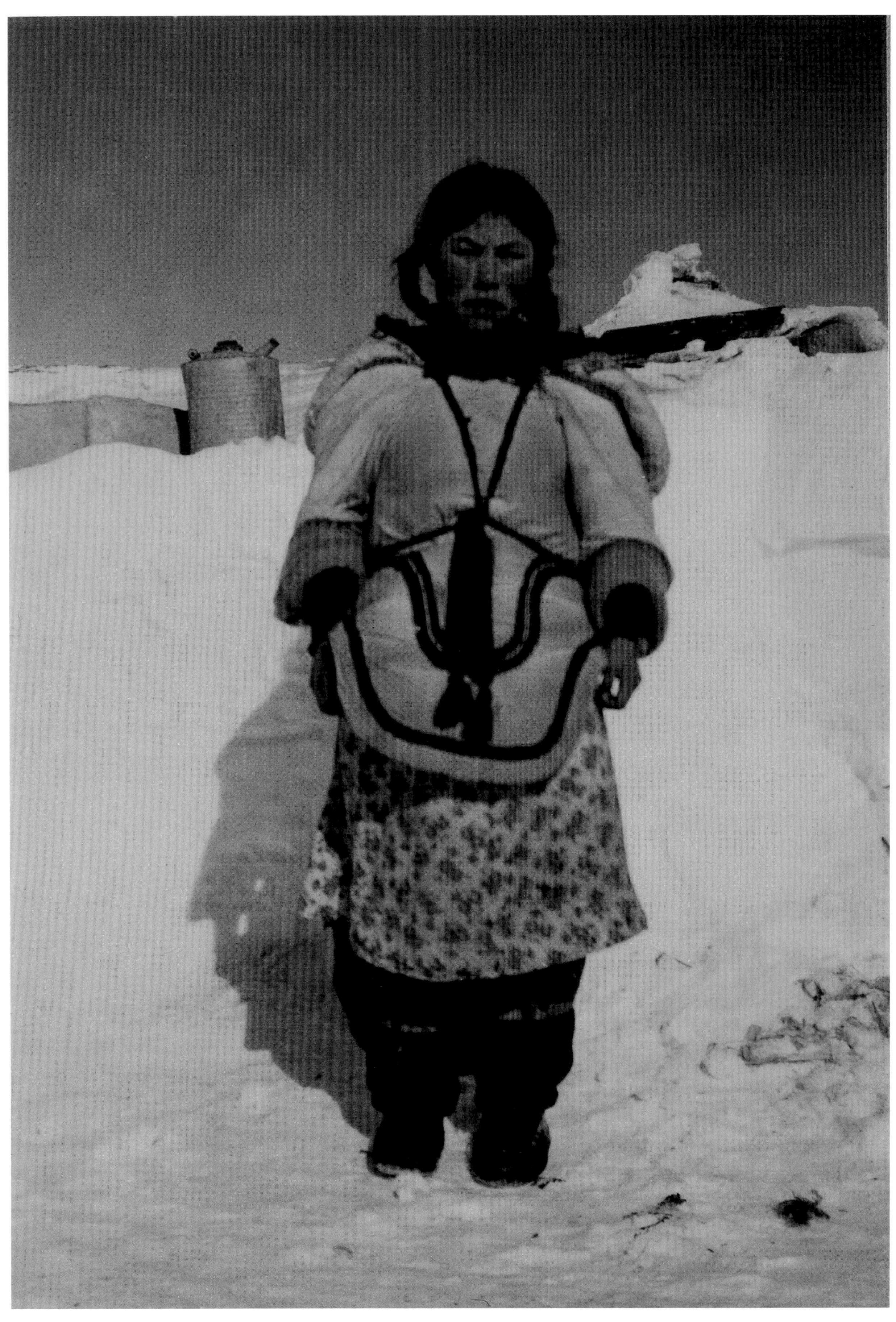

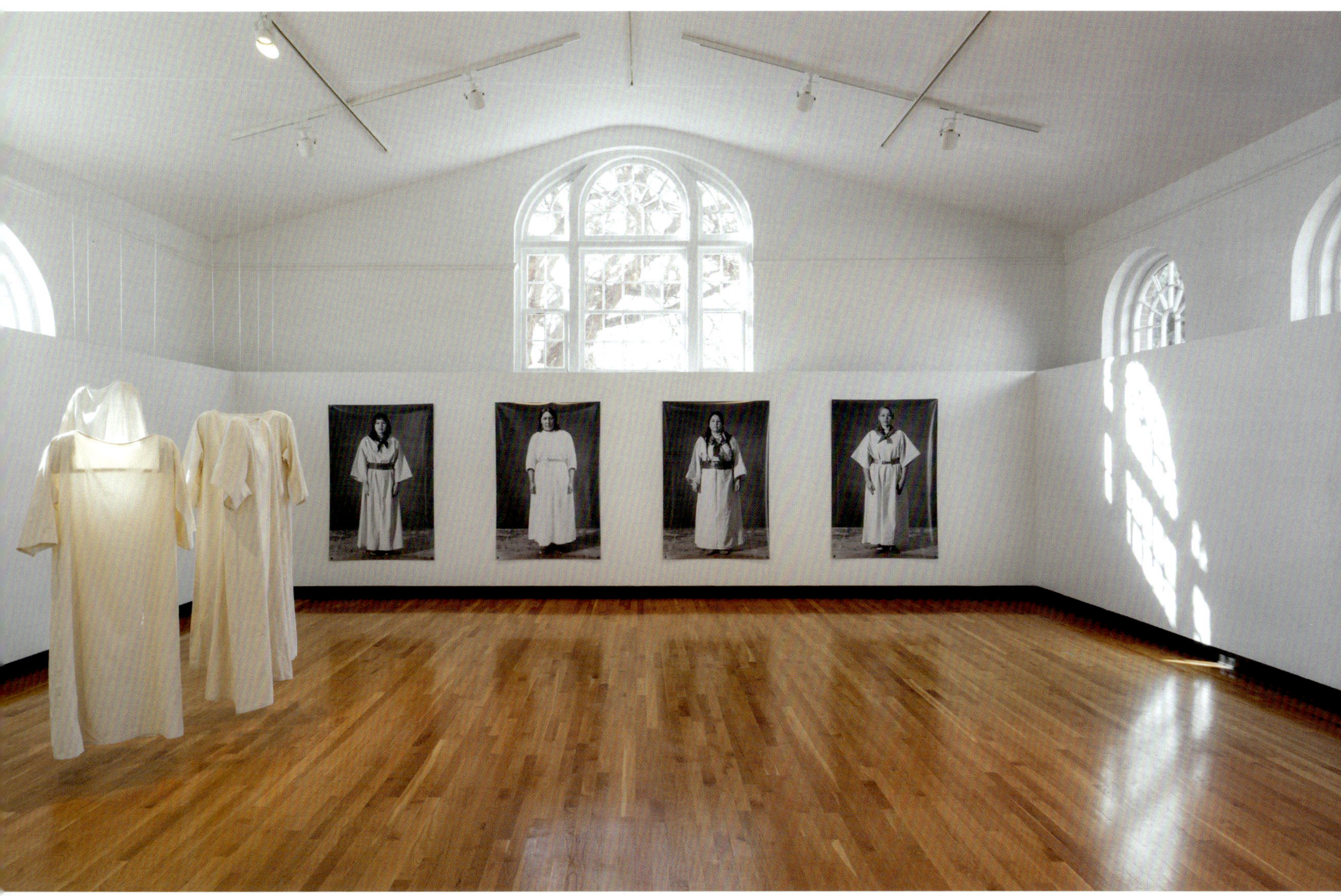

Faye HeavyShield
Kainaiwa Nation, Blackfoot Confederacy
Blood Reserve, born 1953
Clan, 2020
Inkjet prints, canvas dress,
canvas flags, and wood support
Courtesy of the artist
photography courtesy of
Southern Alberta Art Gallery
Photo: Blaine Campbell
© Faye HeavyShield

Page 116:
Peter Pitseolak
Inuit, 1902-1973
Untitled (Kenojuak Ashevak, artist), c. 1940-45
Gelatin silver print
Courtesy of the CMCP Collection,
National Gallery of Canada, Ottawa

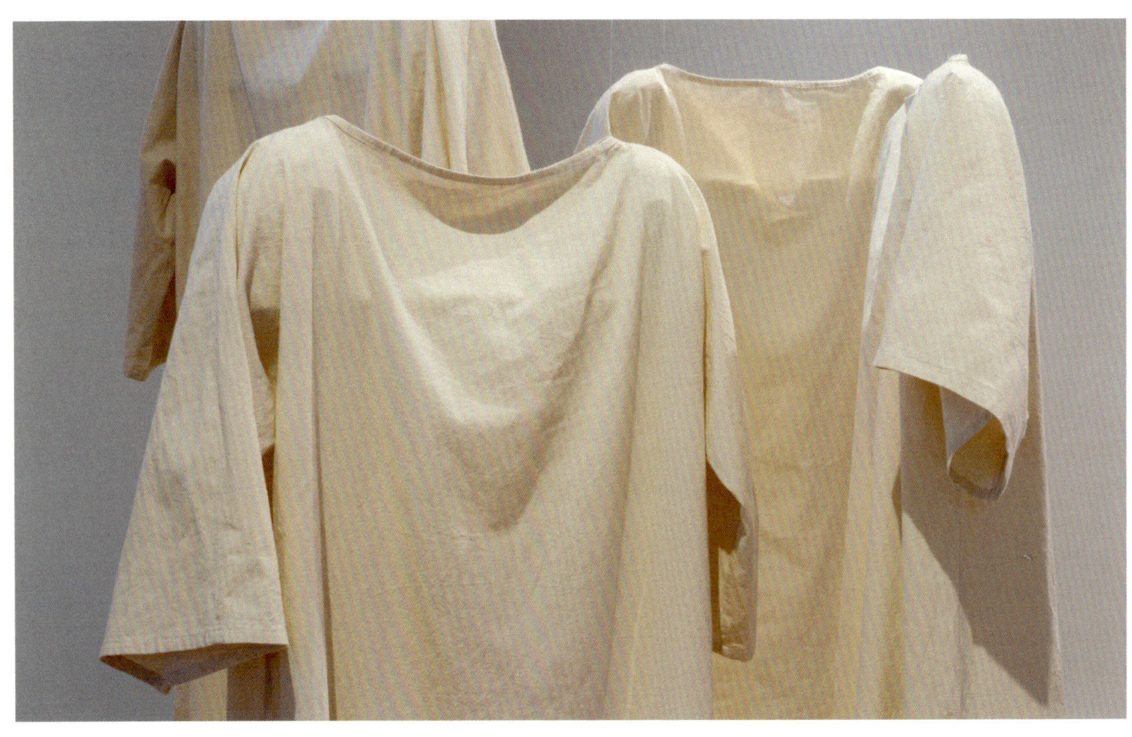

Faye HeavyShield
Kainaiwa Nation, Blackfoot Confederacy
Blood Reserve, born 1953
[detail of Clan]
The grandmothers, 2020
Canvas dresses
Photography courtesy of
Southern Alberta Art Gallery
Photo: Blaine Campbell

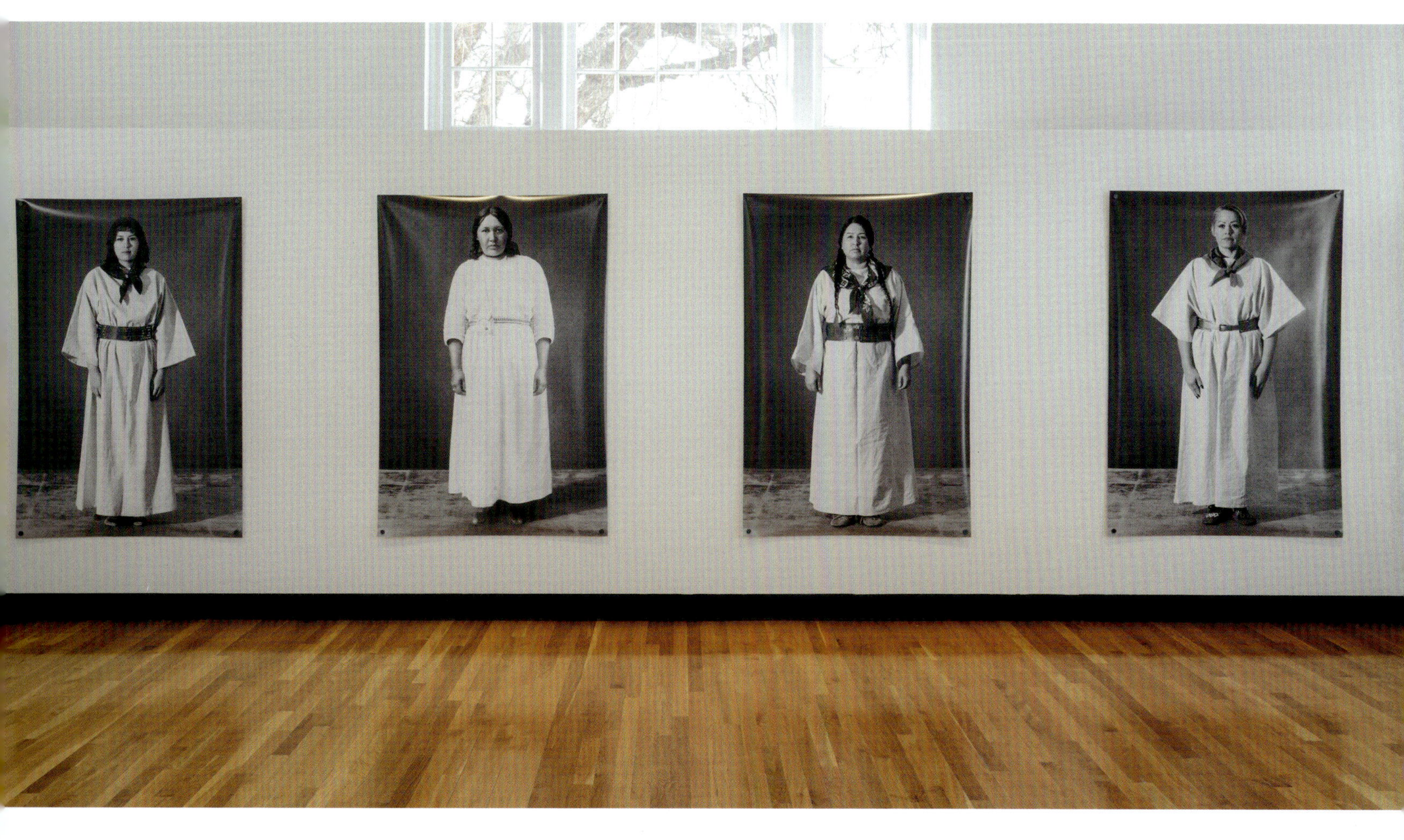

Faye HeavyShield
Kainaiwa Nation, Blackfoot Confederacy
Blood Reserve, born 1953
[detail of Clan]
matri-liminal, 2020
Inkjet prints on paper
photography courtesy of
Southern Alberta Art Gallery
Photo: Blaine Campbell

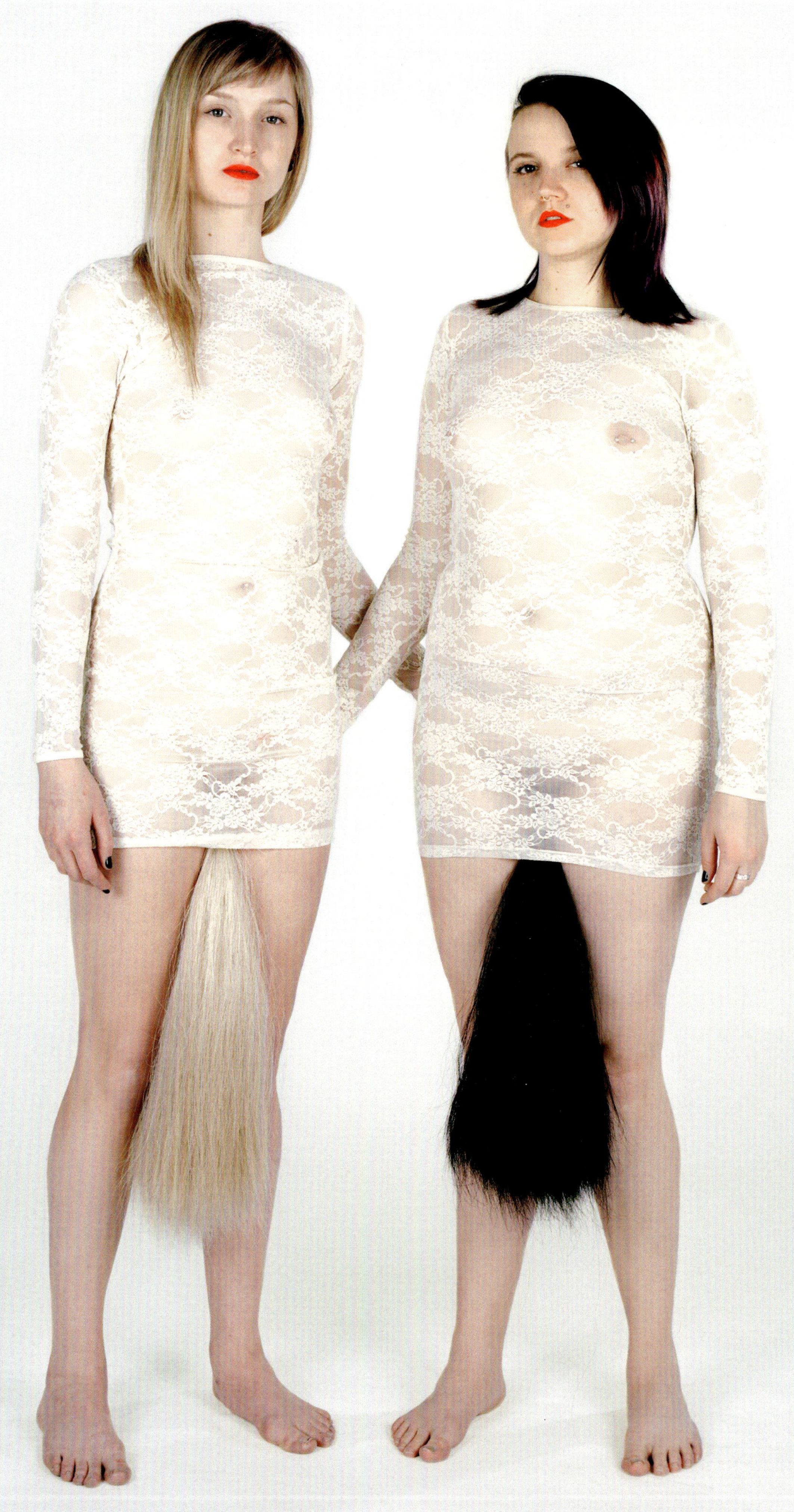

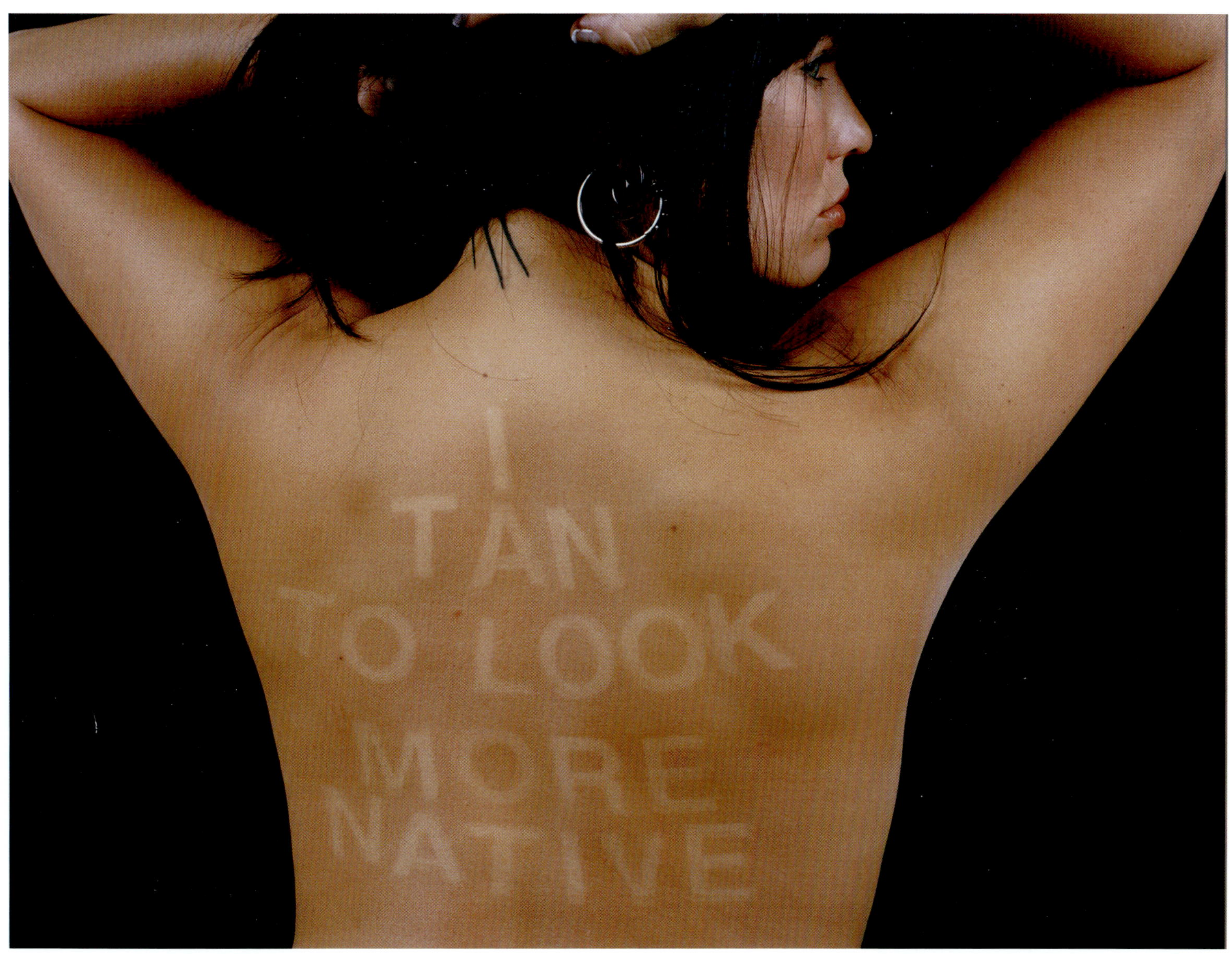

Erica Lord
Athabascan / Iñupiat / Finnish,
Swedish, Japanese-American, born 1978
Untitled (I Tan to Look More Native), 2006
from The Tanning Project
Inkjet print
Courtesy the Artist

Page 120:
Dayna Danger
Métis / Saulteaux / Polish, born 1987
Siostra, 2013
from Sisters series
Archival inkjet print on rag paper

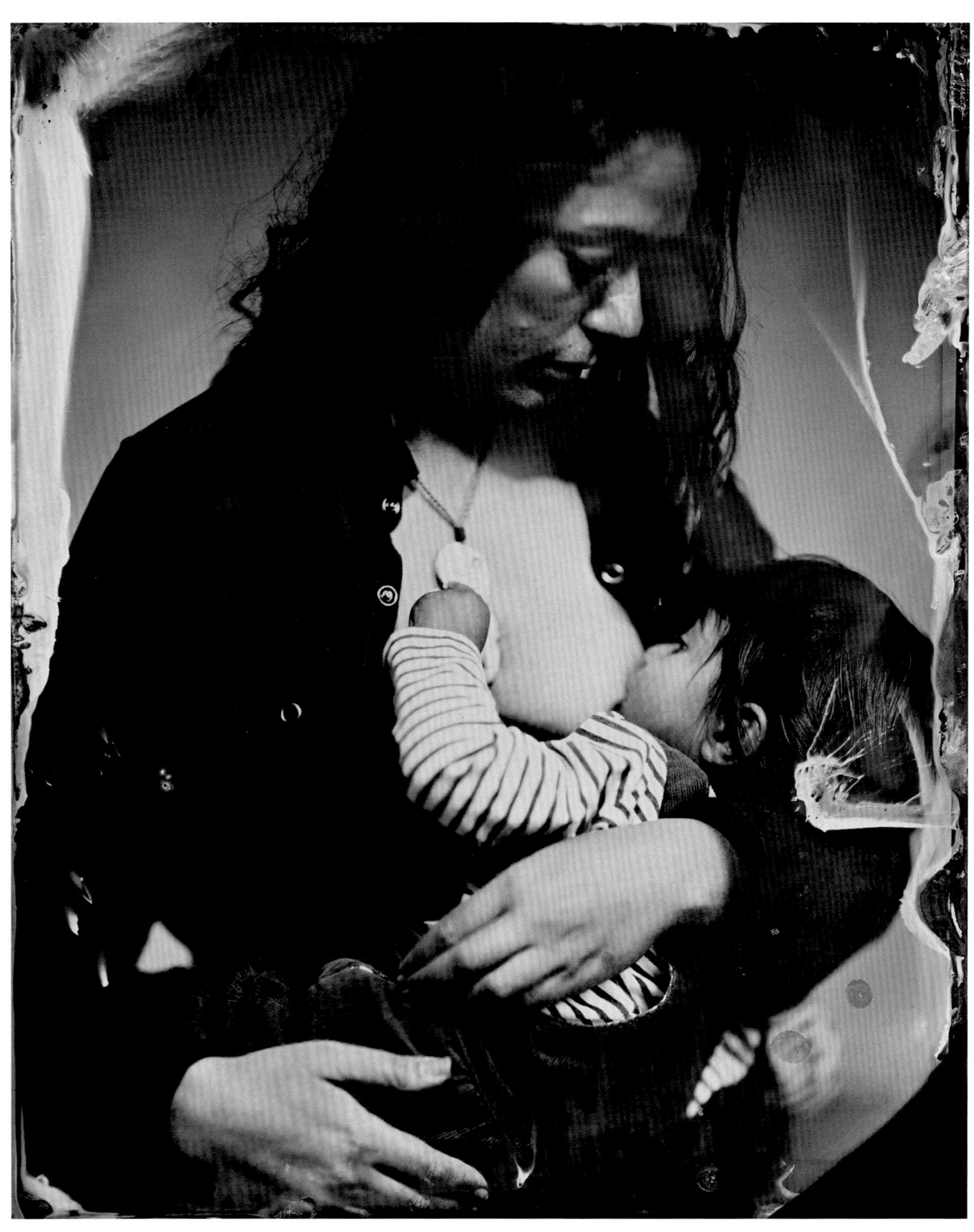

Kali Spitzer
Kaska Dena / Jewish, born 1987
Erena Arapere and Daughter Parekohatu
Arapere, 2018
Archival c-print of scanned tintype
Courtesy of the artist

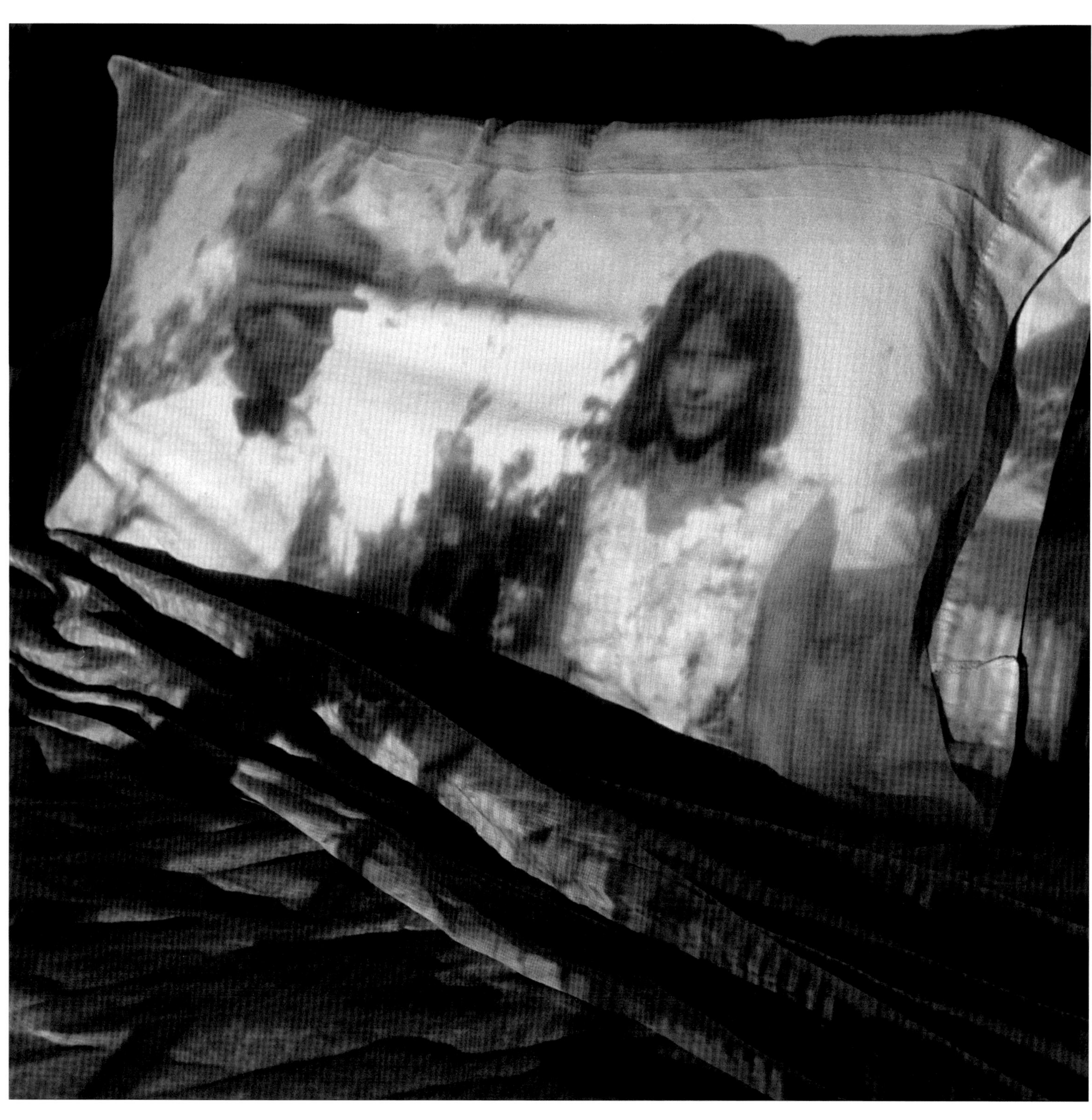

Mercedes Dorame
Gabrielino-Tongva, born 1980
My Ancestors Always Here, 2008
from Living Proof series
Gelatin silver print
Courtesy of the artist

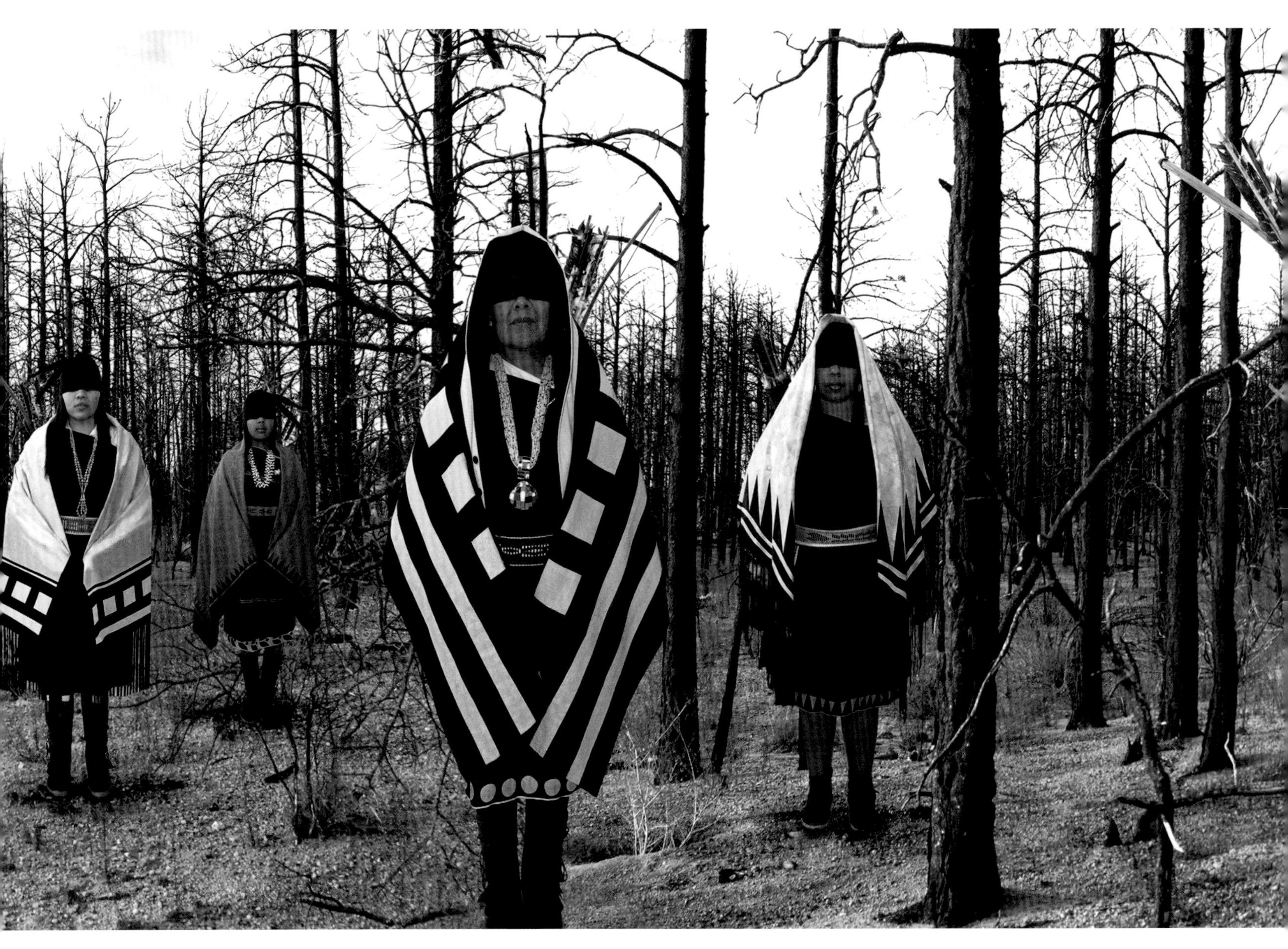

Virgil Ortiz
Cochiti Pueblo, born 1969
Tahu, and her Army of Blind Archers, 2013
Inkjet print
Courtesy of the artist

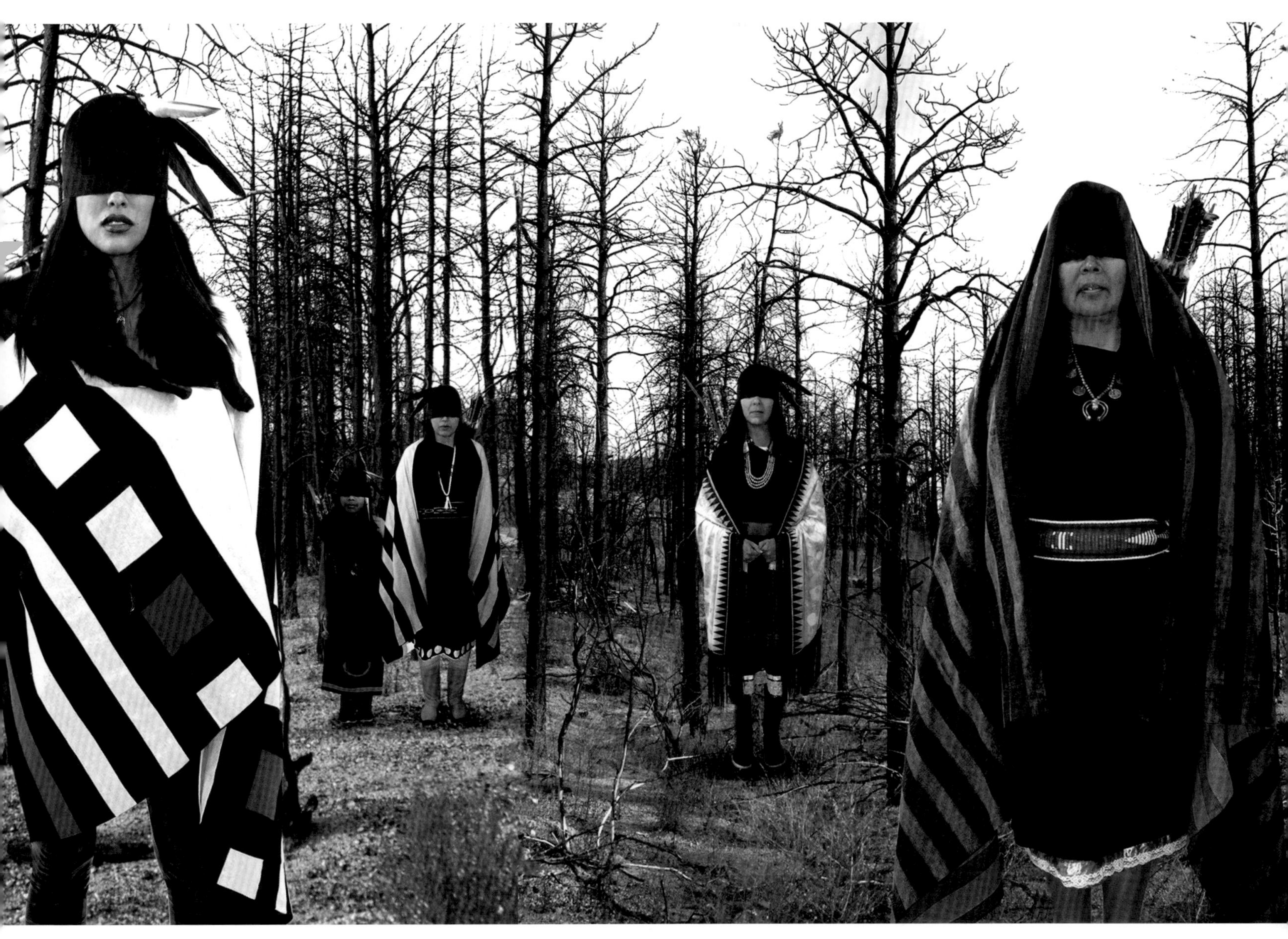

Pages 126-127:
Sarah Sense
Chitimacha / Choctaw, born 1980
Custer and the Cowgirl with Her Gun, 2018
Woven archival inkjet prints on
rice paper, pen and ink, wax, tape
Courtesy of the Collection Pamela and
Kevin Wolf, Courtesy of Bruce Silverstein
Gallery, New York

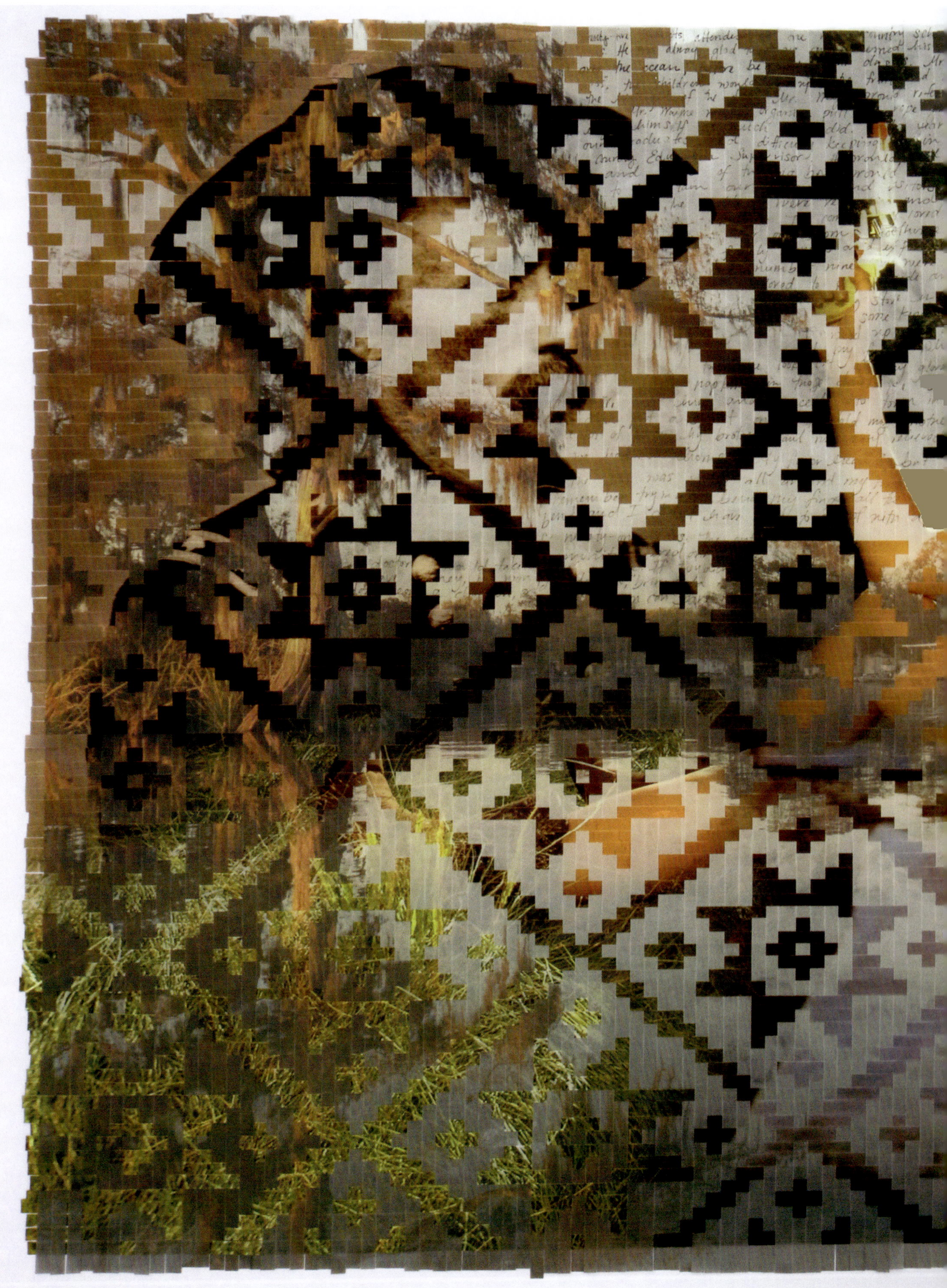

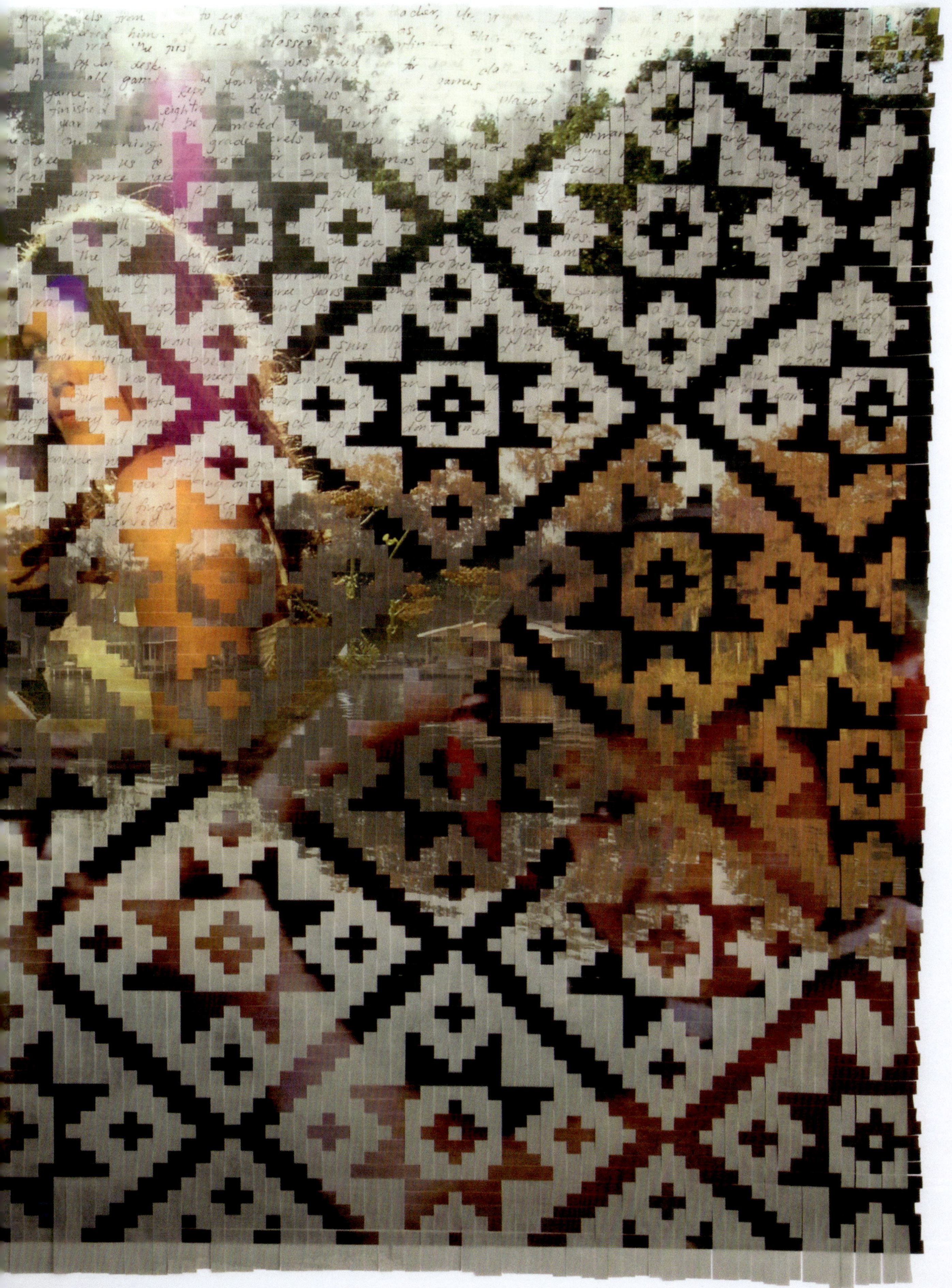

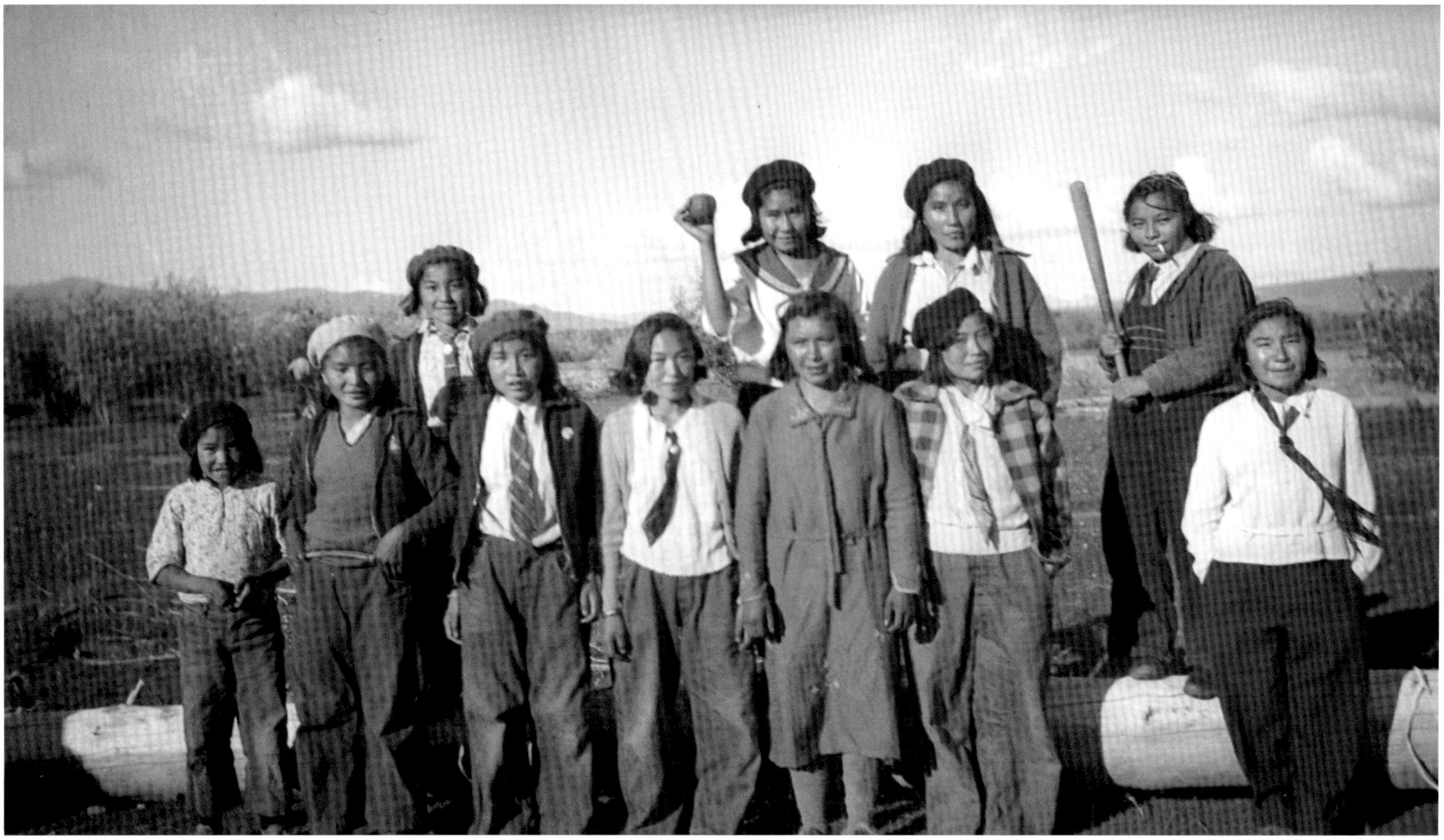

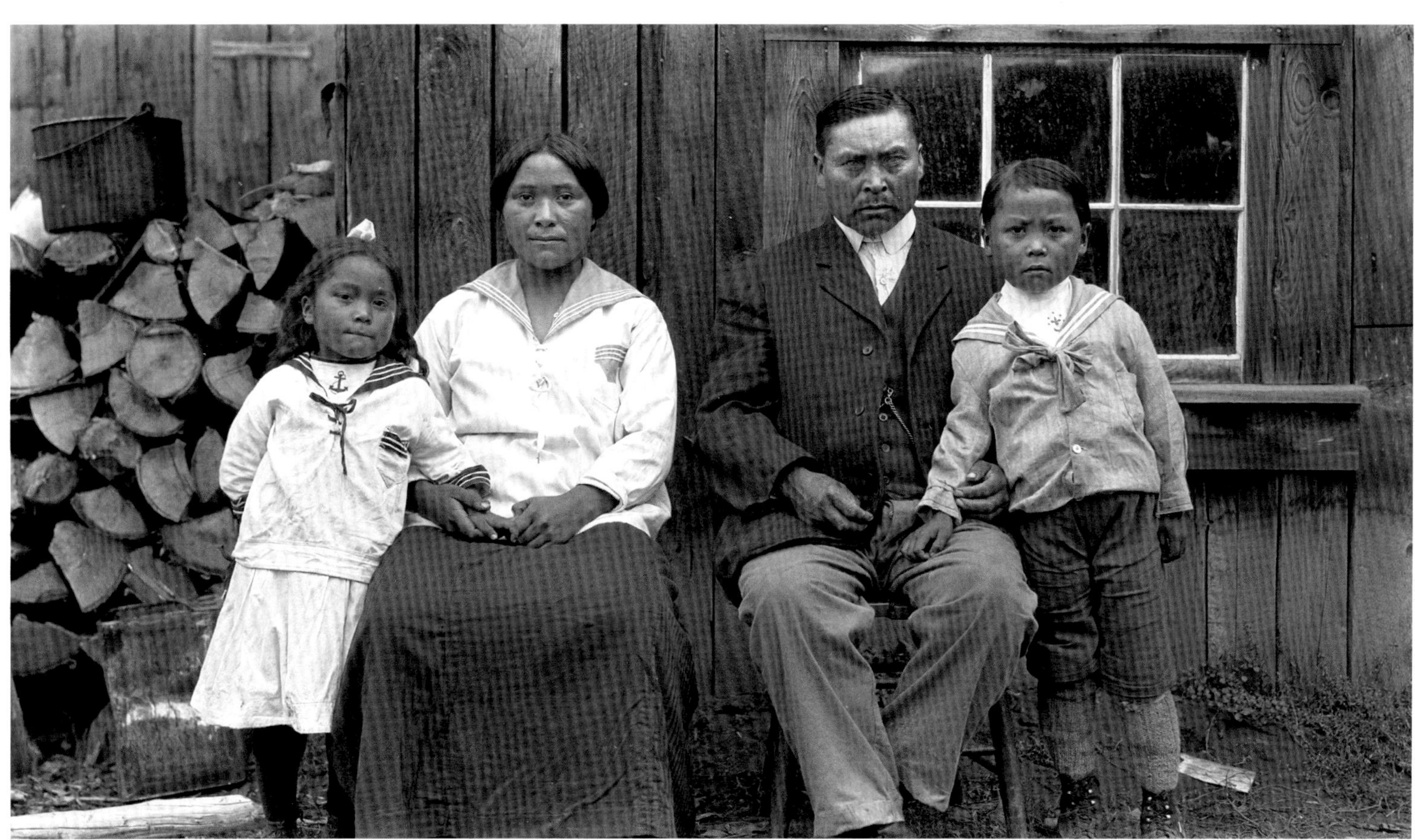

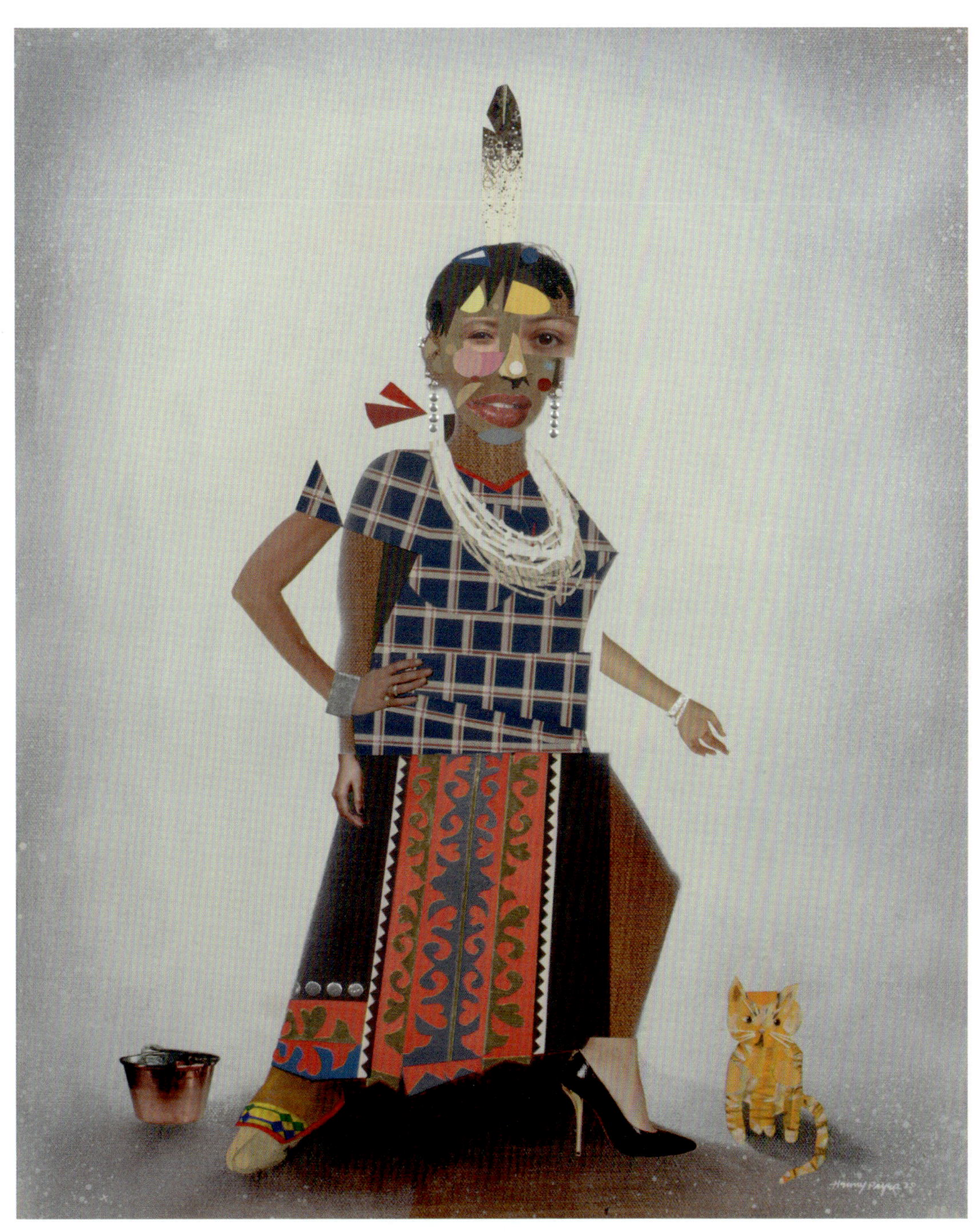

George Johnston
Tlingit, 1894-1972
Church Picnic at Mouth Nisutlin River
Around 1941, c. 1941
Courtesy of Yukon Archives, 82/428, #33

Louis Situwuka Shotridge, Stoowukháa
(Astute Man)
Tlingit, 1882-1937
A Native Family, Git-ten-mekl, 1918
Courtesy of the Penn Museum, image no. 14960

Henry Payer, Jr.
Ho-Chunk, born 1986
a[MUSE] II, 2021
Mixed media and collage on canvas
Courtesy of J.W. Wiggins Native American Art,
University of Arkansas, Little Rock
© Henry Payer, Jr.

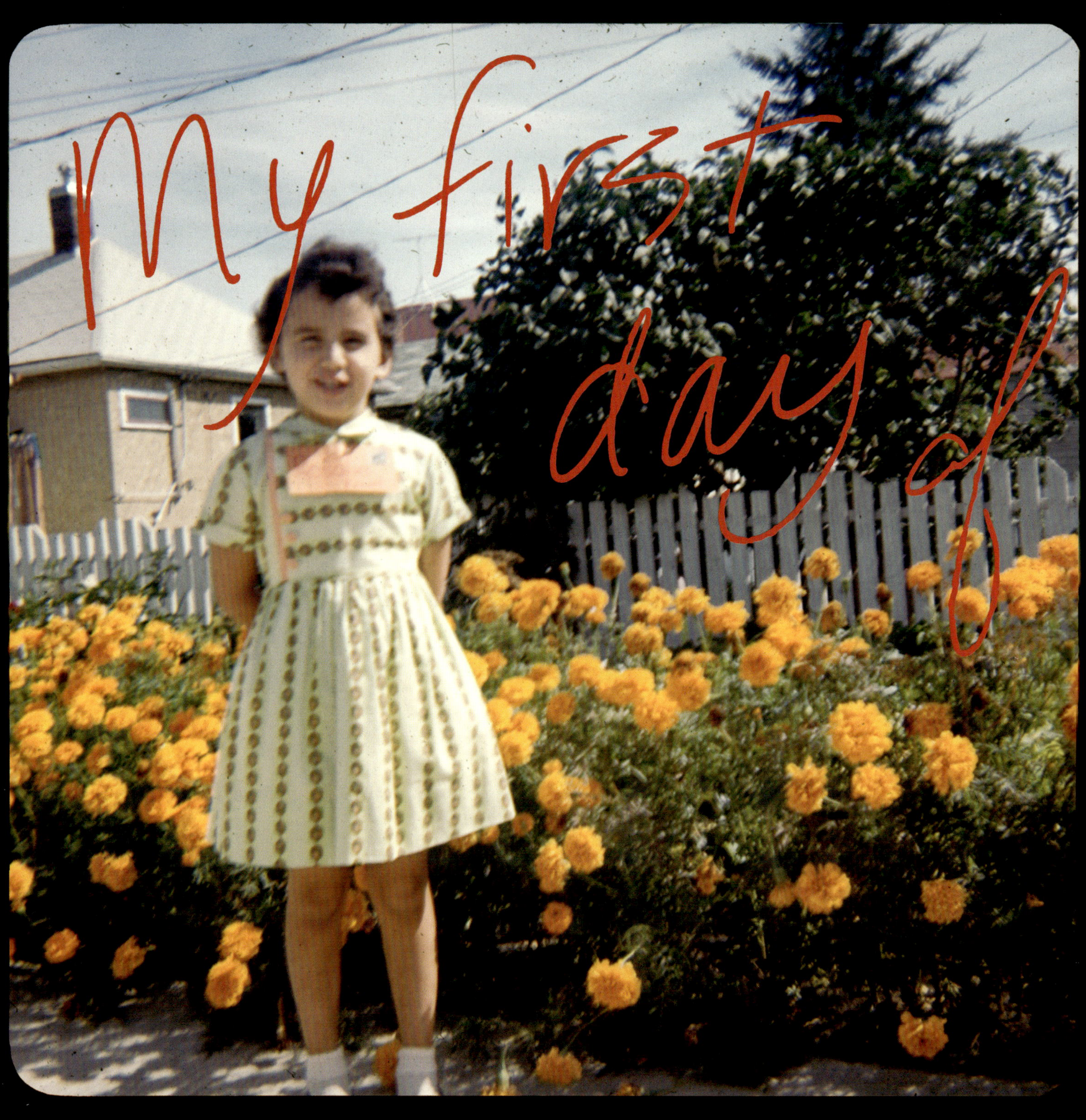

assimulation

AN ENDURING PASSION

BY ROSALIE FAVELL

MY LOVE OF PHOTOGRAPHS AND PHOTOGRAPHY STARTED EARLY. Whenever the camera appeared, I started running towards it (or maybe the person taking the picture). I also loved looking at photographs. My parents valued their world and wished to share special moments just by pointing them out. Family snapshots, photo albums, and evenings spent projecting slides set the stage for my love of looking.

I began taking "real" photos as a child on a camera my sister gave me. It was unlike today's cell phone cameras that are easily available and make picture taking so simple that even an infant can do it. The mystery of the roll of film that you loaded into the camera was equal to the thrill and surprise of opening the envelope of prints from the camera shop.

I became more intentional in my picture taking when I was a teenager. The camera gave me a way to interact with the world from a distance. I hid behind the viewfinder. I was able to safely observe the world with detachment and try to make sense of it. It was not till much later that I realized I had been looking for acceptance and seeing my place in my family and family photographs brought me home to myself. My searching for clues to my identity grew from and was informed by snapshots both my family's and my own.

The more photos I made, the more I wanted to learn about photography. I was riveted. I took a night class at the local high school and learned how to develop film and make prints and use my camera more proficiently. I also experienced agony for the images that did not turn out for any of many technical reasons.

Plate and Fig. 1
Rosalie Favell
Metis, born 1958
my first day of assimulation, 1996/2022
from from an early age series
Inkjet print
Courtesy of the artist
© Rosalie Favell

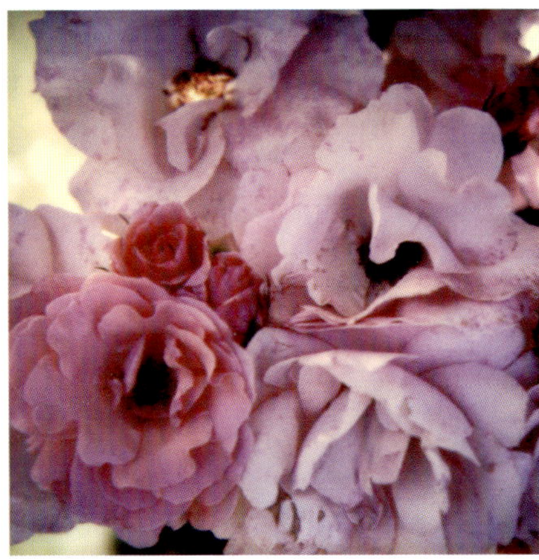 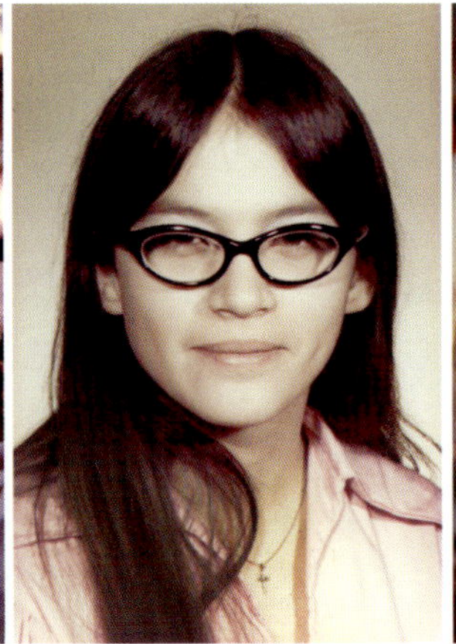 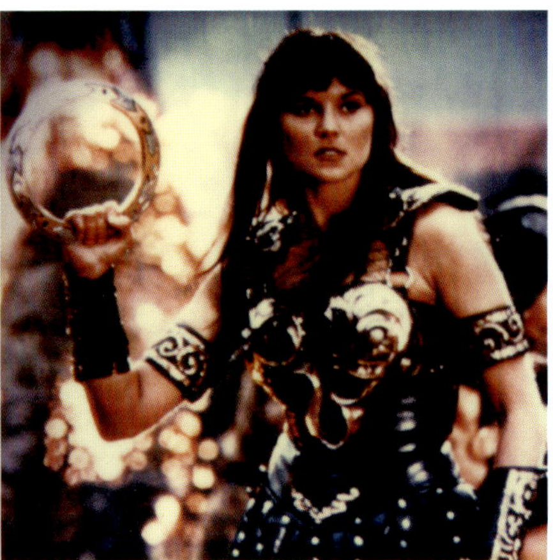

Fig. 2. *Longing and Not Belonging #4,* 1998. (Courtesy of the author).

I kept seeking out more places to learn about photography. I had no idea that my love of the medium would become my lifelong passion. Or that it would take me around the world. As a teenager I took evening classes and my appetite for learning more about photography exploded. I found my way to more formal photography studies in the '80s at Toronto Metropolitan University in Toronto and in the '90s at the University of New Mexico in Albuquerque where I was taught by incredible photographers: Betty Hahn, Dave Heath, Patrick Nagitani, Thomas Barrow, and Marta Braun to name a few.

After my family, my love of photography was deepened by my studies in the history of the medium. Because I loved photographing people, I was drawn to documentary photography and portraiture: Diane Arbus, Richard Avedon, Imogen Cunningham, Julia Margaret Cameron, Henri Cartier-Bresson, Robert Frank, Dorothea Lange, W. Eugene Smith ... and the list goes on.

After studying and working in the field of photography, I learned about a larger community of Indigenous photographers that expanded my sense of belonging and the bringing together of my worlds that up to that point had seemed separate: my firm grounding in the technical and historical aspects of the medium; my larger Indigenous community; and my personal struggle to understand my identity. My world expanded and I made lifelong friends. Although, at that time, I did not understand my Metis identity and I did not connect with any Metis photographers I found a sense of connecting family, photography, and community.

My photographic practice was deepened through my admiration for photographers such as Avedon, especially his portraits. His images are incredible for their simplicity and handling of

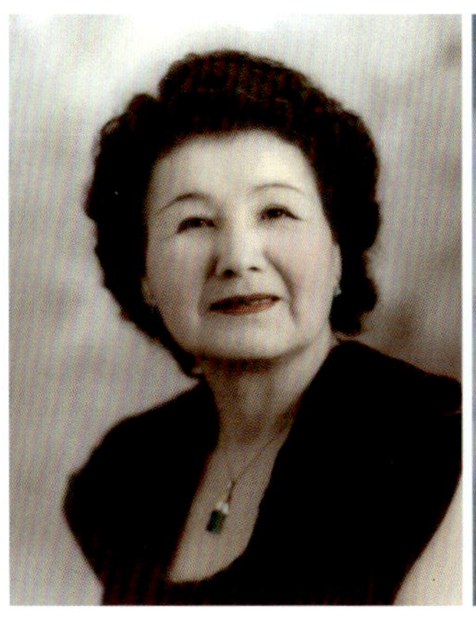
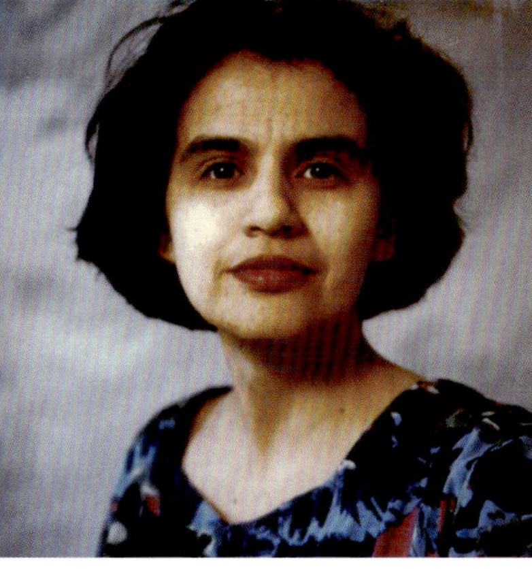
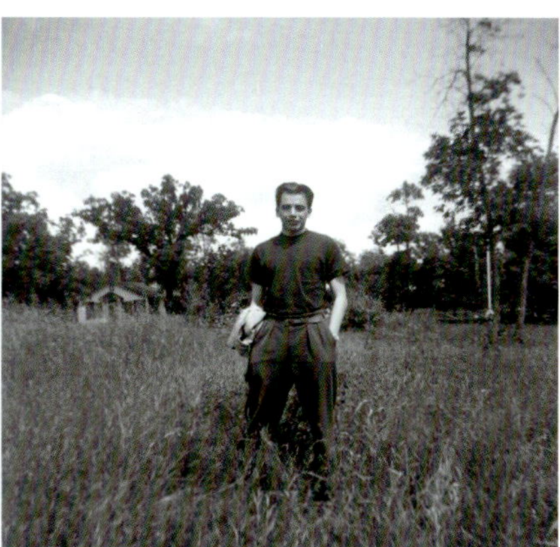

Fig. 3. *Longing and Not Belonging #34,* 1998. (Courtesy of the author).

the gaze that directs the look of the individual back to me. His style of white background with black border edge decontextualizes the subject and compels the viewer to connect with the person in the frame. This style of portraiture is particularly important in my major body of work, *Facing the Camera* (2008–2018) (see pg. 135) which was initiated by my desire to photograph my community. One portrait grew into 500 portraits of Indigenous artists, curators, writers, academics, and community advocates, and as occurs in Avedon's work, my subjects often look directly into the camera and by extension at the viewer. Through this project, and my continuing studies, travel, creating, and connecting with artists and Indigenous arts communities, my understanding of myself and the world expanded yet again.

My fascination and love of family snapshots has held my attention my entire life. I realize that I am very privileged to have negatives and prints from my parents and grandparents. This family archive feeds my spirit. I feel a responsibility to keep my family alive through my mining and re-presenting them. The history of the Métis is complex and perplexing even for many Métis individuals. Through my process of working with my family's archive I have been able to work through this history situating myself in the simple context of family.

My Nanny's photographs have been especially inspiring. What I remember of her is childhood memories mixed with the innocence of childhood. She treasured her photographs of family and friends, keeping them in albums that kept her company until her last days. I discovered them decades after she was gone. I am still passionate about looking at them. I am searching them to understand her and the complexities of the times she lived in. These albums are ev-

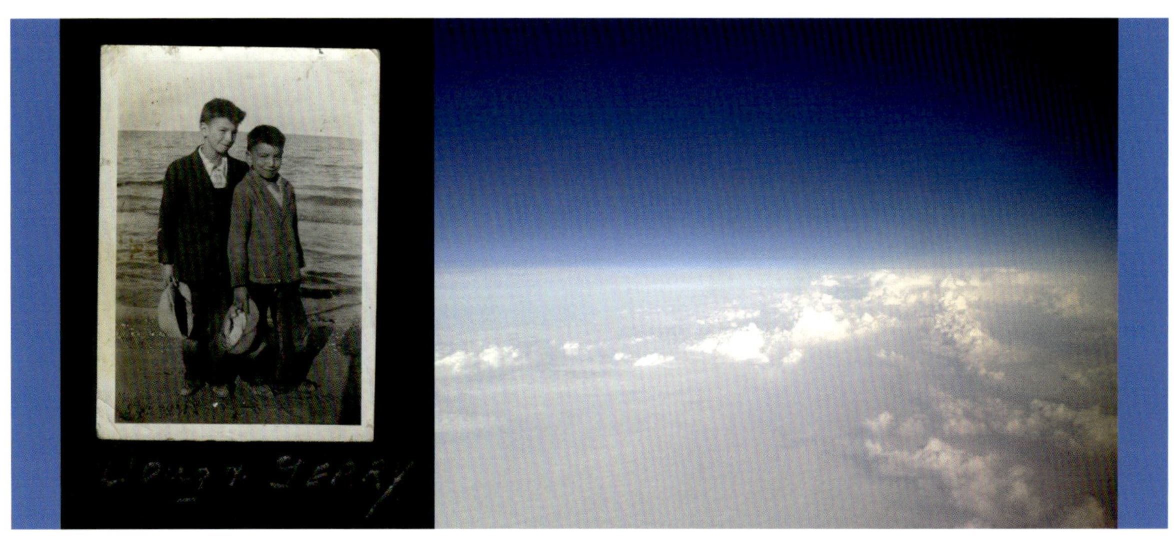

Fig. 4. *Doug & Gerry*, from the series *Closer to Heaven*, 2012. (Courtesy of the author).

erything to me. They speak to me, who I am, my family and my heritage. But more, they are part of a history of an area we all share and call home. Images from my family's albums (from my parents and both sets of grandparents) indicate the rich history of my part of the universe.

My family's history in the Red River area runs deep. My Cree grandmother met an English fur trader in the late 1700s and my family's legacy started. The Métis, as a distinct people, began when Louis Riel defended those of mixed Indigenous and European heritage in the Red River area. This proud generation of peoples changed over the years to a Defeated generation, and then a Shamed one, which was my grandparent's generation. The next generation of my father's was a Hidden one. My generation was the Lost generation. The present generation of my nieces and nephews are the Found generation. I am humbled by their growing appreciation of my journey and my efforts to illuminate our heritage and light the way for their children to come.

Throughout my career, I have created work to reveal and sustain our presence. We have been hiding in plain sight. Throughout my many projects and artworks, I have felt the coming together of my search for myself. Like Dorothy in *The Wizard of Oz* and as I depict myself in the photograph, "I Awoke to Find My Spirit Had Returned" (1999), I always return to my family and our archive.

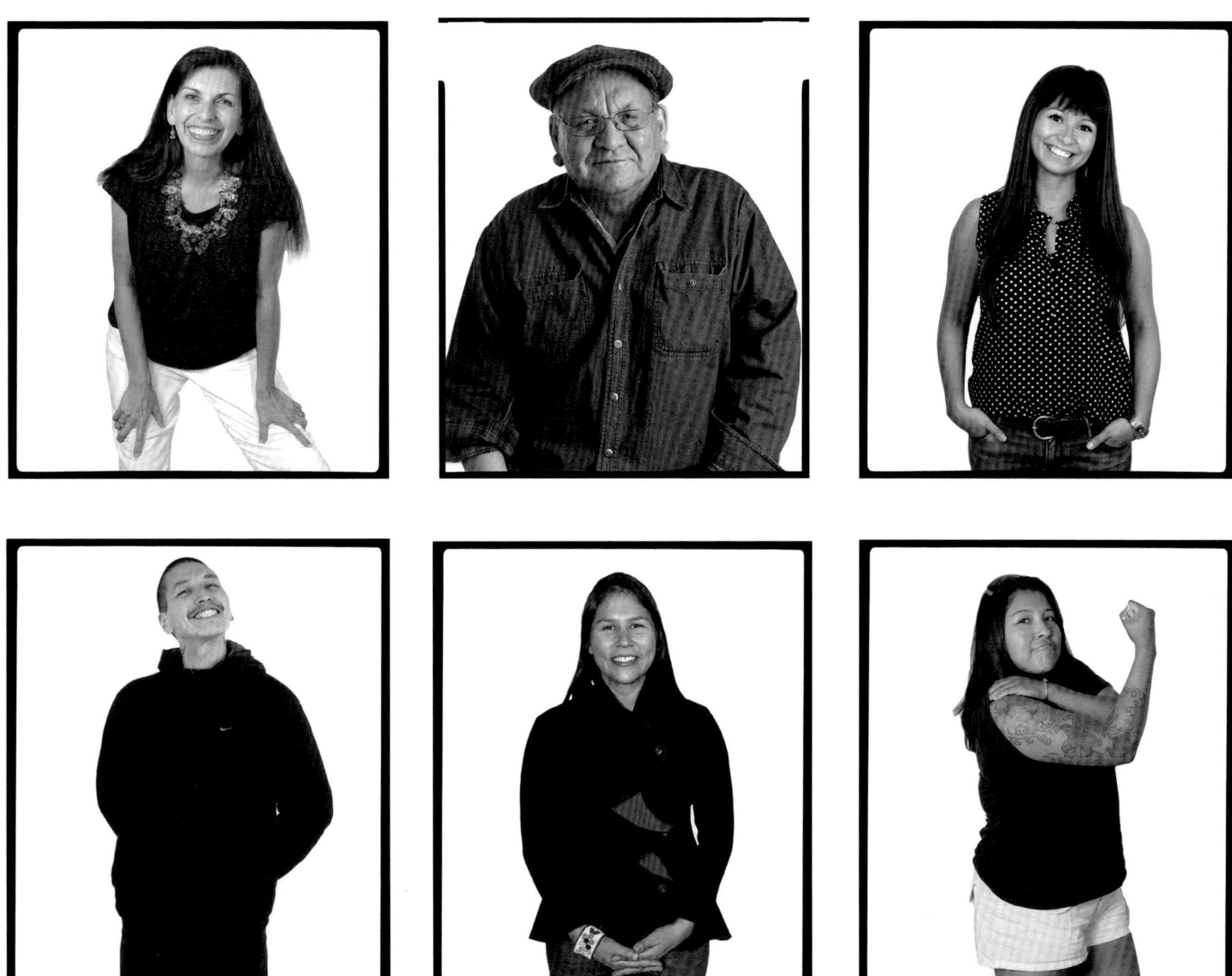

Top row, from left: **Fig. 5-7** *Shan Goshorn*, Santa Fe, NM, 2012; *Alex Janvier,* Banff, AB, 2008; *Alex Nahwegahabow*, Ottawa, ON, 2014, *Bottom row, from left:* **Fig. 8-10** *Patrick Ross*, Winnipeg, MB, 2012; *Meryl McMaster*, Winnipeg, MB, 2017; *Rondee Graham*, Santa Fe, NM, 2012, from the series *Facing the Camera*, 2008–2018. (Courtesy of the author).

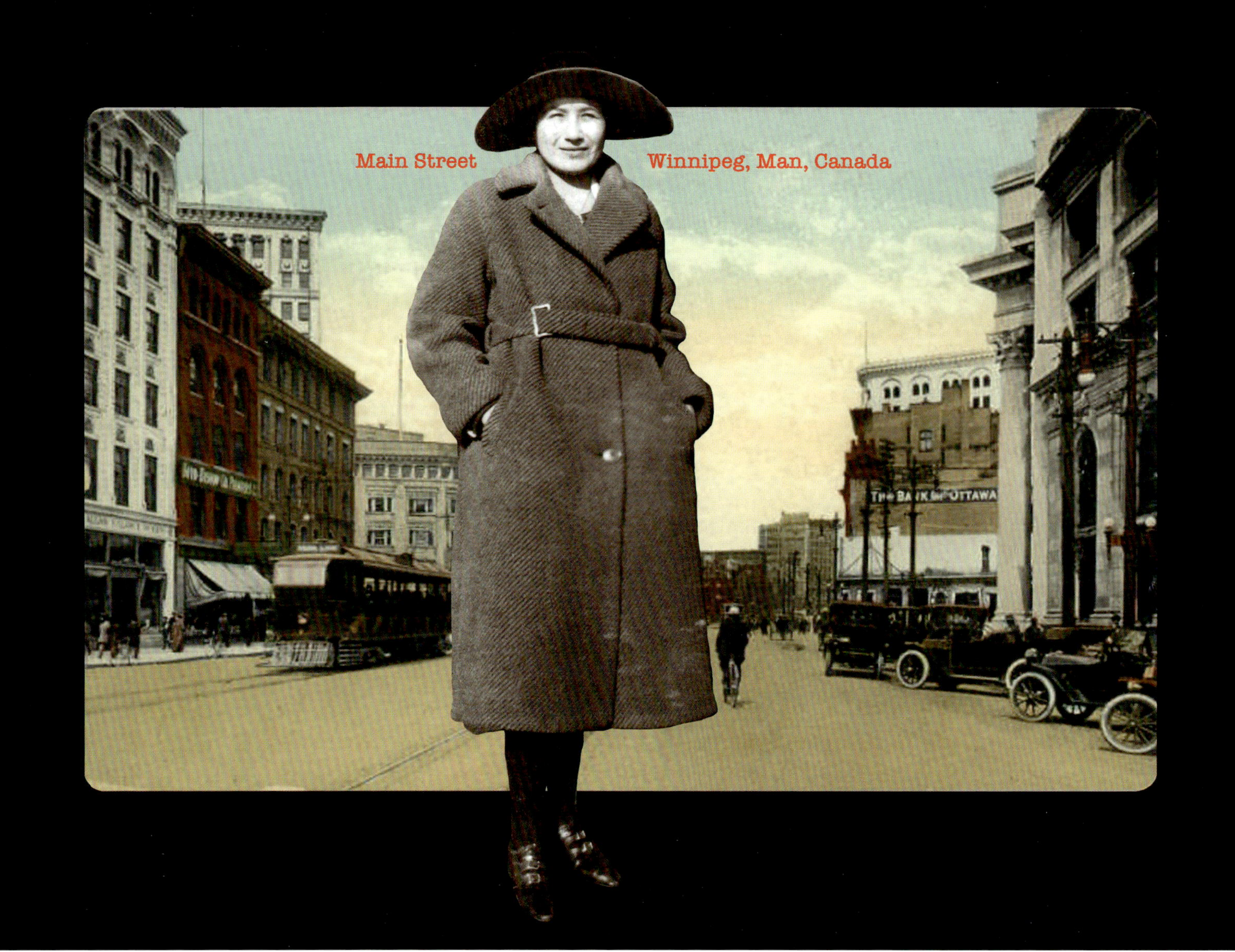

Plate and Fig. 1
Rosalie Favell
Metis, born 1958
Holding Her Ground, 2021
from Family Legacy series
Inkjet print
Minneapolis Institute of Art, Gift of funds
from Nancy and Rolf Engh 2022.42
© Rosalie Favell

ROSALIE FAVELL'S PHOTOGRAPHIC REVISITATIONS

INDIGENOUS FAMILY ARCHIVES & HISTORICAL MEMORY

BY EMILY L. VOELKER

METIS ARTIST ROSALIE FAVELL POIGNANTLY DESCRIBES "looking through the old black pages" of her family's photographic albums, invoking the turning of thick, bound sheets pasted with pictures of beloved relatives.[42] The nearly intangible way in which we now experience photographs in the digital age, even of our most intimate relations, adds nostalgia to her evocation, conjuring folios full of tenderly hand-placed and annotated images. She continues, "I keep finding images of my family that I just love. I keep going back to these images."[43] In many ways, this assertion—and the act of revisitation it describes—conveys a central aspect of the artist's practice. Born and based in Winnipeg, Manitoba, Rosalie has worked primarily with photography since the 1980s. In the early 1990s she began to explore her Indigenous identity as a Metis woman of Cree and English ancestry for the first time—having not self-identified in this way before—using the camera as the principal tool for her investigation.[44] Initially making straight photographs, the artist has since turned more heavily to centering and reexamining archival images in numerous series, many of them featuring her own family. In this approach, and across distinct bodies of work, Rosalie returns repeatedly to a corpus of ancestors, themes, and imagery to reenact the experience of seeking and negotiating herself through photographic archives and images.

Rosalie's practice operates as an act of generosity with a medium that has historically been particularly fraught for Indigenous peoples and communities. Photography emerged in widely dispersible formats in the second half of the nineteenth century along with the height of global colonial empires, coinciding with and instrumental in international imperialisms. Across North America the creation of photographs of Native peoples occurred simultaneously with government-funded projects that surveyed territories for European and Euro-American settlement, directly facilitating this process. State photographic archives of Indigenous peoples are therefore intimately tied to the colonization process, and the dispossession and surveillance of the creation of reserve (Canada) and reservation (United States) systems. Metis people lost their lands during this period and were effectively erased from federal records; thus displaced, they were forced into rootlessness or absorbed into settler property structures.[45]

As Rosalie shows us, however, Indigenous family archives complicate state archival formations and classificatory schemes, as well as top-down conceptions of the photographic medium. Her works center life and connections to demonstrate the gaps, silences, and spaces in between in "official" records, and by extension the settler historical narrative itself. The artist's deeply personal and quietly radical work creates visibility for lived complexities, populating historical memory with rich and multifaceted family stories. Employing and integrating a range of different photographic technologies and strategies, Rosalie's practice visually and materially enacts how we make meaning of photographs, in the process affectively demonstrating the medium as the vehicle through which she has consistently located herself in relation to place, family, and history.

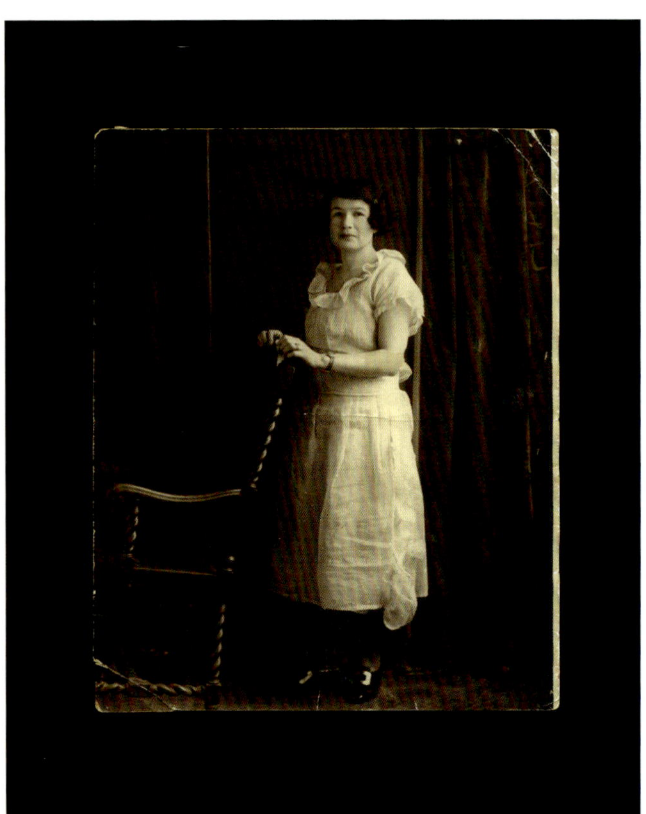

Fig. 2. Rosalie Favell (Metis, born 1958), *Anne Favell (1896–1976)* from the series *Forging a New Path, Anne Favell (1896–1976)*, Inkjet print, 2021. (Courtesy of the artist).

The family member to whom the artist most often returns in these artistic revisitations is her paternal grandmother, or Nanny, who represents a kind of familial anchor, rooting her in ancestral relations and histories throughout her photographic explorations (plate and fig. 1). In *Holding Her Ground*, dating to 2021, Anne Favell, lovingly known to the artist as Nanny, appears superimposed against the center of a receding street in Winnipeg. She stands larger than life, before the bustling figures and city view behind, which as we read in the red text on either side of her head in the background image is "Main Street," suggesting processes of urbanization and industrialization. The artist's family, as the image evokes, has deep roots in the land that became Winnipeg and the larger province of Manitoba in present-day Canada. Rosalie and her Nanny's Cree ancestors had long lived in this area before the advent of colonization, while those descendants on the English Favell side arrived through work in the fur trade. The artist's family lineage on her maternal side is English and Scottish.[46] As the artist describes herself, she is the "seventh generation of this mixed blood culture."[47] The monumentalized and centralized place of Nanny—representing the Aboriginal side of Rosalie's family—visualizes both the longstanding familial connections to this place and the ongoing Indigenous presence within it.

Rosalie's Nanny serves as a recurring, grounding point of references in her practice not only due to these connections of lineage, but also because her grandmother relished being photographed throughout her life. In the work *Forging a New Path, Anne Favell (1896–1976)*, also from 2021, the artist selects and presents a group of her Nanny's portraits made in both photographic studios and with a hand-held camera in the early decades of the twentieth century (fig.2). In the piece, these pictures are isolated from the original volumes in which they were initially held and hung together in a dazzling assemblage. Anne Favell kept numerous albums during her life full of photographs of friends, family, and herself, and Rosalie refers to the last of these as her "self-portraits."[48] In these pictures Anne Favell appears consistently fashionably dressed and centered within the image, as apparent in this example made in a studio of her standing in a light gauzy dress trimmed with ruffles around the neck and posing with her hands on the back of a chair. She looks directly at the camera, her straight face, framed by a clipped bob, illuminated from a light source to the right that captures the diaphanous fall of her skirt and the sheen of the brass buckles on her shoes. The creased edges of the object, apparent in the digital inkjet version printed by the artist, show evidence of a history of interaction, handling, and use of the treasured item. Terming these works self-portraits acknowledges the self-possession and sophistication Anne Favell brought to opportunities of self-presentation in the photographic exchange.

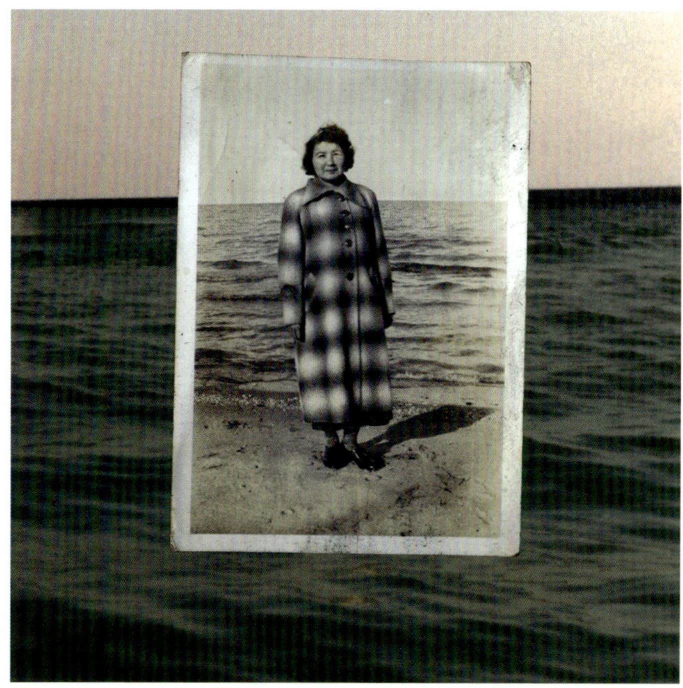

Fig. 3. Rosalie Favell (Metis, born 1958), *Annie*, from the series *Wish You Were Here*, 2011. (Courtesy of the artist).

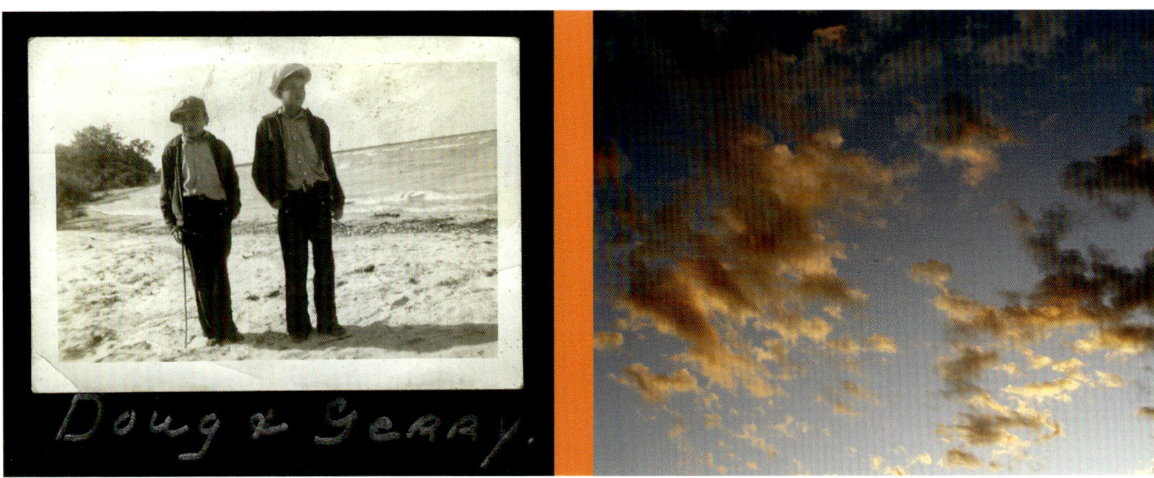

Fig. 4. Rosalie Favell (Metis, born 1958), *Doug & Gerry*, from the series *Closer to Heaven*, 2012. (Courtesy of the artist).

The self-portraits of Anne Favell made with a hand-held camera in *Forging a New Path* similarly demonstrate the radical potential of presenting the self, and Rosalie consistently looks to her Nanny as inspiration for her own photographic performances and explorations. Pictures created with a hand-held camera in the series showcase a range of facets of Anne Favell's identity: as a mother, in the midst of working, and as an independent and stylish woman. In many she appears outdoors, against a backdrop of framing foliage, and while in a number she dons the same serious expression as in the studio portrait discussed above, in others her smile communicates effusive joy. The incredible collection resonates with photography historian and theorist Tina Campt's discussion of the African diaspora and vernacular uses of the medium as a rich counterarchive—containing expressions rarely preserved in written records—for experiences and enunciations of self. She suggests that we engage with such images "as sites of articulation and aspiration; as personal and social statements that express how ordinary individuals envisioned their sense of self, their subjectivity, and their social status; and as objects that capture and preserve those articulations in the present as well as the future."[49] Indeed, Rosalie's practice brings her Nanny's articulations of identity into the future as a multivalent archive that expresses the particulars of Metis experience throughout much of the twentieth century. As the artist explains, in her revisitation of these archives, she is consistently looking for "evidence...[and] clues of who we are" as Metis people.[50] The myriad details in the images in *Forging a New Path* reveal Anne Favell as "fashionable, restless, and worldly," according to Rosalie, as well as conveying her "love of photography and imaging herself," which the artist describes as imbricated in her own.[51]

In her approach, the artist commonly uses the technique of digital photocollage to bring pictures and scenes from her family archive into conversation with other visual materials and each other in new ways, a technique utilized in the creation of *Holding Her Ground* (plate and fig. 1). Here, Rosalie has combined an early twentieth century postcard of Winnipeg with one of her Nanny's many self-portraits. The cityscape contains gradations of color articulating buildings, sky, and street typical of chromolithography, while Anne Favell stands in front of the scene's frame in the range of gray tones characteristic of gelatin silver prints (the medium of the original photographic image), overlaid and larger than the scene beyond. In placing her in the burgeoning urban space, Rosalie suggests the cosmopolitanism of her Nanny and by extension the way in which Indigenous peoples have long adapted to changing social and political circumstances. As the artist points out, mobility appears as a common theme in her family's photographs, and here Anne Favell stands with automobiles and a bike streaking into the background to the right, as well as a streetcar gliding into the foreground at left.[52] Anne Favell herself is dressed to ambulate through the city, with her fashionable overcoat, wide brimmed hat, and buckled shoes. The conveyance of independence and beauty we see repeatedly in the self-portraits of Nanny is here matched through the stitching together of these two image worlds by a rootedness in place. Nanny's placement visualizes the ongoing presence of the artist's family—and Indigenous peoples—within this modernizing place, particularly powerful in confrontation of histories of Metis displacement. Her frontality expresses continuity and futurity, and indeed Rosalie steadfastly looks to her Nanny to continue to hold her own ground, as she describes.[53]

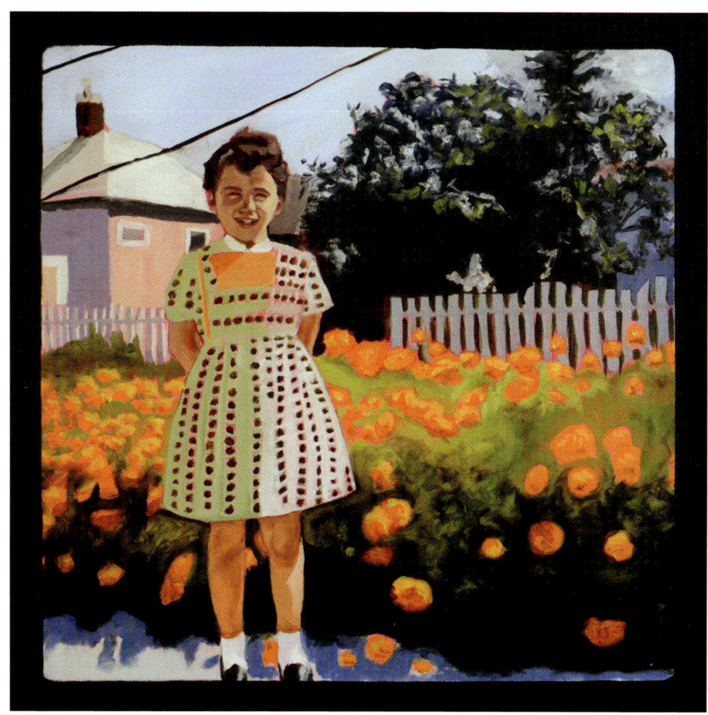

Fig. 5. Rosalie Favell (Metis, born 1958), *First Day*, from the series *from an early age revisited*, 2014, oil on canvas. (Courtesy of the artist).

The artist's series, *Wish You Were Here* (2011) similarly revisits and integrates photographs of her Nanny, collapsing linear settler constructs of time to instead explore reverberations rooted in ancestry and place. Again revisiting her Nanny's albums, Rosalie selects pictures from the volumes of her grandmother's travels (fig. 3, see pg. 139). In pieces such as "Annie," we see one of these snapshots isolated from the original compilation and superimposed against a contemporary photograph, taken by the artist, of the same place. Here, Anne Favell appears at the edge of the shore of Lake Winnipeg, her feet crunched into the sand with the water lapping to the edge in gentle waves behind her. She wears a plaid overcoat, and the wind tousles her hair. This historical picture appears slightly yellowed and faded, especially along the right edge of the image, and the viewer notes the marks of time and use. Gentle creases are evident in the upper left and signs of wear characterize the object's edges. These visible and tactile dimensions of the print conjure the artist's material engagement with the photograph. The work's placement at a slight tilt against the backdrop of the artist's own later picture of the lakeshore—a place she frequently visited her grandmother while growing up—imaginatively reenacts the wistful handling, sorting through, and emotive responses to such images. Indeed, the title of the series doubles to evoke Rosalie's feelings for her grandmother, as well as the operation of travel images sent as, or visually recalling, postcards. The work, with Rosalie's later framing photograph depicting the same expanse of water, but in color as the background, connects the two makers across time but rooted in a single, charged place. The undulating, buoyant waves on the surface of the blue gray water and the stretch of pinkish sky above the horizon express an expansiveness—of affective ties and intergenerational echoes—contained within this landscape. The piece intimates the relationship of the artist's photographic revisitations to both personal and historical memory; in her relationship to this place: she carries her Nanny and by extension her Metis past with her. These processes of archival mining and activation act as a sort of excavation of these pasts that are woven into the present.

Rosalie's series *Closer to Heaven* (2012) (see pg. 140) also centers family pictures and suggests the way that the tactile dimensions of these objects, their handling and use, open to their revelatory meanings. The series features photographs of the artist's father Gerry and his brother Doug, who as she realized in returning to her mother's albums, were consistently imaged together throughout their lives (fig. 4). Always appearing as a pair in pictures, the two of them passed away within a week of each other, indicating their enduring interconnection. Following her father's passing, Rosalie describes feeling that "the ground beneath my feet disappeared" and during a flight soon afterward turned her camera to the fleeting spread and play of sky outside the window.[54] These images, one of which appears on the right, she ultimately paired with Gerry and Doug's childhood photographs, as seen on the left. The work suggests not only a restless, ungrounded period of searching after the loss of a parent, but also the way our most intimate, familial connections link us to the expansive and all encompassing. The artist shares personal and highly specific objects, not just in image content but also physicality. In this work, handwritten text appears on the black of the original album page beneath the picture of Doug and Gerry. The labeling in graphite under their photographs, such as this one, always reflects the order in which they were born, regardless of their arrangement in the image. Echoing the earlier piece "Annie," they stand on the sandy shore of Lake Winnipeg. The artist indicates, "as an Indigenous artist, I am inviting the viewer into my world where Indigenous peoples claim the right to exhibit their own culture and history."[55] Indeed, the artist brings us into her family archives, and her search through them for her Metis roots. As she asserts regarding the power of this generosity, "imaging my family is making Metis experience visible." Rosalie continues in acknowledgment of the highly specific and personal nature of her work, "but this is the experience of *my* family, every Metis family is different."[56]

Throughout her practice Rosalie has turned to her family's photographic archives, especially those featuring her Nanny, as a model for her own self-imaging strategies, which interrogate identity and at times suppressed, unspoken histories. In the series *from an early age* (1994), including works such as *my first day of assimulation* (plate and fig. 1, see pg. 130), we see the artist turning her archival excavation to representations of herself in childhood. The body of work reexamines color slides from the 1960s, a particularly popular format during this era for recording and viewing family pictures, activated when illuminated and rhythmically perused through a projector. Here, Rosalie revisits an image of her first day of kindergarten. She stands to the left side of the photograph as a small child, her arms crossed behind her back, and the skirt of her starched, white patterned dress floating down above her knees. The black background framing the rounded edges of the image content gives away the slide format but also heightens the specificity of the glowing, Kodachrome color that imparts an almost hallucinatory quality to the picture. The sunlit marigolds hover as a field of bursting blossoms behind the lower half of the figure's small body, while the white picket fence cuts across the back of the image just behind her waist. The artist reveals more complex, sinister undertones to the photograph through her overlay of scrawling handwritten red text that reads, "my first day of assimulation." The words raise the specter of the history of Indigenous cultural genocide through educational systems in Canada in the form of Residential Schools that, beginning in the 1880s, removed Aboriginal children from their communities and forbid all forms of embodied cultural expression.[57] Rosalie's work probes the suppression of these traumatic yet insidious histories in settler social systems and identity performances through the tensions in the image, with the swooping red lettering caving in on the small, primly dressed body from above and to the left. The artist's spelling of "assimulation" also works to underscore the simulated settler likenesses, or mimicry, that colonial acculturation policies aimed to forcefully imprint on Indigenous bodies.[58]

At the time of the series *from an early age* in the early 1990s, the artist had begun to explore her Indigenous identity in new ways, revisiting childhood photographs in the process and mining silenced and sublimated aspects of the past. She acknowledges becoming "increasingly aware of the colour of my skin" and recalling memories of trying to "scrub her tan off," as well as her mother's explanation that her and her father had "Indian blood" but not speaking much further about it.[59] Family photographic archives became a rich repository to search for aspects of this personal lineage that remained largely unspoken. Having done extensive genealogical research, Rosalie traces her mixed ancestry on her paternal side to the marriage of Englishman John Favel, who worked for the Hudson Bay Company, to a Cree woman named Titameg in 1773. Although written records document John Favel's place in the company, Titameg and their children are listed merely along with him, and it is this intergenerational suppression of Indigenous presences that the artist confronts throughout her work.[60] Rosalie explores, and lays bare, this denial through her revisitation, and textual annotation, of her mother's slides from the 1960s, in the process illuminating how photographs themselves are being used to imagine mainstream cultural belonging in mid-twentieth century Winnipeg.[61] In returning to such archives, the artist continues to use the photographic medium to negotiate issues of identity and belonging in new and evolving ways.

Rosalie's recursive practices with both family archives and previous bodies of work foster an ongoing process of becoming in the excavation of identity. In the series *from an early age revisited* (2016), the artist reconsiders another time the works included in the earlier, *from an early age*, this time translating the original photographs into oil paint and removing her prior textual inscriptions (fig. 6). Here again, we see the image of Rosalie on her first day of kindergarten, this time transferred in scale and media. The artist has kept the same black border in the slide, but the orange of the marigolds now radiates even more brilliantly, the warm tones carried to the outline of the fence, the dots on the figure's dress, the shades of her skin, and the illumination on the pink house behind. Working in the medium of paint enables Rosalie to go back to straight photographs but also visually and materially embodies the processing of these images. This remaking enacts a working through that reproduces the experience of sorting, holding, and making meaning with such pictures. Rosalie shows this process to be never settled and draws us into the experience of historical and personal meaning around these objects themselves. In this later body of work reconsidering her first day of kindergarten, the artist's perspective seems to have softened and shifted, with the figure enlarged and the annotations removed, as she locates herself through the photograph anew.

Rosalie Favell's revisitation of family photographic archives doubles as interrogation of the intergenerational, embodied histories she carries within herself. As Indigenous identity for Metis peoples is familial rather than communal, these collections serve as a rich repository to explore the complexities of this experience and make them visible. Rosalie's practice of return embraces both the silences and evidence in these photographic collections, which cross eras and vernacular formats. Moreover, her recursive engagements with family pictures serve as an act of generosity and materially draw their viewers into an experience of personal and historical meaning-making that is never complete or fixed. Throughout her practice Rosalie's Nanny and her uses of photography function as a guide for the artist's own probing self-imagining strategies; offering a point of connection between past, present, and the evolving future.

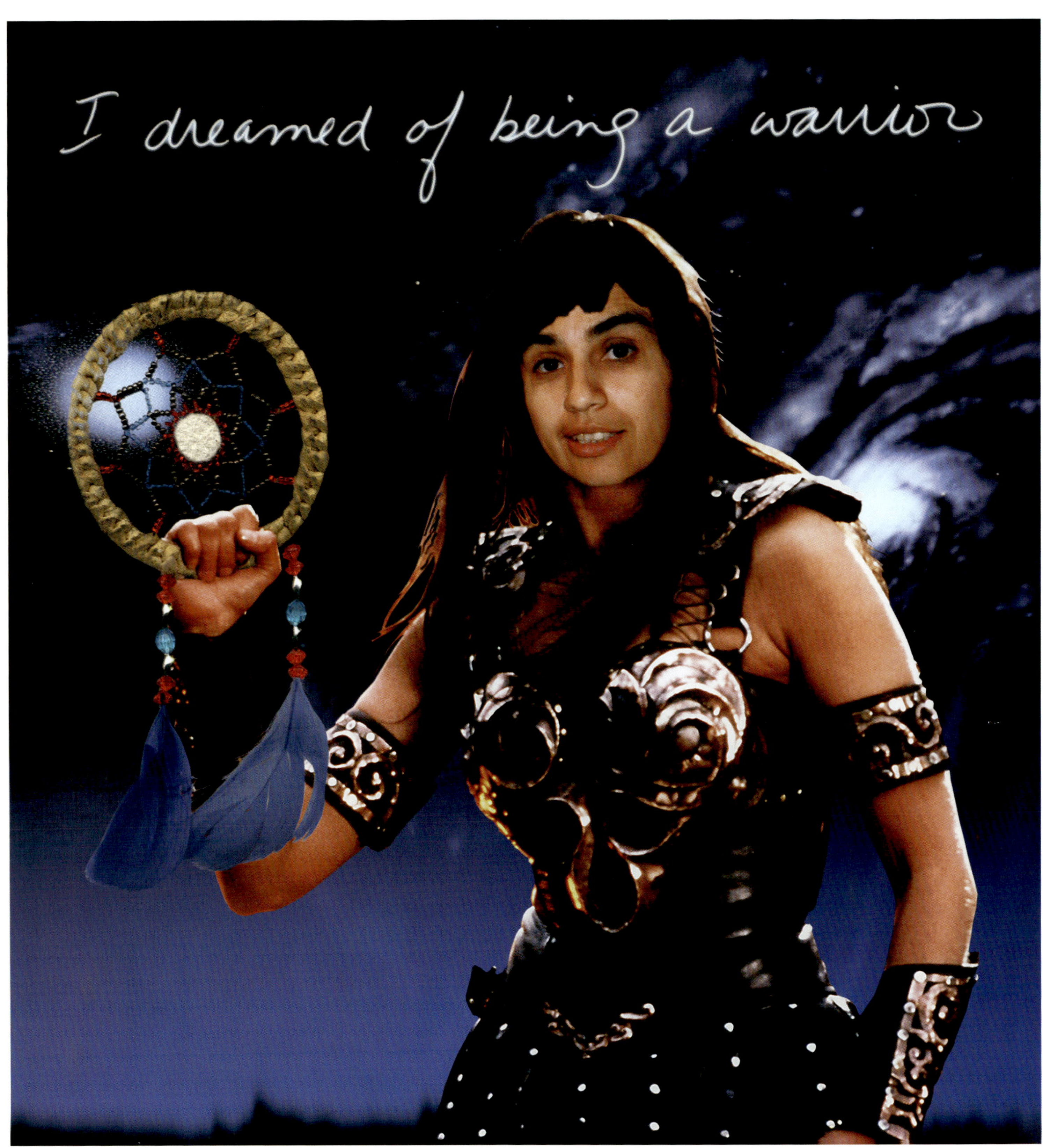

Rosalie Favell
Metis, born 1958
I Dreamed of Being a Warrior, 1999
from Plain(s) Warrior Artist series
Inkjet print
Courtesy of the artist

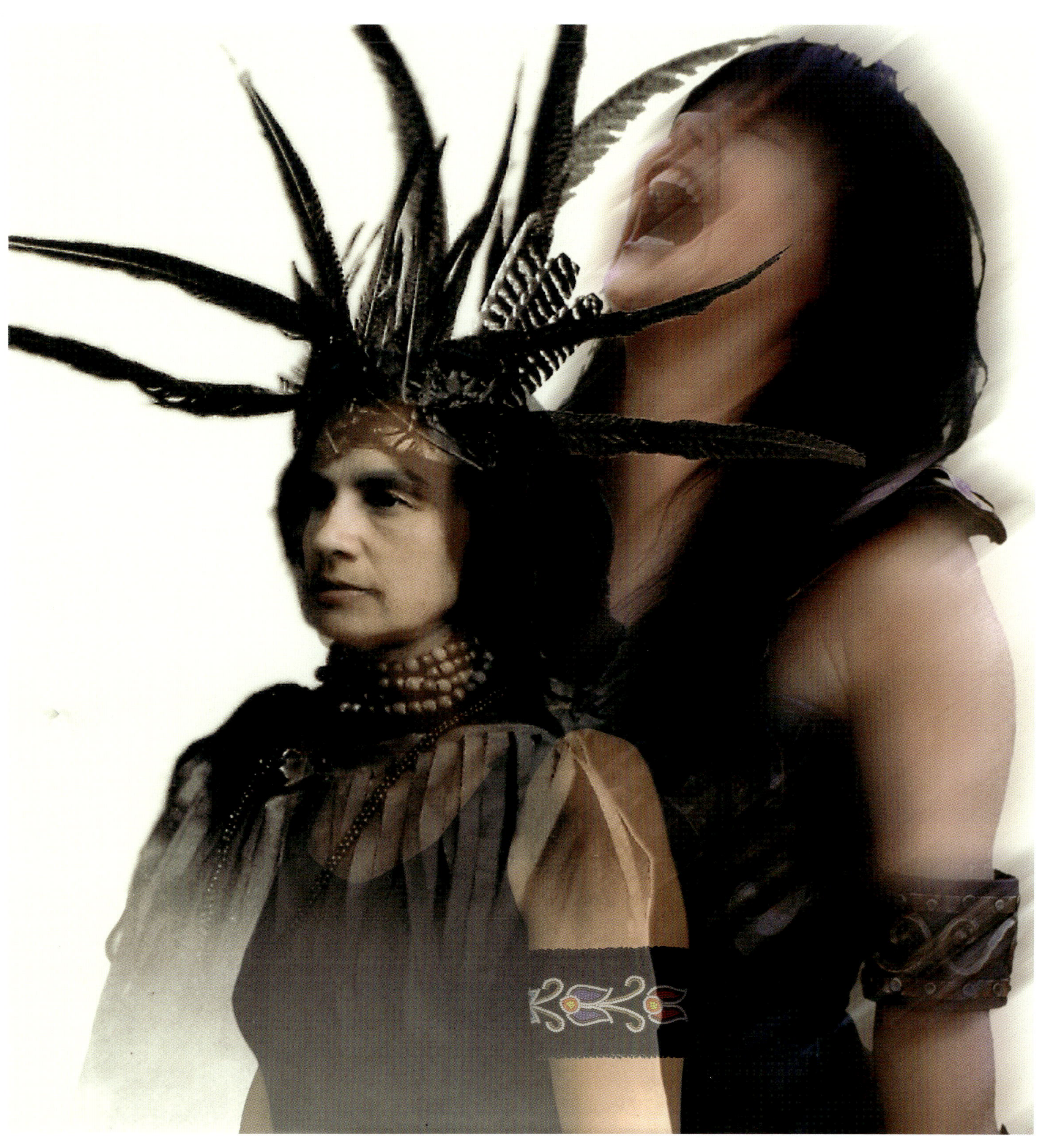

Rosalie Favell
Metis, born 1958
Transformation, 1999
from Plain(s) Warrior Artist series
Inkjet print
Courtesy of the artist

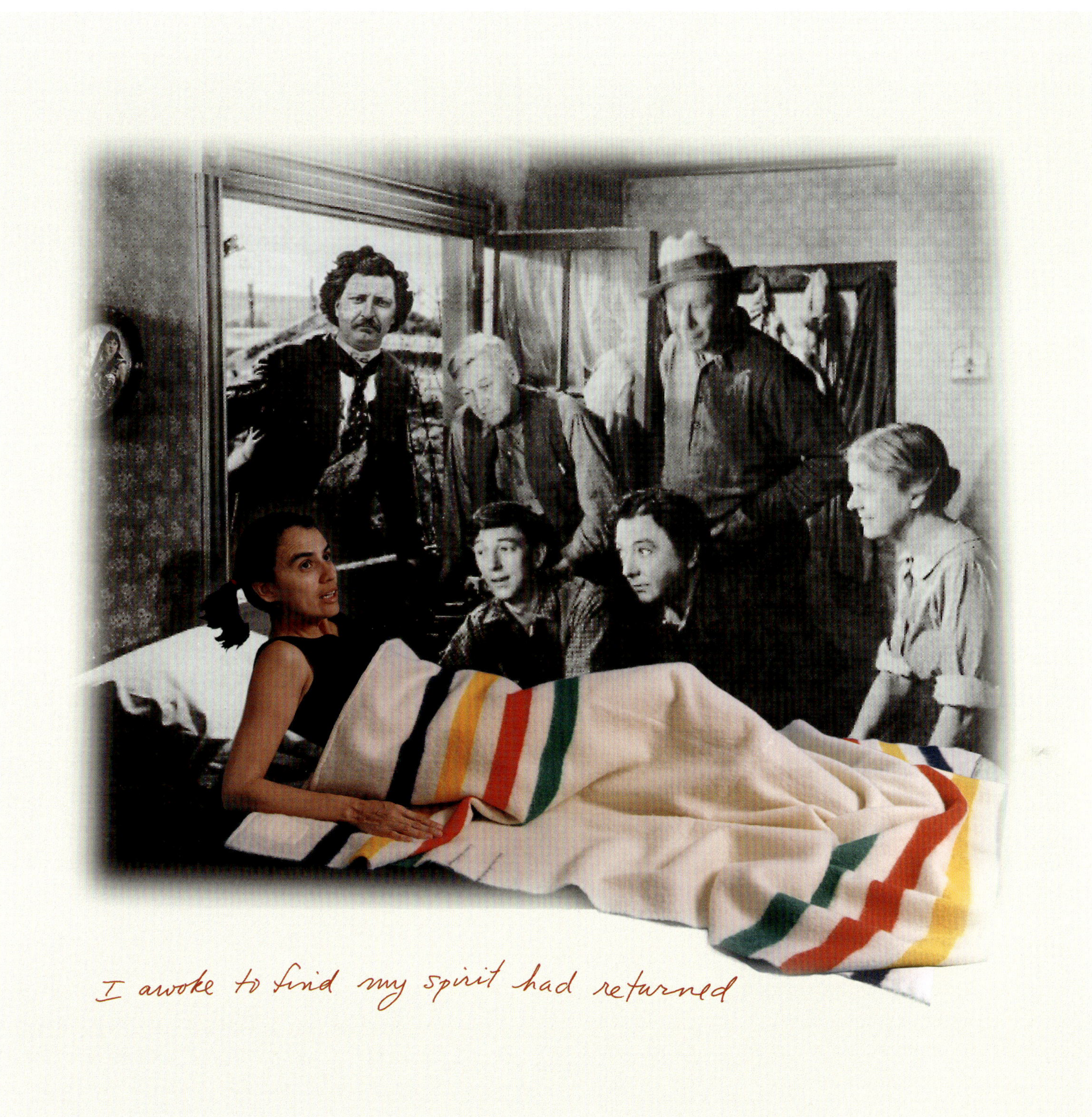

Rosalie Favell
Metis, born 1958
I Awoke to Find My Spirit Had Returned, 1999
from Plain(s) Warrior Artist series
Inkjet print
Courtesy of the artist

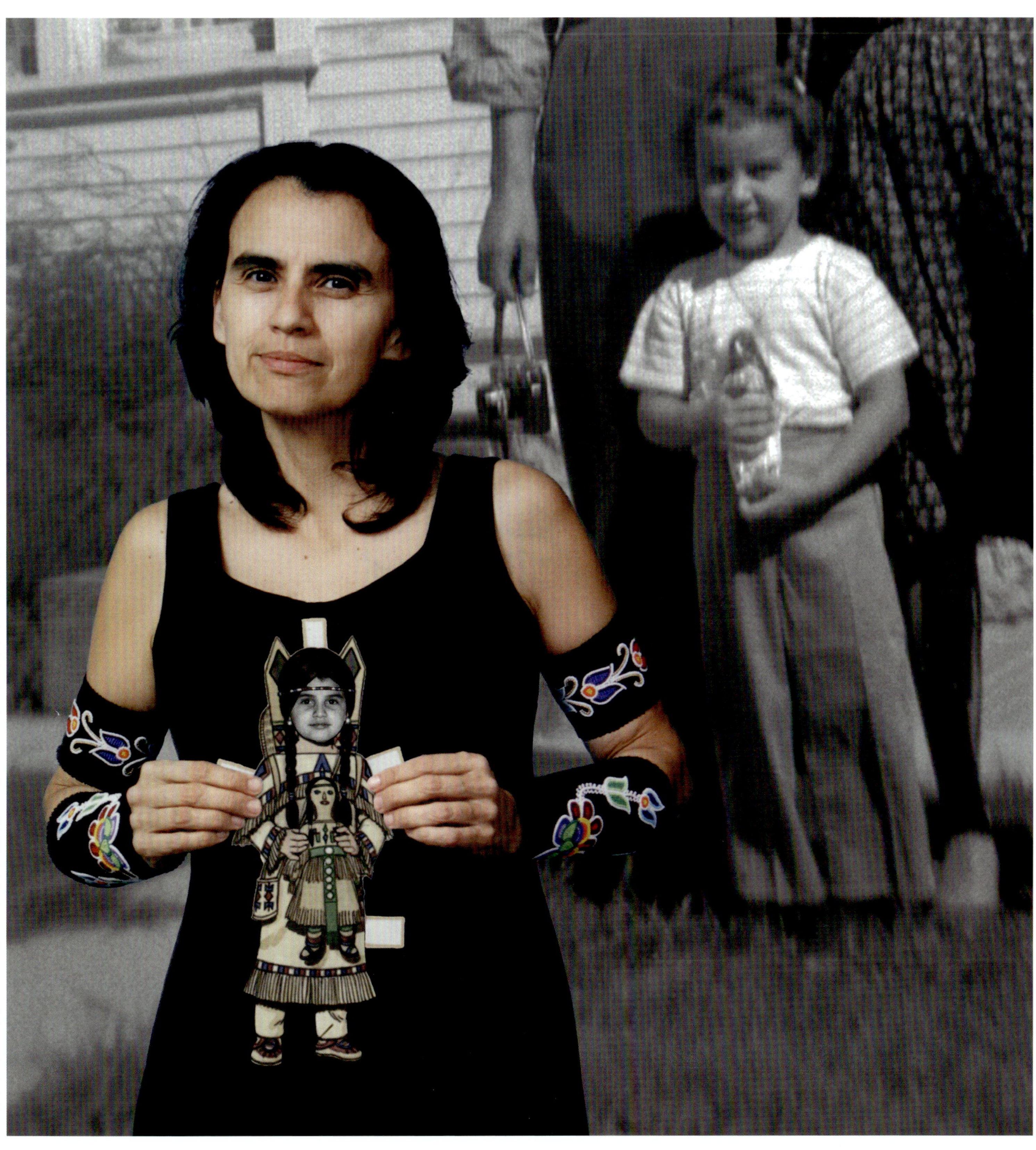

Rosalie Favell
Metis, born 1958
Paper Dolls, 1999
from Plain(s) Warrior Artist series
Inkjet print
Courtesy of the artist
© Rosalie Favell

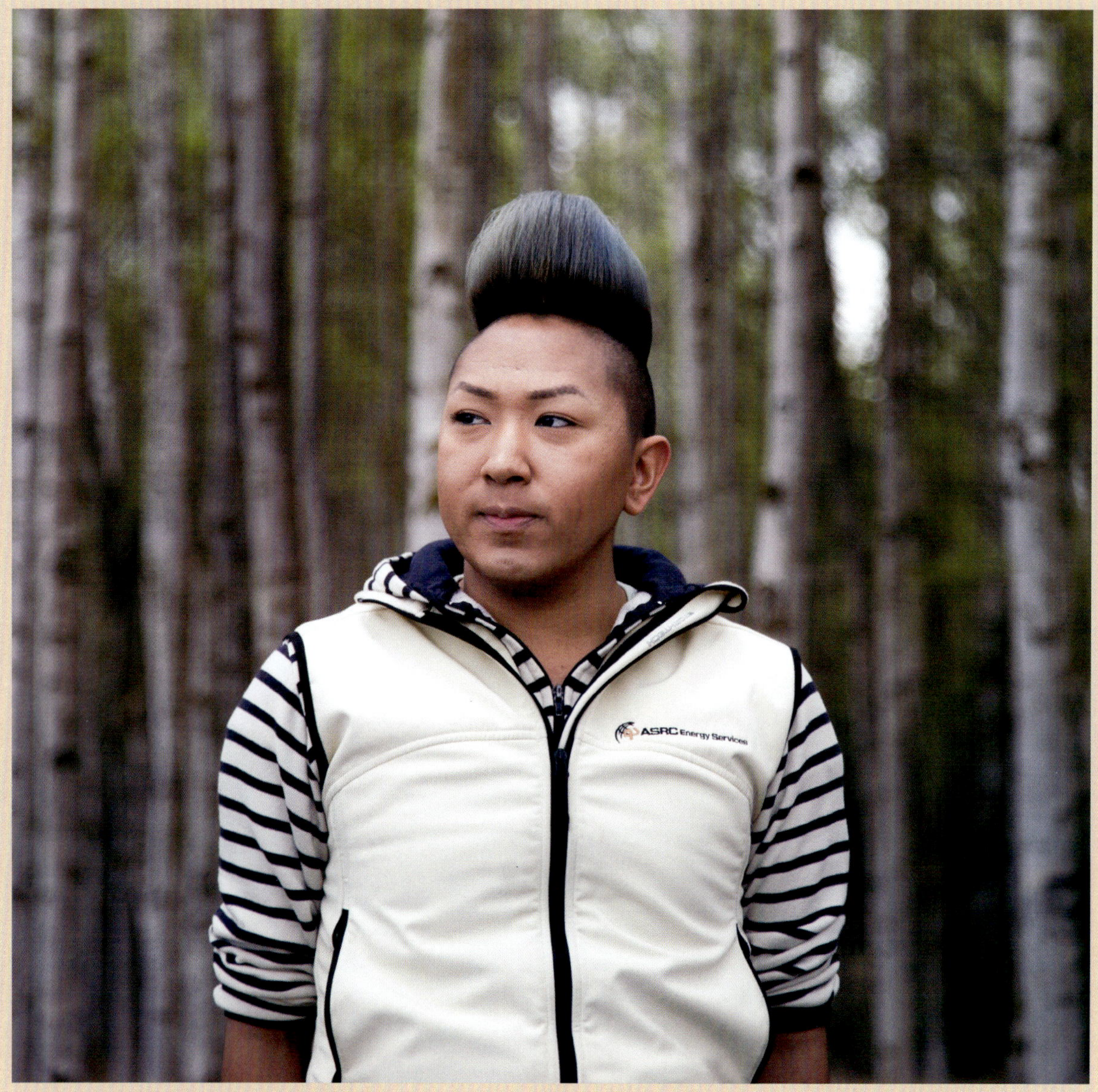

My name is Cam. I live in Anchorage, Alaska, and my family is from Wainwright, Alaska. I am Inupiaq, Aleut, and Athabaskan.

Cam is passionate about projects like Continuous, which strengthen the LGBTQ2 community that currently lacks quality conversations about being queer:

"By increasing our visibility, I hope it will inspire other LGBTQ2 Alaska Native persons to become more comfortable with their own identity. I think if we learn the words our peoples have used for persons like us, we can bring together Alaska Natives and LGBTQ2 identities to create a strong and thriving community."

"It's important to be visible to various communities, especially for the youth. I mention the youth because I, myself, didn't know any adult LGBTQ2 persons and the ones I did see were on Logo TV. That took a toll on my self-confidence because I didn't fit within that limited perspective of what a gay male is supposed to look or sound like."

For Cam being part of Continuous, "allows me to look inwardly to examine where these two identities come together and from that I draw personal strength. I believe the more you know about yourself, the stronger you can be as a person. I don't just say, 'I am queer' or 'I am Alaska Native,' but proudly state, 'I am a queer Alaska Native' and I feel empowered by that. I've struggled with being queer and being Alaska Native but I'm realizing that I'm neither but both together and I am proud to be a part of these beautiful communities."

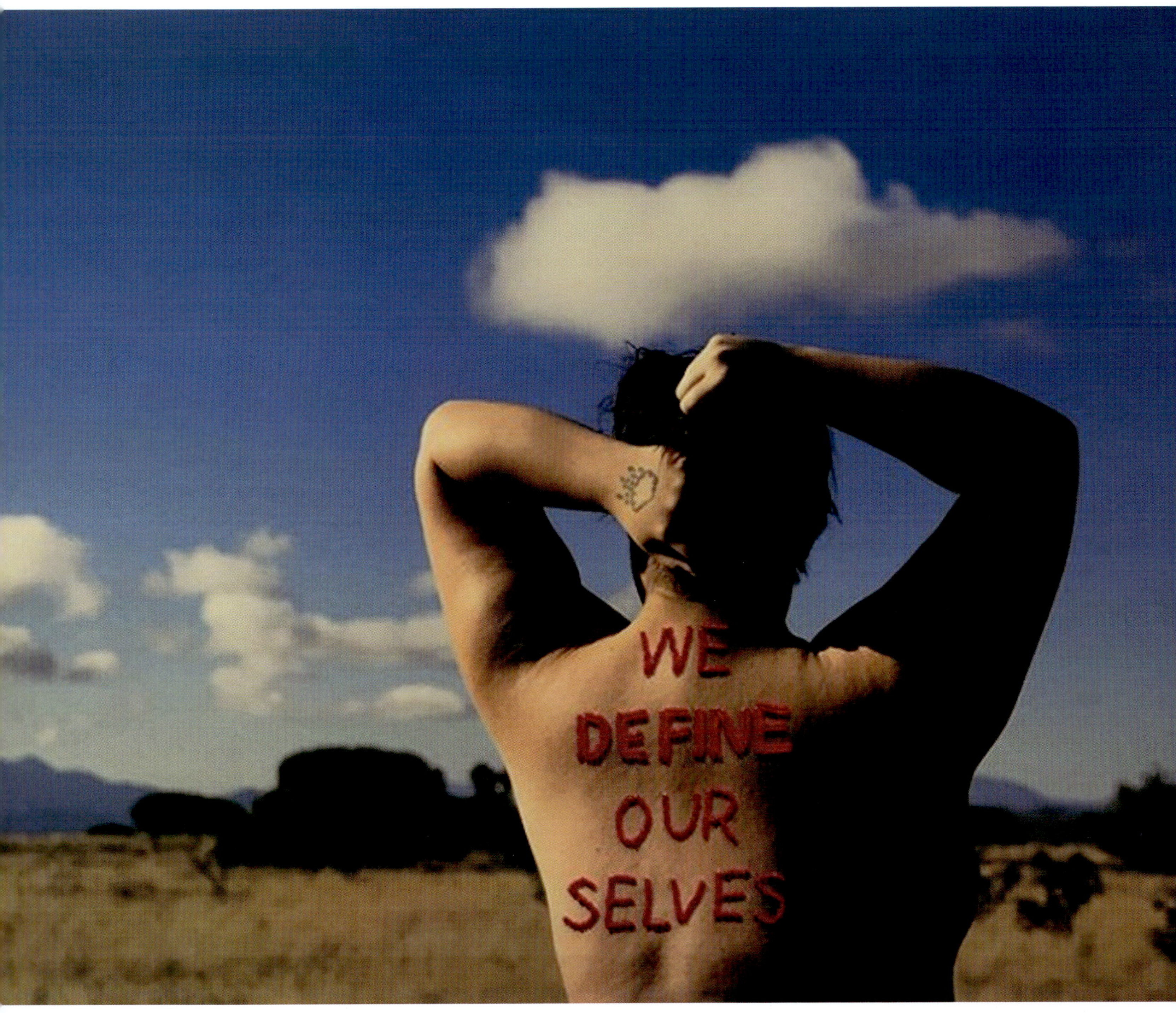

Page 150:
Jenny Irene Miller
Inupiaq, born 1988
Cam from Continuous (2015-2018), 2016
Archival inkjet print
Courtesy of the artist
© Jenny Irene Miller 2016

Ryan Young
Lac du Flambeau Ojibwe,
We Define Ourselves, 2018
Beadwork on canvas print
Courtesy of the artist
© Ryan Young

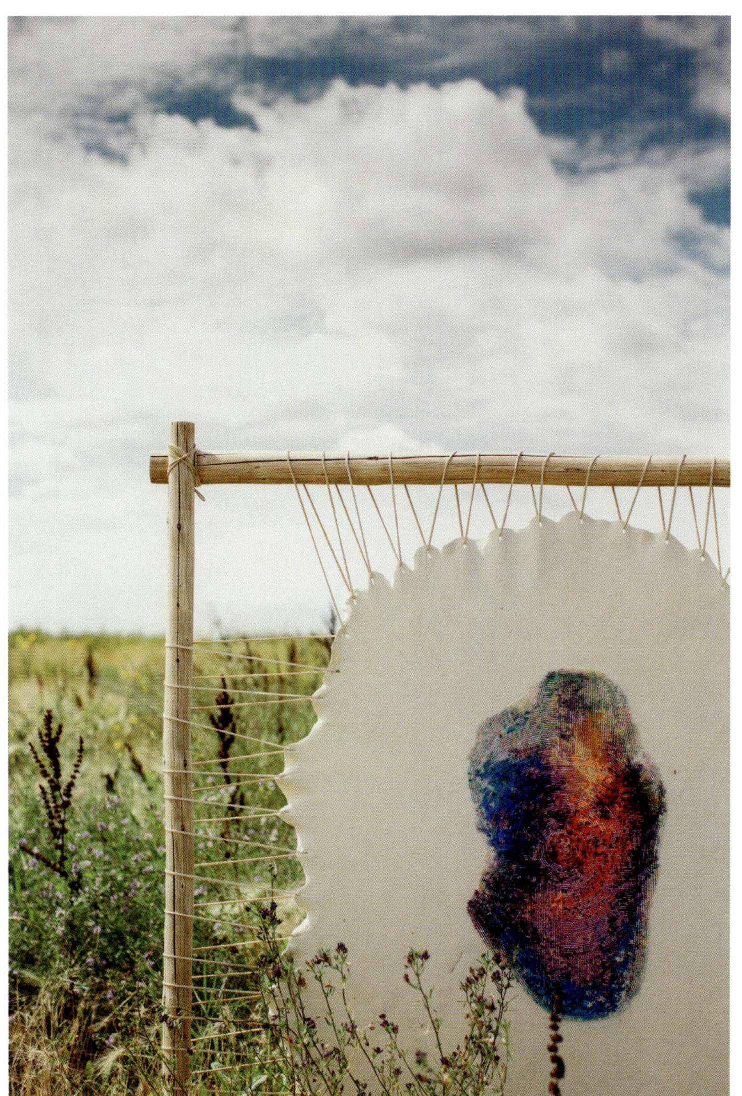

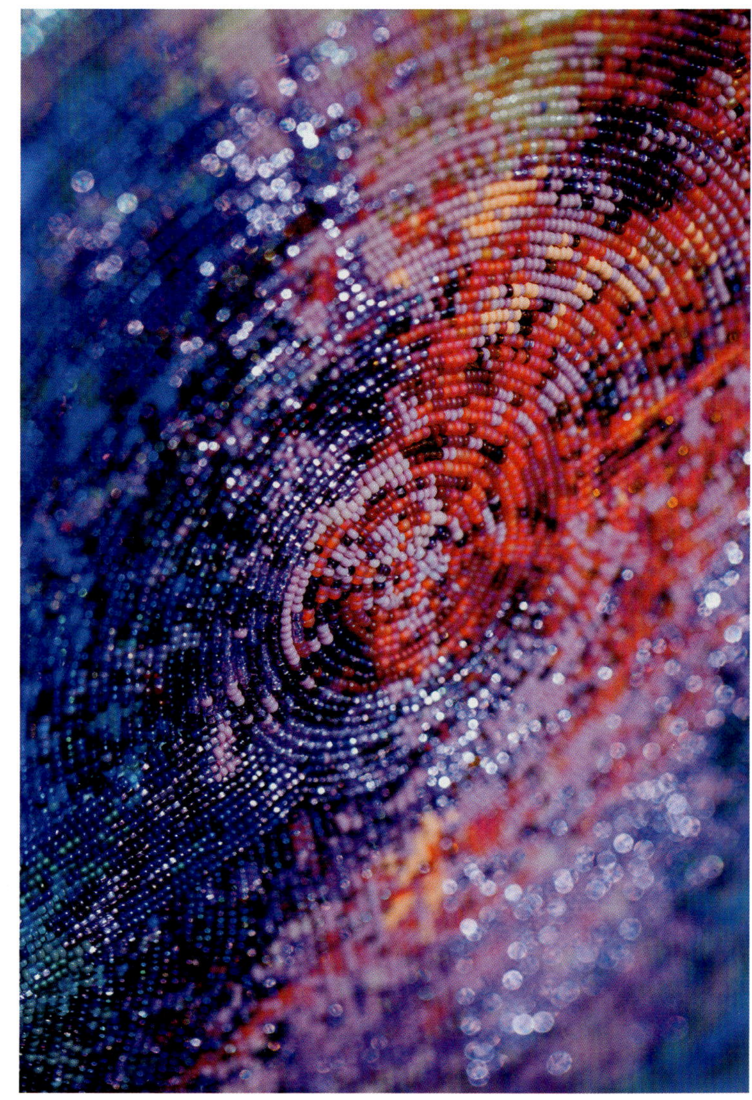

Catherine Blackburn
English River First Nation Dene/European
But There's No Scar?, 2017
Glass beads, deer hide, wood, leather,
canvas, and nylon thread
Courtesy of National Gallery of Canada, Ottawa
Photo by Tenille Campbell
© Catherine Blackburn

But There's No Scar? [detail], 2017

Catherine Blackburn
English River First Nation Dene/European
Tenille Campbell (photo credit)
English River First Nation Dene/Métis
But There's No Scar II, 2019
Transparency in light box
Courtesy of Kenderdine Art Gallery
© Catherine Blackburn

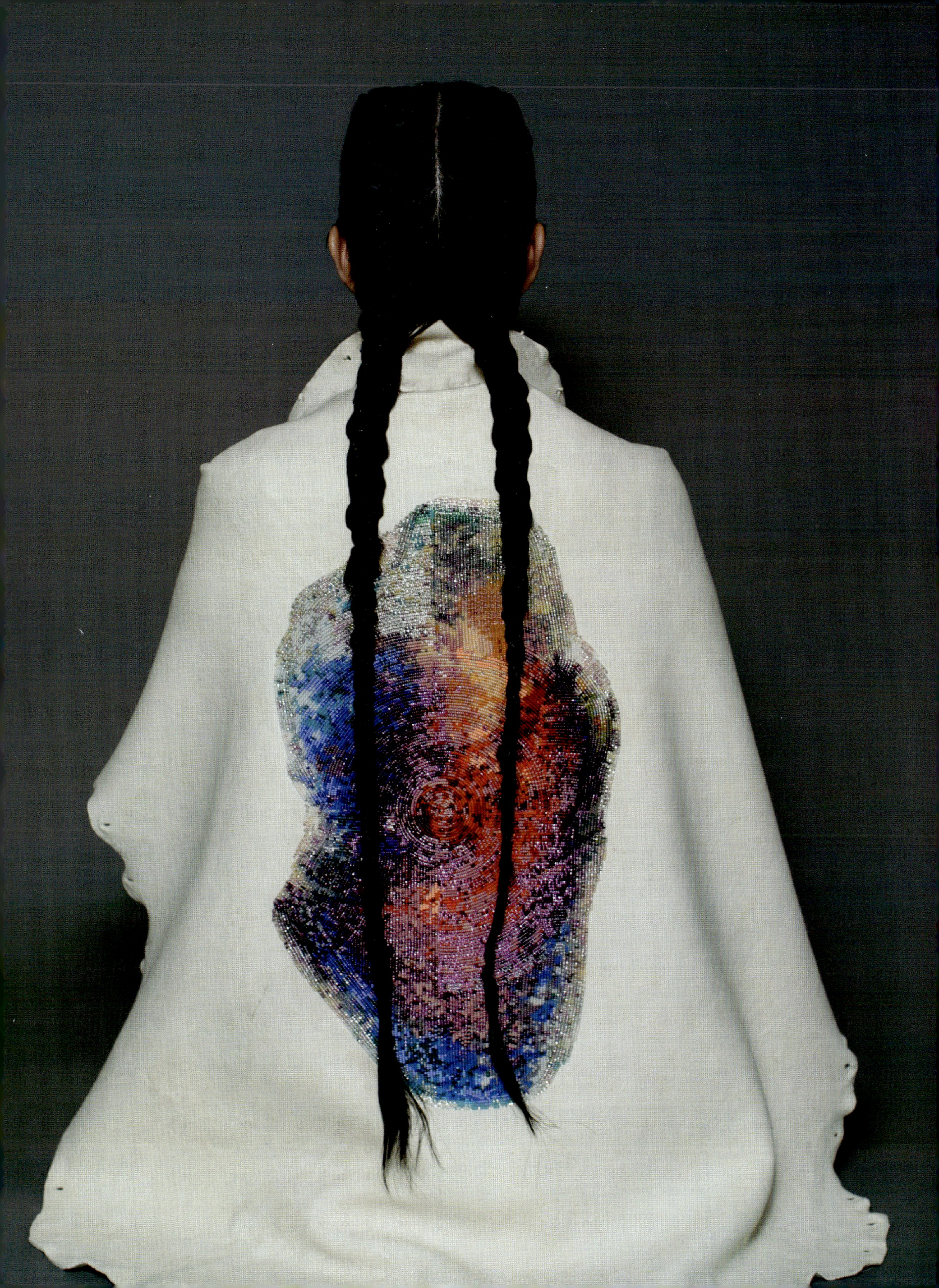

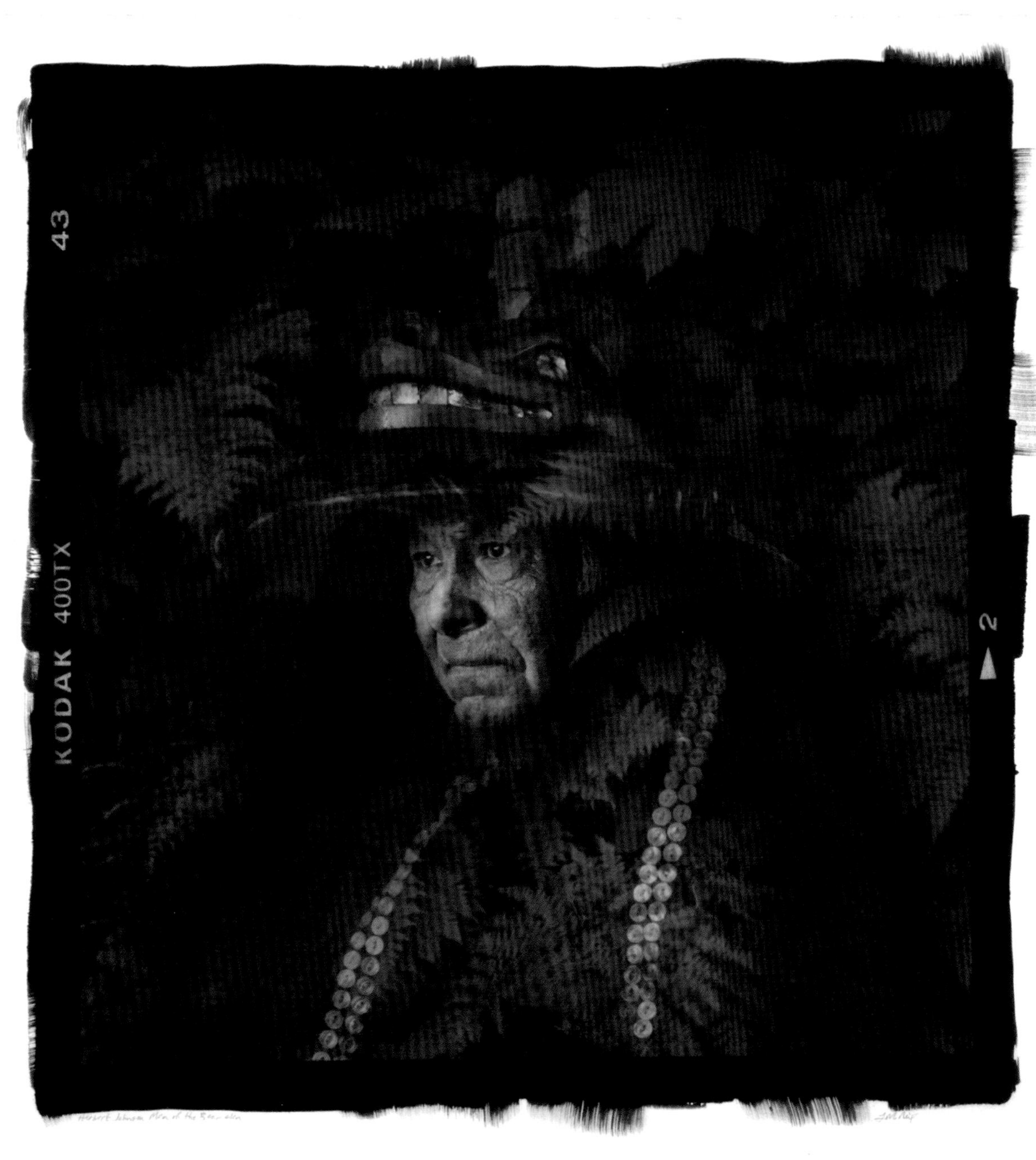

Larry McNeil
Dakl'aweidi K'eet Gooshi H'it, Killer Whale Fin House Tlingit / Nisga'a, born 1955
Herbert Johnson, Man of the Bear Clan, 2018
Palladium print
Courtesy of the artist
© Larry McNeil

Dugan Aguilar
Walker River Paiute / Mountain Maidu / Pit River Achomawi, 1947–2018
Mimi Mullen (Maidu), Grand Marshal of Greenville Gold Digger Days Parade, 1997
Gelatin silver print
Courtesy of C.N. Gorman Museum
© Dugan Aguilar

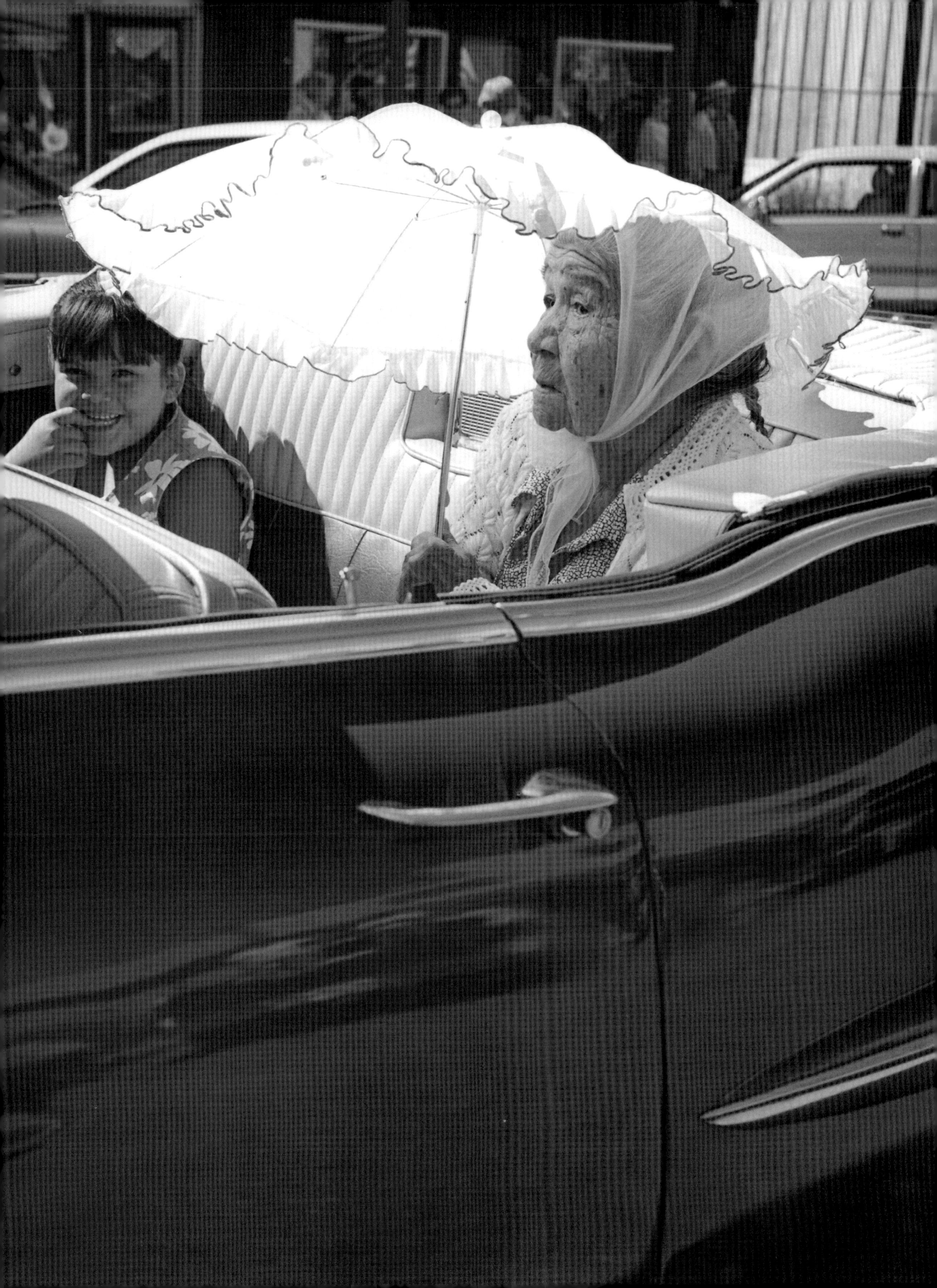

ANOTHER WAY: VERNACULAR

BY LAURA WEXLER

IN NOVEMBER 2016, a week after the election of Donald Trump to the presidency of the United States, I traveled with my small seminar of Yale Public Humanities students from New Haven, CT to Washington, DC, to visit museums and memorials. Barack Obama was still in office at the time, and it seemed to me everyone we met in the city was as anxious and morose as I was, and fearful of the coming change. Having long planned our trip, I was hoping we would find public art that would inspire new stories and generate hopeful approaches to the future. Our first visit was to the National Museum of the American Indian on the Mall, and it addressed this hope in a powerful and, for me, entirely unanticipated way.

Nora Naranjo-Morse's group of clay sculptures, entitled *Always Becoming*, stood in a small garden on the south side of the building. A Tewa Pueblo Indian from Santa Clara Pueblo, sculptor Nora Naranjo-Morse had won the NMAI outdoor sculpture design competition ten years earlier. The work was installed and dedicated on September 1, 2007, the first outdoor public sculpture by a Native American artist to be displayed in Washington. Humble in scale, multiple rather than monumental, the pieces a decade later were already crumbling a little, sprouting weeds, shifting shapes. The museum curator who was giving us a tour invited us to step into the garden's enclosure. From that position it was easy to see the enormous white marble dome of the US Capitol far behind them on Pennsylvania Avenue, framed by trees, heavy with pride. Here were two examples of endurance that coincided and collided with one another. Given the historical moment, I immediately understood the sculpture as a theory of governance. Naranjo-Morse predicted the American empire's inevitable decay and asserted the greater permanence of thousands of years of native forms more amenable to change. My eyes and my perspective widened. Here was the art I was looking for.

What then, of the photograph? Ernest Amoroso, the museum's staff photographer, was careful to record just this vision in an installation photograph that is used to introduce the site. It is an

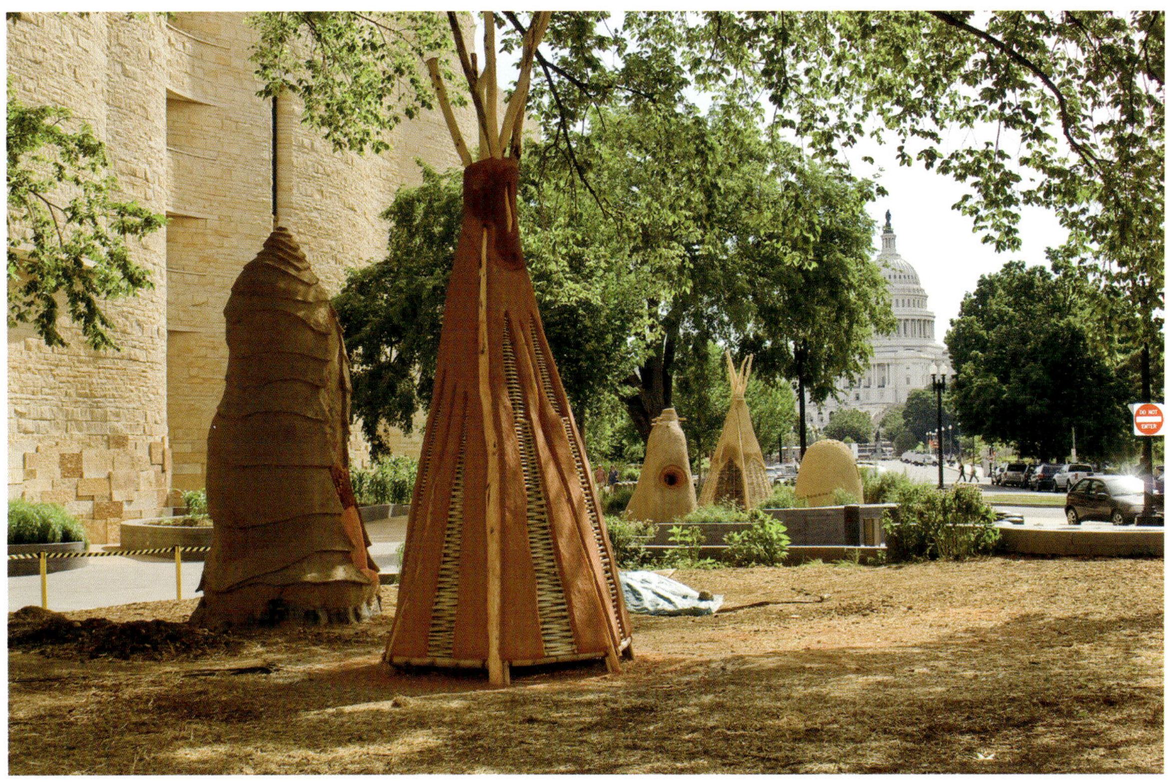

Fig. 1. Nora Naranjo-Morse, K'apovi (Santa Clara Pueblo), b. 1953, Always Becoming, 2007, Cob (mixed clay, soil, sand, and vegetal material), unfired clay, locust wood, bamboo, pottery sherd/sherds, agave/maguey fiber, stone. National Museum of The American Indian, Smithsonian Institution (26/5840). Photo by NMAI Photo Services. © Nora Naranjo-Morse

excellent record of the magnificent sculptural display, but it goes further than that. The image sharply juxtaposes the Greco-Roman (presumed to be white) marble to the red clay architectural forms, making sure they both are in clear focus.[62] It plays the multiple, biomorphic, sometimes bulging, domestic, human-scaled shapes of the sculpture against the smooth regular surface of the giant, single, empty circular dome. It is undecidable if the small encampment faces the Capitol in assertion, accusation, or supplication, or ambiguous attitudes that invoke the ghosts of the past. In highlighting the relationship of his work to the sense, form, and feeling of the object, Amoroso demonstrates why what scholars call "instrumental images" should be read along with the art of the past into the record of Native American photography.*

Instrumental images comprise genres of the vernacular that are traditionally excluded from what is considered art: "the aerial view in military photography, corporate advertising, paparazzi celebrity photography, commercial portraiture, industrial photography, police photography, and, crucially, documentary photography," according to Allan Sekula.[63] Installation photographs made by a staff photographer for a museum would be another such genre. It is true that most professional photographers who work in that way are seldom free to choose their own assignments. But the workaday images that photographers, including Indigenous and non-Indigenous photographers, have made for institutions and organizations are a crucial part of the conversation. Both Indigenous and non-Indigenous photographers who are conversant with the artists and sensitive to the goals of Native institutions are engaged in the work. And given that few Indigenous photographers have been able to make their way as solo artists, or studio proprietors, the photographs made in such employment are also a logical place to extend the search for their hand. Because of the injunction given to staff to communicate a perspective for work that is sometimes a critique, vernacular photographs that appear in brochures, broadsides, catalogues, and websites, like this one, are interwoven with Indigenous histories and viewpoints.

In a recent book, *Imagining Everyday Life: Engagements with Vernacular Photography,* the editors, Tina M. Campt, Marianne Hirsch, Gil Hochberg, and Brian Wallis recommend understanding the vernacular photograph as "rooted in an understanding of everyday life that acknowledges the value of the banal and overlooked, the boring and passive, and the significance of the quotidian, often repetitive micro-events showcased in commonplace photography."[64] I subscribe to this understanding, but I want to underline that often, as here, there is nothing passive about such a photograph. Rather, a mind is looking, and inviting viewers to join in. Like the living sentinel forms in Nora Naranjo-Morse's sculpture that are surveying the Capitol, Amoroso's photograph is also guarding how the sculpture appears to the public. It is an element of a yet to be consolidated archive of Indigenous photographs that demonstrate who is watching, and how. I have elsewhere named this form a "chrysalis archive."[65]

I have another, more personal, reason for highlighting Amoroso's image of Naranjo-Morse's sculpture. One afternoon nearly forty years ago, I walked out of my field. I was originally an "Early Americanist." I had just read the following in a manuscript account by Captain John Mason of the massacre of hundreds of Pequot men, women, and children near Mystic, Connecticut, where the English set their fort on fire:

> Thus were they now at their Wits End, who not many Hours before exalted themselves in their great Pride, threatening and resolving the utter Ruin and Destruction of all the *English*, Exulting and Rejoycing with Songs and Dances: But GOD was above them, who laughed his Enemies and the Enemies of His People to Scorn, making them as a fiery Oven: Thus were

the Stout Hearted spoiled, having slept their last Sleep, and none of their Men could find their Hands: Thus did the Lord judge among the Heathen, filling the Place with dead Bodies![66]

When I grasped the smallest sense of what this sentence was about, I realized that I could not work far into the future with the sound of such a voice speaking in my ear. I returned my book, walked down and out of the long central nave of Yale University's cathedral-like library, and deliberately left my years of graduate student scholarship on "Colonial American Literature" behind, vowing not to return.

Still, the memory of that manuscript remained etched into my memory. In the manuscript was a map drawn by Captain John Underhill, like Mason an English perpetrator. He depicts the massacre in a map drawn from the killers' point of view:[67]

The map burned in my mind. *The figure of the Indiens' fort or Palisadio in NEW ENGLAND And the maner of the destroying It by Captayne Underhill and Captayne Mason* is a searing and unselfconscious document of a genocide *in media res*, a virtual snapshot recorded two centuries before such an exposure became technically possible in and as photography.

Ariella Aïsha Azoulay proposes in *Potential History: Unlearning Imperialism*, that we should "unlearn ... the accepted origins of photography and those of the 'new world' as disconnected in European historiography." Instead, we should see how they are entangled. We should "imagine the origins of photography go back to 1492."[68]

> The invention of photography and the invention of the new world are not unrelated. Suggesting that the origins of photography go back to 1492 is an attempt to undermine the imperial temporality that was imposed at that time, enabling people to believe, experience, and describe interconnected things as if they were separate, each defined by newness. To put it another way, for photography to emerge as a new technology in the late 1830s, the centrality of the imperial rights on which photography was predicated had to be ignored, denied, or sublimated, or in any case pushed into the background and not perceived as constitutive of its operation as a technology.
>
> Foregrounding these rights requires a simultaneous exercise—unlearning the accepted origins of photography and those of the "new world," their familiar temporal and spatial connotations, which even today are still closely associated with modernity and the "era of discoveries," and attending instead to the configuration of imperial violence and its manifestation in rights. ... Among these rights are *the right to destroy*

> *existing worlds*, *the right to manufacture a new world* in their place, *the rights over others* whose worlds are destroyed together with the rights they enjoyed in their communities and the *right to declare what is new and consequently what is obsolete*.[69]

Underhill's map certainly registers the imposition of "*the right to destroy existing worlds*" along the lines of which the invention of the camera-made image as a record-keeping social practice would be predicated two hundred years later. In solidarity with what Azoulay terms, "unlearning imperialism," or "unlearning the process of destruction that became possible: the knowledge, norms, procedures, and routines through which worlds are destroyed in order for people to become citizens of a differentially ruled body politic."[70] I take it to be a foundational image of the origins of American photography. Yet, although the study of "colonial America" has now become what it should have been in the first place, that is, decolonial studies, it is complicated to center such a violent configuration of imperial rights at the heart of photography without reimposing further violence.

Indigenous work addresses this problem. By constructing such a village in the US Capitol and building Indigenous dwellings that exist there freely not as history but as a present lifeway, one that even offers shelter to contemporary unhoused citizens who are not so well served by the current regime, Naranjo-Morse rebalances accounts. By foregrounding the handmade dwellings as the center (though not the subject) of his image—the way they first appeared even in Underhill's drawing ("the Indians houses," "their streets") before Underhill added soldiers shooting the people in that space, Amoroso's photograph of Naranjo-Morse's sculpture restores the gravitas of existing Indigenous worlds in a metropolis that generally disregards them, unwinding the relations of imperial power that Underhill had mapped. In Amoroso's image, the viewer stands level with the people, not outside or above, this living way. The photograph is no mere record. It offers potential companionship staked against the violence of the present and the past.

PART III

A WORLD OF RELATIONS

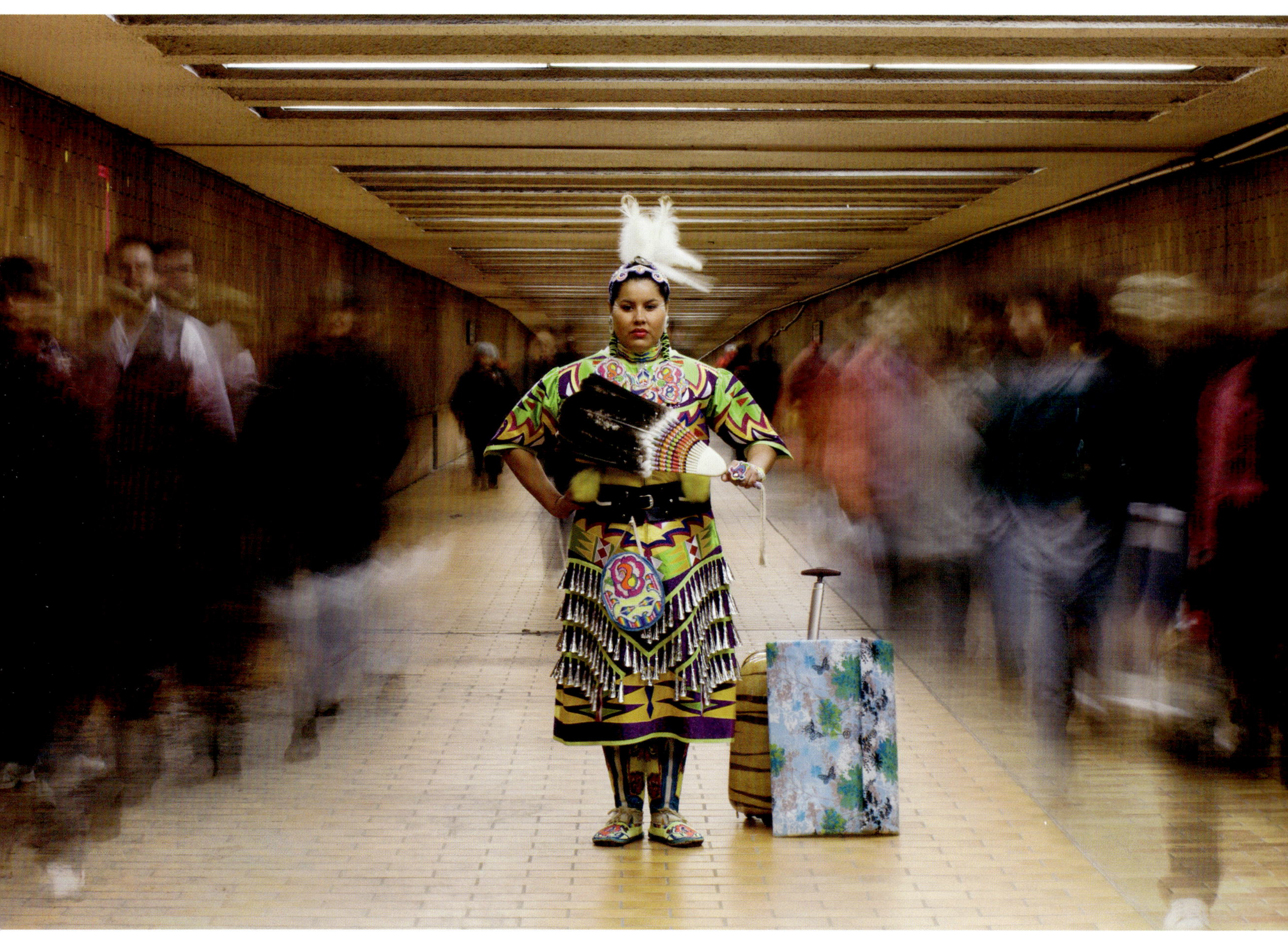

Nadya Kwandibens
Animakee Wa Zhing #37
First Nation Anishinaabe
Tee Lyn Duke (née Copenace)
Toronto, ON, March 2010
from Concrete Indians series
Courtesy the Artist / Red Works Photography

Page 165:
Ossie Michelin
Inuit, born 1983
Fracking protest, Elsipogtog, New Brunswick, 2013
Courtesy of the artist

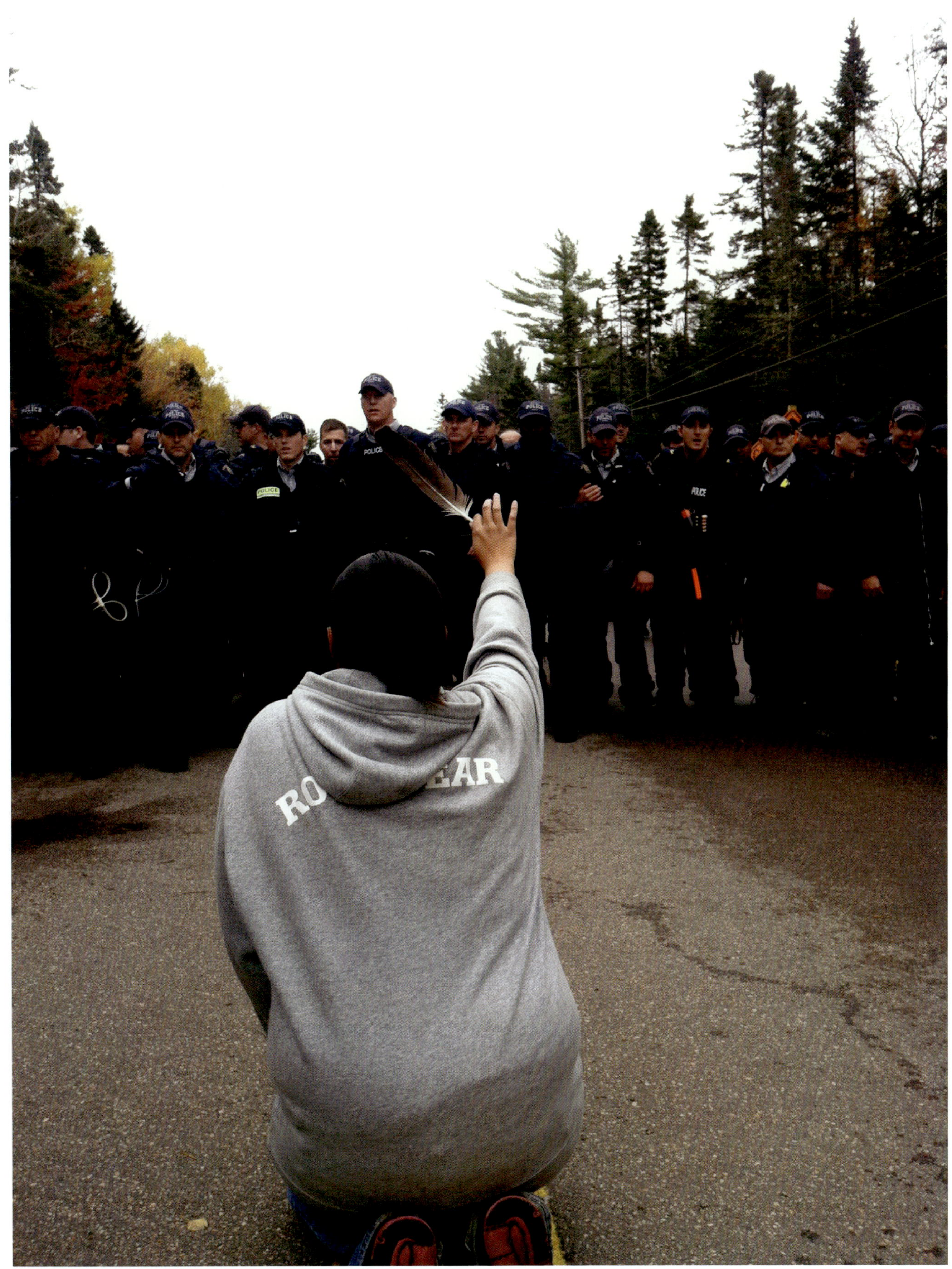
POLICE

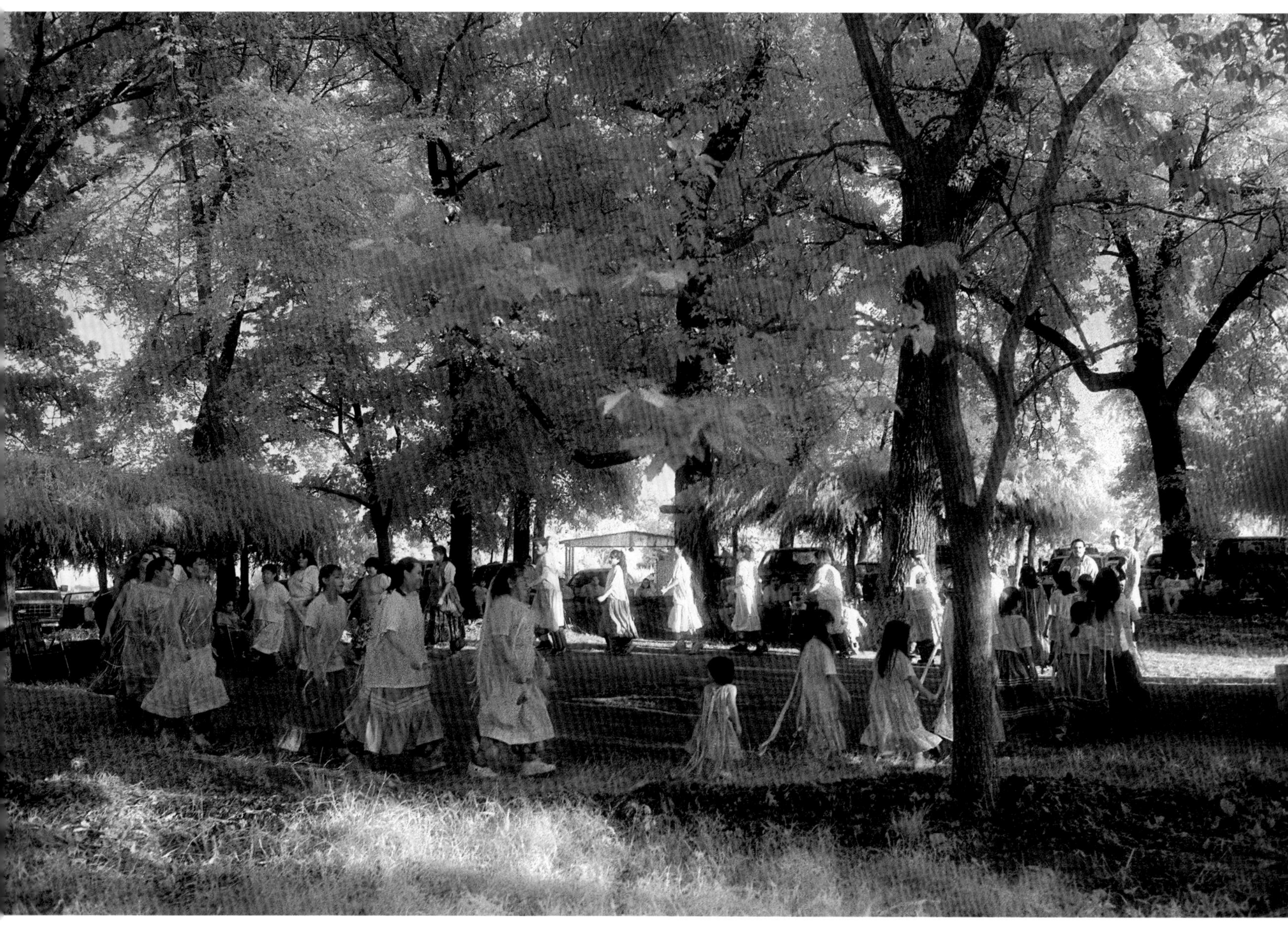

Thomas Fields
Muscogee Creek/Cherokee, born 1951
Dancing in the Sunlight, 1999
Digital black and white print on archival paper.
originally shot with 35mm infrared film
to explore the tonality of the image.
Courtesy of the artist

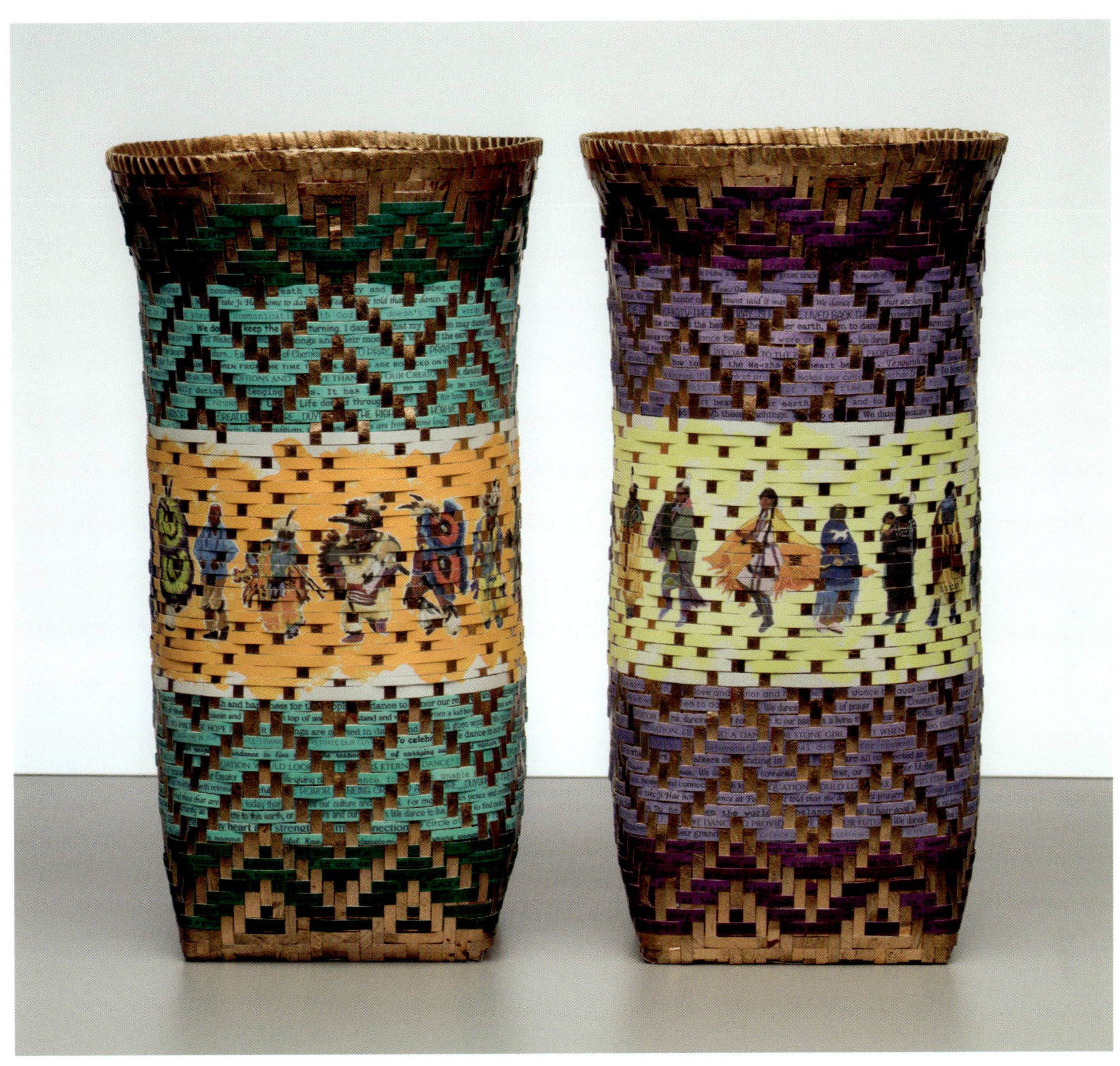

Shan Goshorn
Eastern Band Cherokee, 1957-2018
Why We Dance, 2016
Arches watercolor paper splints
printed with archival inks,
acrylic paint, artificial sinew
Detroit Institute of Arts, Museum Purchase,
Flint Ink Endowment Fund, 2021.286.1

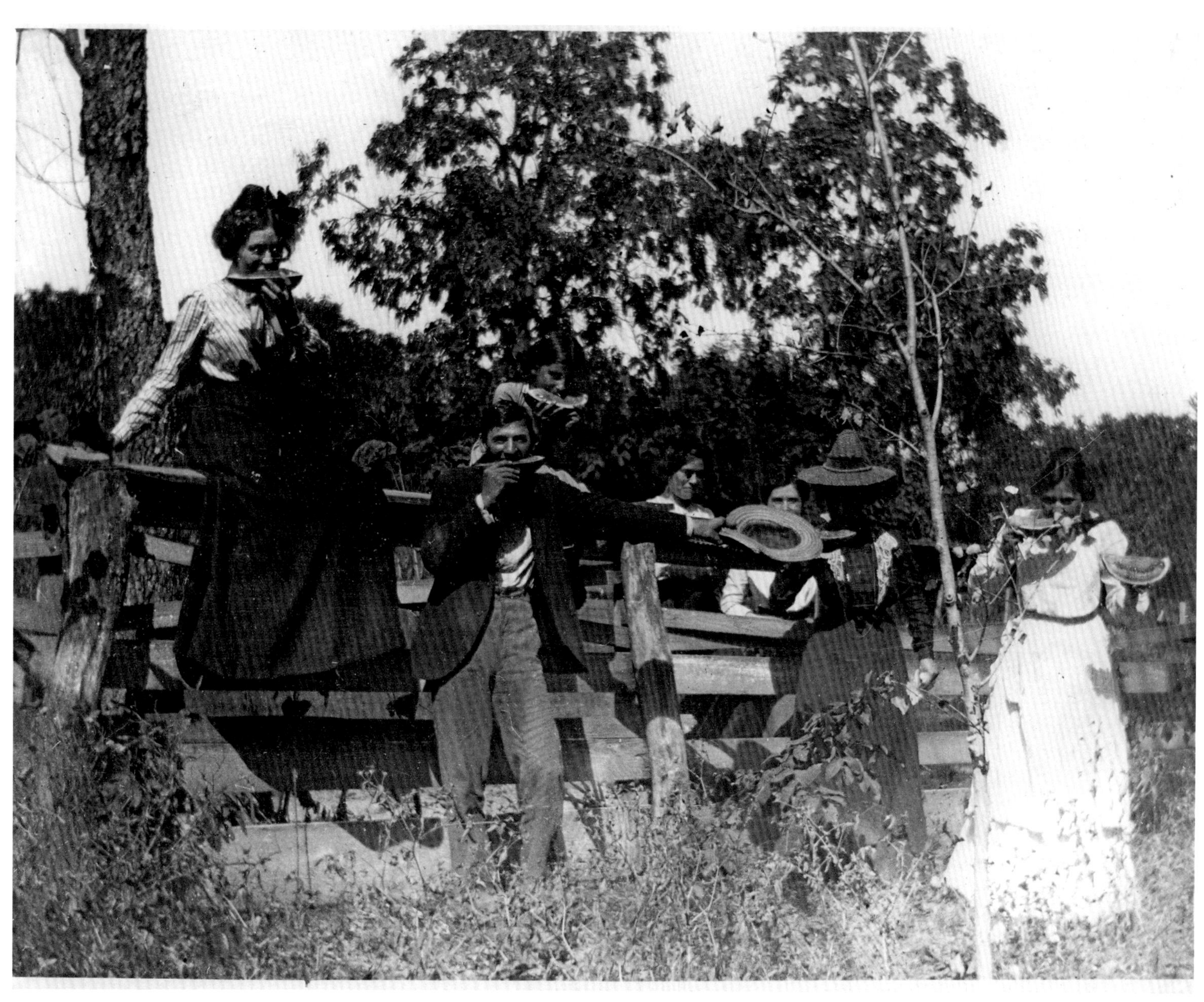

Jennie Ross Cobb
Cherokee, 1881 - 1959
Park Hill, Indian Territory, c. 1896-1906
Courtesy of the Oklahoma Historical Society,
Jennie Ross Cobb Collection, 20661.21

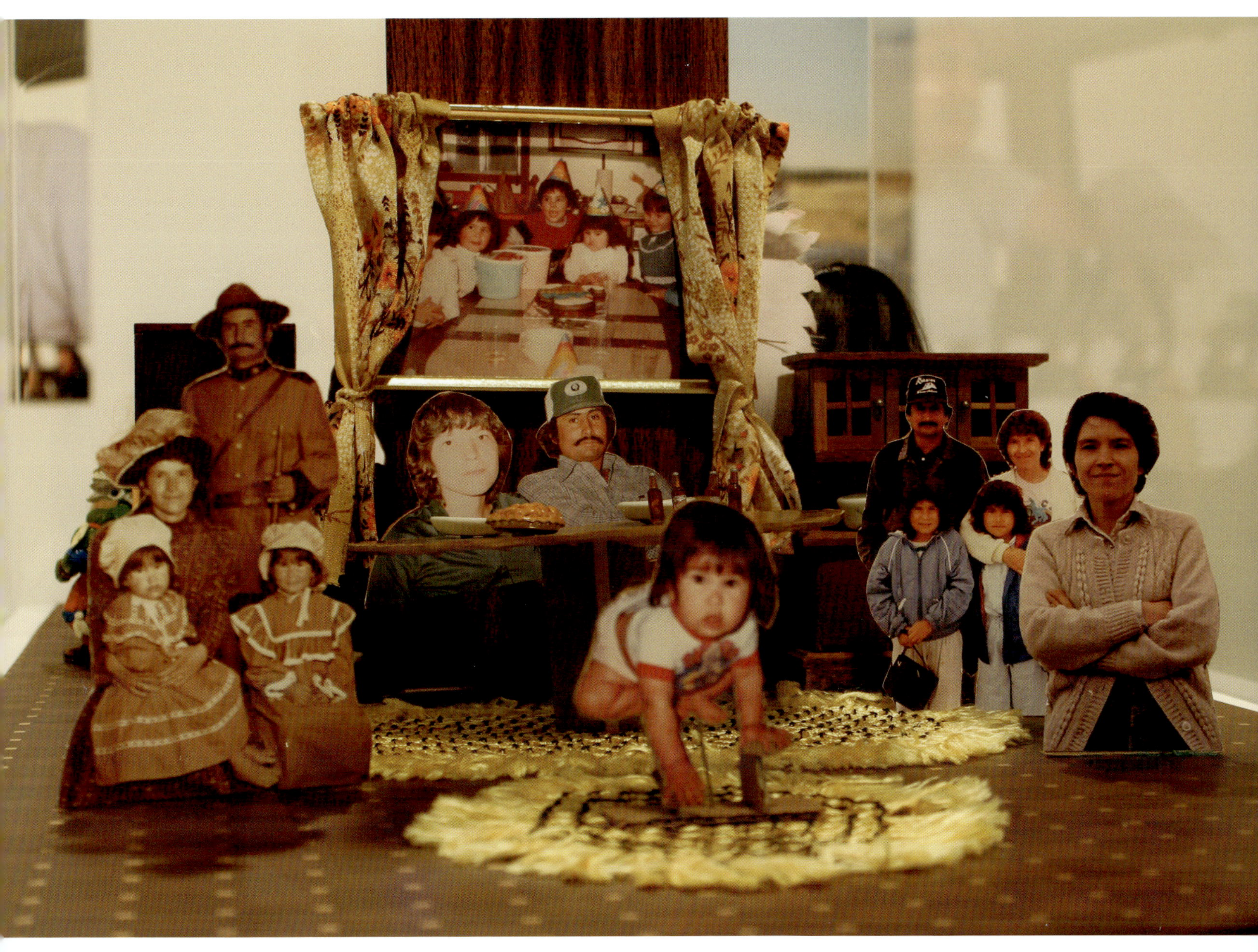

Joi T. Arcand
Muskeg Lake Cree Nation, born 1982
[Diorama 8], 2014 - ongoing
from Through That Which is Scene series
Mixed media
Courtesy of the artist

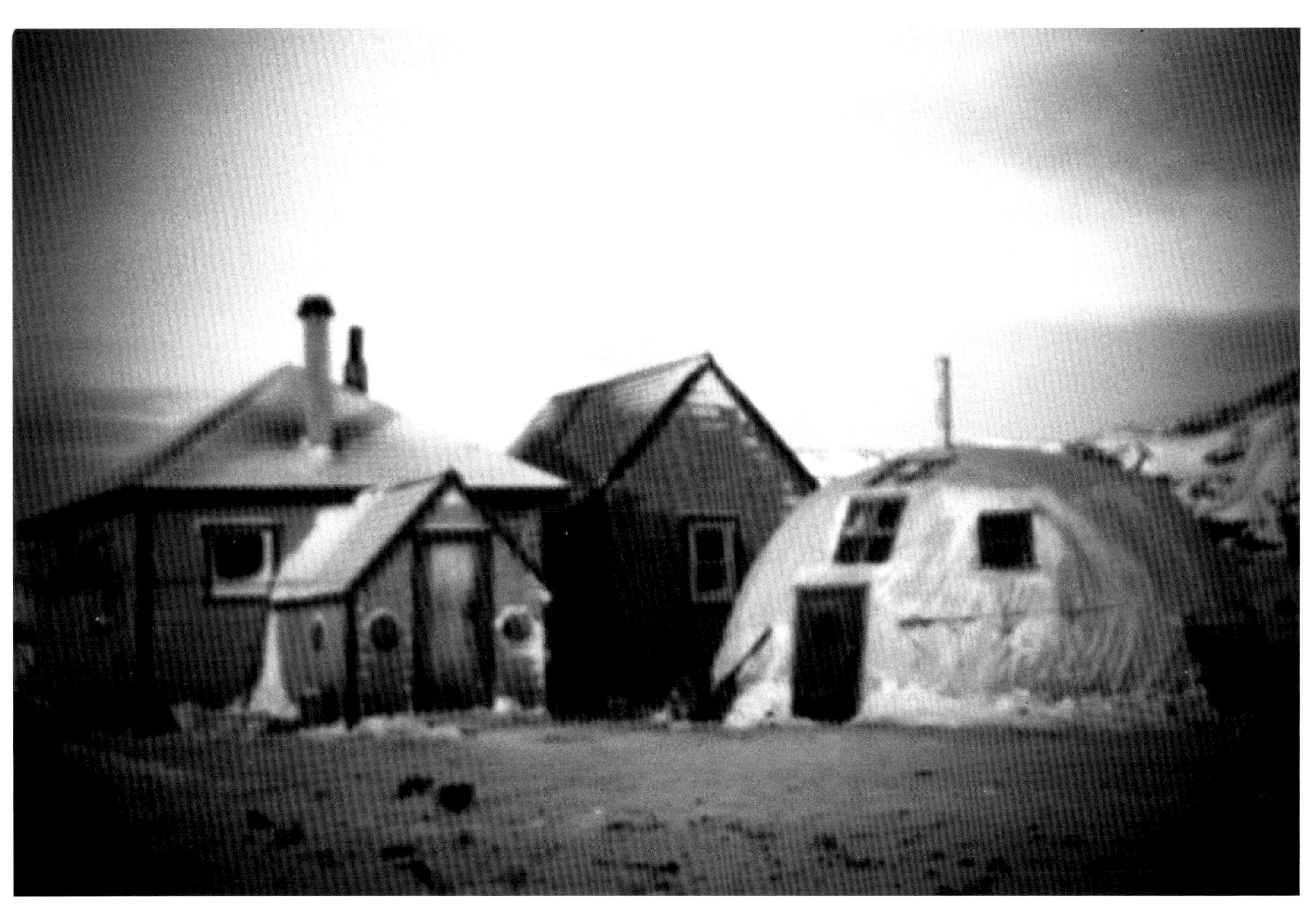

Peter Pitseolak
Inuit, 1902-1973
Pitseolak's wooden house and quarmak,
c. 1940-60
Canadian Museum of History, 2000-255,
CD2000-224-018

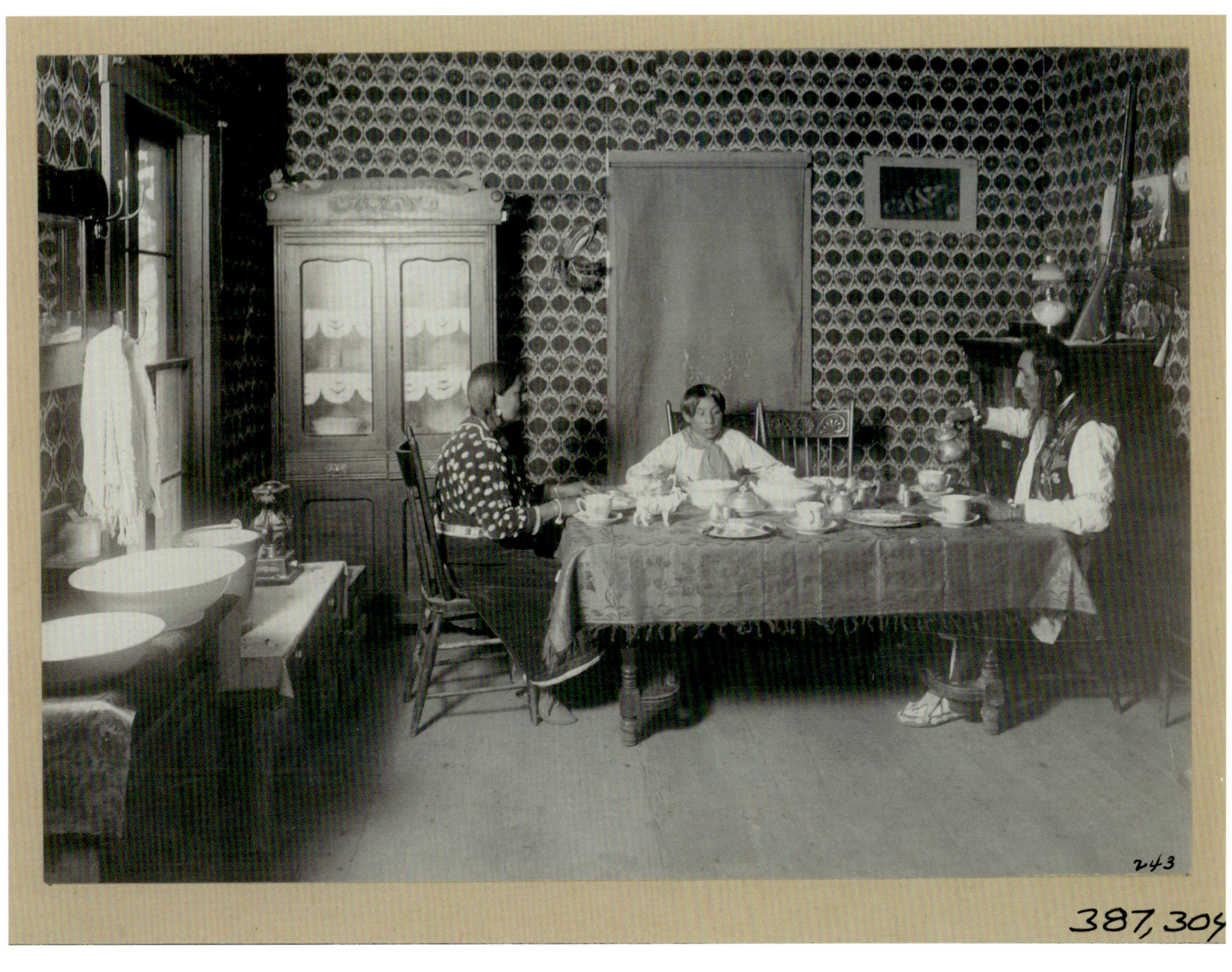

Richard Throssel
Nehiyawak (Cree) / Adopted Apsáalooke, 1882–1933
Interior of the Best Indian Kitchen on the Crow Reservation, 1910
Gelatin silver print
Courtesy of the National Anthropological Archives, Smithsonian Institution, Washington, D.C.
(00486700)

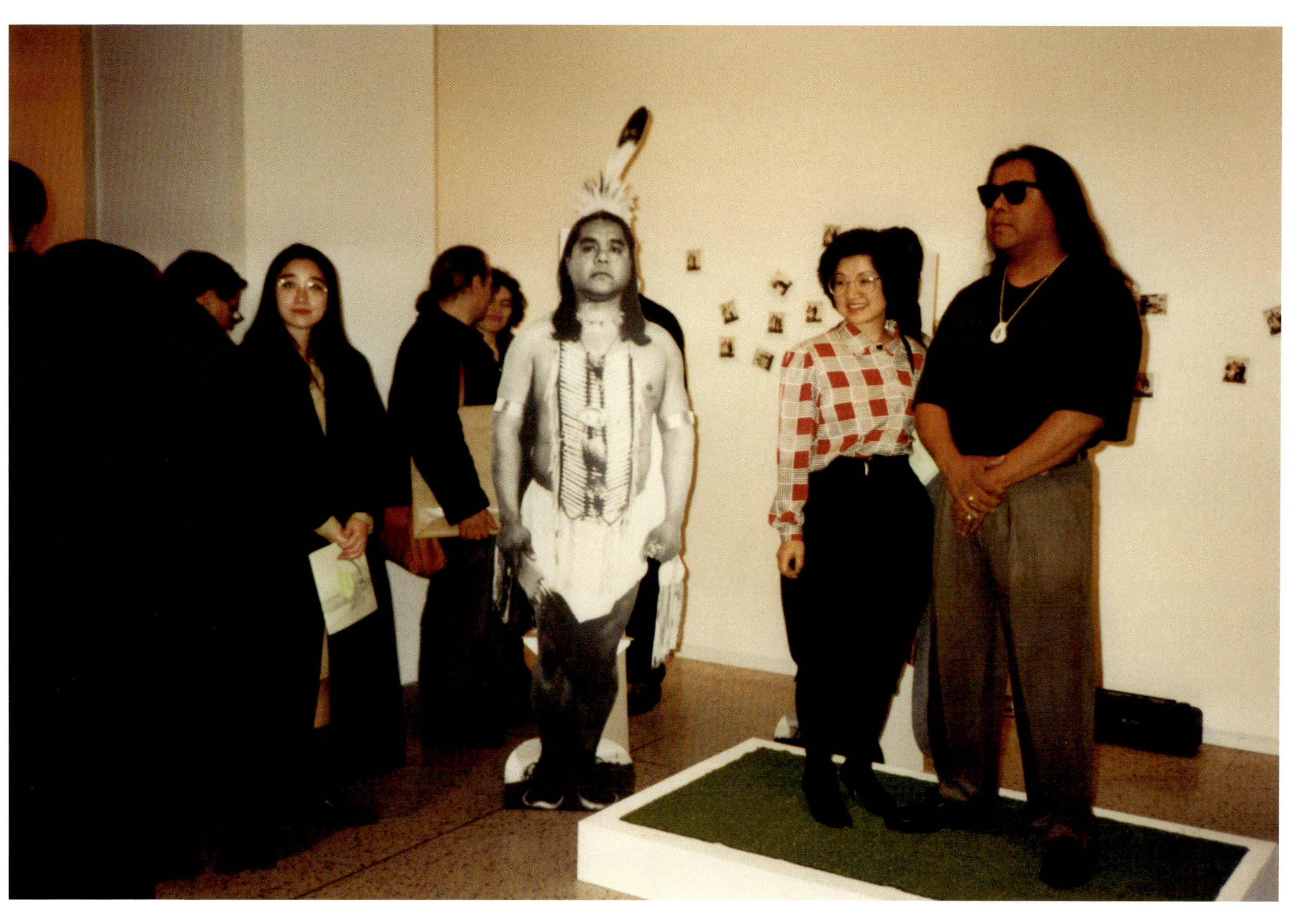

James Luna
Payómkawichum Luiseño / Ipi /
Mexican-American, 1950-2018
Take a Picture with a Real Indian, 1991
Courtesy the Estate of James Luna and
Garth Greenan Gallery, New York

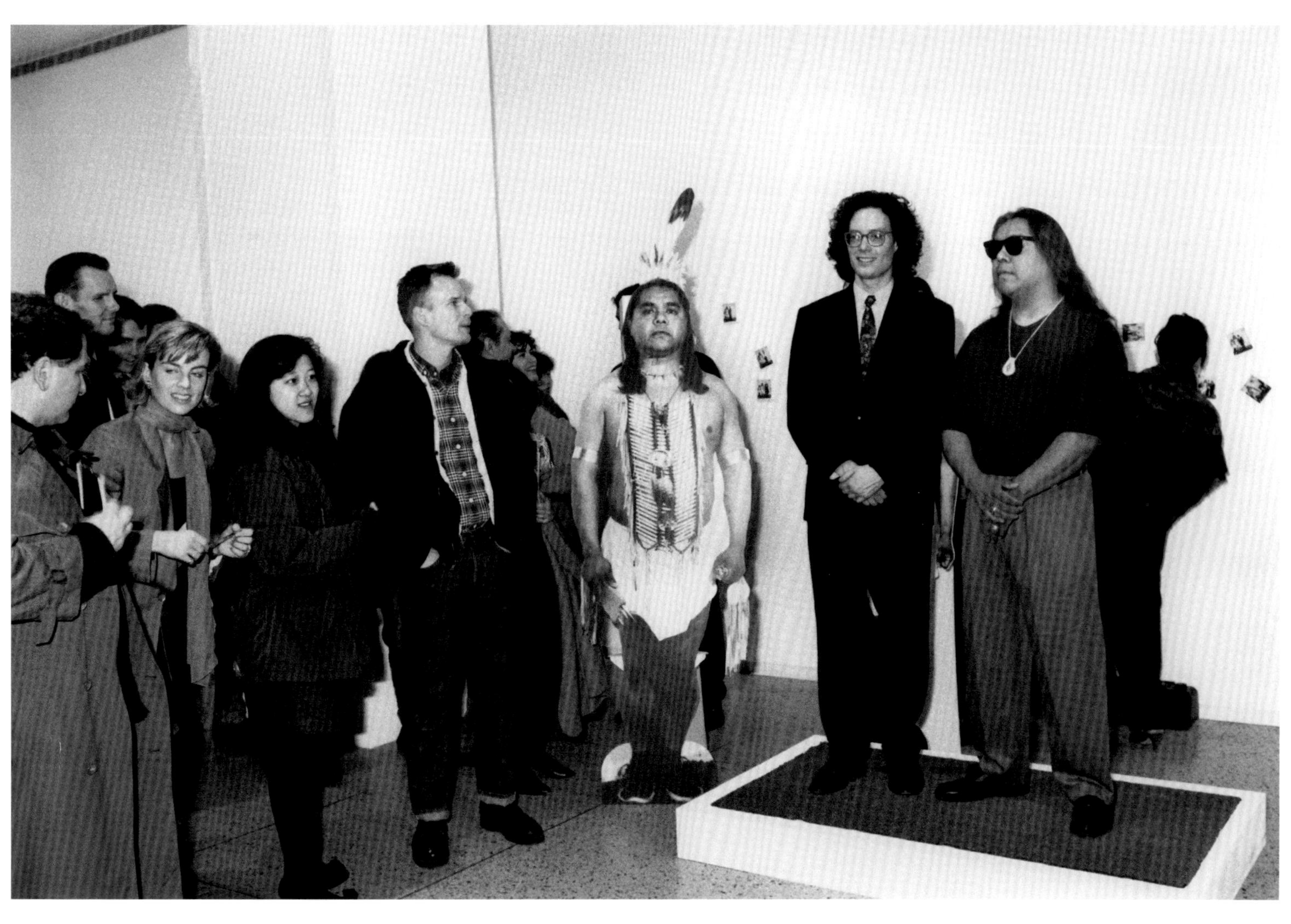

James Luna
Payómkawichum Luiseño / Ipi /
Mexican-American, 1950-2018
Take a Picture with a Real Indian, 1991
Courtesy the Estate of James Luna and
Garth Greenan Gallery, New York

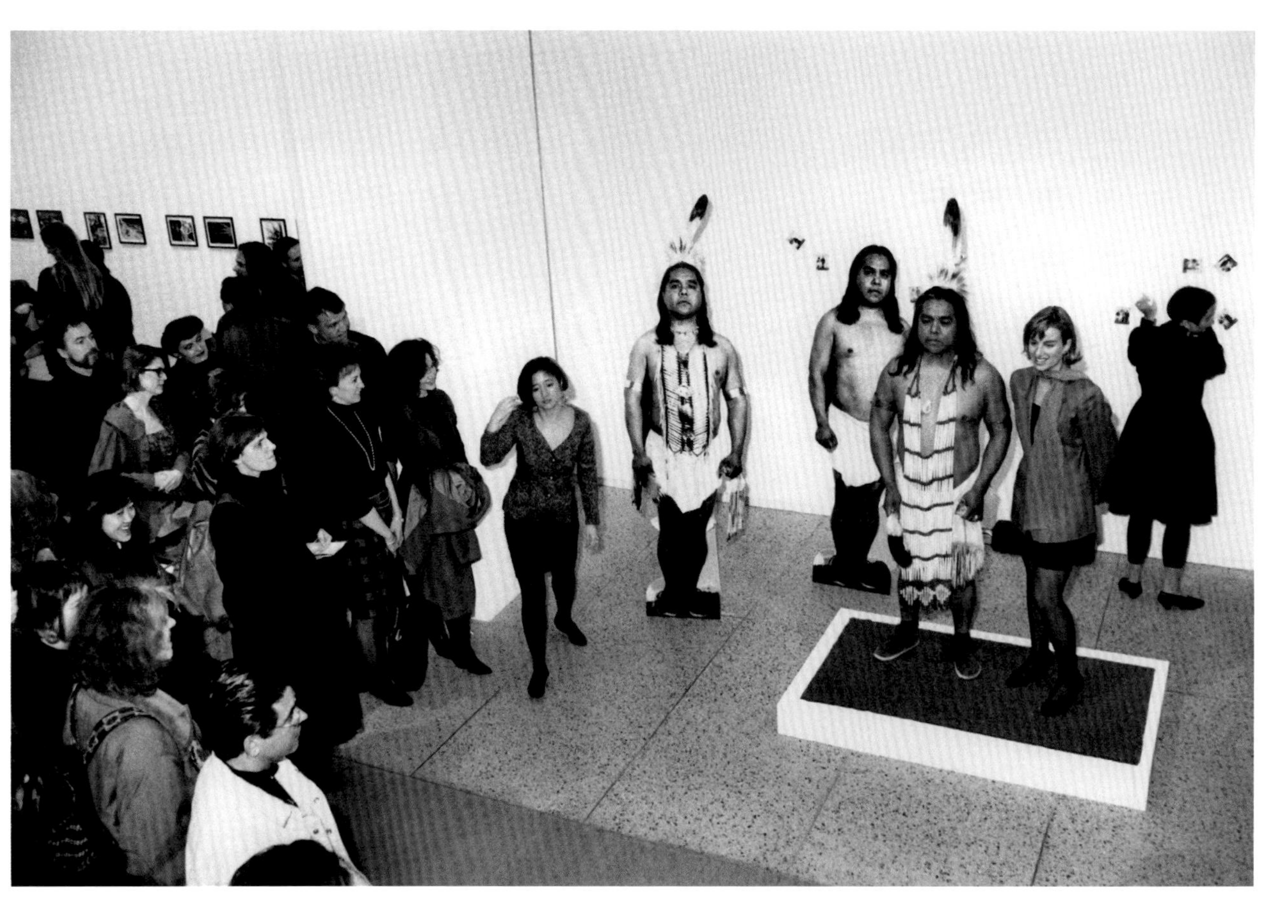

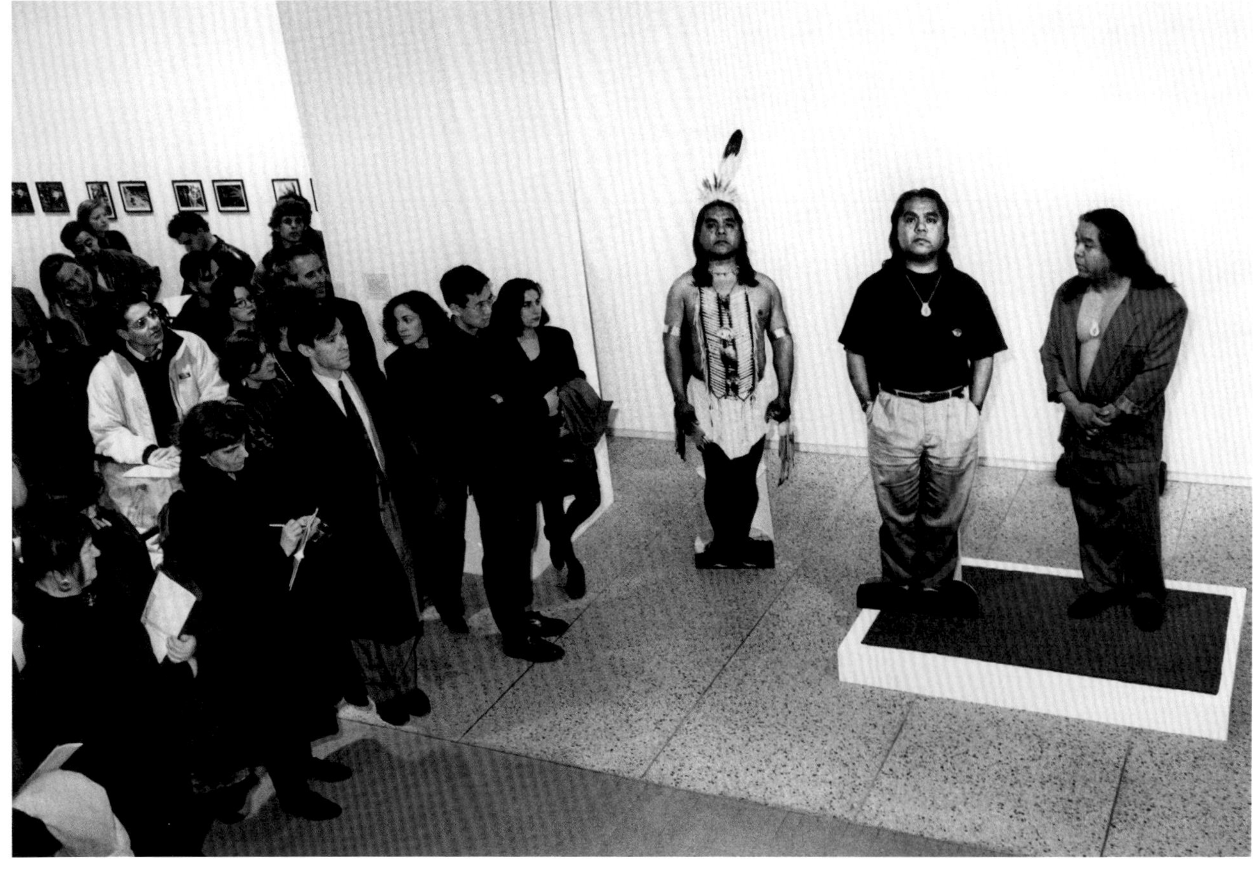

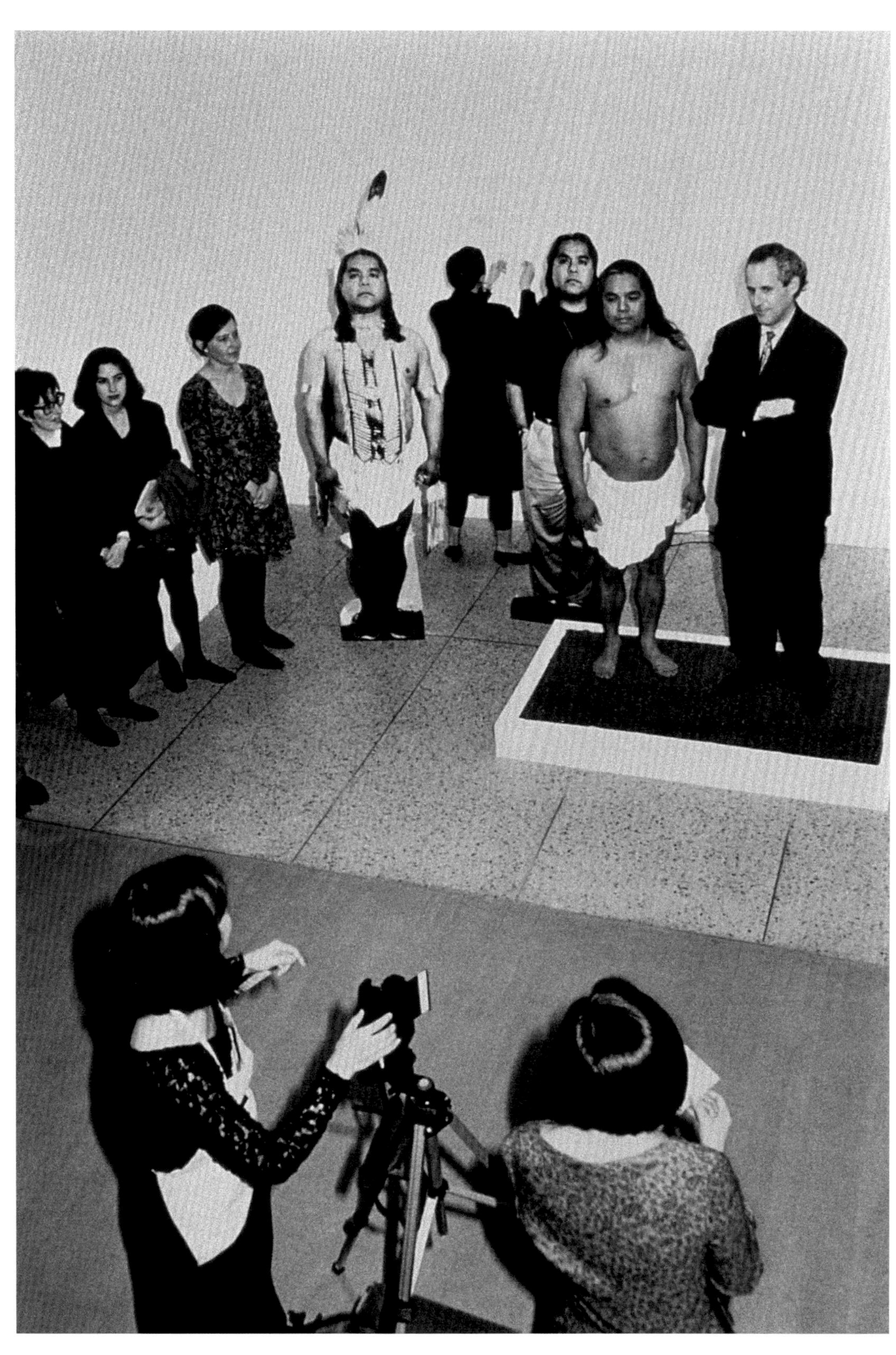

James Luna
Payómkawichum Luiseño / Ipi /
Mexican-American, 1950-2018
Take a Picture with a Real Indian, 1991
Courtesy the Estate of James Luna and
Garth Greenan Gallery, New York

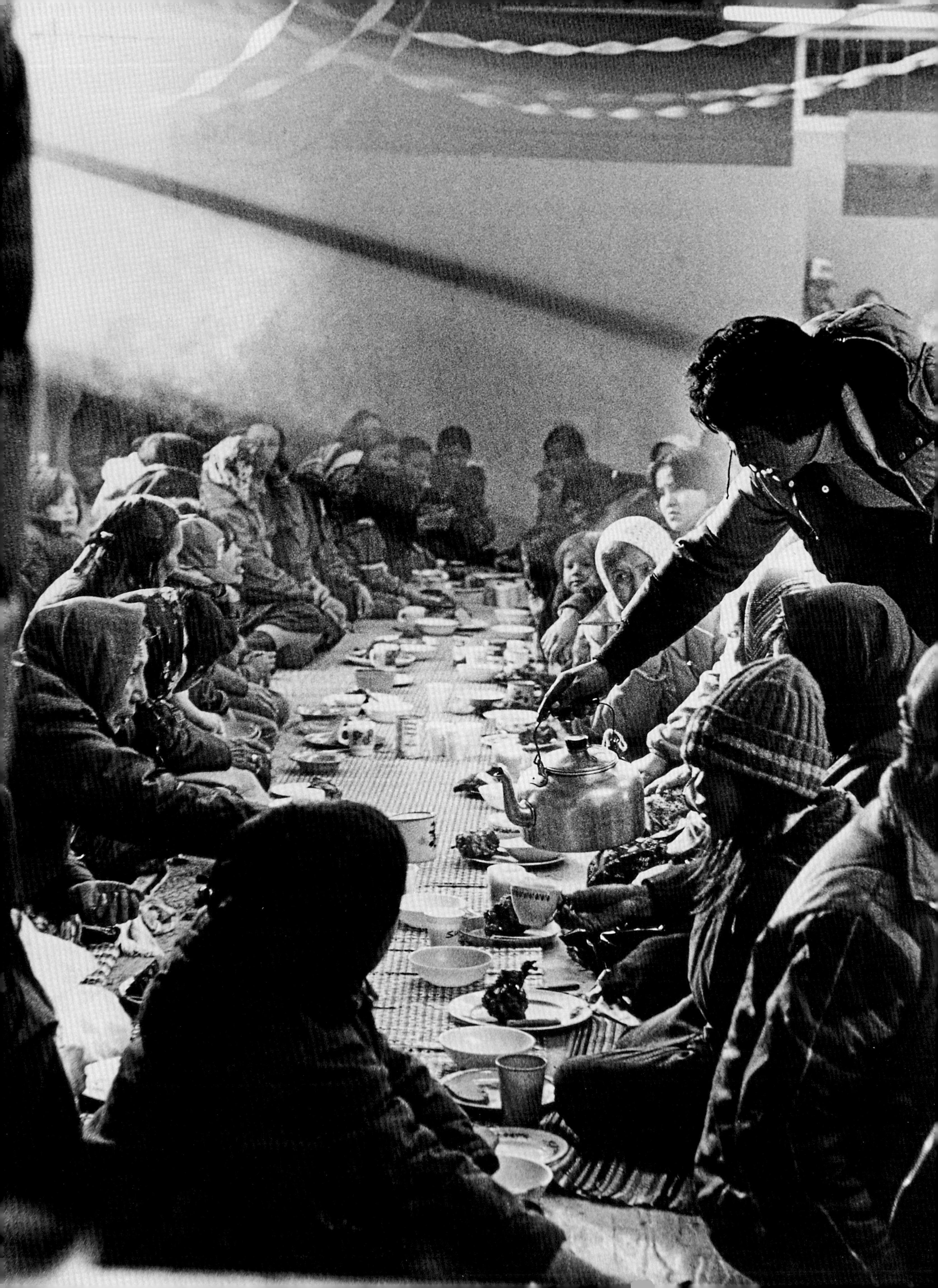

RESEARCHING THE LEGACY OF THE NATIVE INDIAN/ INUIT PHOTOGRAPHERS' ASSOCIATION (NIIPA)

AN INTERVIEW WITH RHÉANNE CHARTRAND AND CASEY RILEY

Casey Riley: Rhéanne, thanks so much for joining me in conversation. Could you begin by sharing how you came to research the Native Indian/Inuit Photographers' Association?

Rhéanne Chartrand: Yes. Actually, I learned about NIIPA (Native Indian/Inuit Photographers' Association) in the course of working on my very first exhibition for McMaster Museum of Art, which was called *Unapologetic: Acts of Survivance*. It was one of two exhibitions I produced during my residency year at the museum. Shelley Niro and Jeff Thomas were a part of that exhibition. In the course of doing research on the two of them in late 2016, I came across an article from 1990, which was a one-page essay written by Yvonne Maracle about the Native Indian/ Inuit Photographers' Association, in which Shelley was cited as a member. I thought, "What is the Native Indian/Inuit Photographers' Association? Why have I never heard of this group?"

The article said that NIIPA started in Hamilton [Ontario] in 1985 and all these folks were involved, and this is what we did, and this is how we supported Native photographers. So, I called up Jeff Thomas, with whom I still have a very good working relationship. When I asked about NIIPA, Jeff said, "Oh, yeah, that was a collective we started in the eighties." I was intrigued.

When we opened *Unapologetic: Acts of Survivance* in January 2017, Kevin Sakolinsky from the Indigenous Art Centre at CIRNAC (Crown-Indigenous Relations and Northern Affairs Canada) came to the opening because the centre was a partner for that exhibition, and I said, "Hey, Kevin, do you know anything about this NIIPA group?" He said, "Oh, yeah, we have a bunch of works by the NIIPA members in our collection." From there it became an obsession for me, learning all I could about NIIPA. I started the deep dive in 2017, and in August 2017, I went to see the work at CIRNAC. It was at that point that I realized how exciting the material would be to research further.

Dorothy Chocolate Carseen
Tłı̨chǫ, born 1959
Feast at Fort Franklin, Northwest Territories, 1981
Gelatin silver print
Indigenous Art Centre Collection at
Crown-Indigenous Relations and
Northern Affairs Canada

Casey Riley: So this collective was not necessarily on your radar as an Indigenous scholar, even though you were interested in photographic history as it pertained to Indigenous peoples in Canada?

Rhéanne Chartrand: No, it wasn't.

Casey Riley: I wanted to ask you a question about the name, which we're referring to as NIIPA. Tell me about the distinction between Native, Indian, and Inuit. How was that designation made, and would that designation still cohere in a contemporary Canadian context? I think as we're talking about all the different ways that we denote culture and identity and affiliation, it's valuable to historicize it and to hear a little bit about it from your research.

Rhéanne Chartrand: The name is a bit redundant in some sense, but I also think Native was the common term used by Indigenous folks in referring to one another, whereas Indian and Inuit were more legal terms. Métis obviously being the third in the group of defined Indigenous identities in the Canadian context. I think it had to do with these photographers recognizing that there was already a legacy of Indigenous image making, and that some of the more established or historical Indigenous photographers were Indian and Inuit. So, I think that might have been why they came up with this sort of ... what's the word I'm looking for?

Casey Riley: They amalgamated the two.

Rhéanne Chartrand: The amalgamated name for the organization.

Casey Riley: As you know, in the course of the Mia project on Native photography we've been talking about ways to identify status through federally issued identity cards.

Rhéanne Chartrand: Indian status cards. Yes.

Casey Riley: Yes, that the federal governments in the United States and Canada issue to Indigenous people as a qualifier or a marker of affiliation. I was just curious if NIIPA's name was also a political statement because we are still in the early to mid-1980s, and we're still talking about a time of activism and organization around identity as it pertains to Indigenous peoples.

I'm looking at this wonderful photograph of many NIIPA members seated around the television, which appeared in an article you wrote on NIIPA. It struck me as I was reading your article that women were very important to this organization, perhaps even central to it. I wonder if you could talk about that, because that's not something that is explored in this article, and I find it interesting that the Photographer's Union and the Hamilton Regional Indian Friendship Centre, as well as the Native Women's Centre, all had a part in the establishment of NIIPA.

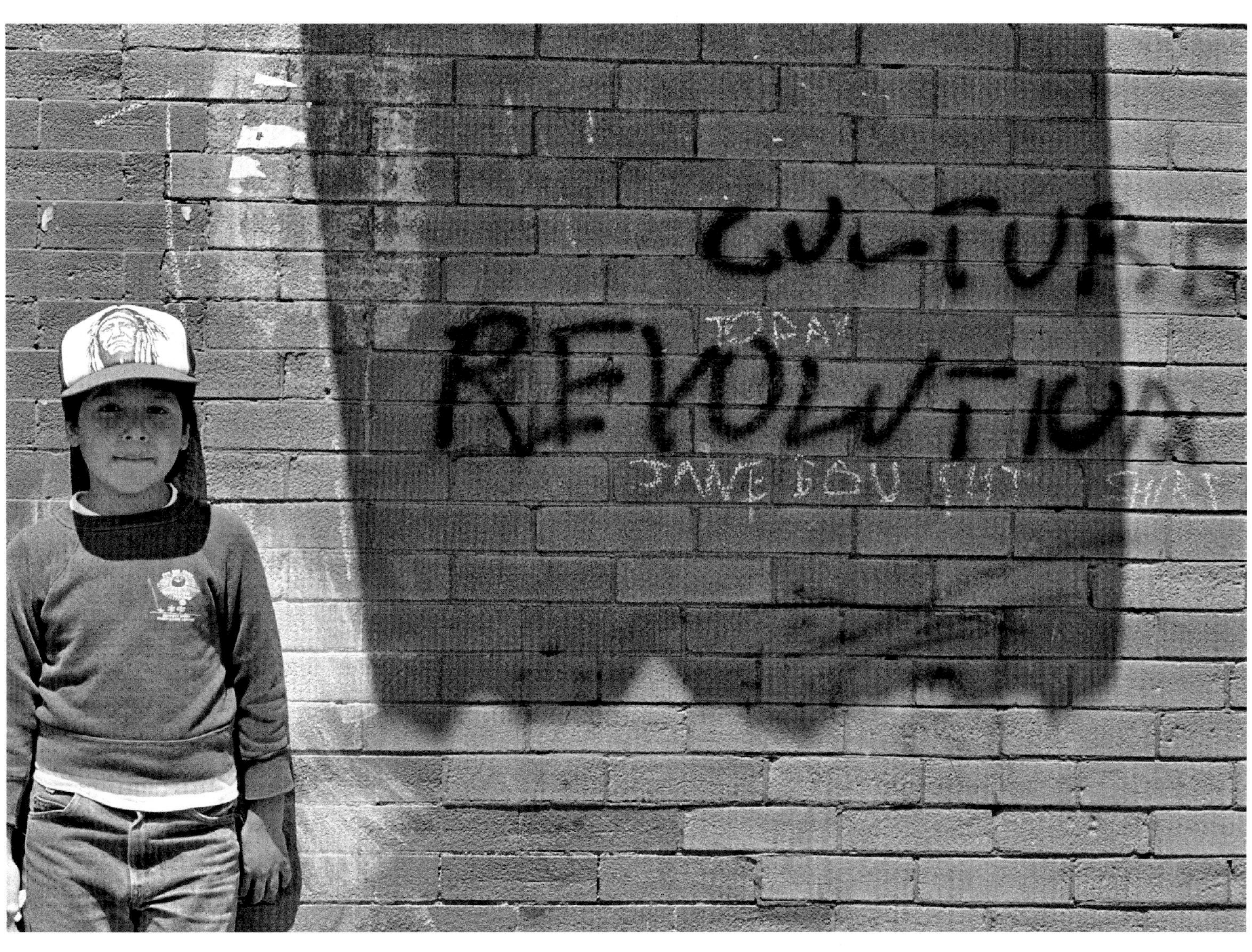

Jeffrey M. Thomas
Urban-Iroquois / Onondaga, born 1956
Culture Revolution Today Toronto, ON, GPS:
43.6493 -79.393967, 1984-2021
Archival pigment print
Courtesy of the artist
© Jeffrey M. Thomas

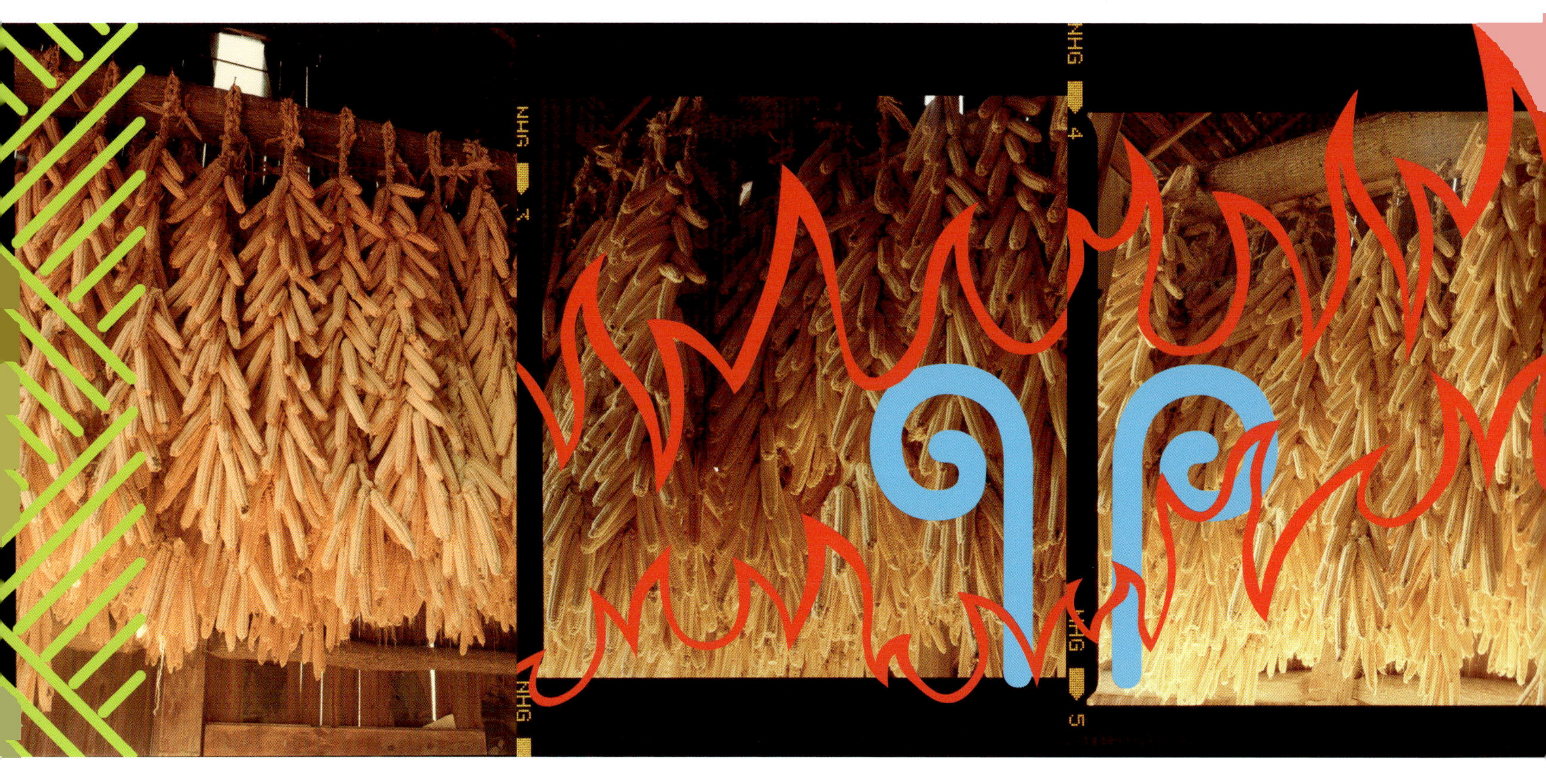

Jolene Rickard
Tuscarora Nation, Turtle Clan, born 1956
Scorched Earth 1779: Gayogo̱hó:nǫ' Return, 2023
Inkjet print
Courtesy of the artist

Rhéanne Chartrand: Yes, absolutely. NIIPA kind of started through a program run by Lynne Sharman, who at the time was the director of the Photographer's Union, and who found Yvonne. Yvonne had produced a student exhibition of her photographic works, and Lynne saw it and said, "I want you to come work for me." So, Lynne brought Yvonne in to work at the Photo Union as an employee. Then this idea kind of came about to host a conference of Native photography. Eventually they decided they needed more help, and so they got money to support Brenda Mitten's role. Brenda came in to work with Yvonne and to produce this first ever conference of Native photography in Canada. When the conference happened and it was clear that there was an interest amongst the photographers present to establish a photography collective, and then subsequently an arts service organization, Brenda and Yvonne became the cofounders and codirectors.

So yes, you're right, women have led NIIPA from the beginning and have continued to lead NIIPA throughout its entire history. When Brenda stepped away in 1987, Yvonne stayed on as the sole director until 1998. Then after Yvonne left, Carol Hill became the administrative director for NIIPA until its closing around 2005/2006.

Women have been central to NIIPA's story, and they have definitely been the ones doing the care taking and keeping the doors open, sometimes at the expense of their own salaries or caring for their families. Really, they're owed a lot of gratitude for fighting to keep NIIPA alive. NIIPA itself was born out of that conference and the photographers present. That's why Jolene Rickard was a founding member. That's why Shelly Niro was a founding member. These women played a role in establishing and growing NIIPA.

Casey Riley: You noted the sacrifice of their salaries and I'm having two conflicting thoughts. On the one hand, there are these incredible women who have always been leaders and matriarchs and the centers of their communities. At the same time, we know that women are historically more easily exploited for our free labor. I wonder what you think about that, or I wonder if there's a kind of confluence of things happening that tell a bigger story about women as organizers, and the sacrifices we make to do that labor. More specifically, I wonder if you can connect that to Indigenous histories as well or contextualize it within colonization.

Rhéanne Chartrand: Indeed, these things are interconnected. As the NIIPA archives show, fairly soon after the first conference, they made the decision to incorporate and establish the organization. But they actually had to wait a few months to incorporate, because Yvonne was only nineteen and couldn't legally take on that responsibility (in order to become an executive director of an organization in Canada you must be over nineteen). When they did establish themselves, funding became a perpetual issue—funding was always a problem for NIIPA.

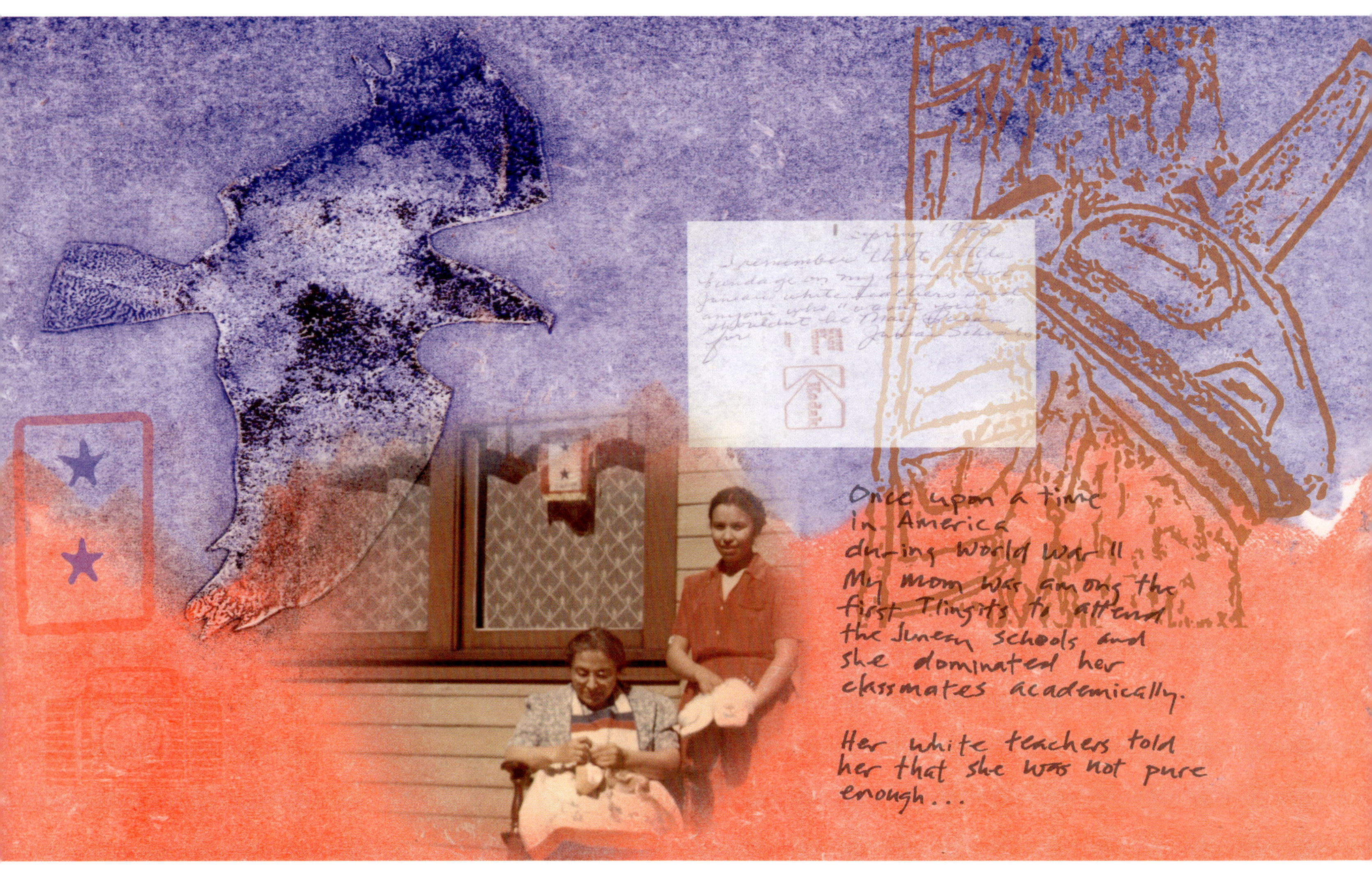

Larry McNeil
Dakl'aweidi K'eet Gooshi H'it, Killer Whale
Fin House Tlingit / Nisga'a, born 1955
Once Upon a Time in America, 2002
from Fly by Night Mythology series
Courtesy of the artist
© Larry McNeil

I don't think that it helped that the leadership was female, because as you rightly point out, there probably was a lack of recognition of the hard labor involved in getting an organization going, coupled with the lack of funding that was available to Indigenous organizations meant that these women leaders were always forced into a position of having to choose between putting food on the table for their families or making the vision of a photography collective a reality.

That's why, in part, Brenda left in 1987: She had young children and couldn't get a stable income from NIIPA because of the broader funding issues for Indigenous art service organizations. So, Brenda actually left because NIIPA couldn't offer her a stable salary. When Yvonne had her daughter in 1990, she only took a six-month maternity leave because NIIPA needed her so badly that she had to come back.

Yvonne jokingly always says that she raised her daughter Shannon under her desk at NIIPA. Shannon was always at the NIIPA office, and so Yvonne was playing mom as well as executive director at the same time. At various points in NIIPA's history through the nineties, Yvonne had to reduce her salary because there wasn't enough money to keep the organization afloat. So she would reduce her salary to help keep the doors open. NIIPA funding issues are symptomatic of a wider lack of support for Indigenous arts at that time.

Casey Riley: And photography specifically.

Rhéanne Chartrand: And photography specifically, yeah.

And then how that trickles down to the female Indigenous experience of having to constantly juggle responsibilities to community, to your family, and then to doing something that you think is important.

Casey Riley: This is so fascinating to hear about; women were uniquely positioned to serve as leaders in this realm, and at the same time, were expected to make sacrifices in a modern economic construct that weren't necessarily advantageous or fair to them or their families.

Rhéanne Chartrand: Yes, absolutely.

Casey Riley: I guess my next question is, why Hamilton? Maybe even more importantly, why did this happen in Canada and not the United States? What are some of the factors that you attribute to the success of the establishment of this organization, as difficult as it was, as it started there.

Rhéanne Chartrand: I'll quote Yvonne when she says, "Why not Hamilton?" In terms of NIIPA starting here, Hamilton has a strong union culture, and the Photographer's Union, we can't leave them out of the equation—they were NIIPA's launching pad. NIIPA grew out of what the Photographer's Union was doing, and eventually eclipsed the Union itself, which didn't exist very long. Certainly Lynne Sharman bringing in Yvonne and then Brenda jumpstarted things, and then cosponsoring that first conference ... but I want to give credit where credit is due: The Native photographers present at that conference themselves made the choice to establish NIIPA.

A lot of the founding members were practicing photographers, and many were also from Six Nations, which is just outside of Hamilton. So, there was also that connection. In terms of it happening in Canada, Brenda was able to leverage the national Indian Friendship Centre network to call up the centres and ask, "Hey, who are the Native photographers in your community?" And use that kind of communication chain to find photographers across Canada and then bring them to Hamilton. Right from the outset, the intention was always to be cross-border, and maybe you didn't see that necessarily reflected in the first conference and those that were present at it, but certainly as you move into '86, '87, '88, and most certainly into the nineties, you see the presence of Indigenous photographers from the US as part of NIIPA's core membership.

I think that just kind of came through engaging with photographers south of the border through attending events in the United States and bringing them into the fold. I think the reason why, perhaps, NIIPA started in Canada and not in the US, is despite the funding challenges that NIIPA experienced, there definitely was (and is) more public funding and support for Indigenous art or Indigenous peoples in Canada than there is in the US. So, despite the struggles, I think perhaps it was easier to launch the organization in Canada than it would've been in the United States.

Casey Riley: It's interesting to hear you confirm that because that was my suspicion. You were talking about the networks that were so crucial to the formation of this group, and in our council, we've talked about those networks and about how there's this thriving parallel ecosystem that's been self-sustaining and self-nurturing and growing over the decades in Native photography. I wonder, as you've talked to some of your counterparts, or some of the early founders about this work, what it was like for them? I mean, they reached out to people through their friendship centres, but what did that look like? Were they driving? Were they calling people on the phone? I mean, this is the 1980s, so it's not like you could send an email or a text.

Rhéanne Chartrand: This is pre-internet.

Casey Riley: Yeah.

Rhéanne Chartrand: Brenda would cold call friendship centres and just simply ask, "Who are the Native photographers in your community?"

Casey Riley: Ah, okay.

Rheanne Chartrand: And then slowly but surely, names and contact info for Indigenous photographers started to trickle in.

Casey Riley: Got it.

Rhéanne Chartrand: There were some member photographers that were a bit more established and well known who had connections with other photographers. So what NIIPA did, what that first conference did, was bring together all these photographers working in different parts of the country, thinking that they were the only ones doing photography. If you look at the archives, you see that there's this common response of, "I thought I was the only one doing this, and now I realize that there's actually the whole community of photographers that are doing this work."

So, NIIPA was an incubator, launchpad, and network; it brought everybody together, it created opportunities for conversation, exchanging ideas on photographic practices and techniques, approaches to image making, but then it also acted as a launchpad for a lot of photographers who were lesser known, or photographers who were still emerging. NIIPA really did support that emerging group, not just in terms of its membership, but also creating employment opportunities for Indigenous folks in the region. It also helped launch a lot of people's careers; former members now work for other Indigenous art service organizations, some work at galleries now, and others work in film and TV and radio broadcasting.

Casey Riley: I was going to say, or journalism.

Rhéanne Chartrand: NIIPA really was this incubator, launchpad, and network for a lot of early image makers working in photojournalism. I think that's what's so special about it because it wasn't just focused on advocacy. NIIPA wasn't only focused on, as their first organizational objective says, "to promote this positive, realistic, and contemporary image of Native peoples," which is an amazing objective, but it was also about building capacity and building relationships. So, it's interesting when you look at the early members, some of these folks still are collaborators to this day. They are still friends. They've continued to show together. You know what I mean?

Casey Riley: Yes.

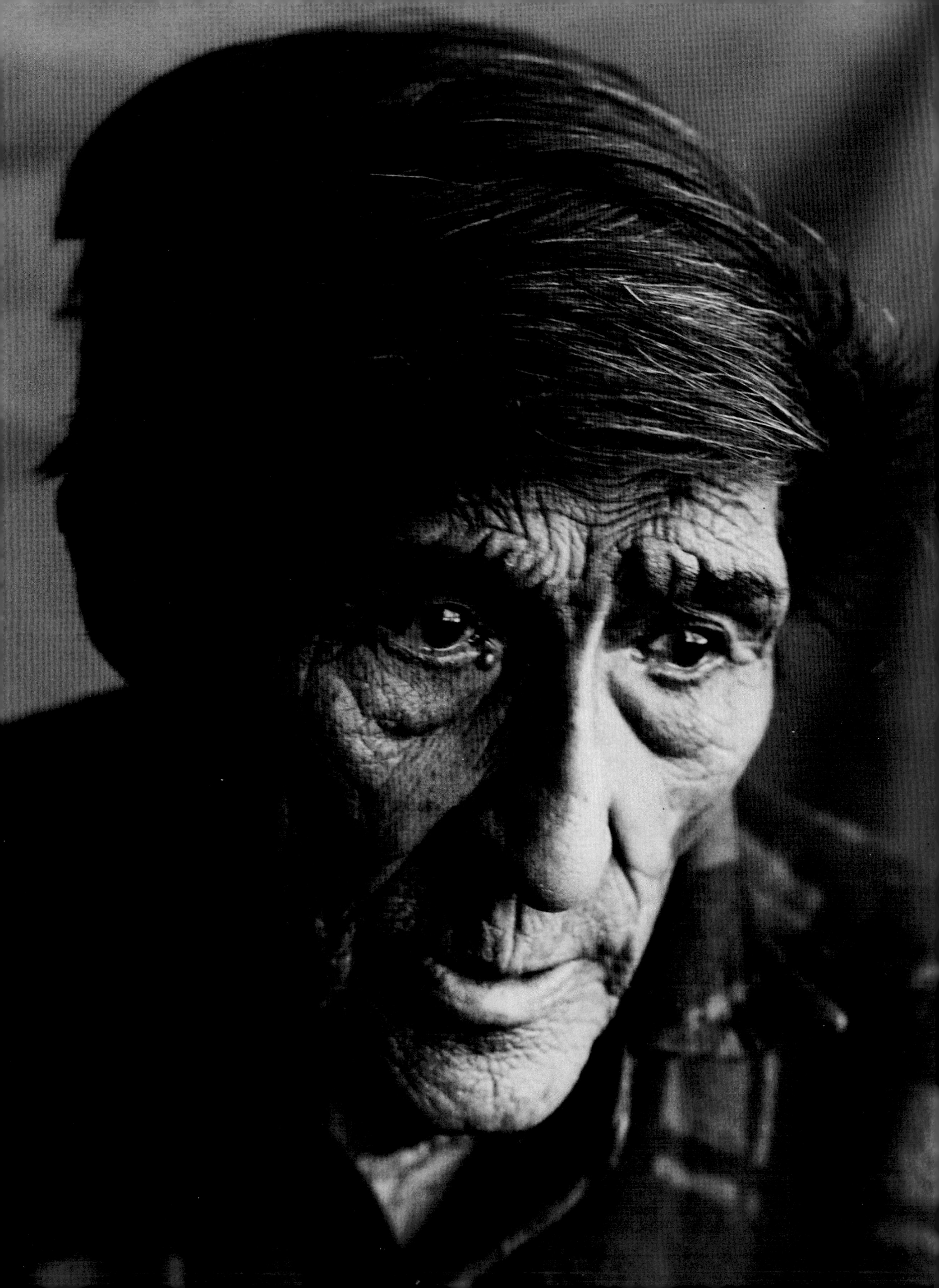

Rhéanne Chartrand: So, those relationships that started in the eighties, particularly in those early years of NIIPA, have actually only strengthened over time.

Casey Riley: I love that too. I mean, knowing the deep history that exists between Shelley and Jolene from decades of literally working together in the trenches to establish these important opportunities and networks and to keep them thriving.

Rhéanne Chartrand: Yeah, Shelley worked for NIIPA in the eighties, and Jolene was an active member at the same time.

Casey Riley: I love how you defined the activities or the identity for NIIPA, in addition to its very high minded mission of presenting themselves and their communities, but also this very pragmatic function, which is, "Okay, we're being left out of all of these opportunities and spaces, so it's a safe space to grow and get feedback and portfolio sessions and technical review, and then it's a launchpad in that for folks who are interested in employing or learning more about Native photographic practice or just playing who's out there working, they can attend VISIONS or another conference or another NIIPA conversation."

This idea of networking was so forward thinking for its time. As you stress in your research, that kind of collective action wasn't necessarily something that a lot of professional photographers around the world were doing. I mean, there's Magnum, right? There's the Kamoinge workshop here in the US that would be another close parallel for African American artists and artists of the African diaspora here in the states. But it strikes me that there's really something special about NIIPA.

Rhéanne Chartrand: NIIPA was ahead of its time in many ways, but I also want to historically situate it, because we also know that there is this longer Indigenous photographic history that has been ignored.

Casey Riley: Exactly.

Rhéanne Chartrand: So, there were those senior "grandfather" photographers that existed that gave NIIPA a precedent for the photographic practices it wished to support, and a basis on which to build. Some of them were actually involved in NIIPA's founding, like Murray McKenzie, who was the organization's first board president.

Casey Riley: I was going to say, like Murray McKenzie. Or Larry McNeil, right?

Murray McKenzie
Cree, 1927-2007
Daniel Spence, Lonesome Trapper, age 102, 1984
from Native Studies series
Gelatin silver print
Courtesy of Indigenous Art Collection, Crown-Indigenous Relations and Northern Affairs Canada 306226

Rhéanne Chartrand: Larry was involved. He got involved in '86, and then in the nineties became NIIPA's board president. So, he was an important NIIPA champion through the late eighties and early nineties.

Casey Riley: Right.

Rhéanne Chartrand: Some noteworthy Indigenous photographers have played a role in NIIPA's history, like Murray McKenzie. He's a bridge; he's a link to that older generation of photographers who are doing community photojournalism, social documentary work. But the beautiful thing about NIIPA is the work itself and the works that the member photographers were producing literally run the gamut in terms of styles, techniques, and approaches to image making.

Casey Riley: Yes.

Rhéanne Chartrand: You can't pigeonhole it, even though that's oftentimes what happened with the funders. The funders would simply say: "Oh, you're doing social documentary photography. It's social history. It's not interesting. It's not artistically rigorous enough." And I really feel like that criticism is frankly, prejudicial and misplaced, because as we see, for example, say you take one photographer in the course of their time with NIIPA, and you'll observe this willingness to experiment and change creative direction and to adapt to new techniques and to try things out and to eventually find their artistic voice, to find their aesthetic. You see that with photographers like Greg Staats or Jeff Thomas. These photographers dipped in and out of NIIPA, but you see changes in their work, aesthetic shifts in their practice. I think why NIIPA is so special is because they would do photo-critiques at conferences. They would provide darkroom facilities to their members. They would show members' works in their gallery space and invite folks in from the community. So it was, as you say, this tool to develop one's skills, both technically, conceptually, and artistically.

Casey Riley: I'm just looking at the photographs of Jeff Thomas and Dorothy Chocolate in front of their work and thinking about the process of receiving feedback from one's peers and how crucial that is for any artist's practice, but it is really an important part of the photographic community and tradition here in North America. I like what you were just talking about in terms of the inclusivity of picture making, for lack of a better term, that existed in NIIPA. At the same time, it strikes me from what you've written that one of the key aims for NIIPA was also

Dorothy Chocolate Carseen
Tłı̨chǫ, born 1959
Judith Charlo carrying a hide,
T'èɂehdaà (Dettah) NWT, 1988
TIFF digital image from original
35mm colour slide
NWT Archives/©GNWT.
Dept of PW&S/G-1995-001-2774
© Dorothy Chocolate Carseen

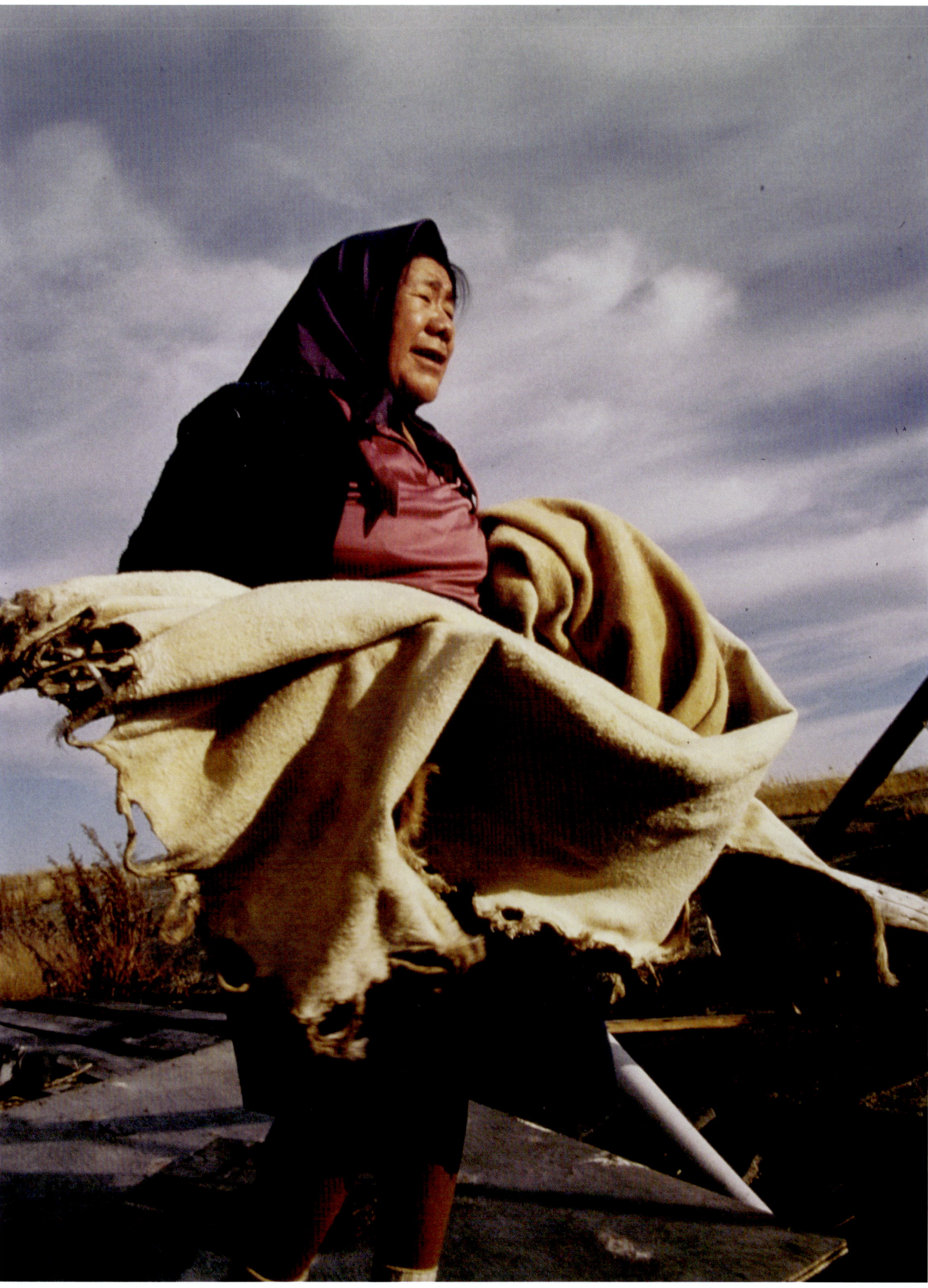

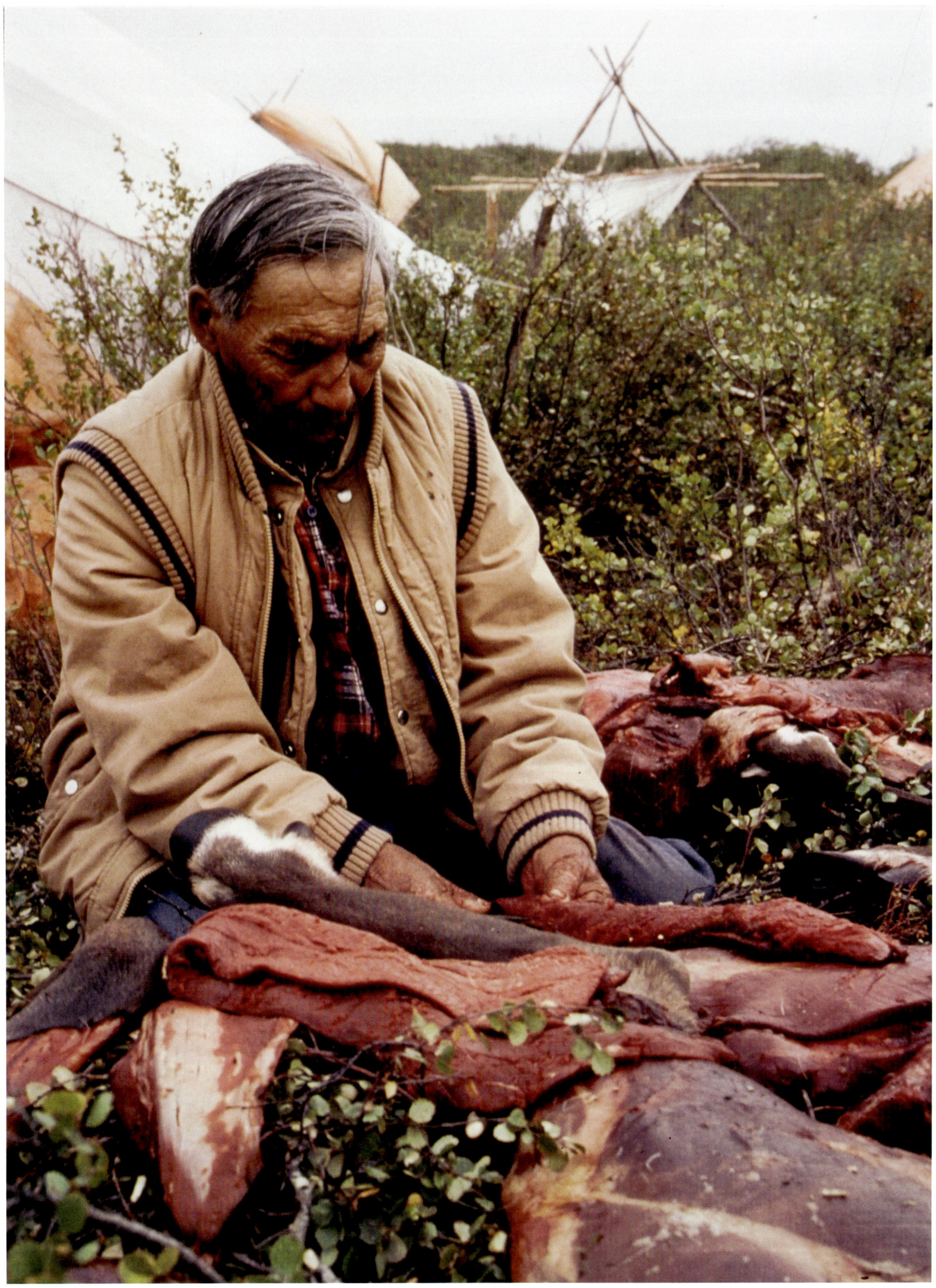

to assert Indigenous photography as art, as something that was a creative artistic practice. I wonder if you could contextualize some of the challenges, because you and I were talking before we started recording about the kind of layers of barriers and marginalization that presented challenges to the photography community when they were beginning this endeavor.

Rhéanne Chartrand: I mean, you know as well as I do that prior to the late eighties, photography was not very widely supported by mainstream art institutions. There were a handful of photographers that maybe were having mainstream success, but you didn't really start seeing huge acquisitions of photographic works until, I'd say, the nineties, and much less by Native photographers. They were not even on the map of mainstream institutions, yet there was (and remains) this image bank within American visual culture of Indigenous peoples, and Indigenous photographers were constantly finding themselves butting up against this image bank.

I do think that some of the early motivations for establishing NIIPA were to redress stereotypes and misconceptions, not just historical, but also contemporaneous to their moment in terms of the homeless Indian or the "drunken Indian" or misrepresentations of political movements (i.e., the American Indian Movement). NIIPA members were really set on wanting to represent themselves, to use the camera in a way that was empowering, and to some within the mainstream art world, that wasn't rigorous enough or it wasn't "art" enough. I think that NIIPA really pushed back on that in order to have the work of their members taken seriously as art.

The way they did that was by building capacity and building up technical skills, actually showing people how to properly use equipment to refine their practice, and to offer critique to one another like, "Okay, this is good, but you can make it better," or "You can try this," or "Use our facilities to test this out." So, when we get to the nineties, there is a critical mass of Indigenous photographers who are producing quality photographic works and making that statement is no longer tenable, but still they're being marginalized.

I really don't think that it was until after I'd say, the mid '90s, that you really start to see the mainstream art world actually turning their head and looking at what was happening in Indigenous photography. But there had already been ten years of work to build that capacity up. As we know from Mia's exhibition *In Our Hands: Native Photography, 1890 to Now,* there's a much longer legacy of exceptional photographic work by Native photographers, it's just that those photographers of earlier generations were working in isolation. That's what distinguishes NIIPA: it brought folks together. These photographers were no longer isolated, they had a community, and that's what makes NIIPA so special.

Dorothy Chocolate Carseen
Tłı̨chǫ, born 1959
Victor Rabesca skinning a caribou at Gots'ǫkàtì
(Mesa Lake) NWT, 1988(Dettah) NWT, 1988
TIFF digital image from
original 35mm colour slide
NWT Archives/©GNWT.
Dept of PW&S/G-1995-001-2774
© Dorothy Chocolate Carseen

Casey Riley: You said something just a moment ago about community that made me think about some of the challenges that still exist for artists, especially artists of color and women, basically any non-white male artists, and that is the matter of access to studio space, the financial means to have access to a darkroom, or today a high-end digital camera and so on. It sounded to me like maybe there was also some sharing of resources or teaching people about where they could develop their work. Could you speak to some of those practices and how NIIPA supported its members in that way?

Rhéanne Chartrand: Members would provide workshops for other members. Shan Goshorn would come up and do workshops on hand tinting; Bert Crowfoot would come and do workshops in photojournalism and event photography; Shelley would do workshops on infrared photography. So they were not only members of this organization, but they were also offering their knowledge and expertise back to each other through the workshops that they would be invited to do at the NIIPA space. So, yeah, they were kind of collaboratively building capacity.

Casey Riley: Were there studio spaces or darkrooms that were specifically for members?

Rhéanne Chartrand: Yep.

Casey Riley: Amazing.

Rhéanne Chartrand: Members could rent out NIIPA's darkrooms to produce their work.

Casey Riley: Okay. That's really important too, in terms of building an infrastructure for their practice.

Rhéanne Chartrand: Yeah, NIIPA operated a darkroom facility in all the locations that it operated from. It had three locations over its lifetime, and at each, Yvonne's husband built a darkroom. NIIPA was kind of divided up into three areas: the front area that was the gallery, the office administration area, and then the darkroom facilities that could be rented out.

NIIPA also solicited sponsorship from photography companies. In the early nineties when they were working on *See Through Our Eyes: A Native Perspective*, Kodak and Lowepro USA came in as sponsors for that project. Oftentimes, NIIPA had better luck getting support from the corporate world and, at least here in Canada, from the Secretary of State or Employment and Immigration Canada as opposed to from actual arts funders, which is kind of the sad part of the story. The arts funders, or art councils, really didn't support NIIPA to the extent that they probably needed to remain viable forever.

But despite all those challenges, NIIPA existed for twenty years, so they're still one of the longest existing Indigenous art service organizations in Canada. They will soon be eclipsed by others, but nevertheless, up until a few years ago, they were the second oldest organization, even though they no longer exist. That's significant.

Casey Riley: I'm glad you clarified that about the infrastructure surrounding NIIPA. It's nothing short of revolutionary.

One thing that stuck out to me when I was reading your article was, in talking about acquisitions of work for the Visions project, was that you noted it wasn't possible to acquire Jolene's work because she was a US-based artist. To what extent did you see this arbitrary division based on colonial national boundaries?

Rhéanne Chartrand: Yeah.

Casey Riley: These national boundaries don't necessarily represent the relationships or affiliations among Native people involved with NIIPA. So I wonder if you could speak to some of those challenges, if they existed beyond that example, and what are some of the creative ways that NIIPA members overcame those challenges?

Rhéanne Chartrand: There are a couple of examples: One is going back to that first conference, VISIONS, out of which the organization was born, and VISIONS also birthed *Visions* the exhibition, and that was organized with help from Rick Hill.

Casey Riley: Right.

Rhéanne Chartrand: So, if you look at the archive, Rick Hill's work wasn't acquired either, nor was Simon Brascoupé's. That had to do with the fact that they both worked for the Indian Art Centre (now called the Indigenous Art Centre) at CIRNAC at that time, so it was a conflict of interest to purchase their work. Because Jolene was based in the United States (and still is), she was also impacted. In subsequent years, the Centre ended up acquiring Rick's work, but Simon's was never acquired, nor was Jolene's. That was because at that time, they only collected Canadian artists. They did not collect Indigenous artists from the US. That mandate has since changed. That's why now with all the photographic works we are currently stewarding at the McMaster Museum of Art, some of the US members works can actually be advanced to CIRNAC for donation/acquisition because their mandate has changed. So, that's very exciting.

Going back to what you're talking about with the US members, that was a persistent issue for NIIPA in terms of getting public funds, because all the funders were Canadian, yet half of their membership and half of the board by the nineties were American. That was always to their detriment, in some sense, in terms of getting funding from Canadian sources. They still fought around it. They said: "This border doesn't apply to us. Our community is across Turtle

Island and we're going to make it work." And what they would oftentimes do, especially around the early nineties, is they would host sessions in Canada and then go host sessions in the US.

With respect to the *See Through Our Eyes* project, there were working committee meetings in Canada, and working committee meetings in the US, and then they would bring all of that together and that shaped the nature of the project. They also tried to help fund folks to come up from the states too, where they could, so they were always trying to work across that border. A lot of folks have the Jay Treaty (1794) too, so they did have the capacity to move back and forth freely. So they kind of just threw their middle fingers up to the government, I guess. But certainly, for NIIPA as an organization, it made it challenging to get consistent stable funding because the Canadian funders were saying, "Well, half your members are American, so why are we funding you?" It was an ongoing issue, but they just simply forged ahead. They didn't care.

Casey Riley: This is another way in which they are path breakers or visionaries, because they as an artist collective were saying, "The national boundaries that you are ascribing to us don't apply."

Rhéanne Chartrand: Exactly.

Casey Riley: And eventually, it seems, our respective governments listened.

Rhéanne Chartrand: It took a long time …

Casey Riley: Yeah, but again, this is a way in which NIIPA's professional practices added up to advocacy, intentionally or not, and they actually shone a light on better practices for the 21st century.

Rhéanne Chartrand: Certainly, I mean, the American photographers' works could have been collected by CIRNAC back in the eighties, but now here they are collecting it from archives in 2022.

Casey Riley: Yes.

Rheanne Chartrand: To their good fortune, really. Yvonne was able to save all that work when NIIPA closed. Otherwise, all that work would've been lost to history— a huge detriment to our understanding of photographic practices in Canada and in the US.

Casey Riley: Can you talk a little bit about the knowledge keepers and sharers in this dynamic? Aside from you, who's been keeping NIIPA alive in public memory and who's been stewarding this since the organization came to a close?

Rhéanne Chartrand: I would say, first and foremost, Yvonne, maybe not necessarily publicly, but certainly behind the scenes all these years. Once NIIPA closed, she took it upon herself, along with Carol Hill and Martin Loft, to divvy up NIIPA's assets amongst themselves. But the only assets that really survived were the photographs that Yvonne saved in crates, some ephemera and exhibition materials, and paper documentation. Carol kept a lot of organizational documents too. So, we certainly owe a great debt of gratitude to Yvonne for not only saving all this archival material, but also for saving over 350 photographs that she stored in crates and waited for somebody to come along to, and for lack of a better term, give a shit, to start poking around and asking questions.

Yvonne has, without a doubt, been my right hand, my rock, the person to whom I go. The second phase of the project would not have happened without Yvonne bringing it to my attention that she had all this archival material saved. The way she went about it was so nonchalant. We met shortly before the opening of *#nofilterneeded*, which was the first exhibition on NIIPA I curated. We got in touch through Greg Staats, and I owe Greg many thanks for connecting us. Yvonne ended up coming to the opening of *#nofilterneeded*, and casually mentioned "Oh, I have some stuff I'd like to show you. Let me know when you have time to come and see what I have."

It took about a year before it was possible to get together and visit her about what she'd saved. When I saw it all, I was just completely blown away. Here I thought I was one and done with *#nofilterneeded*. I've shone the light on NIIPA, now everyone knows about it, and then Yvonne throws this massive curve ball/gold mine of art and archives at me, and I'm just like, "Oh, I'm not even close to being done here."

So, I've really been supported by the members themselves. Yvonne, first and foremost, in terms of realizing *NIIPA 20/20*, but even being able to turn to Brenda Mitten. Brenda provided her archives, Greg Staats provided his archives, and Carol Hill provided her archives as mentioned before. Once we did *#nofilterneeded*, other members started reaching out to me, stating, "I was involved with NIIPA." Larry McNeil's been very helpful, too, in terms of connecting with US members. I really owe a debt of gratitude to the members themselves in terms of me being able to go to them and say: "You know what? I think this is when you were involved. Do you recall this?" They say memory fades with age, but for the most part, the alumni have very vivid memories of their time with NIIPA.

Another champion of NIIPA from day one is Martin Loft. Martin Loft is probably the one person that keeps the spirit and memory of NIIPA alive in a public way, and he's always willing to talk about his affiliations with NIIPA. In terms of US members, I would say Larry McNeil is really very good at celebrating NIIPA publicly. He will occasionally post his NIIPA press card on his Facebook. Because those two individuals are really active on social media, I would say they definitely do the most talking about NIIPA publicly. But certainly, offline, every member in some way, once you bring it up, has a story to tell about NIIPA and their involvement, and they are very willing to talk about it.

I don't think the project would've ever unfolded the way it had, especially this second half, if not for the members themselves. Even Shan Goshorn, whom I was in communication with before she passed, was going to be involved in the second exhibition. She was cited in the first project (*#nofilterneeded*) as an early US member. We were never able to really get together some work of hers to include in the project at that time, but that's what's so beautiful about what Yvonne saved, because now we have work by Shan that we were able to include in *NIIPA 20/20*.

As Yvonne often shared with me, "We didn't have grandfather photographers ... we had to find them or create them." She sees Murray McKenzie and Larry McNeil as grandfather photographers. Having Robin Armour, a photo technician from the Yukon Archives, come and present on George Johnston at the VISIONS Conference in '85 was exciting for them because everyone realized, "Wow, there's actually a longer legacy to our photographic practice." This is something I've been thinking through a lot in writing this comprehensive history of NIIPA, trying to position it within this longer timeline.

I think what really stands out to me, and I think even *In Our Hands: Native Photography, 1890 to Now* at Mia really shows this: that we have our own art history. We don't have to reference the Western canon. We don't have to talk about Indigenous photography in reference to colonial portraiture. We don't have to do that anymore. There's enough of our own photographers, our own grandfather/grandparent photographers to actually work in an Indigenous space. I think that's what's so important to me about NIIPA and why I care so much. I have a lot of Native friends/peers that are photographers who do event photography, photojournalism, whatever it may be. At one point I asked a few of them, "Do you know what NIIPA is? Have you heard of NIIPA?" And no one knew. I was so shocked. It kind of became my personal mission to make sure my peers know about NIIPA, to share with them that there is a precedent for contemporary practice and contemporary ways of working together.

NIIPA provides that precedent. I feel like that's why its organizational history matters so much, because it's twenty years of Indigenous art history that was completely overlooked, and we need it in order to understand contemporary practice. That's what motivates me, and it's why I'm doing this work.

Casey Riley: Rhéanne, thank you. I think that's the perfect place to end.

Rhéanne Chartrand: Thank you so much.

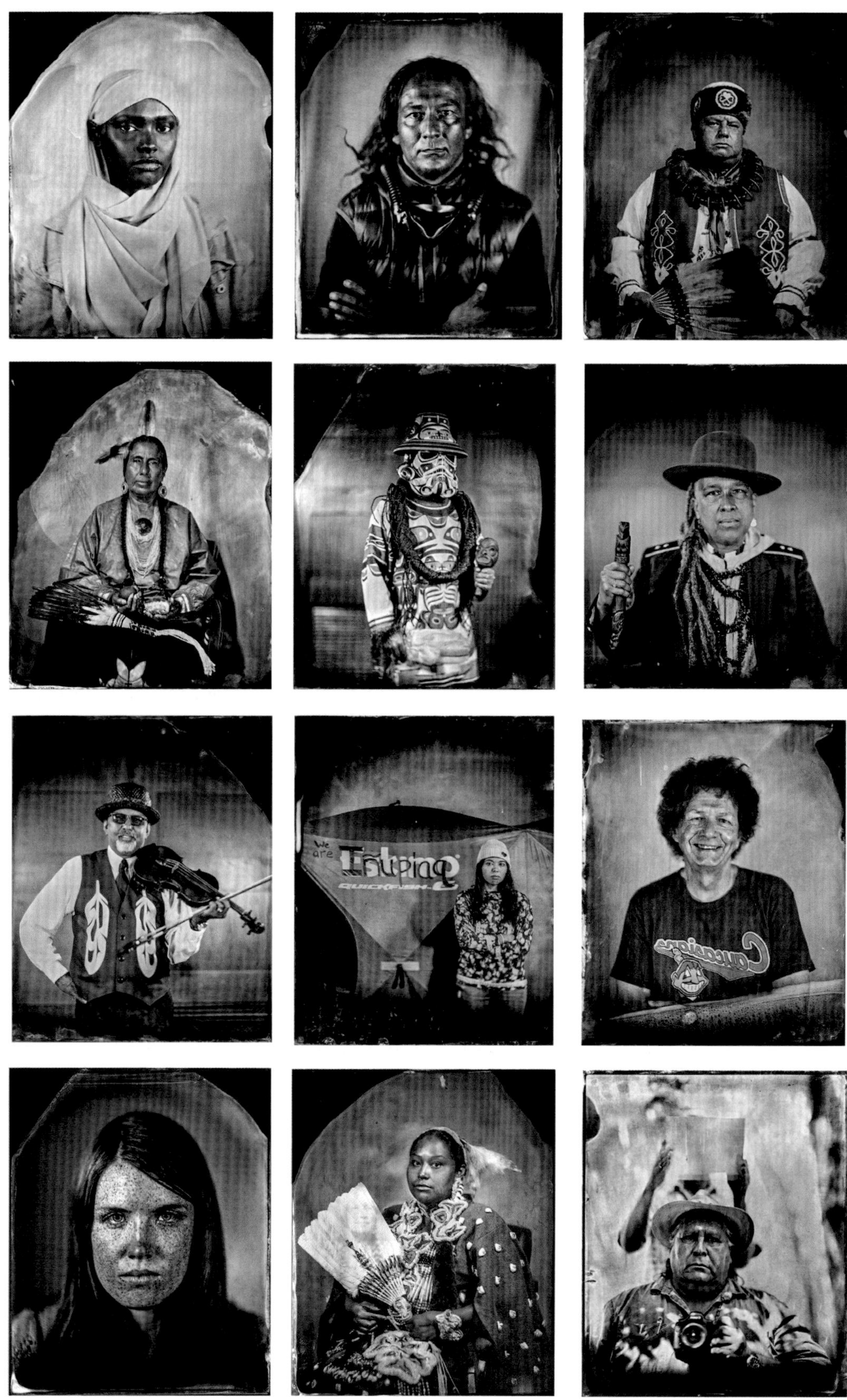

Fig. 1. Grid of CIPX images representative of 10 years of the project (Courtesy of the author).

ON TEN YEARS OF THE CRITICAL INDIGENOUS PHOTOGRAPHIC EXCHANGE

BY WILL WILSON

WHAT IF INDIANS INVENTED PHOTOGRAPHY? What if photography's capacity to indexically register virtually all that comes before it was developed by Indigenous people? How would photography's capacity to stop time and fix the natural world be employed? How would communities that have historically used oral tradition to recall and transmit cultural knowledge, art, literature, and law implement this technology?

These questions and the perspectives they raise frame my understanding of two photographic histories foundational to my practice. In the first place are photographs taken of Diné people during the Long Walk period at Bosque Redondo. Known as *Hwéeldi* to the Diné this place and time of suffering became the stage for the first photographs of the Diné. These photographs attest to the resilience of a people who overcame state-sponsored attempts at ethnic cleansing and negotiated a treaty allowing them to return to Diné Bikeyah, their ancestral homelands. I have often pondered the power relations inherent in the making of these "portraits" and imagined the testimony their subjects might convey. In the second place are photographs that make clear that foundational agreements establishing the United States were made in conjunction with Indigenous national representatives. These photographs, commonly referred to as "Delegation Photography," are a testament to Indigenous sovereignty, and the solemn agreements Indigenous nations entered with a settler-colonial state. Significantly, both the Diné *Hwéeldi* photographs and the delegation photography were produced with the wet-plate collodion photography process. Considering both these early American photographic series or archives through this lens transforms their meaning and opens space to return agency and subjectivity to the Indigenous people they represent.

So how does one set out to establish and engage in a portrait photography project based on this critical Indigenous framework? For me, the answer came in the summer of 2012, during the Santa Fe Indian Market where I proposed the following:

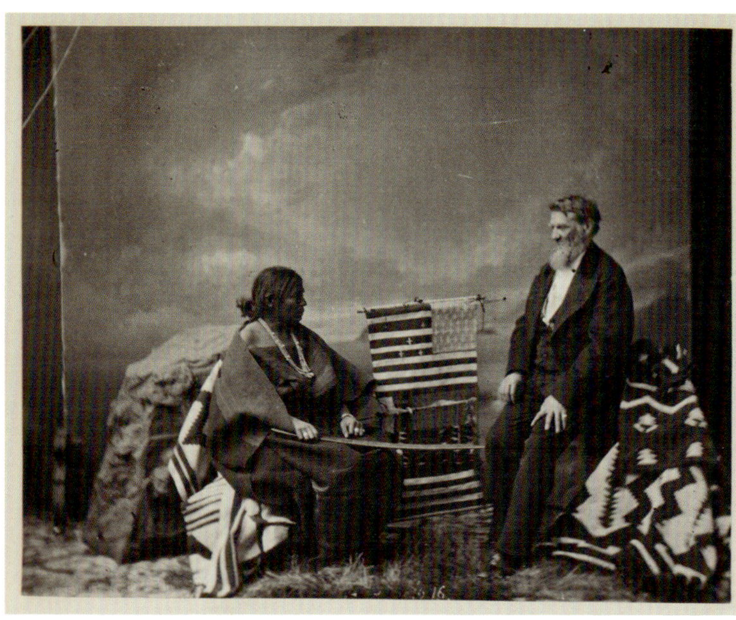

Fig. 2 *Juanita (Navajo) in Native dress and blanket with weaving implements, and Governor William Frederick Milton Arny*, 1874, printed ca. 1900, platinum print. (Courtesy of Amon Carter Museum of American Art, Fort Worth, Texas P1967.2585).

"As an Indigenous artist working in the twenty-first century, employing media that range from historical photographic processes to the randomization and projection of complex visual systems within virtual environments, I am impatient with the way that American culture remains enamored of one particular moment in a photographic exchange between Euro-American and Aboriginal American societies: the decades from 1907 to 1930 when photographer Edward S. Curtis produced *The North American Indian*.[71] For many people, even today, Native people remain frozen in time in Curtis photos. Other Native artists have produced photographic responses to Curtis's oeuvre, usually using humor as a catalyst to melt the lacquered romanticism of these stereotypical portraits.[72] I seek to do something different. I intend to challenge the documentary mission of Curtis from the standpoint of a twenty-first century Indigenous, trans-customary, cultural practitioner. I want to supplant Curtis's Settler gaze with a contemporary vision of 'Native North America.'"

In that same address, I proposed to create a body of photographic inquiry that will stimulate a critical dialogue and reflection around the historic and contemporary "photographic exchange" as it pertains to Native Americans. My aim was and is to convene Indigenous artists, art professionals, government leaders, as well as the public, to engage in the performative ritual that is the studio portrait. This experience would be intensified and refined by the use of large format (8 x 10) wet plate collodion studio photography. This beautifully alchemic photographic process dramatically contributed to our collective understanding of Native American people and, in doing so, our American identity.

In August 2012, at the New Mexico Museum of Art in Santa Fe, I initiated the Critical Indigenous Photographic Exchange (CIPX). This was the initial spark for an ongoing intervention into the history of photography. Throughout the Critical Indigenous Photographic Exchange, I aim to link history, form, and a critical dialogue about Native American representation by engaging participants in dialogue and a portrait session using the wet plate process. This multi-faceted engagement will yield a series of tintypes that's enigmatic, time-traveling aspect demonstrates how an understanding of our world can be acquired through fabricated methods. Through collaboration with my sitters, I seek to Indigenize the photographic exchange.

My work in the Critical Indigenous Photographic Exchange encourages my collaborators to bring items of significance to their portrait sessions to help illustrate our dialogue. As a gesture of reciprocity, I give the sitter the tintype photograph produced during our exchange, with the caveat that I be granted the right to create and use a high-resolution scan of his or her image for my own artistic purposes.

Ultimately, I want to ensure that the subjects of my photographs are participating in the re-inscription of their customs and values in a way that will lead to a more equal distribution of power and influence in the cultural conversation. It is my hope that these Native American photographs will represent an intervention within the contentious and competing visual languages that form today's photographic canon. This critical Indigenous photographic exchange will continue to generate new forms of authority and autonomy. These alone—rather than the old paradigm of assimilation—can form the basis for a reimagined vision of who we are as Native people.

Ten years later, I have had the honor of performing CIPX worldwide, making thousands of portraits in collaboration with an incredible array of individuals interested in photography and the politics of representation. At its core the project is an exchange and engagement with photographic portraiture. The project is about how we see ourselves, how we want to be portrayed, and the collaborative exchange necessary to achieve this. CIPX is a dance around vulnerability, agency, and generosity.

I should highlight two significant developments made possible through this ongoing engagement. The first of these is the *Talking Tintype*, a new photographic form made possible by augmented reality (AR.). In 2013, I linked CIPX portraiture with a commercially available AR platform called LAYAR, building a bridge between nineteenth and twenty-first century imaging technologies. My *Talking Tintypes* enable the rejoining of voice and agency—in the form of web-based film—with the individual portrayed in the historic photographic object. LAYAR went out of business in 2018, which led to the development of my own *Talking Tintypes* app. My vision of returning agency to the subjects of my CIPX project came to fruition. *Talking Tintypes* bridge archive and repertoire through an Indigenous theory of the generative power of representation.

The second development is the collaborative engagement by cultural institutions with the CIPX project to establish relationships with local Indigenous communities. In the age of the "Indigenous Land Acknowledgement," CIPX has created meaningful collaboration between Indigenous communities and museums. One iteration of this development culminated in the exhibition, PHOTO/SYNTHESIS at the Fred Jones Jr. Museum of Art in 2016. Curated by heather ahtone, the project became a model of Indigenous led curation and community engagement and answered the questions, what if Indians invented photography and curatorial practice? In 2022, the Peabody Essex Museum co-produced CIPX with citizens of three Wampanoag communities and redesigned its entrance using CIPX Wampanoag portraiture to acknowledge and honor the original stewards of the land. In 2022, the Delaware Art Museum co-produced CIPX Nanticoke to recognize their developing relations with the Nanticoke and Lenni Lenape communities.

What began as a proposal to answer a simple, but lingering question has become a self-sustaining project contributing to a new ethics-based aesthetic in photographic portraiture rooted in a critical Indigenous understanding of the generative power of representation.

1. Use your smart device to scan QR code
2. This will take you to my Talking Tintypes app on the Apple App Store or Google Play
3. Download and install free TT App
4. Scan any photo from the Talking Tintypes section of my website to reveal AR content: https://willwilson.photoshelter.com/index/G0000n_hiXQrBXNw
5. Scan sample Talking Tintype from this PDF
6. Listen to the voices of remarkable Indigenous people telling their stories through a blending of 19th and 21st century photographic technologies.

Will Wilson
Citizen of the Navajo Nation, born 1969
Insurgent Hopi Maiden, Melissa Pochoema, Citizen of the Hopi Tribe, 2015
Archival inkjet print
Courtesy of the artist

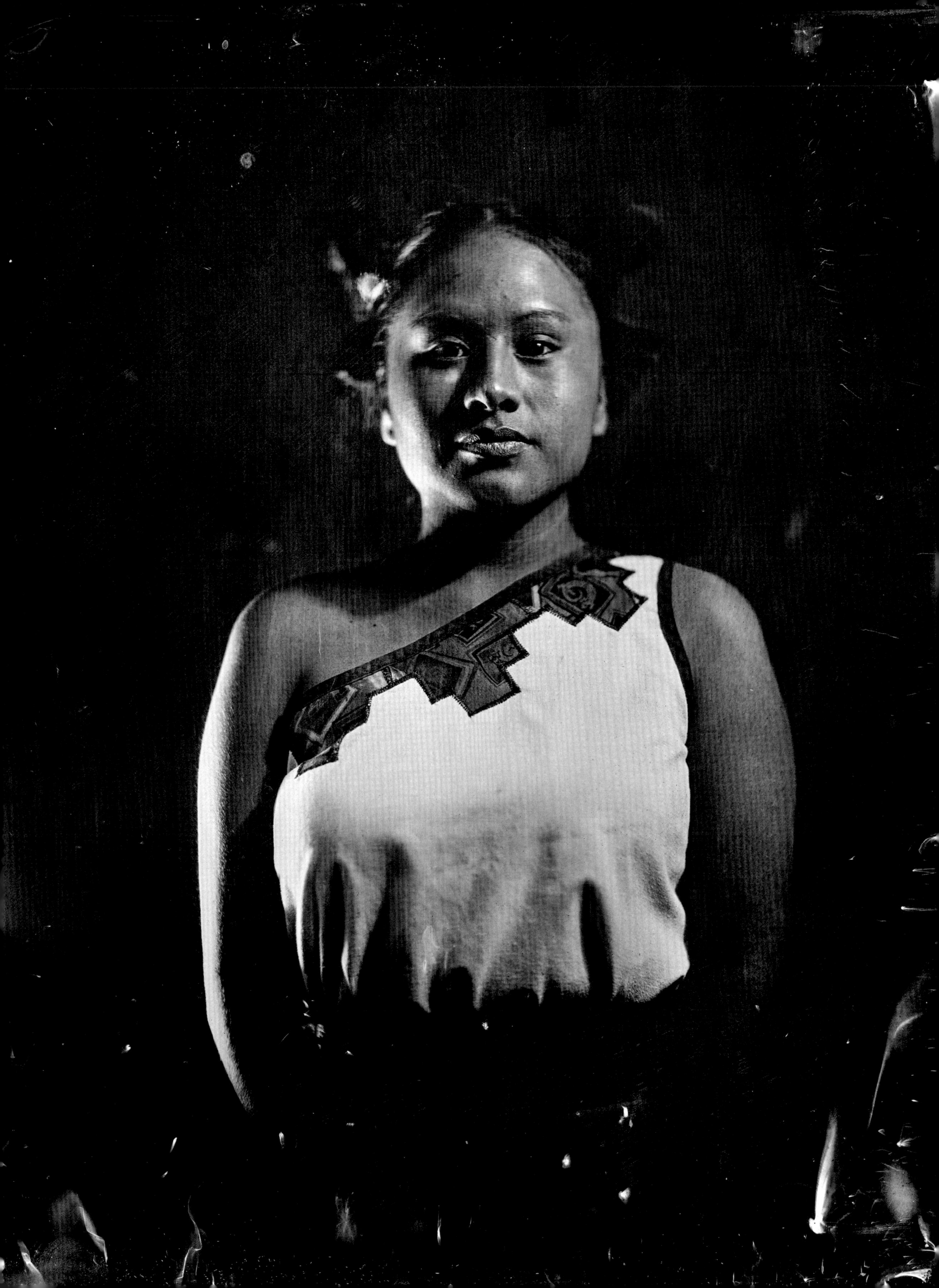

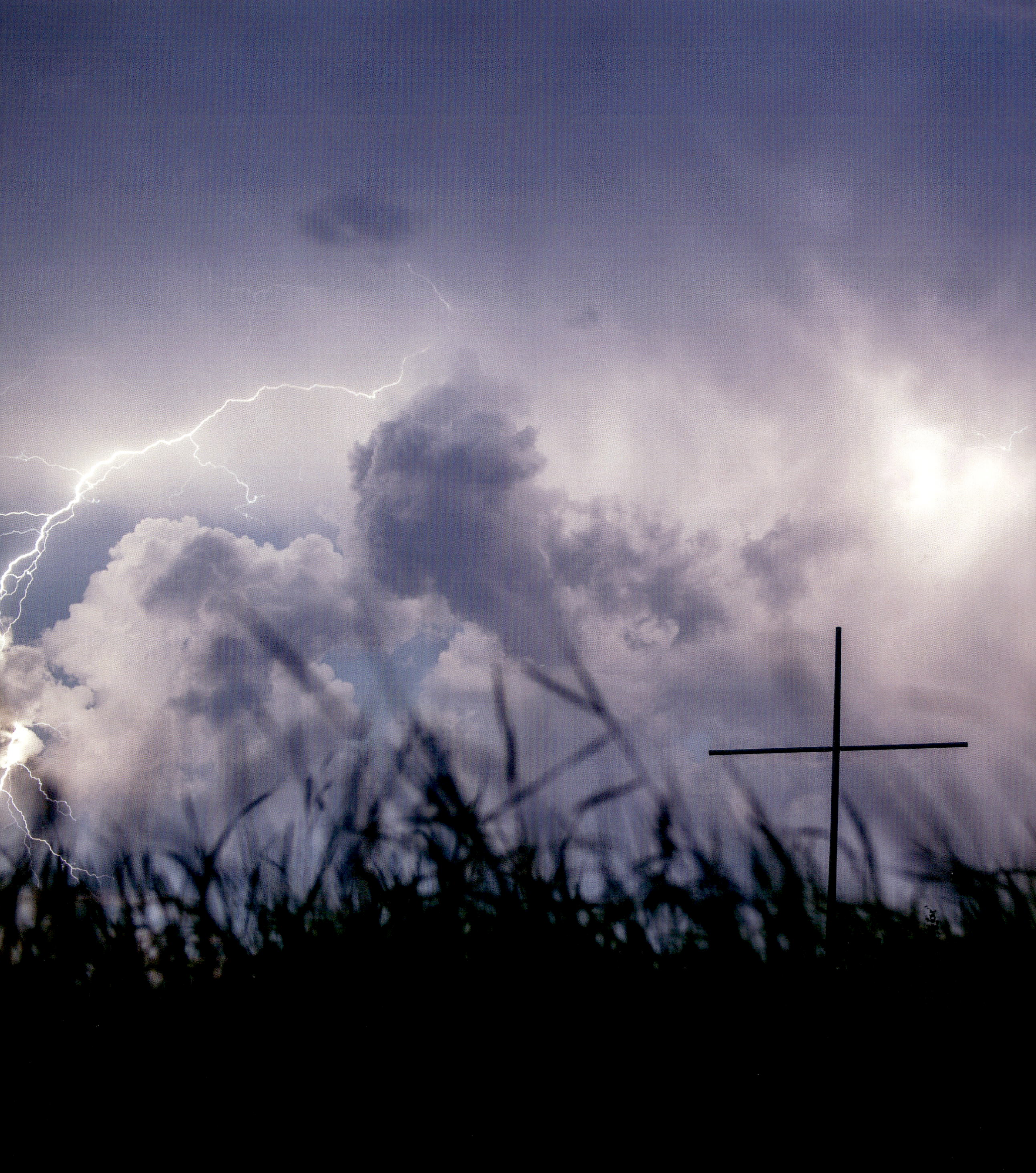

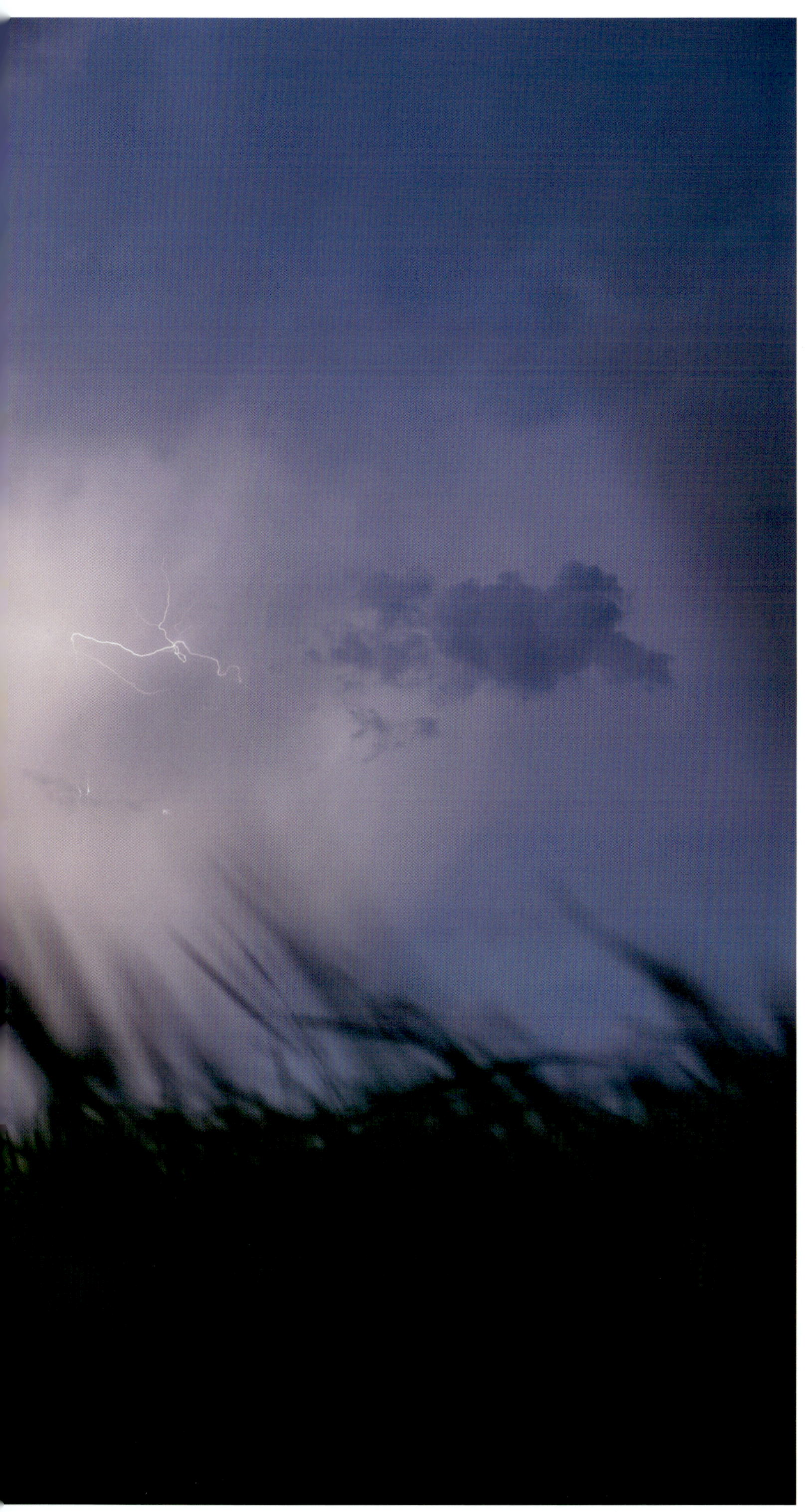

Pat Kane
Algonquin Anishinaabe, Timiskaming
First Nation, born 1979
Łíídlı̨ı̨ Kų́ę́ (Fort Simpson), 2020
Archival inkjet print on rag paper
Courtesy of the artist

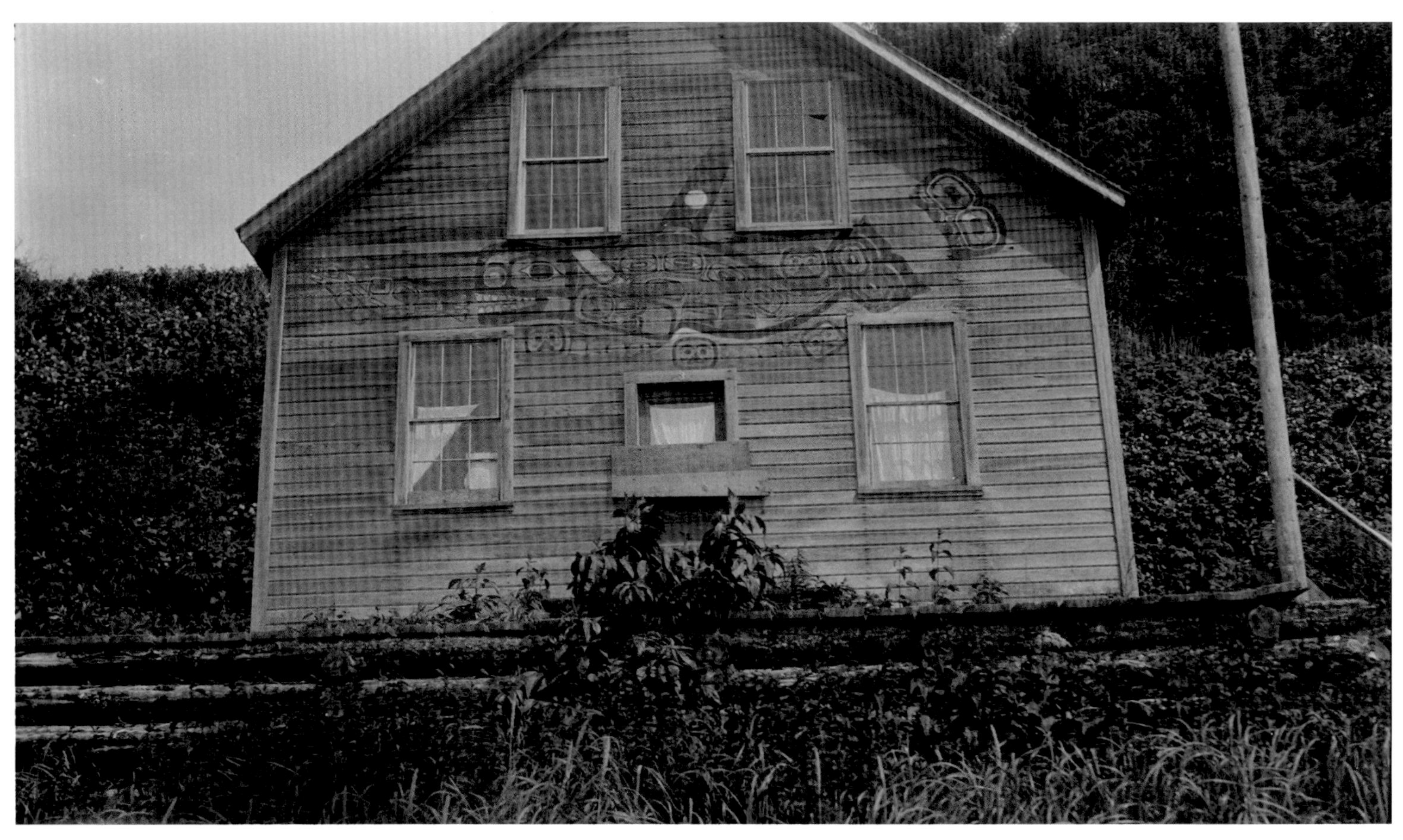

Louis Situwuka Shotridge,
Stoowukháa (Astute Man)
Kaagwaantaan clan Tlingit, 1883-1937
Painted House, Angoon AK, June 23, 1923 , 1923
Courtesy of the Penn Museum, image no. 15046

Page 207:
Louis Situwuka Shotridge,
Stoowukháa (Astute Man)
Kaagwaantaan clan Tlingit, 1883-1937
A Git-Keen young man, Skeena River,
Sept 26, 1918, 1918
Courtesy of the Penn Museum, image no. 14938

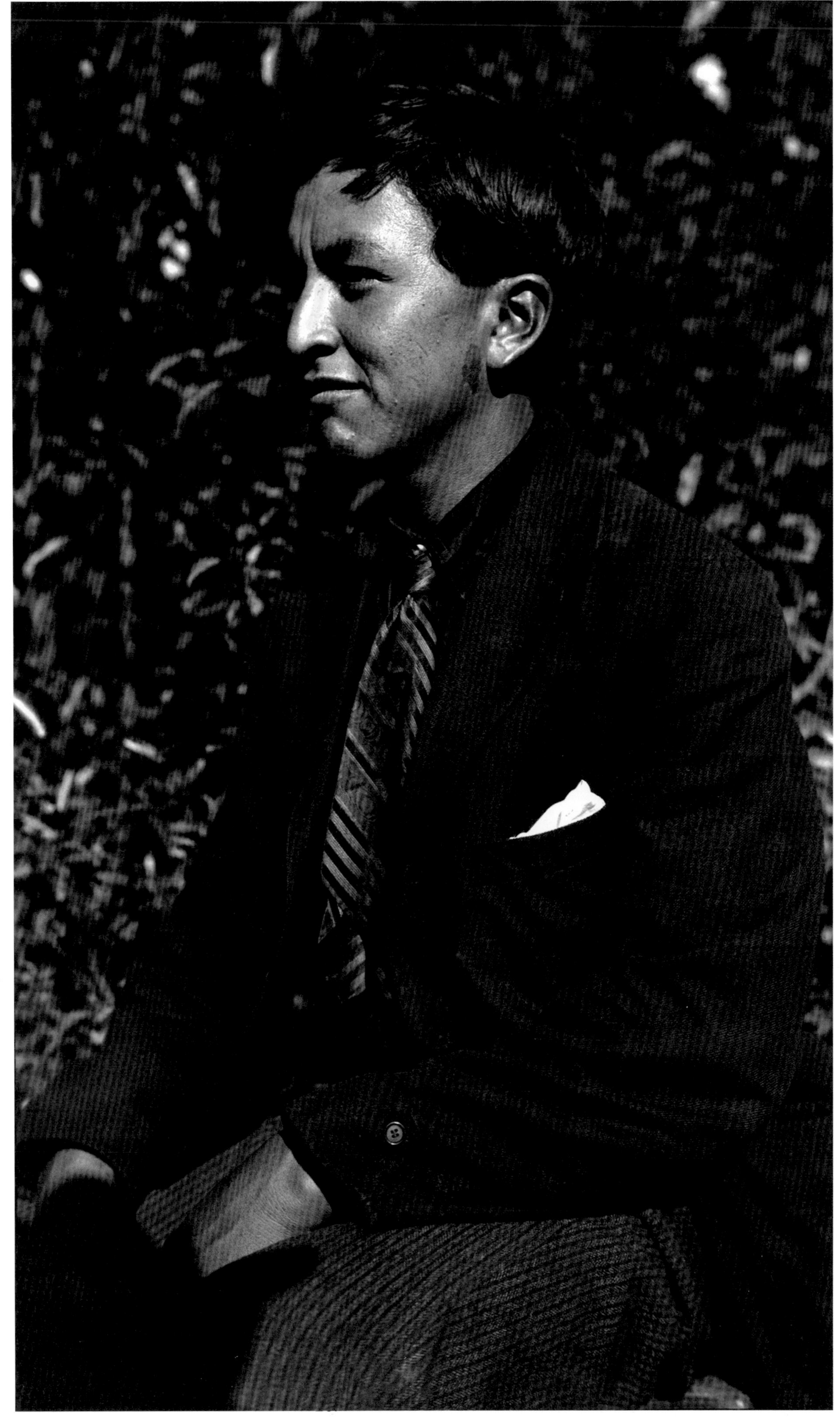

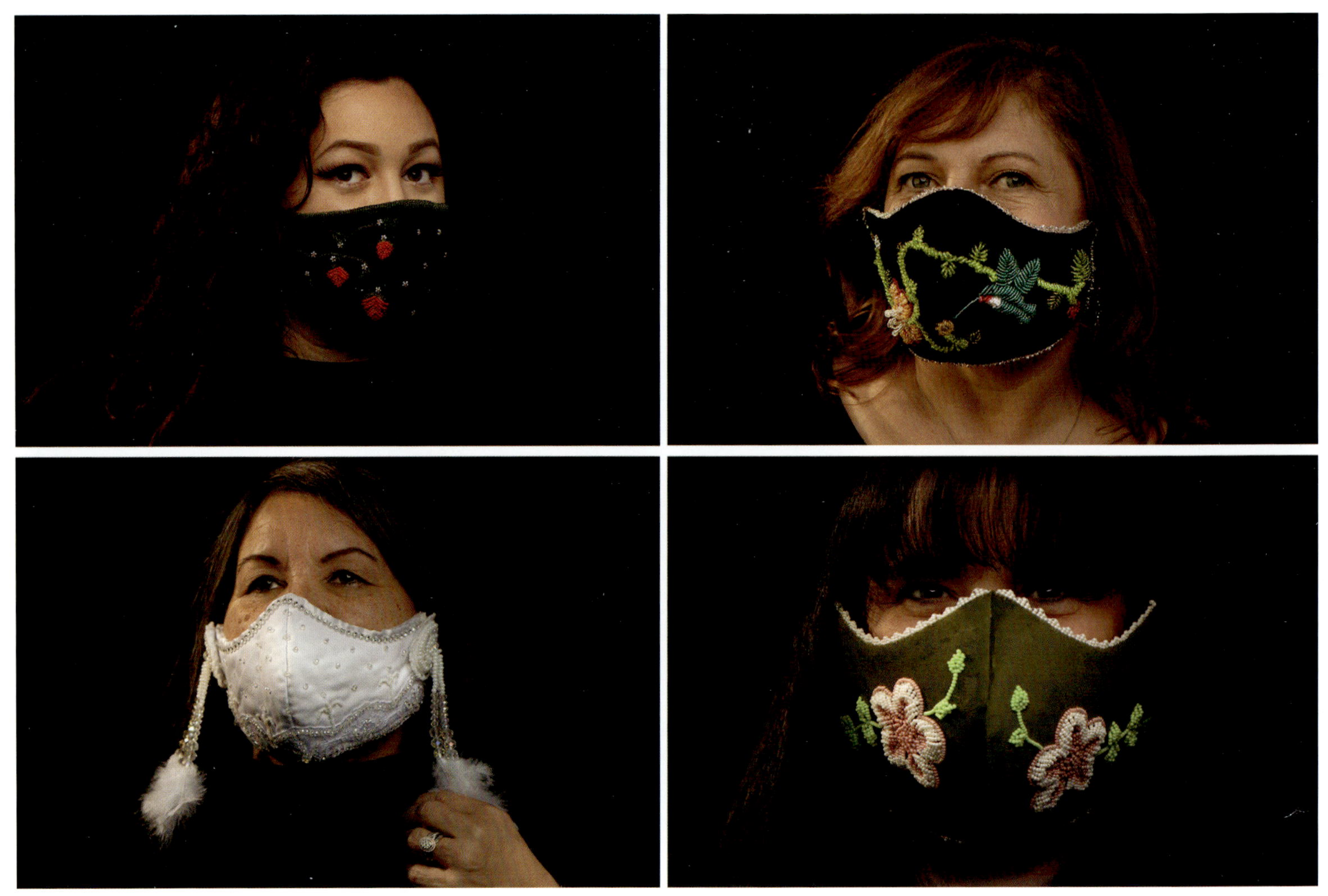

Shelby Lisk
Kanyen'kehá:ka (Mohawk),
Tyendinaga Mohawk Territory, born 1992
Rotinonhsyón:ni style masks
and their makers, 2020
from Breathe series
Courtesy of the artist

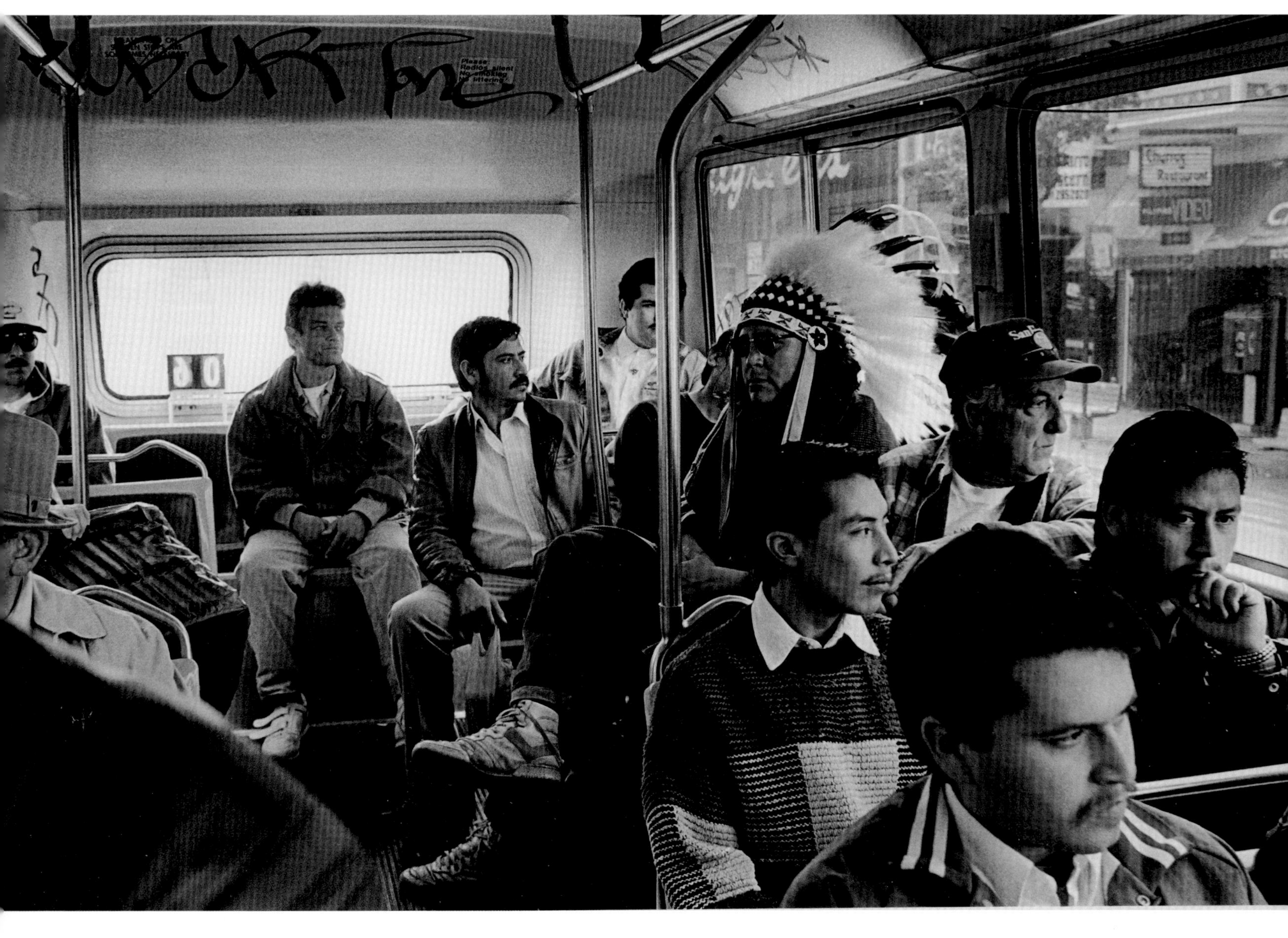

Zig Jackson (Rising Buffalo)
Sahnish (Arikara), Minitari (Hidatsa),
Numakiki (Mandan), born 1957
Indian on Mission Bus, 1994
Gelatin silver print
Courtesy of the artist
© Zig

"WE MAKE THAT CONNECTION"

EIGHT DINÉ (NAVAJO) PHOTOGRAPHERS

BY JILL AHLBERG YOHE

OVER THE COURSE OF SEVERAL MONTHS in the Summer and Fall of 2022, I had conversations with eight photographers of the Navajo Nation. We discussed their practice and their work featured in this exhibition. They also shared what inspires them, motivates them, grounds them, and what they hope viewers may experience and ponder as they encounter and interact with their work.

This is a narrative essay, fundamentally built upon the thoughts and words of each photographer. My analysis occurs through the curation of these conversations. I have lightly edited and streamlined prose, rearranged quotations, and structured the essay into overarching themes. When curating an exhibition, I often seek to remain "hidden" from view, acting instead as a facilitator to allow the artworks and artists to captivate the viewer and draw them into their worlds. This is an attempt to do this in writing.

THE GLITTERING WORLD

Rapheal Begay: As of late, something that I'm very interested in is the role and significance of light. Not necessarily just within the photographic process or the scientific magic that is found in analog photography, photography alone, but within Navajo culture and life. Here in Dinétah, we have four sacred colors that come from the cycle of the sun throughout the day. White is in the morning, the rise of the sun into east. And as it moves throughout the day, takes up space in the sky, it gets blue, referencing the color. And as the sun sets in the west, it turns yellow. And then, as it does completely set it's black.

The significance of light is that it touches everything. It is sort of invisible, yet it allows for such amazing color and magic to exist in the world. I know we have songs in the world. I know we have the elements as a form of transportation and as protection from our deities.

To think about how we reference that in our culture, our community, our design, our outlook, our daily lives, is phenomenal. I'm trying to reference ideas of Indigenous aesthetics, aesthetics indigenous to place, to culture. The aesthetic itself is a self-revolving, self-sustainable idea of culture, of language, internal knowledge, and inside jokes. With all of this, there's something beautiful happening there. More importantly, I look at light as a source of magic, as projection, as prayer. I mean, without it, we wouldn't be able to see, and I think we tend to forget that.

Dakota Mace: I wanted to be able to look at how everything within Diné culture is central to this idea of our four sacred mountains, our four sacred colors and directions. And this concept is still practiced by silversmiths and within the work that they create. I wanted to look at how we are connected to our ancestors through the designs that we create and the memories that are actually embedded within the design itself. I wanted to be able to connect to our creation stories in ways for a younger generation to better understand what it means to be connected to these designs and these relationships, and how these stories would continue on?

These stories have been passed on from one generation to the next, and my family focuses on stories of silversmithing. Each one of these images, forty separate individual chemigrams, all focus on four designs that are important to each silversmith.

That's why I wanted to do the chemigrams process, because it's also working with silver. It is such a beautiful process, but it's also very painterly and every print is one of a kind. And I think that's something special about this particular series. Although there are forty images within the series, each one is individualized by the different textures and designs that are being created within the piece itself. It's very much like thinking of Diné philosophy of being connected with one another. So even though we have our individual thoughts and memories, altogether we're kind of a collective identity. For me, understanding Diné people through silver is the best way to understand us.

A VISUAL LANGUAGE

Will Wilson: I'm not a fluent Navajo speaker, so being in the community and with my family and being a creative person, I didn't really have a great way to express myself. And when I found photography, it instantly became this amazing way to record, as well as think about my life and my family and represent that in a way that fulfilled my need for self-expression.

I also think that there's something about a culture that's rooted in oral tradition. The permanence and descriptive power of photography is so immediate, it can freeze time and is really

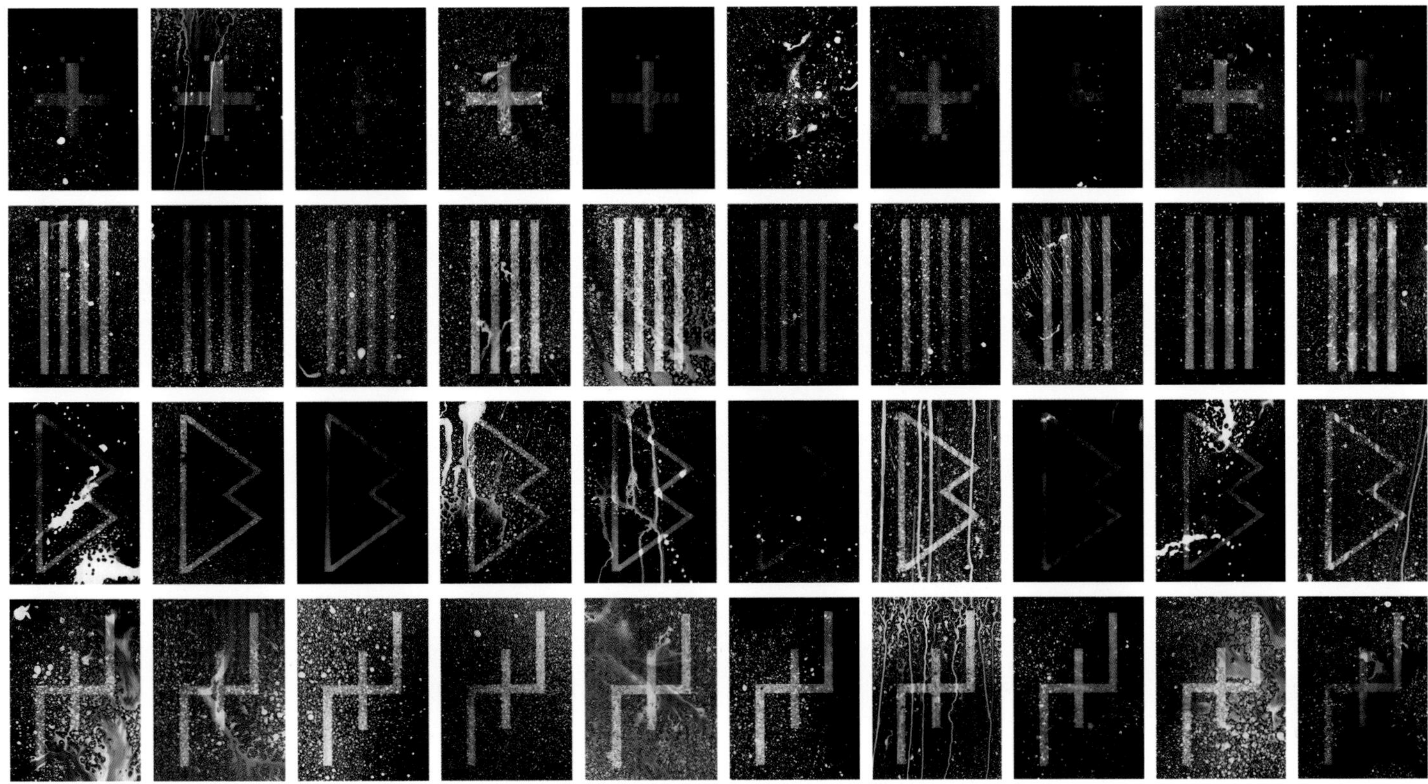

descriptive. And in a place where a kind of representation happens much more, I guess fluidly or ethereally, it's through language, which is not permanent. It's always kind of active and alive and moving. Photography does this thing where it freezes it. It makes a moment endure. For me, I think living in translation became an interesting way to think about, to understand and experience our culture, because it's something that I could revisit through photography.

Dakota Mace: Something that has always been important for me was looking at the narratives through my grandparents' eyes and especially how a lot of our memories exist through objects and especially through photographs. And this was something that as a young child, I didn't get to experience in the same way as other people, who had collections that were in the thousands or hundreds of photographs of their family members.

Dakota Mace
Diné (Navajo), born 1991
So' (Stars), 2022
40 Chemigrams
Courtesy of the Bruce Silverstein Gallery

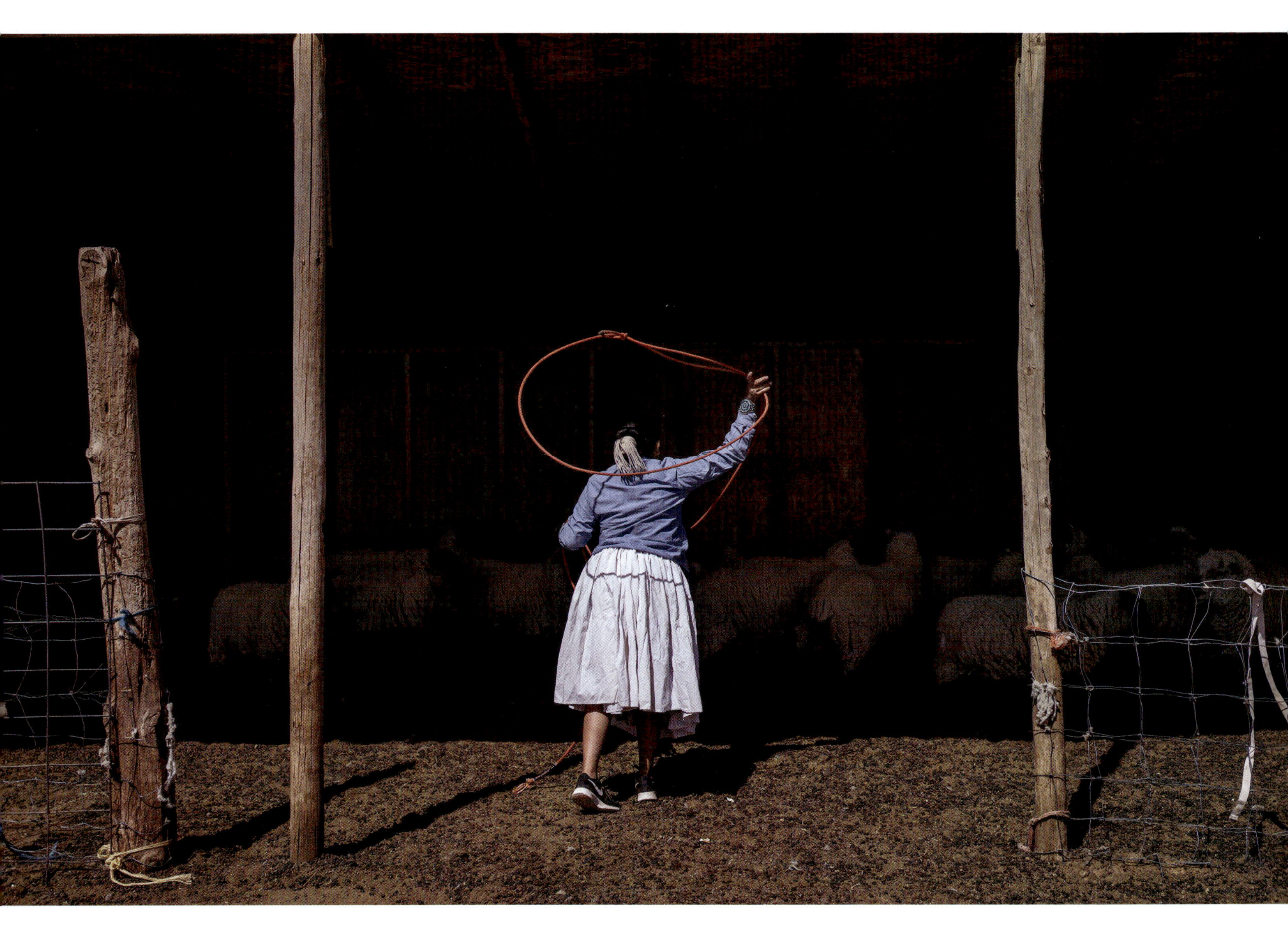

Sharon Chischilly
Diné (Navajo)
Portrait of Naiomi Glasses (Diné [Navajo]), 2021
Courtesy the artist

With my family it was a little bit more complex in that our photos were lost over time, so the few photographs that I do have are really important to me and help me to look at ways that we saw ourselves through that documentation. I look at them as tangible markers of history. This idea was really important for me, and especially for my photos: to translate that our history is one that's unique, one of resilience and survival. Photographs also allow us to open ourselves up and share our stories and to see our history as a continuum of those traditions and our culture.

STORIES IN PLACE

Rapheal Begay: I like to describe my home now as a place between red dirt and blue skies. We are the light that creates that connection. Our feet on the ground, our hands into the air, we make that connection.

I'm really thinking about the land itself as the ultimate source, as the ultimate creator, as the ultimate form of artwork, and everything else is a reflection of that. As I've transitioned throughout this series of images, of ideas, I've come to realize that my work is very elemental. It is very grounded in this ecological relationship that we find ourselves in. And this magic, this sense of alchemy that allows us to transform, to create, and to relate to a project is really beautiful.

My foundation is in Hunter's Point, Navajo Nation [AZ], and I see the legacy of my grandparents all around me. I feel it within me. I understand it when I walk into my grandmother's home, and when I hear the sound of the sheep in the distance as the sun's setting.

I think about them as well as other family members who have passed as I look into the sky and see eagles flying in the area, and just walking in the land ... something that I've learned is that it holds memory. Indicators in our surroundings take us back to a different time, to an emotion, to an experience with someone. And whenever I'm home there, it inspires me. It strengthens me. It gives me energy. It is the source of everything. It is the beginning.

Sharon Chischilly: For this photo with Naomi Glasses, I was on an assignment for the *New York Times* and covered the Navajo Nation reopening during the pandemic. Sheep shearing was one of the subjects that I wanted to photograph. I met Naomi, and they [her family] were doing a sheep shearing camp. I'd never really been to this before. It was really interesting to go and see her environment and see the land and everything. It was fun. I never really photographed people sheep shearing before, so it was interesting to see and watch and learn and see the bonds that the family had with each other.

I just go out and photograph what I see, what's interesting to me. My mom passed away when I was in high school. I didn't really know how to handle that. I just locked myself in a room, didn't go to school. I just did my homework at home, and I didn't really go out and do stuff. I got bad anxiety. Picking up a camera really helped me focus in the moment and not think of anything else, which was very nice for once. I wasn't really thinking about my problems or what happened in the past, or what's going to happen in the future. It just allowed me to live in the moment and explore what was happening around me and meet new people. It's just getting out and being able to take photographs that helped me see new things. I think when I go out and take photos, it's just photographing what I see.

Kalen Goodluck: Land as a character and as a subject, especially when there's added context of history and cultural meaning, can be a particularly impactful visual motivator for a story.

Land is identifiable and even an interpersonal kind of space where tribes really relate and know their own histories and where their own historic ancestral treaty or ancestral homeland boundaries are and where they stand today. This land that you're standing on, doesn't lack meaning in the slightest.

This land has had an economic value that the US settler colonial institutions saw and had appropriated for its own means, and so actually you can trace each parcel's land history from the moment that it was taken to today. The Morrill Act, which had really jumpstarted America's public university system, fifty-two universities that many of us find ourselves in, and go to college in. We really kind of find ourselves and grow up in these schools and meet people. Most of those cultural touchstones in our public institutional systems were directly funded by essentially land theft, by treaties, by massacres, by warfare, forced treaties, executive orders, you name it. *These were people's homes.*

I hope that this work inspires people to learn more about lands, because it doesn't just affect the path that you walk on but really stretches it. And lands have so much more impact in your own personal life than you may have thought.

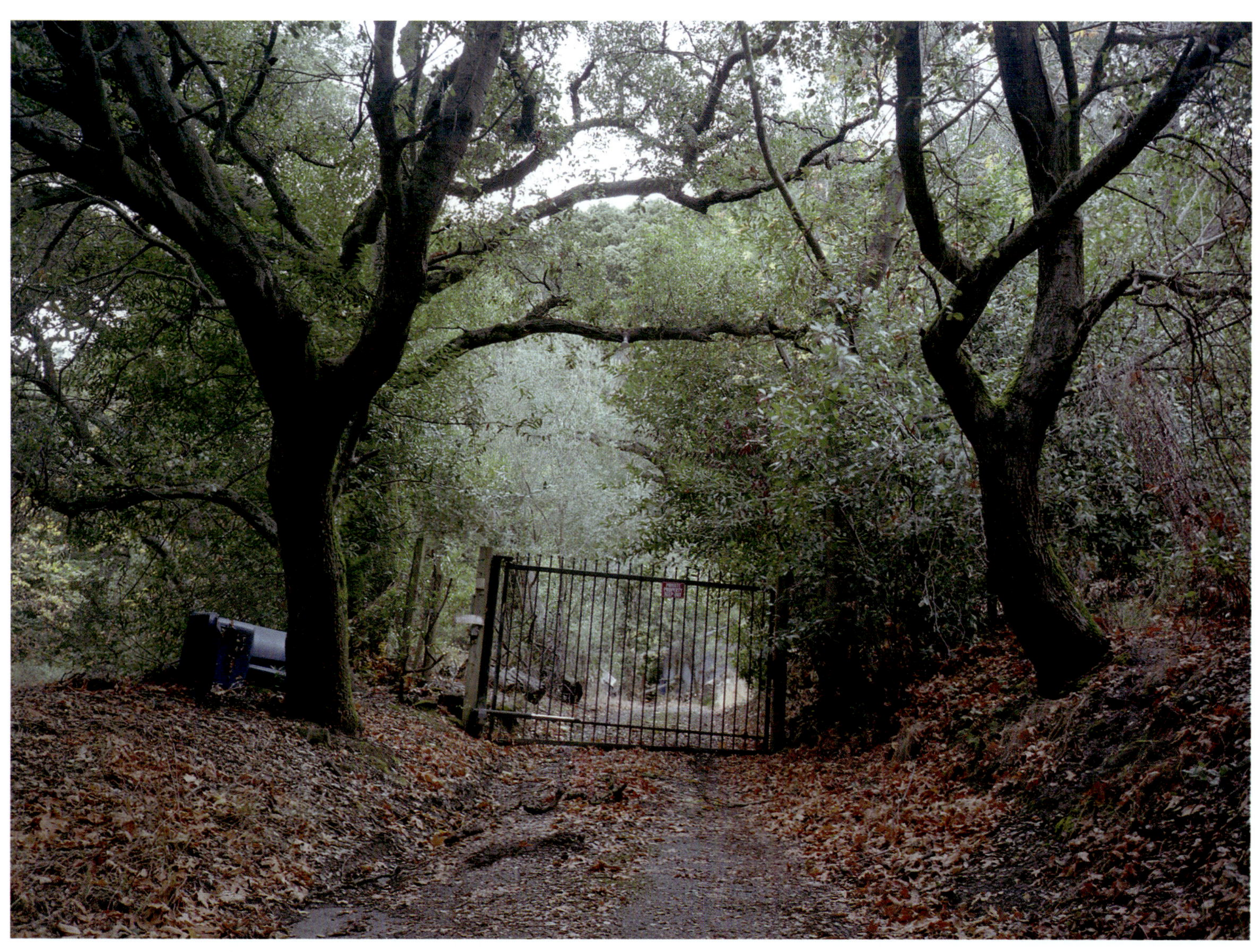

Kalen Goodluck
Diné (Navajo) / Mandan / Hidatsa / Tsimshian, born 1993
(Chap-pah-sim, Co-to-plan-e-nee, I-o-no-hum-ne, Sage-womnee, Su-ca-ah and We-chil-la. The land was seized by unratified treaty in 1851 and granted to Alabama for the benefit of Auburn University), 2020
from Land-Grab Universities series
Courtesy of the artist

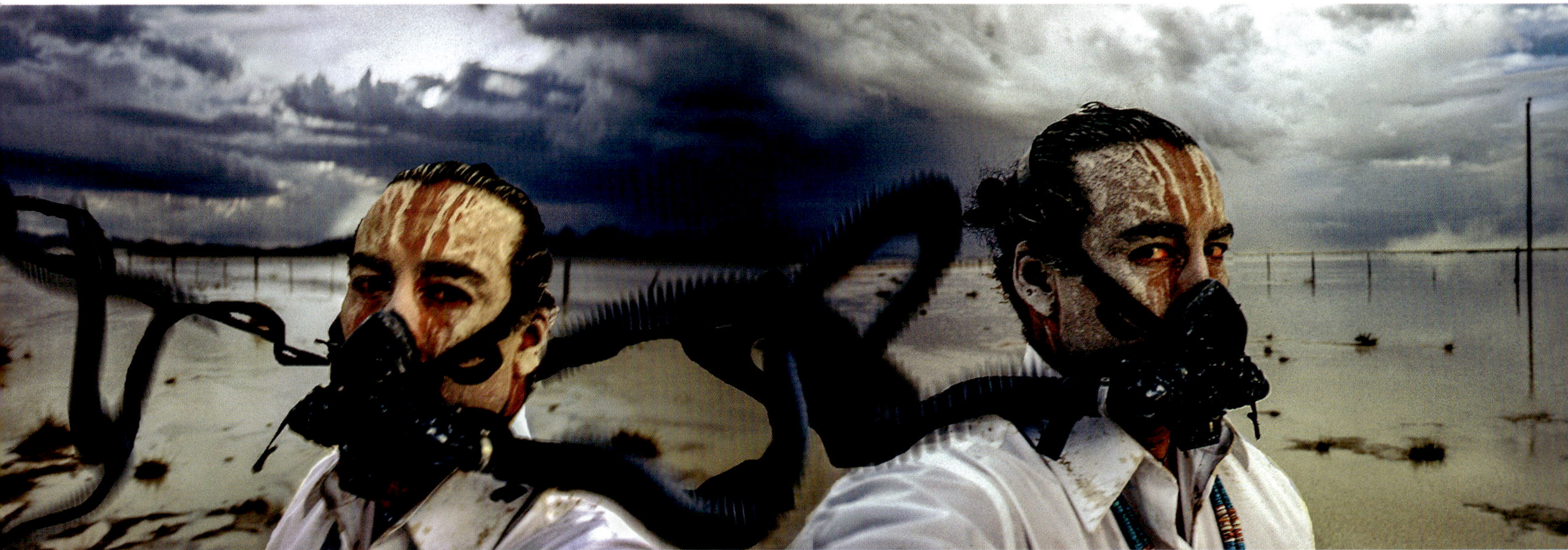

Will Wilson: The issue of abandoned uranium mines on the Navajo Nation is something that I'm really trying to explore and let people know about. And I think everybody on the Rez has pretty much one degree of separation from it.

It's still a very present kind of environmental toxin that people are being exposed to. It's pretty insidious because you can't see it. And it's a slow toxin, so it happens over the course of a long time. And I've thought a lot about what it means to make art around this and to aestheticize this stuff. I think having that kind of critical perspective on the notion of aestheticizing a traumatic issue is to ask myself: "How do I bring this back to folks and let them know about it." On one level it's hopefully a public service announcement.

Eventually this information [of abandoned uranium mines] will be the foundation for an app. I really want to make an app that people can just pull up and see where they are in relation to the sites around them and have quick access to the site screening reports. A quick way to figure out where these places are for people to say to themselves: "Maybe I shouldn't herd my sheep over there. Or there's that area that is a depression in the landscape, and now we know now that it was a pit mine, and where the water comes in, don't let the livestock drink from that."

Will Wilson
Citizen of the Navajo Nation, born 1969
AIR 5, 2005
Archival inkjet print
Courtesy of the artist
© Will Wilson

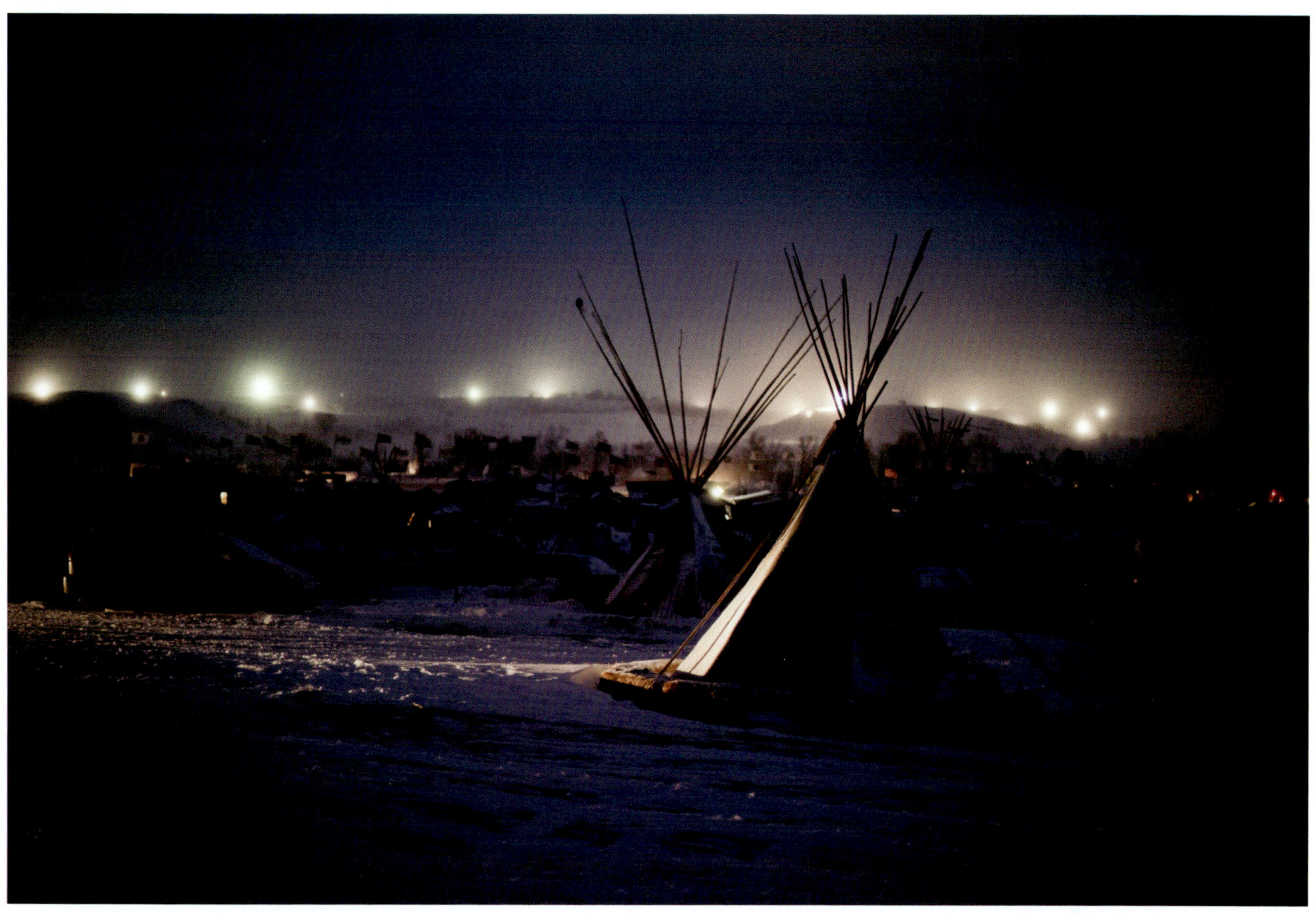

Russel Albert Daniels: This is a photograph of the Oceti Sakowin Camp at Standing Rock Reservation. It's illuminated by the Dakota Access Pipeline security lights in the middle of a December blizzard. To me, it really shows how defiant and committed Native folks are to stand up against genocide, colonization, and imperialism, and to do whatever it takes. You also see this in organizations of people that are doing climate mitigation. Native folks are involved and working for climate change because that's the biggest threat to our whole world. You see folks respecting Indigenous wisdom and Indigenous knowledge in this battle we have against climate change. That's really empowering and inspiring a lot of us to continue telling stories from our culture and other Native cultures that we work within.

Russel Albert Daniels
Diné (Navajo) and Ho-Chunk, born 1974
Blizzard conditions help the DAPL security lights illuminate the Oceti Sakowin camp at the Standing Rock Sioux Nation, December 4, 2016, 2016
Courtesy of the artist

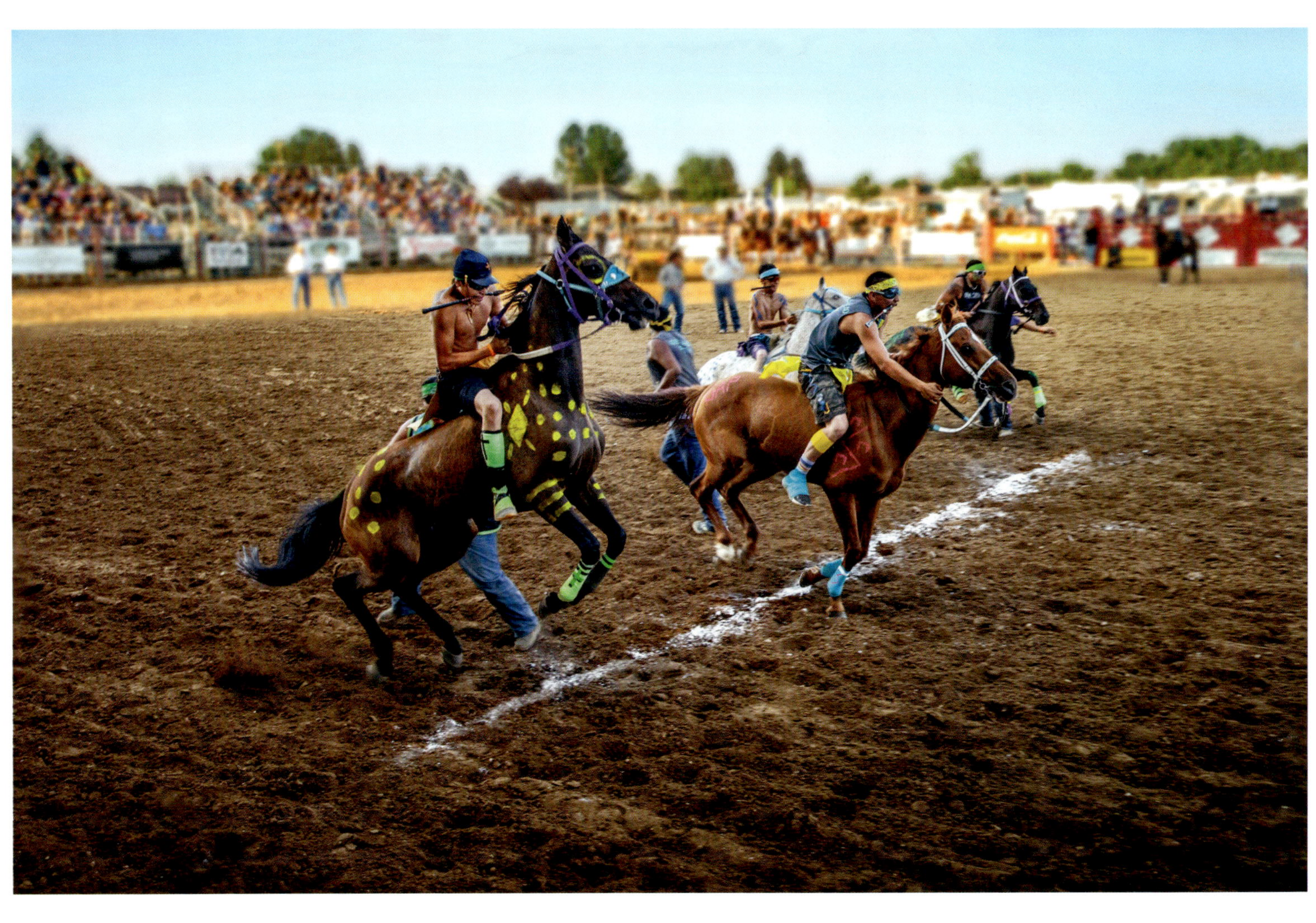

Sam Minkler
Diné (Navajo) , born 1950
My First Indian Relay, Wyoming, 2021
Digital print
Courtesy of the artist

ANIMAL STORIES IN PLACE

Sam Minkler: I grew up on the reservation and I used to ride horses when I was a little kid and I mean, I love horses. I even used to ride donkeys—but mainly horses—and I love going really fast. I love doing tricks on horses, jumping saddles, and going after horses. I used to get up early in the morning, they'd tell me to go get the horses, and I knew the footprint of my horse. I could distinguish it between other horses by tracking it, and just knowing which one's my horse just because of its hoof markings.

There was a program for an Indian Relay in Wyoming that I went to. I just stayed in the Indian Relay alley where they were washing the horses and all the people were cooking and sitting under tents where they camped or had their RVs near where all the horses were kept. They had stalls and they were grooming the horses, and they blessed the horses with sage. And they were marking, putting the different symbols on horses, the different colored teams. The green team would put a green circle or different symbols.

Someone told me that a long time ago, these relays were a way of communication. One group of Natives would send a horse rider to another group of Native people to tell news and that horse and rider would go to the next group. And that's what I learned talking to people in the alley, and I totally love that idea. All the Natives were saying that: "Damn, we glad we have a Native photographer. We used to have other people, they just take pictures and go." So this is the reason I photograph.

I've only actually been to one race and those races went so fast. I could barely think to get my lens on, or a different lens on, just anticipating the horses coming around. I've photographed sports before, but this action is very fast. And I really didn't understand the race until I saw it, and I couldn't predict anything. This photograph is almost perfect in terms of the line. There's a white line at the starting point and the front horse rears up. He's on the first horse [in the relay] and the other guys are still trying to get on the horses, and this photograph is taken probably half a second before they go on. I don't know, within a spectrum of a second, it was a one millionth second of a little part of a second, a one millionth part of it. That's when I took the photograph.

Rapheal Begay: This is a post-butchering process from a celebration and gathering with my family at my late grandmother's home. It had been some time since we had visited my grandmother's home. It's sort of dormant and silent. So, we wanted to bring life back into it. We decided to butcher and bring the family together. As everyone was prepping the meat and cleaning the intestines and moving forward and laughing, I took a moment with my camera. I went outside through the back door and went around my grandmother's home, and around the corner. There, I saw this dog dragging this sheep's head that we left outside. There are other families located or within the community that may have fed the dog, but no one really owned it. It was just there, sort of a wanderer. Just to my left, there's another dog approaching this interaction, and the dog with the sheep's head notices and starts to snarl and gets defensive. So, we begin to see his teeth.

As I've continued to work with this dimension and add to its story, I've learned from it and it teaches me. I feel that it's in conversation with our empathy, our emotional intelligence, and how we relate to our surroundings and our non-human relatives, in this case, a canine.

I look at it in the same light as how we treat our unsheltered relatives. There's this sense of concern, empathy, but there is a lack of responsibility or commitment to help. These two creatures, these two relatives of ours wander the landscape, trying to find what they can to survive. Maybe it's not the best for them. Maybe it's not the most ideal situation, but it is the life that they're living. And I'm not necessarily approaching it with my camera with the sense of judgment, but just allowing myself to document what is merely existing and not necessarily saying it's right to wrong or trying to understand this person's journey but being there to aid in documenting their journey. Hopefully through that journey, it allows me to become more aware of my surroundings, to be more empathetic to what I am seeing that is in front of me, and to remind me of our relationships and our interdependence in this ecological environment that we find ourselves in.

A majority of people who see this image and live off the reservation or live in the city, or who are going to museums and these institutions, are disassociated with its reality. I think there's power in that. And again, as I share this story and as I speak about these ideas that are inspired by the image that was created, I view that as a very important part of my work. My first clan is Honaaghaani, which means one who walks around. That's exactly what I do with my camera. I walk around, into the landscape, into my surroundings, not with the intent of creating an image or documenting, but in responding to it.

Rapheal Begay
Diné (Navajo), 1985
Rez-Dog (Hunter's Point, AZ), 2017
Archival inkjet print
Courtesy of the artist

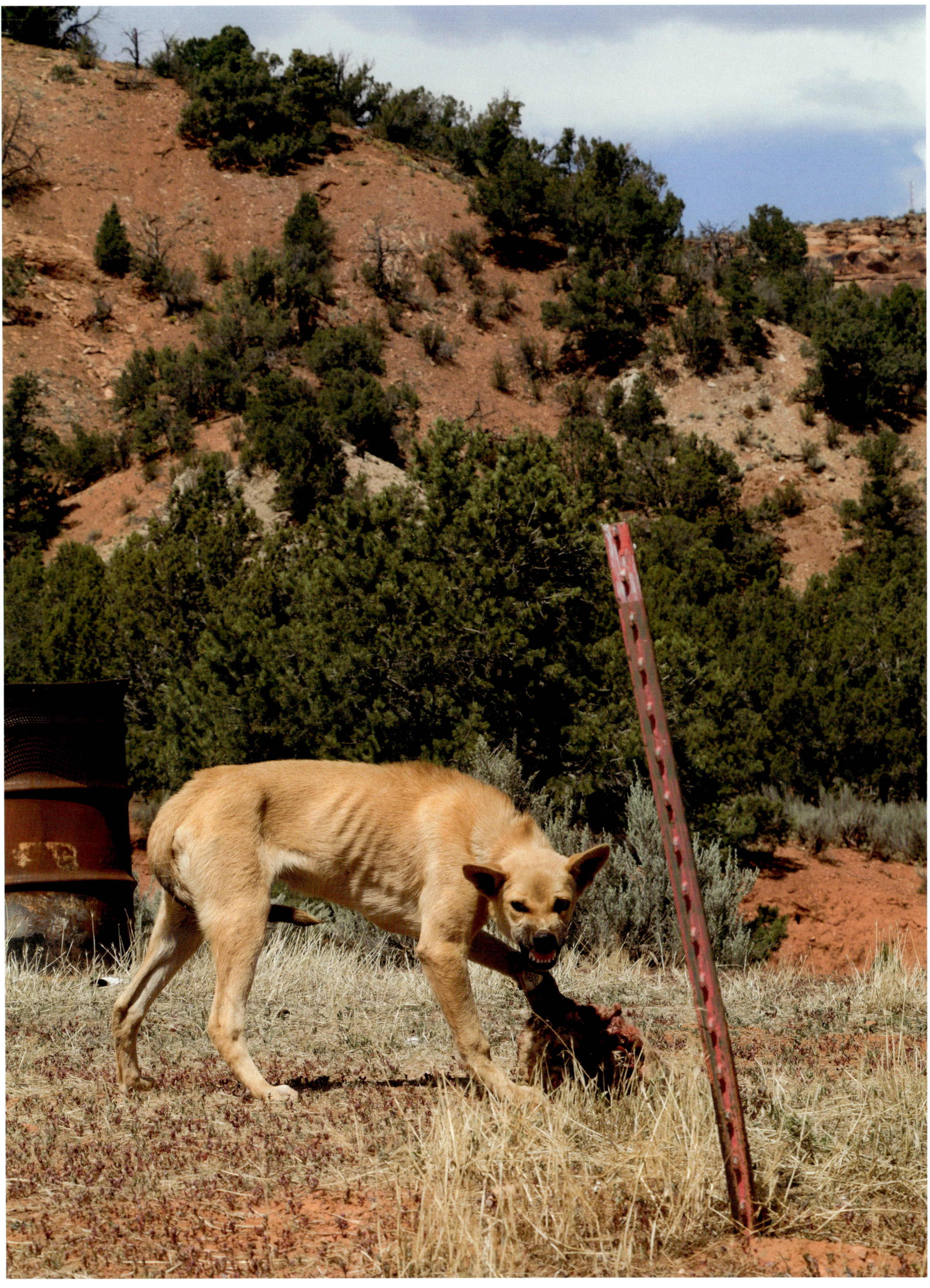

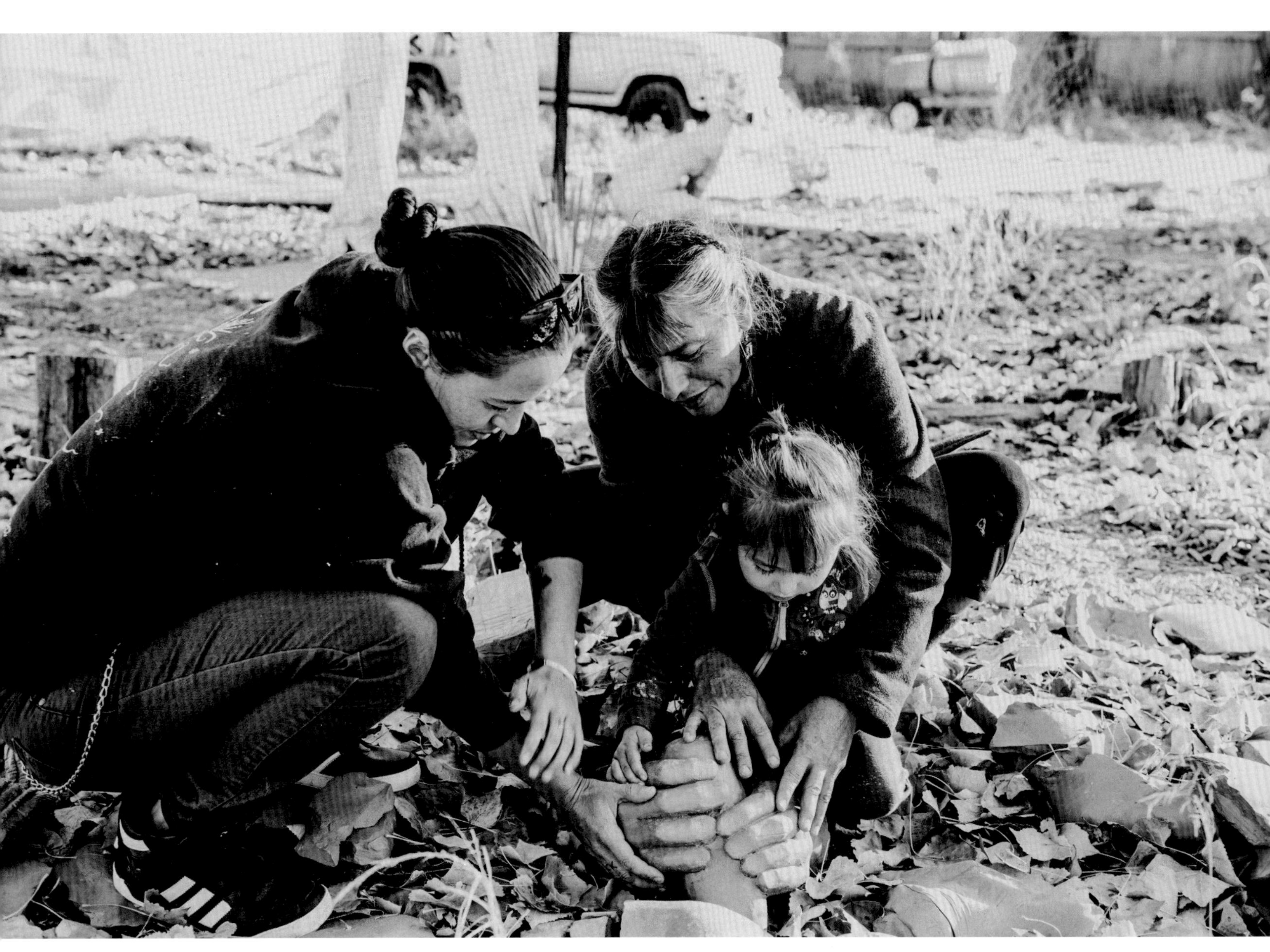

Ungelbah Davila
Diné (Navajo), born 1987
Roxanne, Rose & Cedar,
from Indigenous Artist and Leader series
Inkjet print
Courtesy of the artist

HAND IN HAND

Ungelbah Davila: I felt really honored to take this picture, because I thought it just beautifully represented the generations of artists here in the Southwest. ... And it's always just so remarkable, to me, the legacy and the generational aspect of working with clay that's passed down—from great-grandmother, to grandmother, to mother, to daughter, to granddaughter.

Roxanne [Swentzell] and Rose [Simpson] come from a family of Pueblo potters. They consider themselves potters, sculptors actually. They are taking this generational art form and then making it their own in such a profound and contemporary way, that is so personal to them as women, and as artists. And then seeing that this starts to manifest in a little bit of time I got to spend with Cedar [Rose's daughter and Roxanne's granddaughter], it's exciting to think what she's going to be creating in the future. I just love that moment and that photo and looking back, ten years from now. Notice the hands in the photograph, because with this kind of art, it always comes back to the hands. Creating through the hands.

I'm inspired very much by women. I love photographing women, all women. Each one of them is a goddess. They're so beautiful. And they're so creative. When I'm working with a model or a subject, that moment happens where they reveal their truth to me, and it's such a powerful moment and such a privilege. That's when these beautiful photos happen because there's no facade.

Will Wilson: The tin types are interesting as they are a historic photographic process that gives agency and voice back to sitters. I like what the tin type does, the talking tin type particularly. It still seems to fascinate a little bit or surprise, or there's an aspect of wonder when people suddenly see that still image come to life.

Russel Albert Daniels: I think while doing this work, I find that it's very healing for us. It's also very healing for the communities, individuals, and Indigenous people that are seeing themselves represented in our stories. In these stories, it's often a work of collaboration and not just, "This is mine and you're a subject." It's more of a collaboration, so I think when this is done properly, it's healing for the people in the stories and for ourselves. And in the end, to have it done properly, it's healing for the audience who's receiving this. Because they're finally being told the true stories and seeing that our cultures are full of nuance, individualism, beauty, and wisdom. We're not a monolith. That's been inspiring and is often at the root of a lot of the work that I do.

—

I think one of the exciting things about doing this work right now is that through technology, we've been able to develop organizations and a database of Indigenous storytellers (see indigenousphotograph.com). Our perspectives, our visions, and our voices have been left out for so long. Often, that's due to privilege. We didn't have the privileges or the finances to enter or to be part of the groups that were doing that, or we were intentionally left out of those groups. But now, the power of technology has allowed us to have a voice and to have a community. That's become very powerful. It's been really rewarding to be able to work with that community. I think to be able to be trusted, to tell stories, and to tell our own stories has been very important.

Kalen Goodluck: I think there has been a great push by Native artists to show their own vision and show that they do have stories to tell, whether it is contemporary art or whether it's documentary photography or photojournalism. And to me, it seems like there's this new sort of generational wave of Native photographers, at least, that are really breaking through and making a lot of great strides. The bottom line is I think there are a lot of great Indigenous photographers who are making names for themselves and helping change these institutional problems that we see.

Ungelbah Davila: I think it's just such an exciting time. We are finding bigger, stronger, and more powerful global connections because of social media. Social media has a lot of things that are wrong with it, don't get me wrong. But finding ways to connect as a unified front of Indigenous people, with our relatives to the south, to the north, across the country, across the continents, and across the world. It makes this such an exciting time to be involved in the art world and in Indian country, because the sky's the limit now. We can be an organic people that are growing and living, and experimenting, and promoting ourselves. And being a photographer, getting to capture that moment is such a once in a lifetime kind of thing. This is such a powerful and a pivotal moment in our history and our survival, not just as Indigenous people, but as human beings on this planet.

CLOSING:

Sam Minkler: I really want to encourage anyone who's a Native person to not hold back. Just to do anything, whether it be in music or in the arts, you just have to keep doing it and keep doing it. And just draw from it, we have a history here on this side of the world, much longer than they give us credit for. And our art, I see the quality, the designs, the precision and just the expression and the vibrance of it, the life that we have. If America and the whole world even recognized that just a little bit more and gave us more opportunities, I think that is something that they can gain from us.

Rapheal Begay: We as artists and creators have an opportunity to contribute to our surroundings, to create something, to add to the beauty that is behind us, above us, below us, and within us. We are that light. And I think there's a sense of stewardship that comes with my work, but also maybe just as an Indigenous tribal Native American, American Indian community member, I feel there's inherent responsibility to my language, to my culture, to this lived experience. There is so much to share from what is my perspective, not only as the creator, but as someone who lives within the environment, the cultural landscape that's being documented. I felt that it was important to share my story with it.

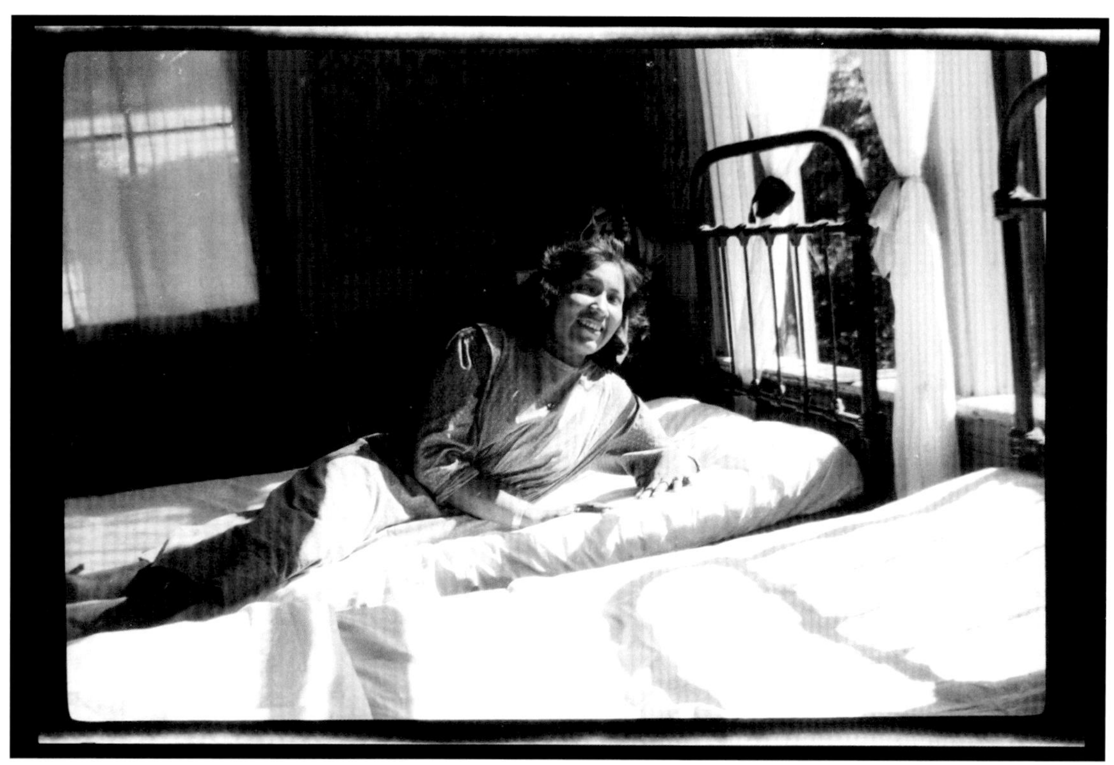

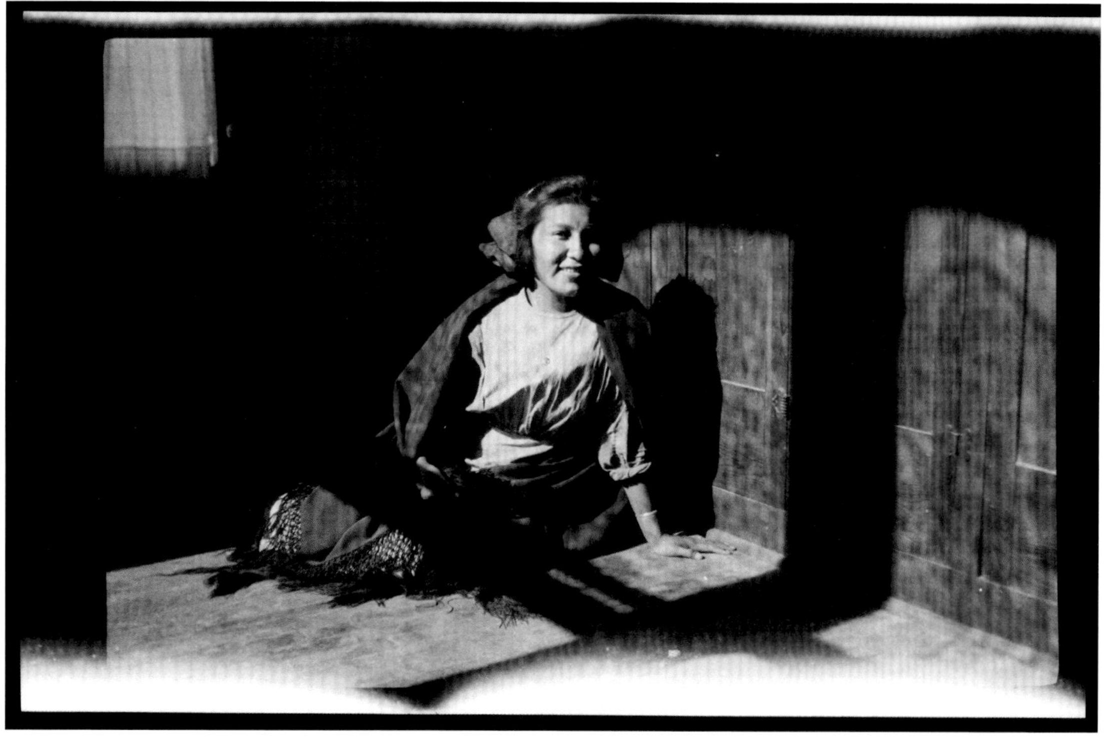

Lucy Sumpty
Nettie Odlety, c. 1915
Courtesy of the Oklahoma Historical Society,
Parker McKenzie Collection, 19650.97 and 19650.86

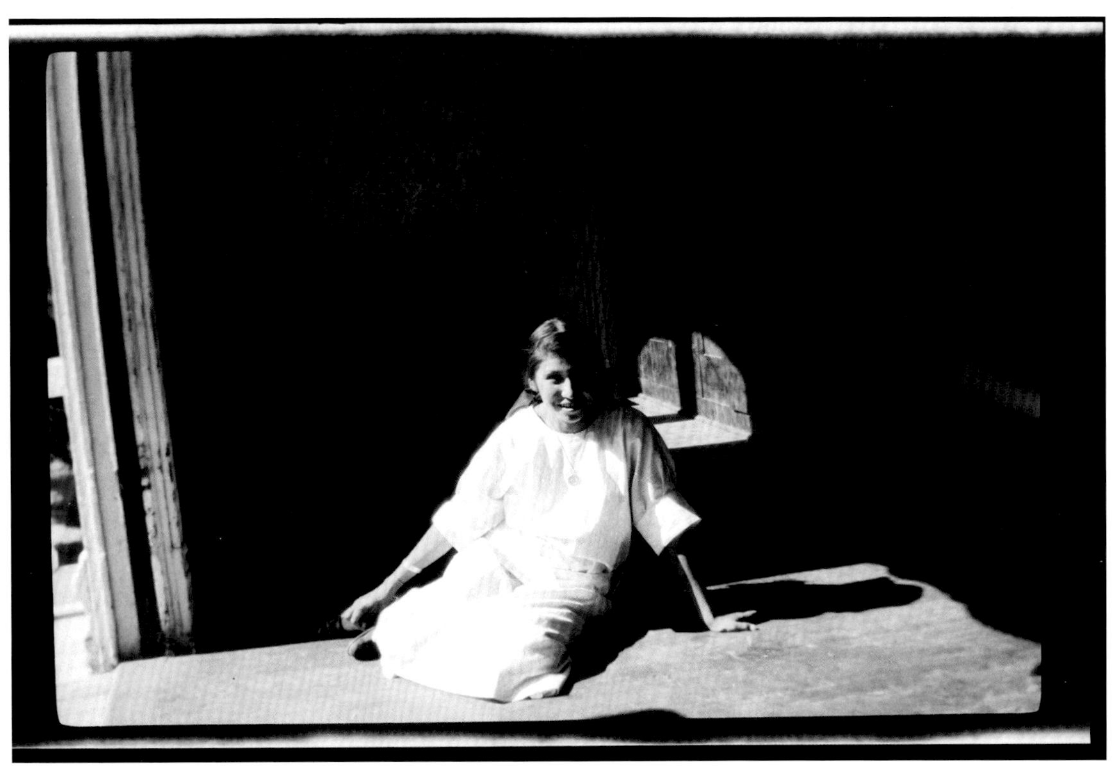

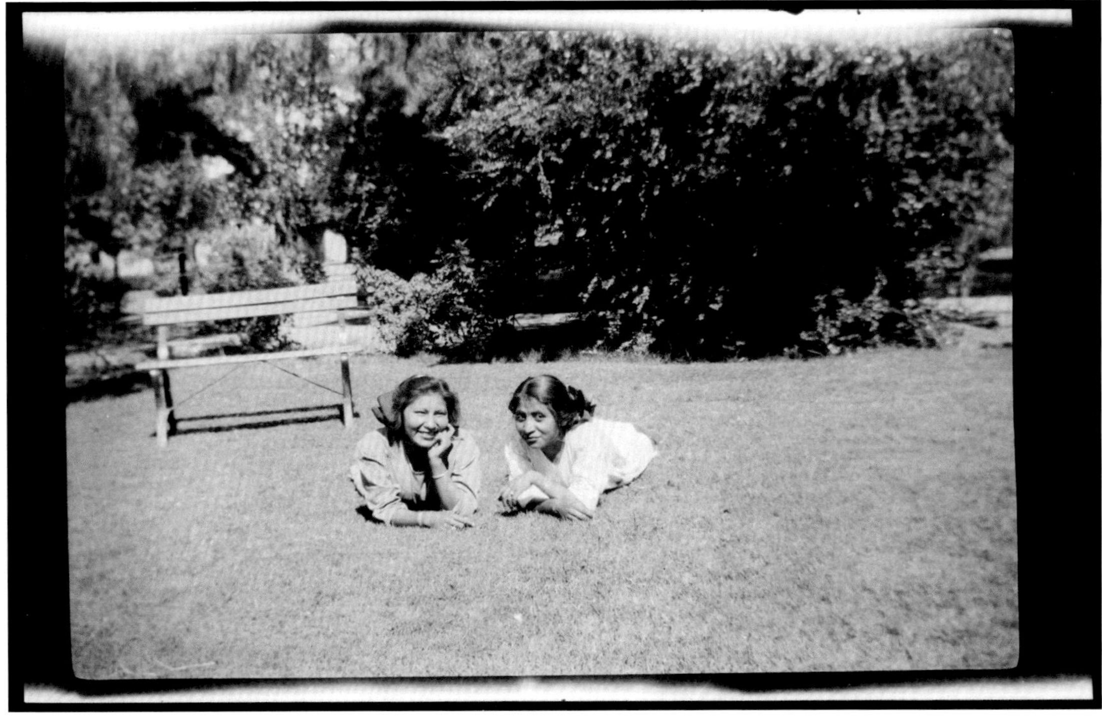

Nettie Odlety
Kiowa, c. 1896–1978
Lucy Sumpty, c. 1916
Courtesy of the Oklahoma
Historical Society 19650.117

Parker McKenzie
Kiowa, 1897-1999
Nettie Odlety and Frances Ross, c. 1915
Courtesy of the Oklahoma Historical Society,
Parker McKenzie Collection,19650.102

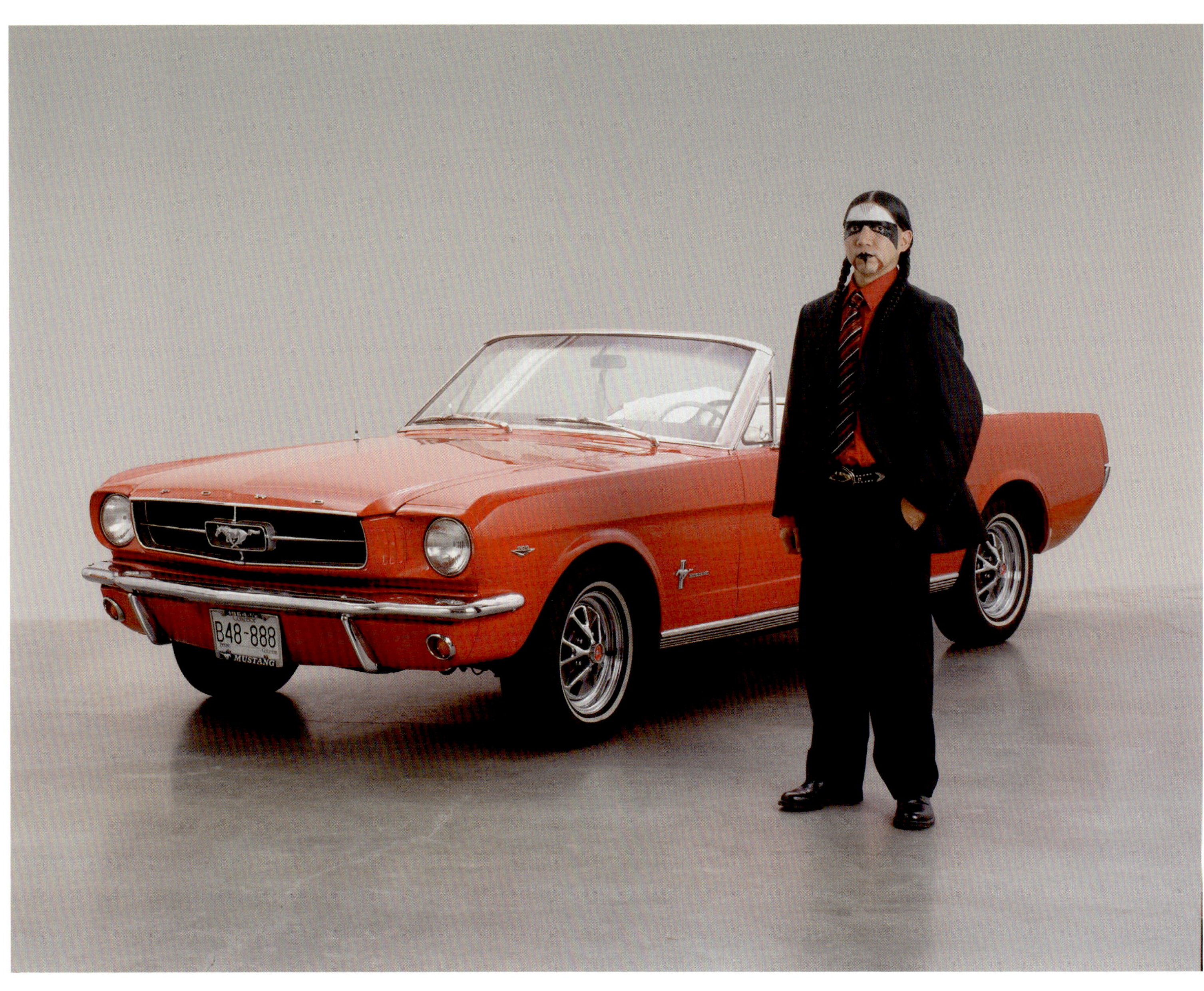

Dana Claxton
Húŋkpapȟa Lakhóta/Wood Mountain Lakota
First Nation, born 1959
Daddy's Gotta New Ride, 2008
from The Mustang Suite
Dye coupler print
Courtesy of the National Gallery of Canada, Ottawa
Photo: NGC
© Dana Claxton

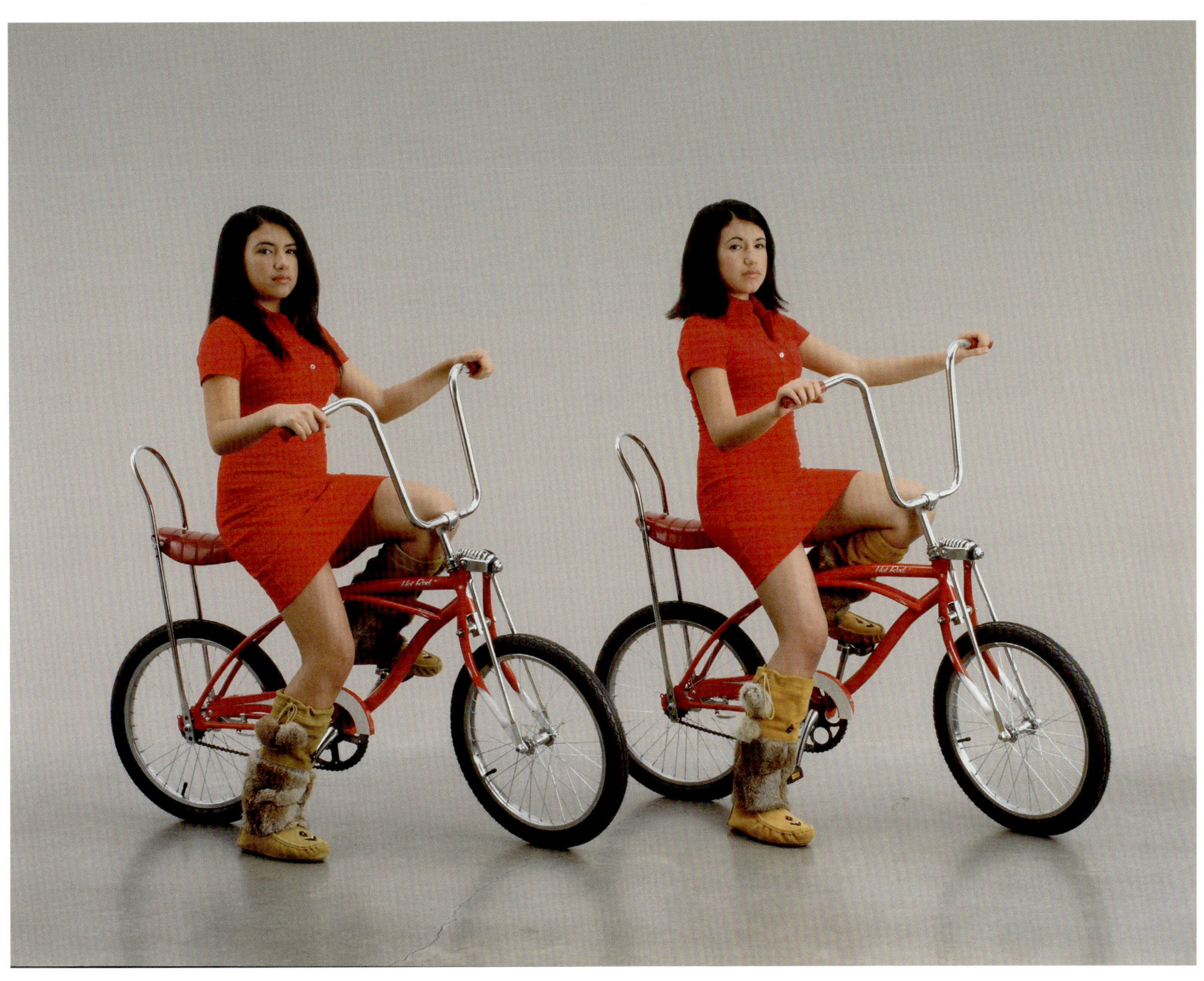

Dana Claxton
Húŋkpapȟa Lakhóta/Wood Mountain Lakota
First Nation, born 1959
Baby Girlz Gotta Mustang, 2008
from The Mustang Suite
Dye coupler print
Courtesy of the National Gallery of Canada, Ottawa
Photo: NGC
© Dana Claxton

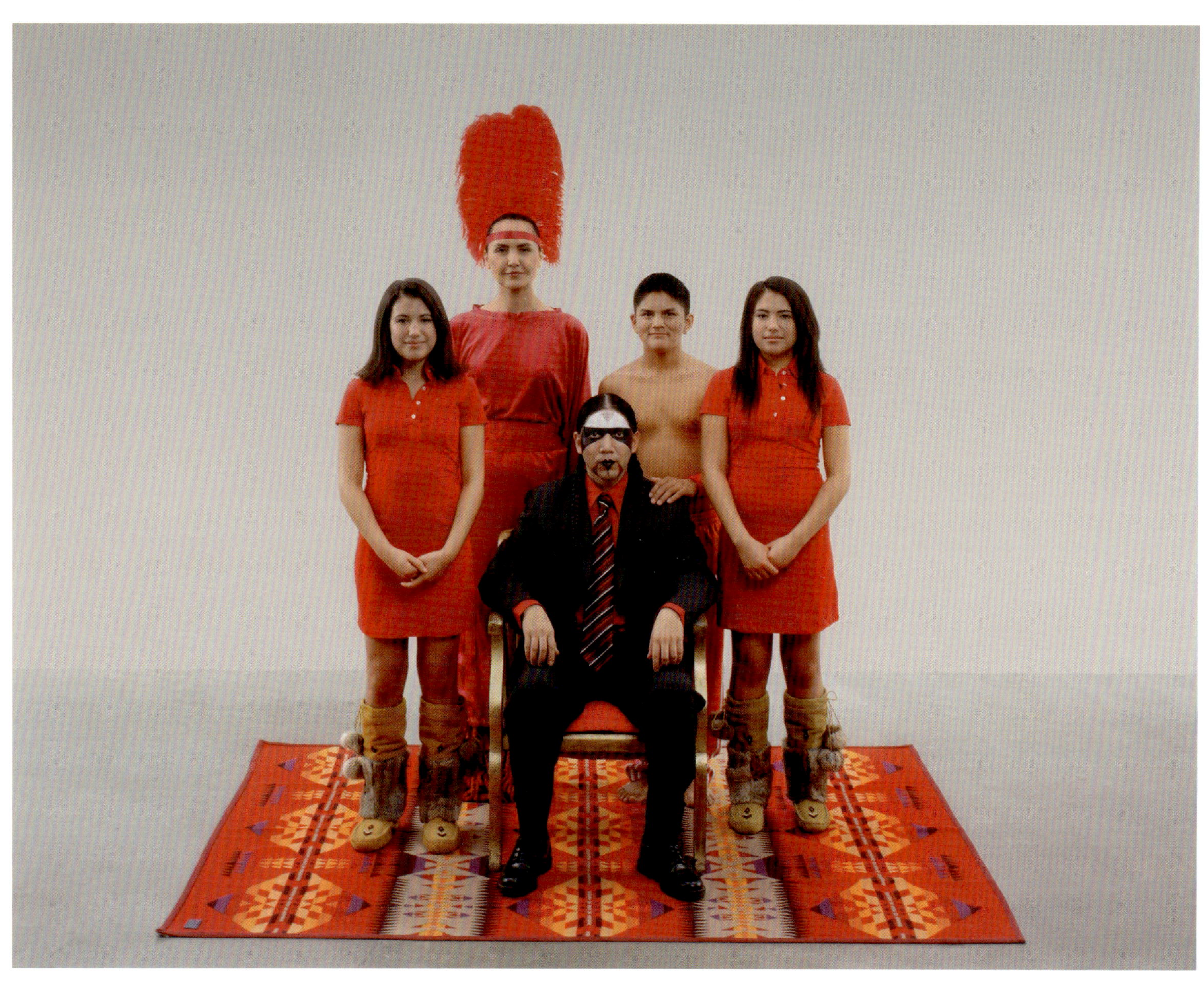

Dana Claxton
Húŋkpapȟa Lakhóta/Wood Mountain Lakota
First Nation, born 1959
Family Portrait (Indians on a Blanket), 2008
from The Mustang Suite
Dye coupler print
Courtesy of the National Gallery of Canada, Ottawa
Photo: NGC

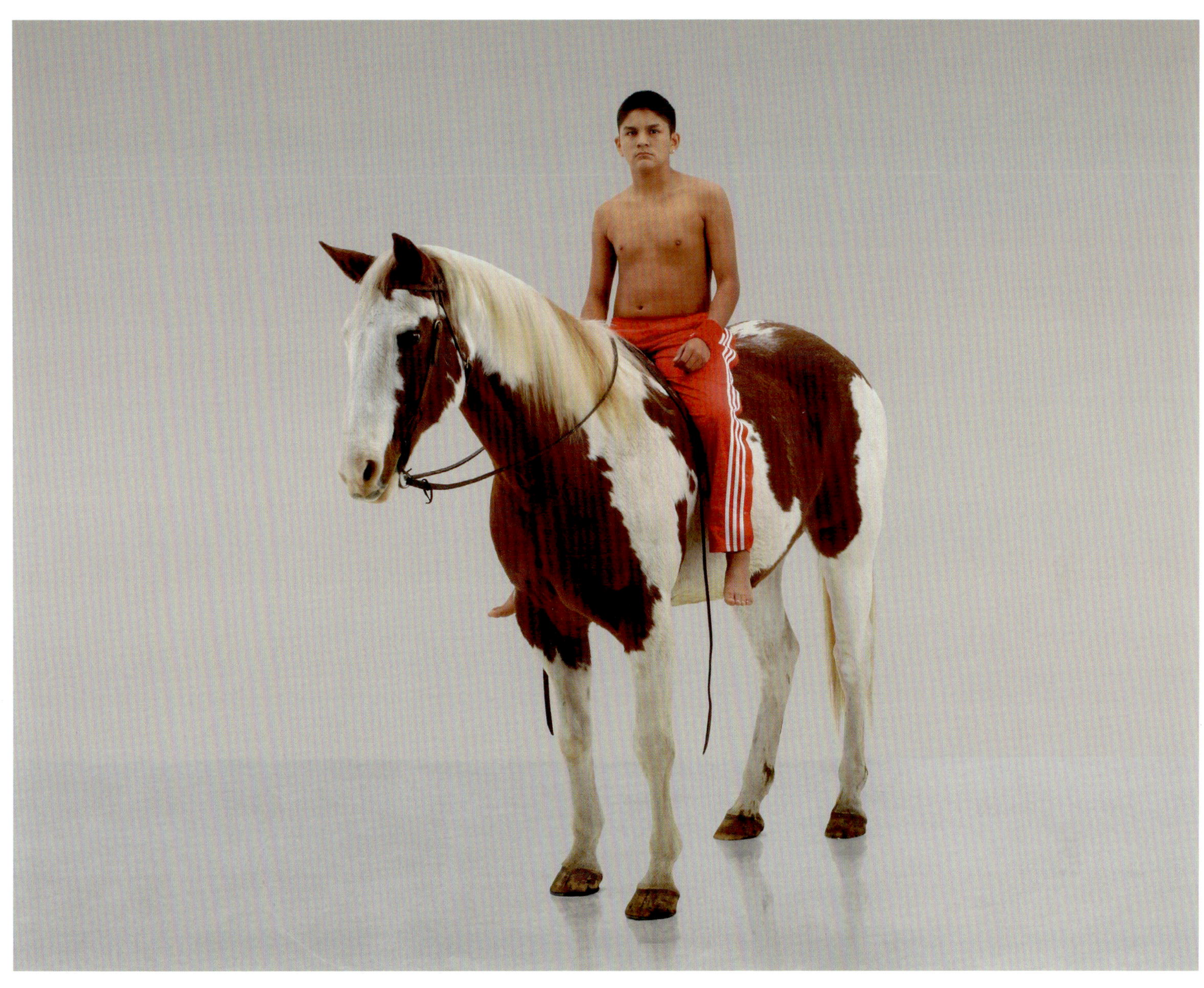

Dana Claxton
Húŋkpapȟa Lakhóta/Wood Mountain Lakota
First Nation, born 1959
Baby Boyz Gotta Indian Horse, 2008
from The Mustang Suite
Dye coupler print
Courtesy of the National Gallery of Canada, Ottawa
Photo: NGC

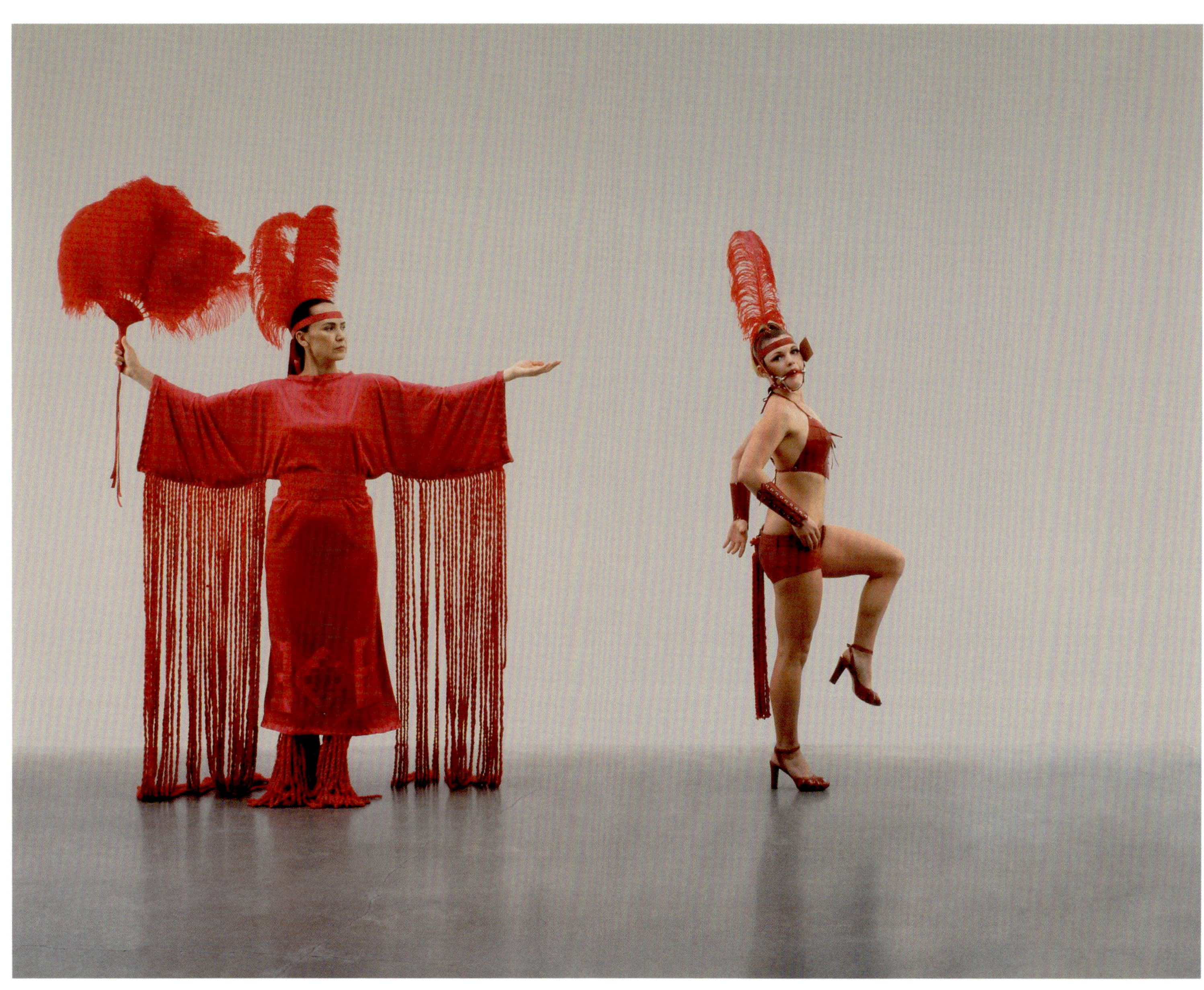

Dana Claxton
Húŋkpapȟa Lakhóta/Wood Mountain Lakota
First Nation, born 1959
Momma Has a Pony Girl (named History and sets her free), 2008
from The Mustang Suite
Dye coupler print
Courtesy of the National Gallery of Canada, Ottawa
Photo: NGC

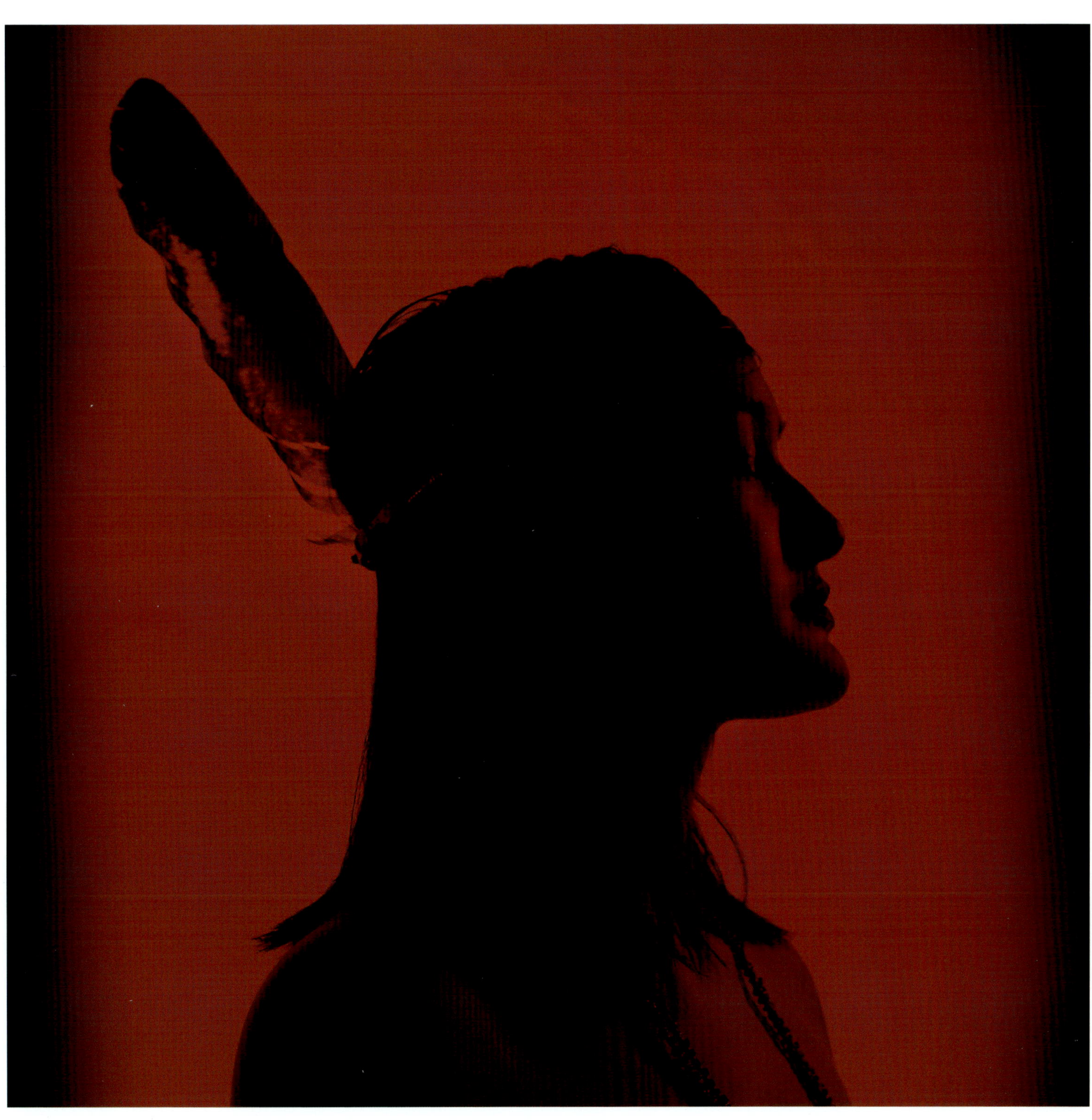

Leah Rose Kolakowski
Keweenaw Bay Ojibwa, born 1989
Bring Her Home, 2018
Courtesy of the artist

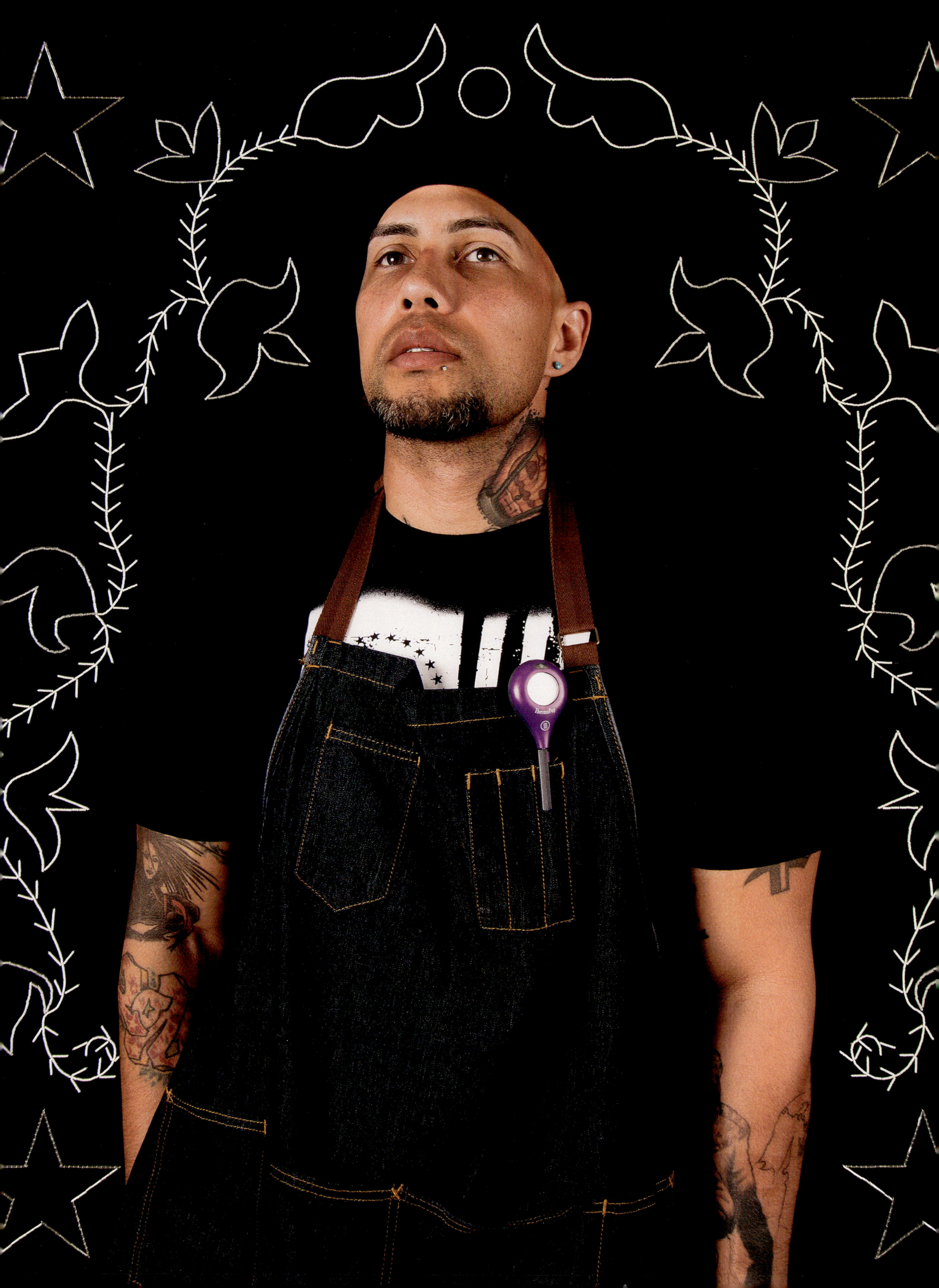

"INDIGENOUS STORYWORK" AND NATIVE AMERICAN PHOTOGRAPHY

BY AMY LONETREE

HISTORICAL PHOTOGRAPHS ARE MOVING DOCUMENTS that provide a glimpse into the past—a past that for Indigenous people has been relegated to the periphery of the American story. The project for many of us in the field of Native American history is to center our communities and our stories in a world that has willfully sought to marginalize, stereotype, and dehumanize us. For Indigenous historians, writing historical narratives that place our voices and perspectives at the center of the narrative is the goal, and photographs are important primary sources for telling our histories in a manner that accurately reflects the nuance and complexity of our experiences. These narratives help restore our humanity, and photographs are powerful lines of evidence that reflect our family and tribal nation history.

Photographs are also important to contemporary reclamation efforts within Indigenous communities. Over the years I have thought critically about the potential of photographs to inspire an active reclaiming of cultural heritage for Native people. One of the central questions that I grapple with is: "How do we begin to theorize Indigenous engagements with historical photography as heritage resources, especially given their colonial history?" The role that photography has played in the service of colonialism—as a documentary project to convey a vanishing race or in creating the anthropological or exoticized other—has received considerable attention in scholarly literature. My research on late-nineteenth and early twentieth-century Ho-Chunk history involves a "reworking" of the photographic archive to provide visual testimony to the ongoing presence and persistence of the Ho-Chunk people in Wisconsin in the aftermath of colonial invasion, violence, and the devastating forced removals from our homelands in the nineteenth century.

Tom Jones
Ho-Chunk, born 1964
Pendalton Price, 2016
Digital photograph with beadwork
Minneapolis Institute of Art, Gift of funds from Lorraine R Hart 2021.88.1

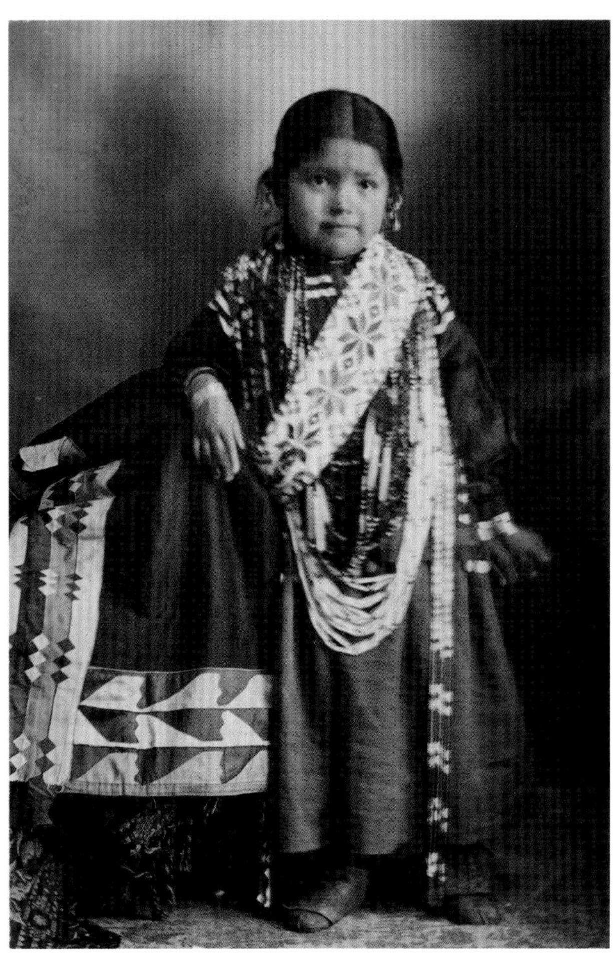

Fig. 1. *Mabel Mary Lonetree (ENooGah)*, ca. 1904. Photo taken by Charles Van Schaick. (Courtesy of the Wisconsin Historical Society, 76694).

I am currently working on a book focusing on Ho-Chunk Nation history and Native American photography. My research explores the intersections of photographic images, family history, tourism, and Ho-Chunk survivance through an examination of two important photographic collections currently housed at the Wisconsin Historical Society: the Charles Van Schaick Collection and the Henry Hamilton (H.H.) Bennett Collection. The Van Schaick collection includes nearly 1,000 photographs of Ho-Chunk people taken between 1879 and 1942. The Bennett Collection is comprised of hundreds of images of tribal members taken from 1865 through the latter part of the twentieth century, and it also contains film reels of the Stand Rock Indian Ceremonial, a major tourist attraction in Wisconsin Dells, WI, from the 1920's to the 1990's. Both collections comprise an amazing visual legacy for Ho-Chunk people documenting a long-neglected period in Native American history—the so-called "Dark Ages" of the late-nineteenth and early twentieth century, and they include visual materials that represent and convey a deep history of Ho-Chunk resilience and survivance, along with the ongoing legacies of settler colonialism.

My own family is well represented in these collections, and I will never forget my first encounter with the Charles Van Schaick photographs in the summer of 1993, while working on a Minnesota Historical Society exhibit featuring the Ho-Chunk Nation. That summer, I had been hired to work on *A Common Ground,* an exhibit that highlighted six different communities from across Minnesota, including the Ho-Chunk Nation. As a Ho-Chunk citizen and museum scholar, my interest in the project was both professional and personal. The exhibit marked one of the first times, if not *the* first time, that a Minnesota cultural institution had presented the Ho-Chunk Nation's story, and I wanted to participate in presenting this much-neglected part of state history. Having the opportunity to conduct research with this treasure trove of historical images of Ho-Chunk families then housed at the Jackson County Historical Society in

Black River Falls, WI, was deeply inspiring, and I will never forget the moment when I held the images of long known but never before seen relatives on both sides of my Ho-Chunk family, who are the source of the pride I hold within me. Seeing these images of my ancestors led to a series of conversations with my grandparents, Ann and Samuel Lonetree, and other Ho-Chunk relatives, and through these conversations I came to know my own family and tribal nation history in new and profoundly meaningful ways.

In the decades since, as I have read the scholarly literature and thought through the significance of Indigenous engagements with historical photography, I find myself returning again and again to these earlier conversations and what they reveal. The knowledge shared by my grandparents in our discussions about the photographs clarified my genealogy and reminded me how deeply and inextricably linked my personal family history is to the history of the Ho-Chunk Nation. What I witnessed in practice is what I call the "storywork of historical photography" and the ways these photographs are working to help us understand connection to community, history, Ho-Chunk knowledge and culture, kinship, and our responsibilities to one another.

Jo-Ann Archibald (Stó:lō) and her collaborators in their scholarship on storywork as methodology argue that: "Indigenous storywork is action, it is process, it is the seeking of meaning in community. ... [it] traverses new theoretical, methodological, and pedagogical realms where Indigenous stories, experiences, and understandings are the core of the meaning-making process."[73] As we engage with the photographs and the stories that they inspire, we are reminded of the central importance of storytelling as a method and how these images are mobilized in the present to "re-right and rewrite" history (to quote Māori scholar Linda Tuhiwai Smith) and reclaim connection to family, place, and tribal nation.

One of the most meaningful images for me from the Charles Van Schaick collection is this one of Mabel Mary Lonetree (see fig. 1). Over the years while working with these collections I have gained important knowledge about my family lineage and heritage, and at times difficult knowledge. Photographs, as we know, have the power to inspire conversations, clarify genealogical and historical information, and raise discussion of painful truths. This image of Mabel Mary Lonetree, one of my ancestors, uncovered some of those painful truths and the knowledge gained from sharing this image is a powerful example of the storywork of historical photography.[74]

We found this photograph when working on *People of the Big Voice: Photographs of Ho-Chunk Families by Charles Van Schaick, 1879–1942,* published by the Wisconsin Historical Society Press in 2011. Mike Schmudlach, one of my co-collaborators, contacted me one evening while we were deep in the development process to convey the story of a recent find. During a

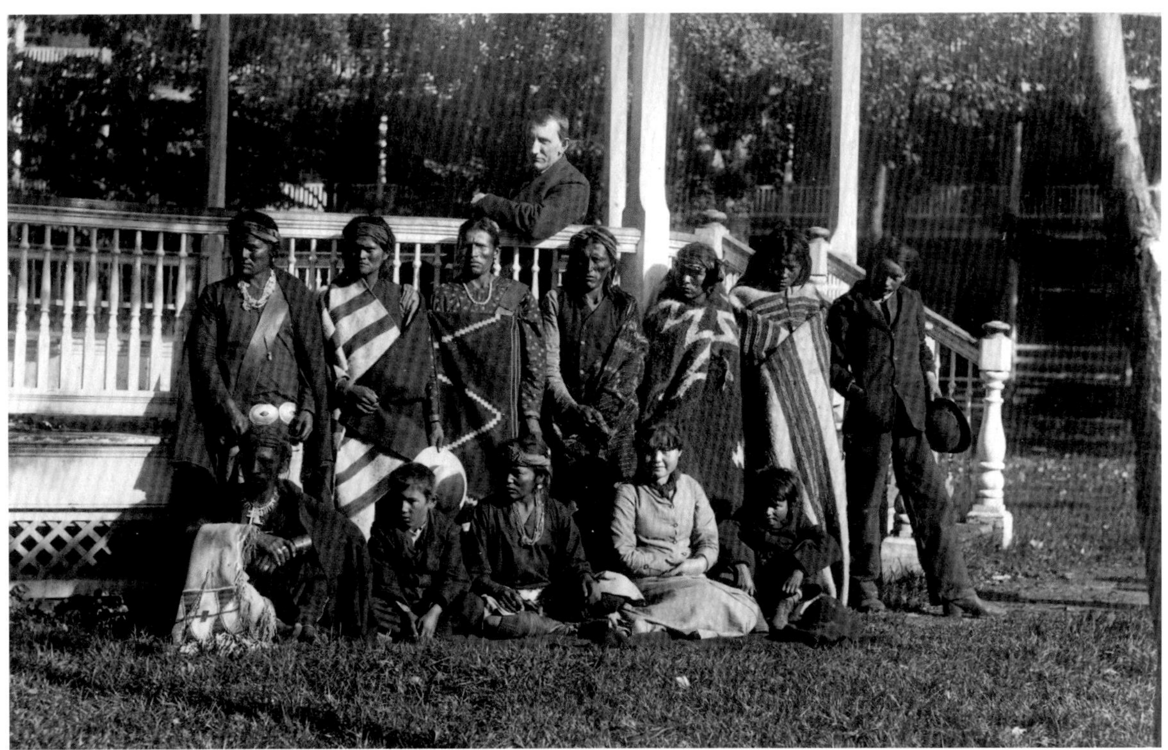

Fig. 2. *Navajo students upon arrival, October 21, 1882.* (Courtesy of the Cumberland County Historical Society, Carlisle, PA.).

trip to Black River Falls, the place where the collection was originally housed before the move to the Wisconsin Historical Society in 1994, he came upon some never before seen images by several of our research team members. The image of Mabel Mary was tucked away in a back room and largely forgotten. Something led him to look in that area and that is when he found it—"It was almost as if she wanted to be discovered," he stated. He sent the photograph to me later, and I smiled as I looked at the picture of this chubby cheeked girl with big dark eyes whose expression and bearing speak to a lively spirit and confidence beyond her years. Mabel Mary is seen in this photograph taken in 1904 in the center of the frame, dressed in the finest Ho-Chunk regalia including necklaces, earrings, paxge, and a beautifully beaded sash, which looks like it could be a bandolier bag turned backwards—with her little arm draped over some Ho-Chunk ribbon applique work.

The family history and genealogical information that was clarified in my later discussions with tribal members revealed a difficult truth, and this information is especially poignant now after the events of the last several years with the Covid-19 pandemic. I learned shortly after viewing this image that Mabel Mary died in 1906 of influenza just a few years after the image was taken. Influenza devastated our community in successive waves in the early twentieth century. Mabel Mary was the oldest daughter of my great-great grandfather, Alex Lonetree, and great-great grandmother, Kate Winneshiek Lonetree. Mabel died at the age of five. Her

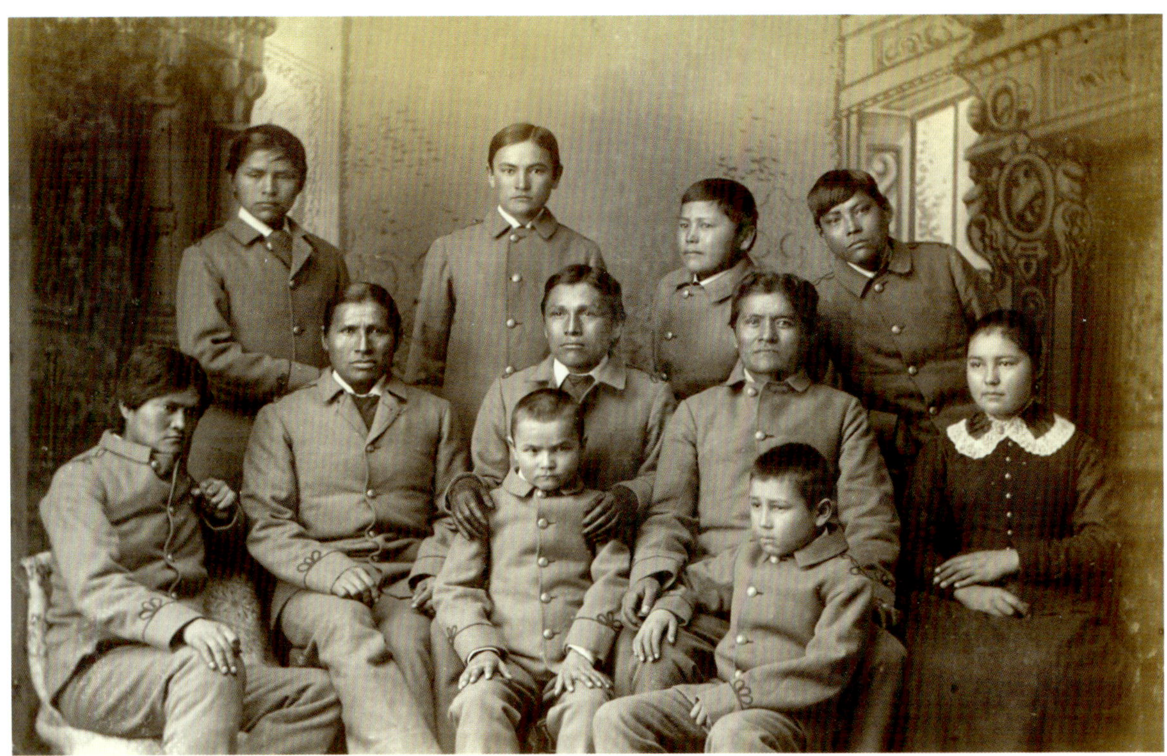

Fig. 3. *Navajo Group who entered Carlisle October 21, 1882, after some time at the school.* (Courtesy of the Cumberland County Historical Society, Carlisle, PA.).

mother had died of influenza four years earlier, as had Mabel's sister Anna in January 1905 and her brother Howard one month after her. My great-grandfather George Lonetree was the only child of Alex and Kate Lonetree to survive the epidemics sweeping Ho-Chunk country during this time.

I should add that I had heard fragments of this story in the past, of the great losses within my family and community during this period, but I did not have the specifics. I did not know the full extent of the losses that Kate and Alex suffered until this image inspired these conversations. My great-great grandfather Alex lost his two daughters, son, and wife in a four-year period. All that remained of his family were his two sons, my great-grandfather George, and his other son, Hugh Lonetree. I cannot help but be overwhelmed with the weight of the loss that my family experienced. But, yet, like our relatives in the nineteenth century, who survived the repeated forced removals from our beloved homelands, somehow through his strong faith and determination, Alex managed to rebuild his life. He married again, and in 1918 had another daughter Sophie, and lived by all accounts a full life as an active member of the community. His story of survivance is one that is shared with many Ho-Chunk people who survived the hardships of settler colonial policies in the late-nineteenth and early twentieth-century, as well as the devastating impact of disease, and who fought to retain our culture in the face of overwhelming odds.

Mabel Mary Lonetree is just one example of the many Ho-Chunk children featured in the Charles Van Schaick Collection. The presence of children in these collections is especially poignant given the ongoing and systematic attacks on our families that continued throughout the twentieth century, as a result of the government's assimilation campaign. The images of our children, either alone or with sisters, brothers, parents, and grandparents, are an important visual testimony of our kinship ties and efforts to keep our families together in the face of ongoing colonial violence. The Van Schaick images also stand in stark contrast to the boarding school before and after photographs that are the most ubiquitous and widely circulated images of Native American children during this period, including the images taken at the most well-known federally run boarding school, the Carlisle Institute in Pennsylvania. We have all seen the "contrast" images of the children, including one of twelve Navajo students with Richard Henry Pratt in 1882, and the "after" photo following "some time at the school." (see figs. 2 & 3)

I find this image of Mabel Mary, a much beloved child in her Ho-Chunk regalia whose life was tragically cut short before her sixth birthday, to have an entirely different feel to it than the images of Native children at boarding school. The boarding school images are also of cherished Native American children, but their images were used as propaganda for the US government's assimilationist efforts and circulated for the purposes of documenting the goals of the boarding school system to assimilate American Indian children. The image of Mabel Mary, dressed in her finest Ho-Chunk clothing and jewelry, was created for her family and fellow Ho-Chunk tribal members. This photograph is now proudly displayed in my own home, and when I see Mabel Mary a mix of emotions are always present. I think of a life taken far too soon and the pain of that loss, but I also feel love and a deep connection to this young ancestor and the knowledge of Ho-Chunk family and tribal nation history that she inspires me to pursue.

I recently attended a conference in Paris hosted by the Institut National d'Histoire de l'Art (INHA), called "Making Pictures Talk" on the power of storytelling from images and how scholars use images to construct narratives. During one of the sessions, an American historian inquired of one of the presenters, "How do we know if our reading of the image is correct, and how do we become confident in our analysis?" She went on to provide a straightforward example regarding her own experience. If one were to look through her family's photo albums, they would see a little girl wearing dresses throughout her young life, leaving future viewers to assume that she loved wearing them. The truth is she hated dresses. Her point is important to keep in mind when pondering, "How do we avoid placing inaccurate assumptions on an individual's personal motivations when engaging with what is happening in the frame?" As she

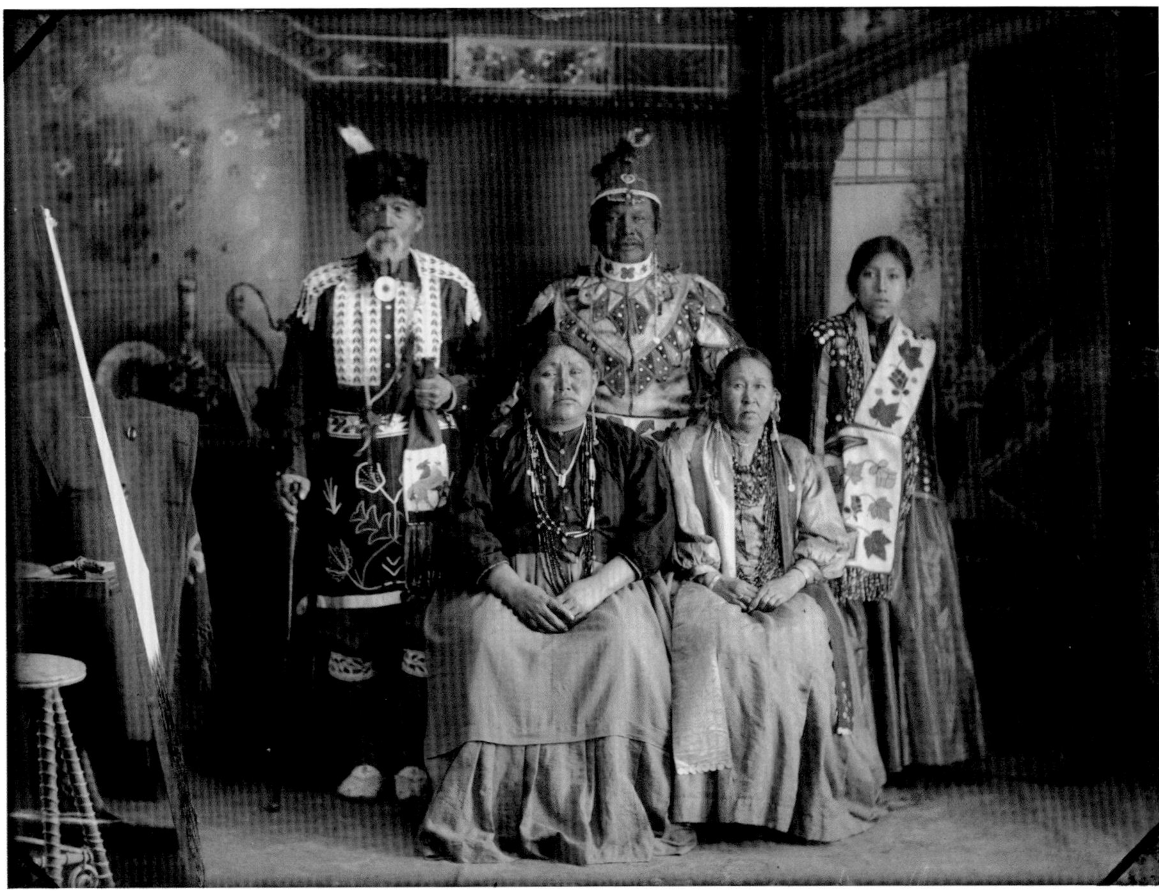

Fig. 4. A studio portrait in front of a painted backdrop of Winnebago Indians: John Hazen Hill, Alex Lonetree, daughter of Alex Lonetree, Mrs. Alex Lonetree, and Wolf Woman., ca. 1890. (Photo taken by Charles Van Schaick. Courtesy of the Wisconsin Historical Society, 3058).

relayed her story, I was reminded of a photograph of one of my ancestors, Alex Lonetree, in his regalia along with other family members and the lessons it provides to not make rigid assumptions or claims regarding one's identity through a quick read of the image. We as scholars and historians must be attentive to the nuances and complexities of how we read images.

This image of Alex Lonetree in a striking shirt also features other relatives in their regalia directly facing the camera in the Van Schaick studio around 1900 (see fig. 4). This photograph has been used in other historical texts and is featured on the back cover of *People of the Big Voice: Photographs of Ho-Chunk Families by Charles Van Schaick, 1879–1942* (Wisconsin Historical Society Press, 2011). It is eye-catching and reflects what Matthew Daniel Mason calls the "accepted conventions of portraiture" during this period, with my great-great grandfather Alex or Alec Lonetree, the family bread winner, in the center of the frame.[75] Standing are John Hazen Hill (Xetenįšarakga), left, Alec (Alex) Lonetree (Nąą linekiga), and Mary Clara Blackhawk (Waxopįnįwįga), daughter of Lucy Emerson Brown; sitting are Lucy Emerson Brown (Peec Kereiga), left, and Lucy Long-Wolf Winneshiek (Šųųkjąkwįga), ca. 1900.[76]

The image reflects the survival of my family and exemplifies our kinship relationships. They are engaging in a process, as other Ho-Chunk families did, of documenting the important people or moments in their lives by having their portraits taken in the Van Schaick studio. These individuals are gazing directly at the camera, standing tall and proud, in what look like carefully planned outfits for the camera. They are standing in front of a typical studio backdrop in Van Schaick's studio; notice that one of the men brought an overcoat and it is in the corner. The presence of the overcoat is a reminder that this photographer was not invested in removing representations of an individual's modernity in these images, as the Van Schaick studio is not about documenting vanishing races. In this image that reflects family cohesion and modernity, one cannot help but notice Alex's attire. I recall a conversation with my relative, George Hushi Greendeer, about this particular shirt.

During our conversation, I told him that everyone who has seen the images, has asked about it over the years with most enquiring, typically in hushed tones, is Alex wearing traditional Ho-Chunk regalia? George then shared a story that has stayed with me and continues to inform my engagements with historical images. He conveyed what his grandmother (and my great-grandmother), Puss White Lonetree, told him about the shirt's history. She shared that Alex saw this shirt in the window of a store in Black River Falls one day and decided to purchase it. The shirt was part of a clown costume, and he later incorporated this jester-style shirt into his outfit for the portrait. The story related to this image, while brief, is informative and layered as it reminds all of us that these individuals were embracing modernity, the quality of being modern, at a moment when others believed they were on the road to extinction and during one of the darkest periods in our history. Alex Lonetree is part of the cultural life of Black River Falls, WI, and embraced an opportunity to incorporate this eye catching and dramatic shirt into his attire for the day along with his intertribal regalia. These people are not resisting change—in some cases they are embracing it. It also instructs us about the complexity of identity and that how one chooses to represent themselves to the camera reflects an evolving notion of culture that is never static. The stories related to this particular image also remind us that during this period of rapid cultural change for Ho-Chunks, when we were believed by some to be on the road to extinction, we are very much present in the ongoing life of the community, and this remains an important act of conveying to the world that we are still here. As James Clifford writes, "For Indigenous people, long marginalized or made to disappear, physically and ideologically, to say 'We exist' in performances and publications is a powerful political act."[77] I would extend that statement to photographs, as well. The motivation of the sitters most likely rests on a desire to document their lives, as all other residents in the town of Black River Falls are doing while posing for portraits in the Van Schaick studio. However, we read these images today as powerful representations of our ongoing presence at the height of the United States government's assimilation campaign and during the ongoing and systematic attacks on our families, cultures, identities, and lifeways.

This is a significant form of self-representation and the Ho-Chunks visiting the Van Schaick studio are choosing how they want to represent themselves to the camera, and for the most part, controlling how these images are circulated, as these images were created for the private collections of Ho-Chunk people and circulated in the intratribal world of Wisconsin and Nebraska. The stereotypes of Native people during this period as victimized, downtrodden, and destitute are pervasive, and must have been painful for our relatives to have to confront every day. While one does not want to ignore the ongoing assaults to Ho-Chunk humanity and families taking place during this time, these images of our ancestors speak to their strength and steadfast determination to persist and do so with a pride of appearance that is uniquely our own. Our ancestors were engaging in a forward-looking act, reflecting their desire to have studio portraits taken for current and future generations. And while these motivations may seem common or universal for all people who have studio portraits taken with family, the images of Native American families during this period must always be read with an understanding of the colonial forces that are seeking to disrupt and destroy those kinship ties. Even though we are facing the ongoing policies of settler colonialism, these images remind us that we are "rich in relations"[78] and this remains one of our greatest strengths.

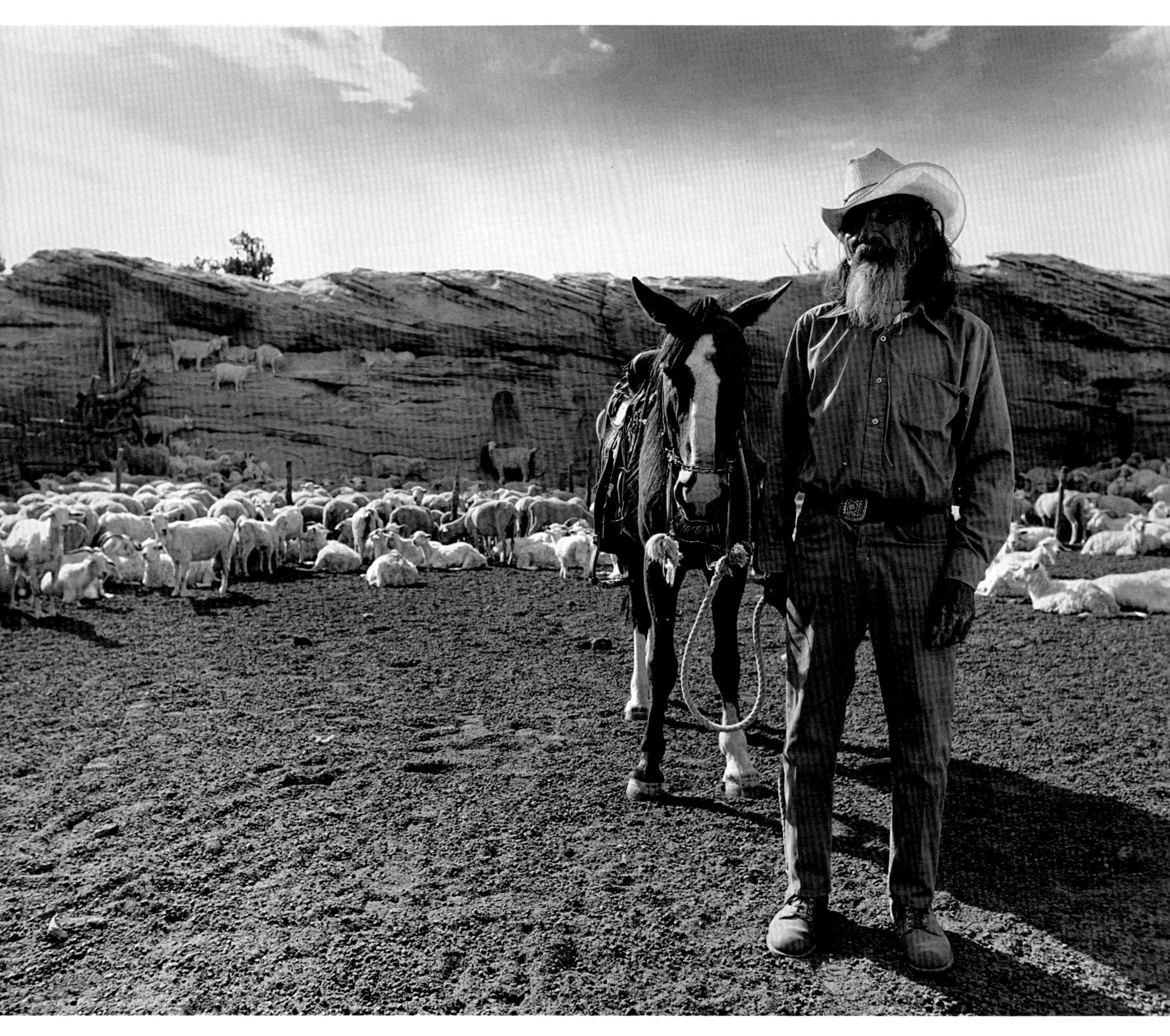

Lee Marmon
Laguna Pueblo, 1925–2021
Bennie at Sheep Camp, 1984
Gelatin silver print
Courtesy of the C.N. Gorman Museum, 2008.20.10.61

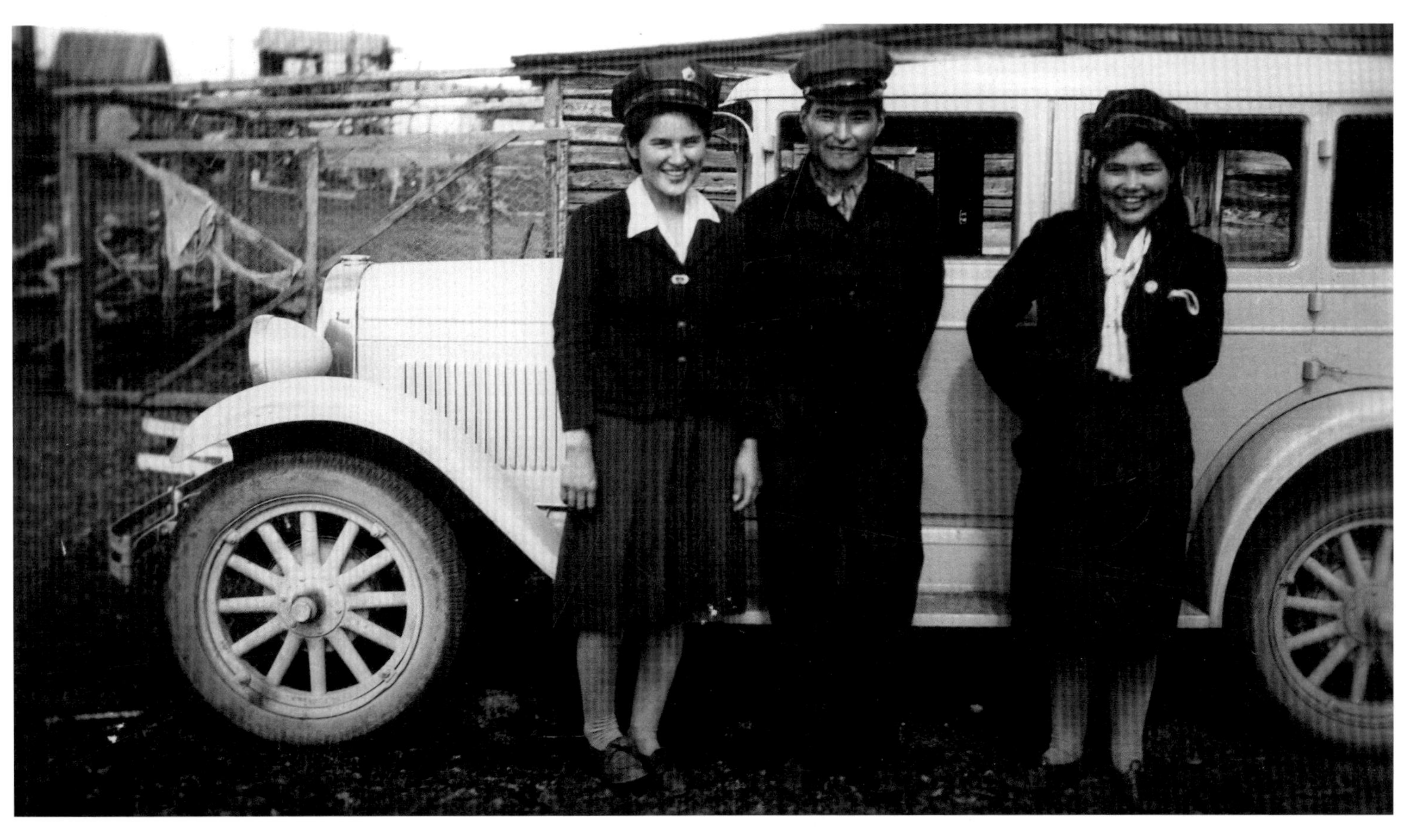

George Johnston
Tlingit, 1894-1972
[George Johnston's Nieces], 1943
Inkjet print
Courtesy of Yukon Archives, 82/428, #19

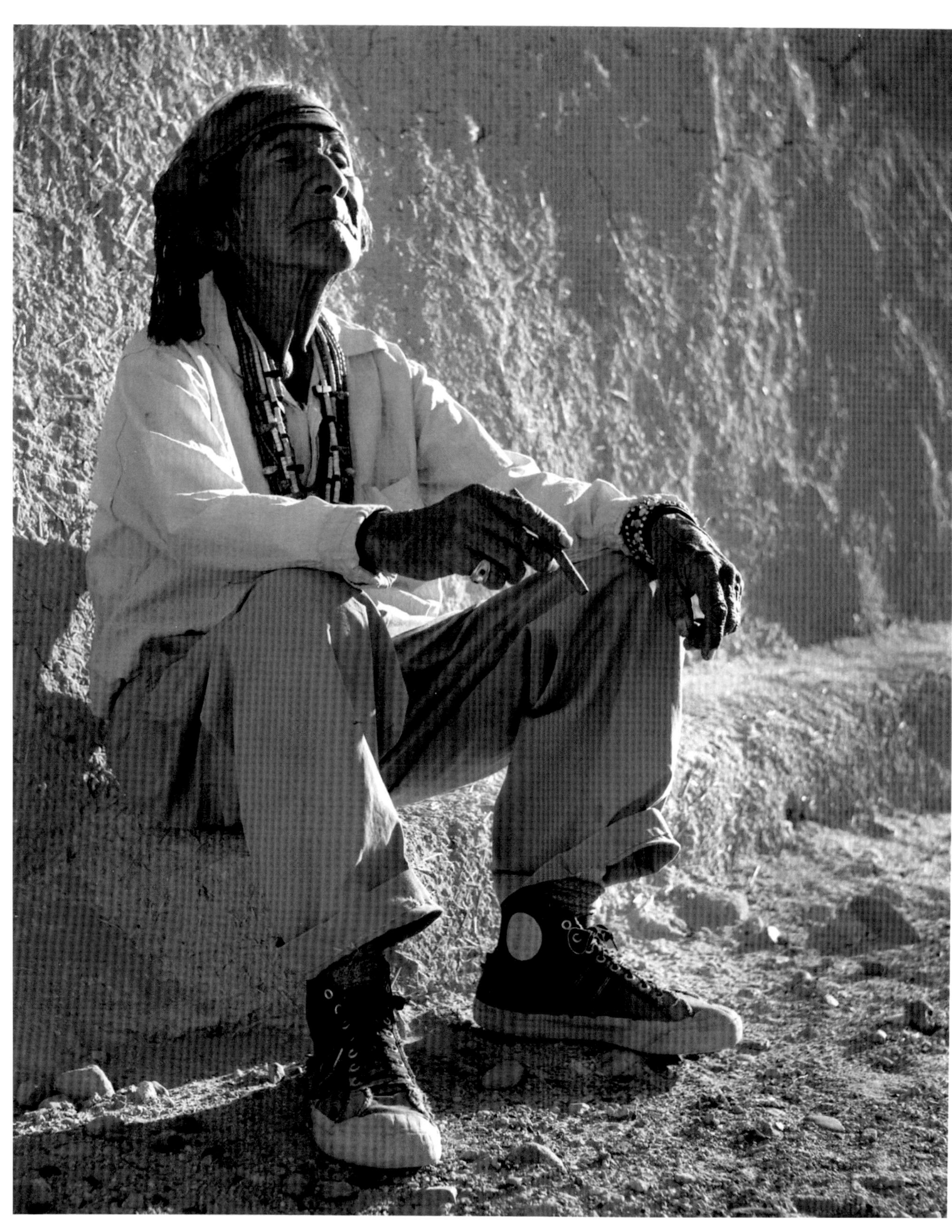

Lee Marmon
Laguna Pueblo, 1925–2021
White Man's Moccasins, 1954
Gelatin silver print
Courtesy of the C.N. Gorman Museum 2008.20.10.67

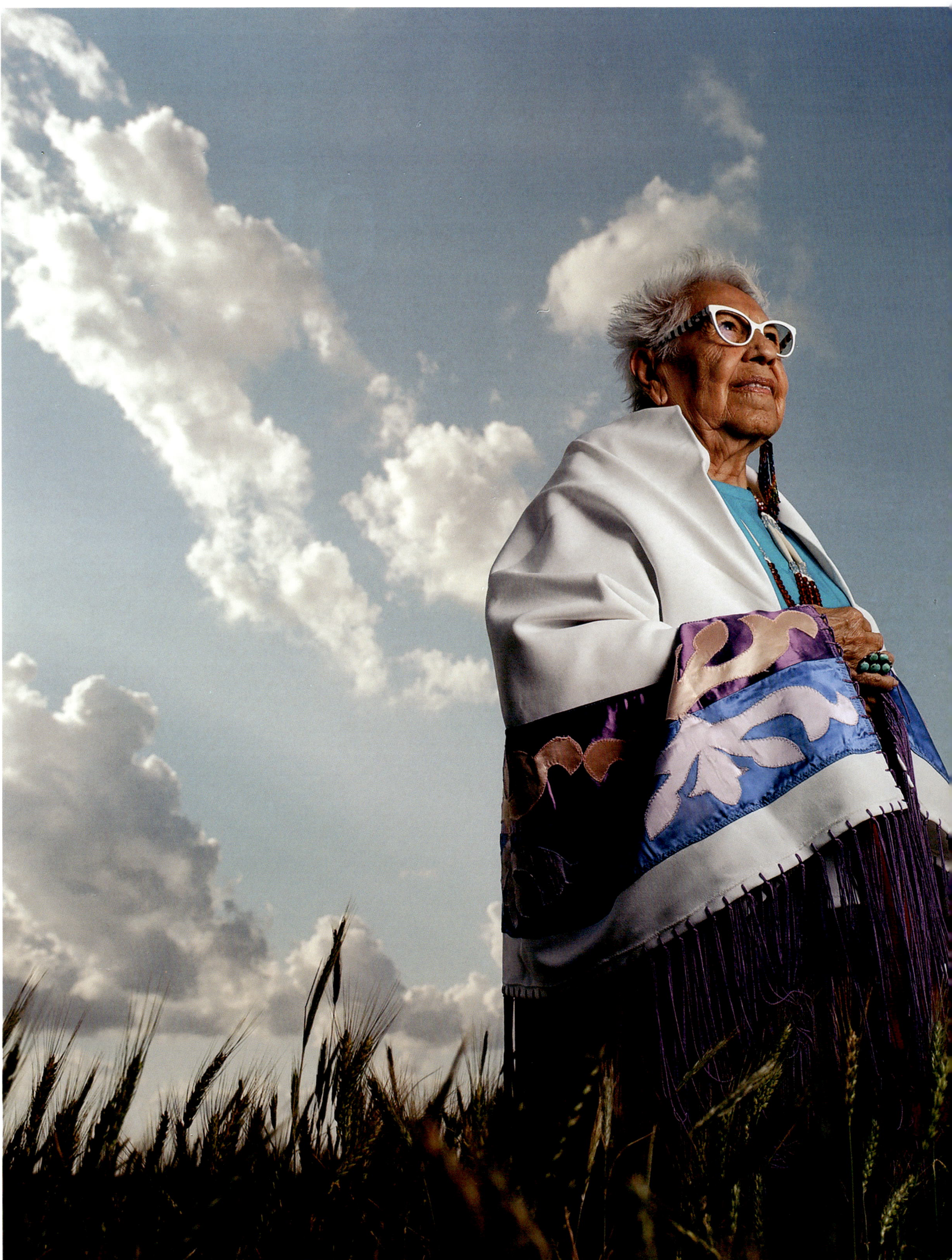

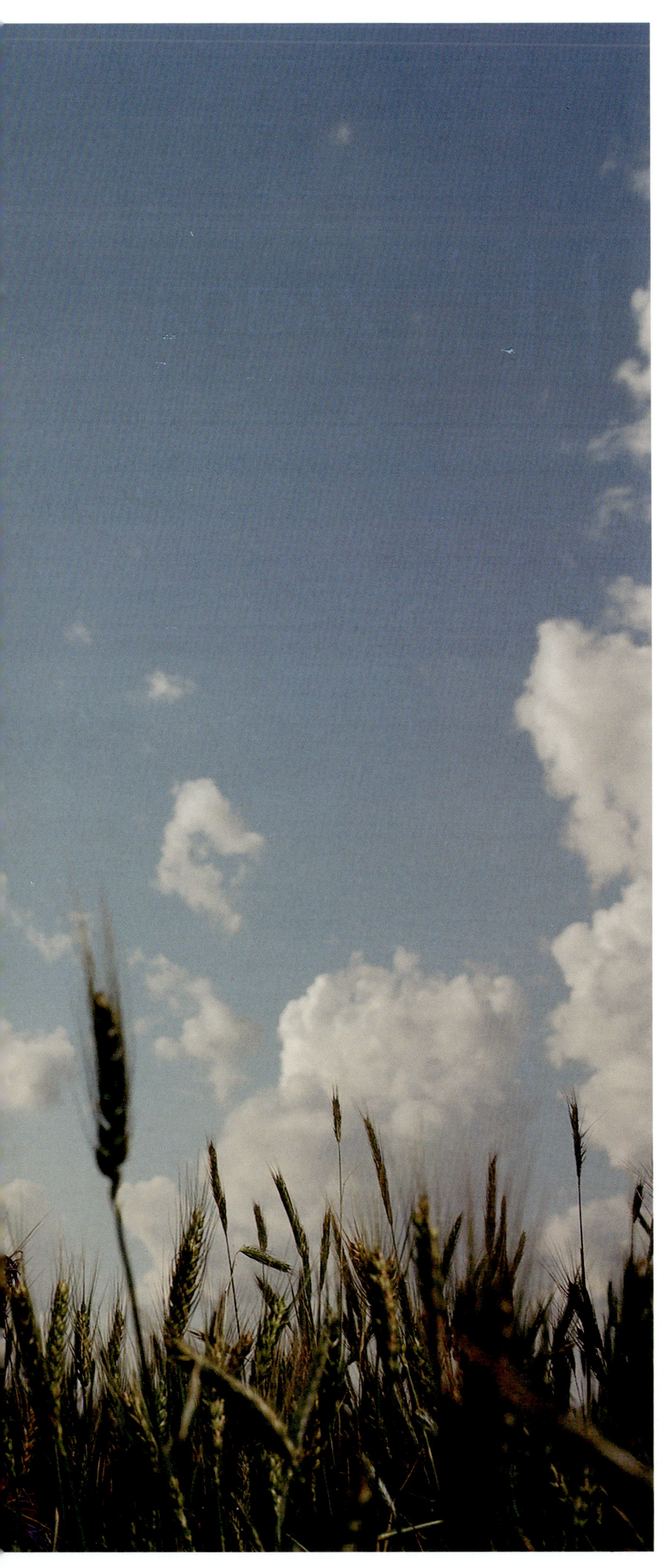

Matika Wilbur (Tsa-Tsiq)
Swinomish and Tulalip, born 1984
Dr. Henrietta Mann (Cheyenne), 2019
Inkjet print
Courtesy of the artist
© Matika Wilbur

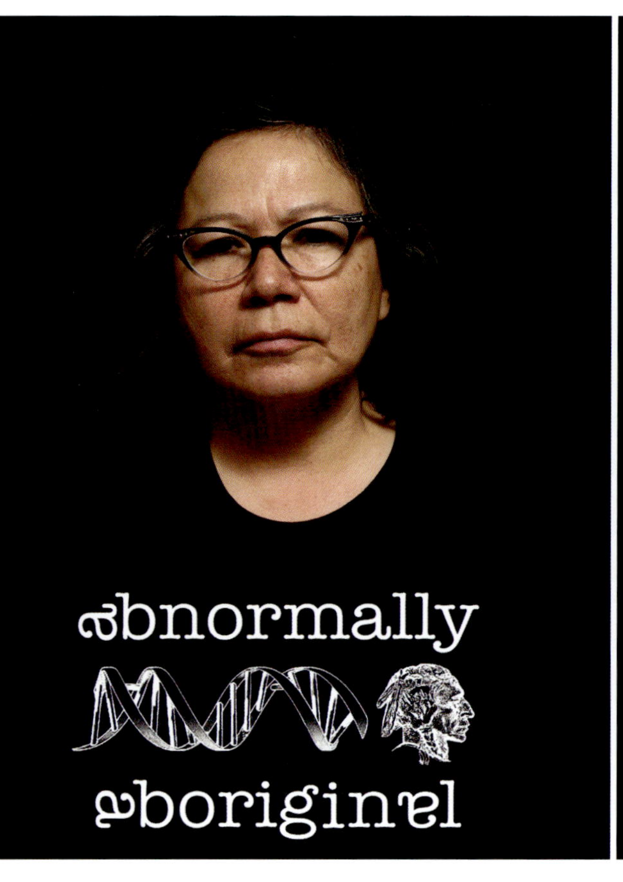

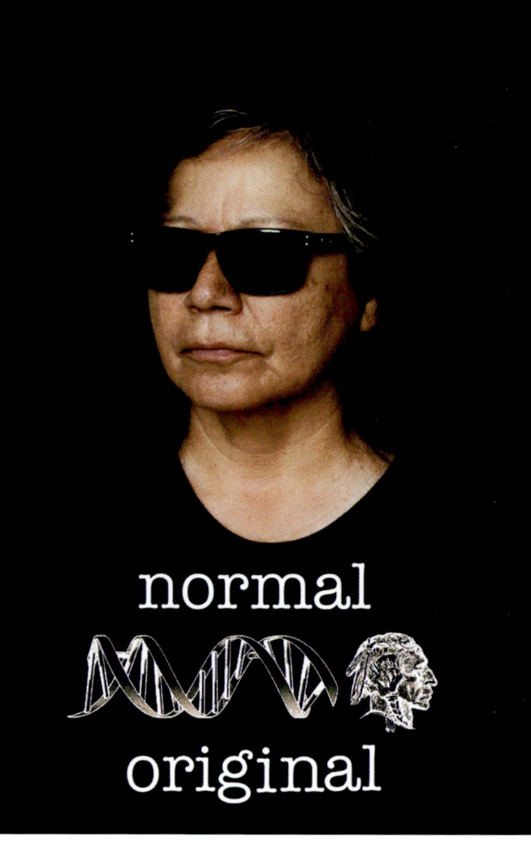

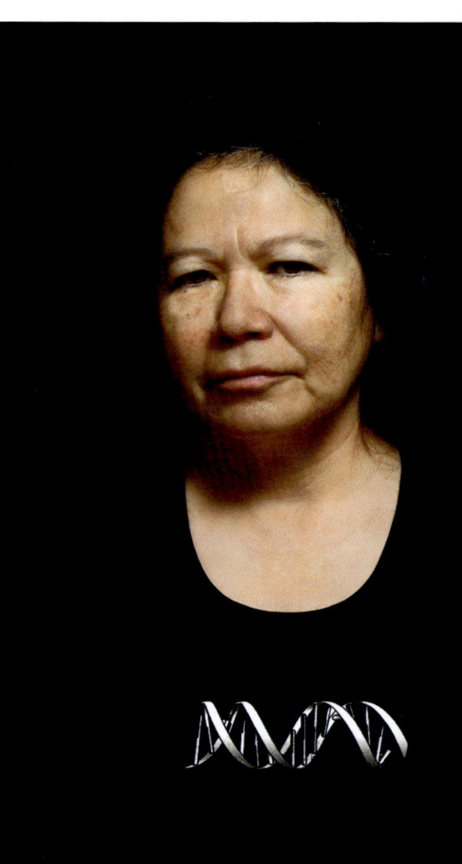

Shelley Niro
Bay of Quinte Mohawk,
Six Nations Turtle clan, born 1954
Abnormally Aboriginal, 2013
Courtesy of the artist
© Shelley Niro

THE LAST ONE HUNDRED YEARS

BY SHELLEY NIRO

ONE HUNDRED YEARS AGO MY FATHER WAS BORN IN 1921. My mother was born in 1930. From then until now, so many changes have occurred. Here, I'm concentrating on the advancement of photography within that time and the influences it's made. They were born into nothing. I was born in 1954. I feel like I was born into nothing. As Indian people we had nothing.

In 1992, the television series *North of 60* was born. It was the first of its kind. Shown on the CBC, in Canada, this became a pivotal time for Indigenous representation on TV and in many other forms.

My parents planned their TV time around Thursday nights at eight o'clock. If they were visiting, they would look at their watches and declare, "We gotta go." They went home to watch *North of 60*. One of the characters, Rosie Deela, was played by a Six Nations resident, Tina Louise Bomberry. They were proud. I mention this series, because it was the first ever to show real Indians playing real situations of Indians on reserves.

I feel that my generation is a bridge between my parents' generation and the youth of today. I did not hold the same awe my parents held however I do know what it feels like to not see any representation of Indigenous visual art production. They grew up in a world where the representation of Indigenous people was limited and not respected if they were not adorned in feathers, furs, and bones.

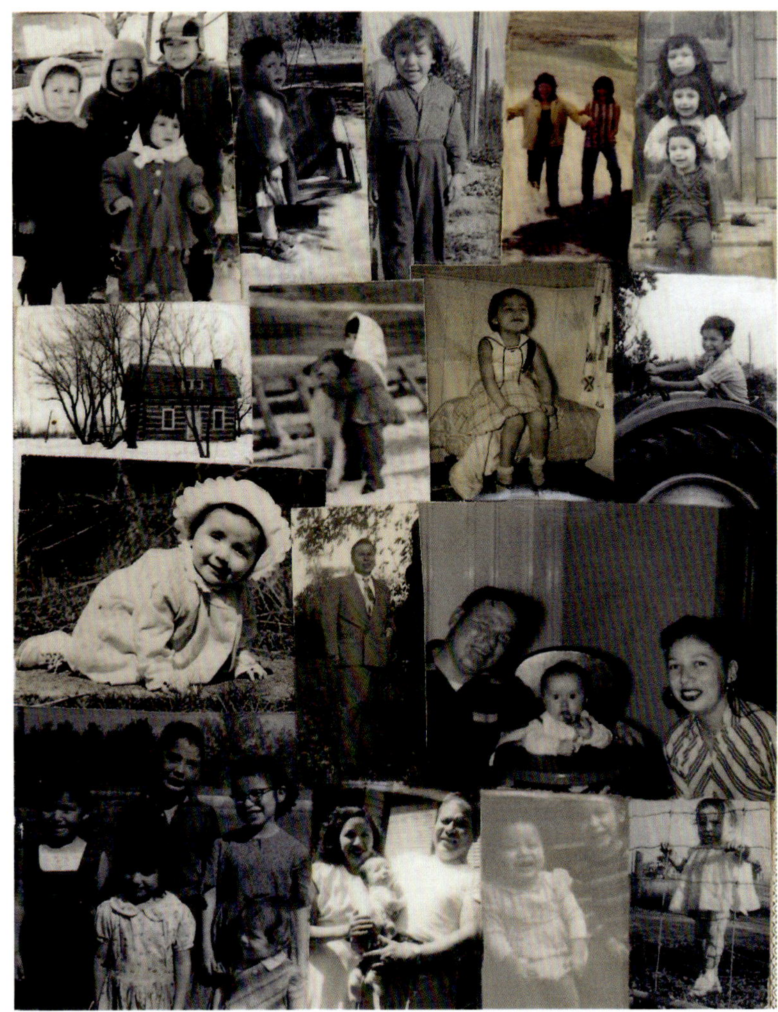

Fig. 1. Montage of family images (provided by author).

My generation had no photographic exhibitions we could go to. There were no books we could use as references. If we were lucky, we could see group photos of church picnics and schools. That was about it.

However, like the rest of the world, we saw the first appearance of the Beatles in 1964 on *The Ed Sullivan Show*, the moon landing, and the Beatles singing "Hey Jude" on the Grammys in 1969. Monumental moments, reminders we had something we held in our hearts to make the days go by sweetly. Images played an important part in the everyday of the anybody and everybody.

I am making statements about the lack of any photographic images made by Indigenous people and how we had nothing. Time has moved on. People from the reserve started to go to art schools, colleges, and universities. We (and I) became aware of the emptiness when images were not there to use as examples of our thinking and perspectives. The melding of art and science became apparent along with its significance.

When I view the expansive array of images that are presented today, I am taken aback to that time. I do not take any of the images for granted. The artists who are making them or the reason why they make them is important. I feel privileged to view them. Of course, I don't always love the images, but I feel akin to the struggle Indian people have had to go through to get to where we are today.

Documentary photography has always been an important art form, especially when there were no cameras pointed in the obscure direction of poverty or the lack of economic resources for most and the impact it has had on communities.

We can now see different Indian nations in their regalia, and we can also see them as ordinary everyday folk. There are serious POVs and humor to lighten the overall mood as we continue towards a world that makes it better for future generations. I am still excited by production in filmmaking and photography.

I don't take for granted the abilities and the intention of this equipment. We as a nation of people are empowered by knowing our statements are important, and now we can document events that will stay permanently as evidence in the continuing cycle of life.

As creative beings, we can extend our imaginations to explore, decipher, and invent our visual languages to include other Indigenous voices working in this space of time. It is exciting to know this is happening.

ARTIST BIOGRAPHIES

BY HEATHER EVERHART (ŁÍÍDLĮĮ KỤ́Ę FIRST NATIONS DESCENDANT) AND JUAN LUCERO (PUEBLO OF ISLETA)

Brian Adams (born 1985) is an Iñupiaq editorial and commercial photographer born, living, and working in Anchorage, Alaska. His work is focused on documenting the region through recording personal stories and creating environmental portraits. Adams is the recipient of fellowships from the Native Arts and Cultures Foundation and the Rasmuson Foundation, which supported his work on projects and the publications *I am Alaskan* (2013) and *I am Inuit* (2017), the latter also sponsored by The Inuit Circum Polar Council of Alaska and the Anchorage Museum. He visited twenty Iñupiat, Yup'ik, and Cup'ik communities over two years to gather stories and make images for the series. His goal was "promoting understanding, dismantling stereotypes as well as misperceptions and connecting the world with Alaskan Inuits, and the Arctic, through common humanity."[79] Included in Mia's exhibition and catalogue is one of Adams' favorites from the series, a portrait of Marie Rexford from the whaling village of Kaktovik. "Marie is such a strong Inuit woman, and I have always felt like she represents the best of what this project is."[80]

Dugan Aguilar (Walker River Paiute/Mountain Maidu/Pit River Achomawi) was a photographer that used his medium to traverse personal traumas and to document the people of his community. The effects of historical traumas, cultural loss due to boarding school, and PTSD are all aspects that informed his craft and acted as a healing mechanism for Aguilar. Through his work he was also able to bring light to the thriving Native communities in California and depicted the celebratory ceremony of existence.

Tomás Karmelo Amaya (Yoeme/A'shiwi/Rarámuri) is a film maker, writer, and visual artist whose work aims to enable healing for issues that affect Native people. His work embodies cultural and traditional teachings to enable viewers to embark on the journey to reconcile the issues that plague Native communities. His works have been featured in various publications nationally and internationally. He is the co-founder of KANION, a media agency and production company, as well as The Indigenous 20 Something Project and Native Love Stories (Instagram).

Arthur Amiotte (Wanblí Ta Hócoka Washté or Good Eagle Center) (Oglala Lakȟóta) is an educator, scholar, and artist, whose works celebrate the ceremonial nature of Lakota culture and identity. Through his exploration of traditional Lakota culture, he creates works that share the oral histories, rituals, and philosophies of his people. He is most notable for his collage works that contrast historical images of his family with photographic and painted elements commenting on Indigenous presence in contemporary 20th Century spaces. Amiotte has worked to bring attention to Native art practices and create relevance in the greater contemporary art canon. His work has been exhibited nationally and internationally in over 100 art shows and in over twenty solo exhibitions.

Artist **Joi T. Arcand's** (born 1982) ongoing photo and diorama series, *Through That Which is Scene,* is a callback to the View-Master—a stereogram device/toy that showed the user eye-catching scenes from tourist attractions. Arcand's dioramas share frozen moments, while also reminding us of the risks of cultural voyeurism. She explores her identity by making work that is reflective of both the personal and political, including stark use of neon and other sign-making materials paired with Cree language and syllabics to Indigenously reclaim public spaces. Arcand is nêhiyaw from Muskeg Lake Cree Nation in Treaty 6 Territory. She holds a BFA with Great Distinction from the University of Saskatchewan and has exhibited in Canada and the United States.

Tyana Arviso (Diné) is a photographer and artist who uses her work to bring positivity and raise the spirits of her audience, utilizing her experience as a creative director to develop narratives in the most impactful manner. Specializing in landscapes, product shots, and contemporary art, she uses her skills to engage her viewers to understand the importance of the spiritual aspect of creativity.

Carl Beam (Carl Edward Migwans, 1943–2005) remains a beloved and internationally acclaimed Anishinaabe artist from M'Chigeeng First Nation. He used a wide variety of media to create his oeuvre of evocative, masterful works that were often focused on the hardships and tensions between Indigenous communities and settlers; yet he was consistently told that the work didn't look "Indigenous enough." Unswayed and committed to his vision, Beam continued to create work that often dealt with abuses of power, informed by his traumatic childhood experience at residential school. His daughter, artist and beloved paint-maker Anong Beam, commented in a 2019 documentary that: "It's hard to feel like he's not here, his agenda (as an artist) is massive."[81]

Rapheal Begay (Diné) approaches his photography as storytellers sharing aspects of Diné culture and traditions. His focus is on landscapes and subjects found on the Navajo Nation. Rapheal also works as a curator and community organizer developing projects that create connections to land and the traditional teachings of his community. He holds a BFA in Art Studio, minor in Arts Management, and a Certificate in Museum Studies from the University of New Mexico.

Frank Big Bear (White Earth Nation) is a multi-media artist best known for his highly detailed colored pencil drawings and large-scale photographic collages. His Anishinaabe culture is highlighted throughout his work with narratives ranging from environmental changes and societal identity to political issues. His works are a mixed theme of emotions and reflections using abstracted images, portraits, and story. His art has been exhibited nationally and internationally with notable works in the permanent collections of the Minneapolis Institute of Art and the Walker Art Center in his hometown of Minneapolis.

James Patrick Brady (1908–1967) was an outspoken Métis leader, political organizer, scholar, and photographer from Lake St. Vincent, AB. He was a devoted advocate for Native rights and democratic socialism, adopting Marxist philosophies in the 1920s. He fought in World War II and upon return began photographing life in Métis settlements in Saskatchewan, always identifying his subjects with their name, date, and location. He later worked to establish mineral resource cooperatives in Métis communities through the Co-operative Commonwealth Federation (CCF)—the first social-democratic government in North America, which formed the provincial government for Saskatchewan. He retired c. 1950. In 1967, Brady and friend Absolum Hackett (Cree) mysteriously disappeared while prospecting near Lower Foster Lake, SK; their case is still cold.[82] Brady's photography was the subject of recent exhibitions at the Glenbow Museum in Calgary, AB, and the Sapp Gallery in Battlefords, SK, both curated by Plains Cree journalist Paul Seesequasis, with Marcel Petit at Sapp. Brady's papers are held at the Métis History Museum.

Tenille Campbell is a Dene/Métis writer and photographer from English River First Nation, SK. Campbell is known for her poetry, and was shortlisted for the Indigenous Voices Award for her 2017 collection, *#IndianLovePoems*. She is also known for being a supportive and collaborative artist—as the co-founder of *tea & bannock,* she hosts a collective online space for Indigenous women's stories shared in the first person. Campbell has an MFA in creative writing from the University of British Columbia and is a PhD candidate at the University of Saskatchewan. She was shortlisted for the 2022 Indigenous Voices Award for her latest work, *need nezu* (*Good Medicine*).[83] As the proprietor of her own business, Sweetmoon Photography (est. 2010), Campbell travels extensively to photograph Indigenous families and communities across Canada.

Dorothy Chocolate Carseen (born 1959) is a Tłı̨chǫ Dene photographer who was raised in the North Slave Region of the Northwest Territories, out on the land near Gamètì. Carseen attended high school in Yellowknife and went on to work for many years as a photographer and editor for *Native Press* newspaper, *Press Independent*, and *Northern Star*. She was a founding board member of the Native Indian/Inuit Photographers' Association (NIIPA) and is dedicated to creating a photographic record of life in trapping camps and contemporary communities. The Northwest Territories archives hold over five-thousand object records of Carseen's body of work spanning 1980–1993.[84]

Dana Claxton (born 1959) is a prolific Húŋkpapȟa Lakhóta artist from Wood Mountain Lakota First Nation and a professor and the head of Art History, Visual Art, and Theory at The University of British Columbia. Her aesthetics of beauty, intentional humor, reverence for Lakhóta cultural memory, and appreciation of the fierceness of Indigenous women are ever-present in each work of film, photography, performance art, and video installation. These values are perfectly represented in Claxton's *Mustang Suite*, a series of five photographs that: "depict a NDN family, each with their own mustang. Collapsing boundaries between the traditional and the contemporary, this family demonstrates a relationship to the horse and freedom. Through these images, the artist relates her own Lakota Sioux heritage, and exposes Indigenous culture's mobility over time."[85]

Jennie Ross Cobb (Cherokee), known as the first Native female photographer, captured images of her community during a pivotal time in their history. During this time, she photographed tribal members with a high sense of detail, making sure the entire photo told the story of that era. Her images are far more than photos, they are the historical documentation of the vulnerability of her tribe's sovereignty as Oklahoma fought for statehood. Her eye allowed for many of her photos to transcend time allowing her relatives, friends, and community to live in relevance through time.

Dayna Danger (they/them) is a Two-Spirit Queer Saulteaux/Polish artist from the Manitoba Métis Federation, residing in Tio'tia:ke (Montreal). Central to their multidisciplinary approach is Indigenous visual and erotic sovereignty.[86] Their projects engage issues of gender, empowerment, objectification, and the complexities of sexuality from a feminist perspective; their work is an offering to and for Queer people.[87] Their series, *Sisters,* was created over two years and is a document of reconnection and relationship between Danger and their sibling Michelle. It is also the first time they turned the camera toward themselves for a project.[88] Danger exhibits broadly and holds an MFA in Photography from Concordia University, serves on the board of the Aboriginal Curatorial Collective, and is a 2022 Mellon Indigenous Artist in Residence at McGill University.

Russel Albert Daniels (Diné/Ho-Chunk Descent) creates works that are used to educate and bring awareness and presence to Native

American and underserved communities. His works delve into issues such as identity, place, and the cultural histories of the Southwestern US. His works have also acted as ways to document current events affecting Indian Country, such as MMIW, Two Spirit communities, and environmental issues. He has worked to create dialogue that helps to reshape the inaccuracies of historical US histories. His works have been exhibited nationally in institutions such as the Smithsonian National Museum of the American Indian in NYC.

Ungelbah Davila (Diné) is a photographer, social media personality, and writer. She received her BFA in Creative Writing from the Institute of American Indian Arts in Santa Fe, NM. Her art is informed by her upbringing, where she learned to be surrounded and influenced by her surroundings and environment. She strives to follow her own authenticity to ensure her creative process is sharing the narrative that is truly of herself. Her approach to creation is that of a storyteller.

Jeremy Dennis (Shinnecock Indian Nation) is a photographer whose works tells the story of the Shinnecock Indian Nation. His images take viewers on a journey through history and navigate the topics of cultural assimilation, identity, and the cultural practices of his people. His work is also a journey of self-exploration, identifying the effects of life on the reservation for him and his community. His photos allow viewers to see through his eyes, and his narrative allows them to empathize with the struggle many Native nations face on reservations. His images are grounded in tradition, land, and ancestral teachings.

Lewis deSoto (Cahuilla) is a multidisciplinary artist who is working as a photographer and installation artist and creates works that draw from his Cahuilla heritage and study of world religions. He began his career in photography as a young child when he would capture images of the world around him. His works tie the cultural stories of his people to modern society by creating large scale installations of nature's evolving landscapes captured through a time-based process of image capture. His works bring the landscapes and nature back to their natural and traditional spaces in a cultural context. Where most people see empty space deSoto sees the original stories and cosmologies of his people.

Mercedes Dorame's (Gabrielino-Tongva/San Gabriel Band of Mission Indians) photos and installations navigate the complexities of culture and ceremony, and its connections to environment. Her work also explores issues of displacement, while living on your own homelands and being unwelcomed in a place you are spiritually connected to. Her images are the documentation of the hardships of lacking the ceremonial spaces that feed and nurture Indigenous identity. Her work allows her to reconnect with her ancestors on a spiritual plane while in the process of creating.

Rosalie Favell* (born 1958) is a revered artist inspired by her Metis heritage and family history. Favell received her first camera at age 10.[89] and for many years enjoyed the black and white format. From that young age, she has explored the relationship between identity and photography, and began her work in the documentary space before transitioning to digital in the nineties. Her collages often include self-portraits, archival family photos, pop-culture references, and reflections on the impacts of colonization. Favell frequently exhibits in Canada and the United States, and is a sought-after advisor, speaker, teacher, and writer.

Thomas Fields (Muscogee Creek/Cherokee) is a photographer, videographer, and digital media educator that works in the field of fine art and commercial practice. He specializes in shooting his community in full frame, black and white photos, that focus on Indigenous presences in modern society. His works document the realities of Native presence in Oklahoma and the issues that impact his community. He considers his work to be visual stories that are captured during moments of spiritual and cultural expressions.

Donna Garcia (Muscogee) is a lens-based artist that creates works that explore methodologies of bringing a natural voice to her subjects by contrasting the way past images were developed. Utilizing movement and slow capture her work has movement that brings her images to life. Throughout her work she explores topics such as gender and race. The life of her images brings to light the concept of sovereignty that takes individuals on a journey through time captured photographs.

Kalen Goodluck (Diné/Mandan, Hidatsa, Tsimshian) is a photographer and investigative journalist whose work explores tribal affairs, health, law, and political issues. His work has been featured in publications such as *The New York Times*, *National Geographic*, and NBC News. Through his work he strives to create an accurate and authentic image of Native peoples. Through his journalism he has investigated the rise of domestic extremist groups and their effects on society. In recent works he documented the impact of the Covid-19 pandemic throughout Indian country. He is a proud member of the Indigenous Photograph and Diversify Photo Collective.

Shan Goshorn (Eastern Band Cherokee) was internationally recognized for her baskets in which she used photographs and historical documents to create traditional basket forms. Her works were recognized and exhibited nationally and internationally and are now housed in the permanent collections of institutions worldwide. Throughout her career she was awarded numerous honors and earned prestige from museums, organizations, and art markets. Her work has continued to inspire and represent her community in a way that allows her pieces to remain timeless creations of Native identity, culture, history, and futures.

B.A. (Benjamin Alfred) Haldane (1874–1941) was a Tsimshian musician and photographer from Metlakatla, AK. Considered one of the first professional Native photographers,[90] he began making portraits of his family at age sixteen. In his mid-twenties, Haldane began a scenic and portrait business, opening a studio in 1899. Indigenous families traveled from their homes to Haldane's studio to sit for portraits that challenged the notion that this "service for the wealthy" was only available to European-Americans.[91] Historian Dr. Mique'l Icesis Dangeli noted: "It is clear that in the socio-political circumstances of both Canada and Alaska that B.A.'s imagery and practice functioned as a dual means of photographic sovereignty both from his perspective as a photographer and from the perspectives of the First Nations people he photographed."[92]

Faye HeavyShield (born 1953) is a revered interdisciplinary artist from Káínawa Nation. She is fluent in Blackfoot and lives on the Blood reserve, where she was born, in Stand Off, AB. Her work is "a reflection of my environment and personal history as lived in the physical geography of southern Alberta with its prairie grass, river coulees and wind, and an upbringing in the Kainai community with a childhood stint in the Catholic residential system." Until the portraits of *matriliminal*, HeavyShield's use of photography was most often in images of skin, water, and land that became a medium of abstraction to create her landscape installations, *Body of Land, Rock paper river, Slivers*, and *Wave*. She is the recipient of the 2022 Gershon Iskowitz Prize which includes a solo exhibition to open in 2024 at the Art Gallery of Ontario. A thirty-year career survey, *The Art of Faye HeavyShield,* premiered at MacKenzie Art Gallery in Regina, SK, in October 2022.

Tailyr Irvine (Confederated Salish/Kootenai) is a photojournalist who documents the complexities and issues that create the diversified identities of Native American nations. Her work has been featured in numerous publications such as the *New York Times* and *Washington Post*, and many others. She has work portraying events such as the Standing Rock Protest. Her work also confronts the highly contentious issue of blood quantum and its impact on American Indian communities.

Zig Jackson [Sahnish (Arikara)/Minitari (Hidatsa)/Numakiki (Mandan)] also known as Rising Buffalo is a multidisciplinary artist whose works encompasses photography and performance. Often placing himself in his photo he explores issues that affect Native communities. Zig began taking photos as a young man while attending secondary school in Brigham City, Utah. Developing his skills for image capture at a young age led Zig, eventually, to becoming the first Native American awarded a Guggenheim, a prestigious photography award. He uses his craft to deconstruct and dismantle the mysticism of the American Indian narrative developed by American museums. He approaches his camera as a teaching mechanism for the histories and cultural components of his people.

Around 1910, **George Johnston** (1894–1972) bought his first camera from an Eaton's catalogue and began making photographs of Tlingit life. He established processes for developing and printing his work and did so for over thirty years. During these years in Teslin, YT, he was also a fur trapper, wolf hunter, the first car owner/taxi driver, builder of the first road, and a single father to daughter Dolly after his wife Lucy died in 1935. Johnston resigned from photography in 1945 after a decade of unwelcome events deeply impacted life in Teslin—the US construction of the Alaska Highway, onset of World War II, American soldiers controlling Tlingit travel, and the arrival of missionary groups, measles, and chicken pox.[93] In his retirement, he continued to study his Tlingit culture as he had done since his teens and operated a general store. A significant contributor to the history of photography, Johnston's work is in the collection of The Smithsonian and the George Johnston Museum opened in Teslin in 1973.

Tom Jones* (Ho-Chunk) is an artist, curator, writer, and educator. He graduated with a Bachelor of Fine Arts in Painting from the University of Wisconsin–Madison, and a Master of Fine Arts in Photography and a Master of Arts in Museum Studies from Columbia College in Chicago, Illinois. He is currently Professor of Photography at the University of Wisconsin-Madison. Jones's artwork is a commentary on the identity, experience, and perception of American Indian communities. For the past 25 years he has worked to create an ongoing photographic essay on his tribe, the Ho-Chunk Nation of Wisconsin. His current work *Strong Unrelenting Spirits* are portraits of tribal members, which incorporates beadwork directly onto the photographs.

Jones co-authored the book *People of the Big Voice, Photographs of Ho-Chunk Families by Charles Van Schaick, 1879–1943*. He is the co-curator for the exhibition and contributing author to the book, *For a Love of His People: The Photography of Horace Poolaw* for the National Museum of the American Indian. His current book project is dedicated to Ho-Chunk baskets and their makers.

His artwork is in forty public collections, most notably: The National Museum of the American Indian, Polaroid Corporation, Sprint Corporation, The Nerman Museum, The Minneapolis Institute of Art, The Museum of Contemporary of Native Arts, The Museum of Contemporary Photography, and Microsoft.

Pat Kane (born 1979) is an award-winning Algonquin Anishinaabe photographer from Timiskaming First Nation, who lives and works in Yellowknife, NT. Kane's mother was a painter—he often watched as she painted landscapes from her own photos—but he didn't begin making photographs until later in life.[94] His work is in relationship with communities, and the resulting projects have improved meaningful connections within the Indigenous peoples of the Northwest Territories, as well as around and outside Canada. As Kane states: "The act of reclaiming culture and identity is ongoing, and my friends here are resilient in a place where symbols and systems of colonization loom large. We can hear colonization when Dene families pray to the Virgin Mary, but we see Indigenization when a young woman holds the hide of a caribou in her arms. In Catholicism we are Children of God, but in the Dene worldview we are One with the Land."[95]

Robert Kautuk (born 1984) is an Inuk photographer from Kangiqtugaapik (Clyde River), NU. Kautuk is committed to the preservation of traditional Inuit knowledge, as evidenced in all his works. He uses a DSLR and drones to document Inuit communities and extraordinary Arctic landscapes. He is most widely known for his arresting drone shot of a traditional harvest atop an ice floe, taken during a Piqqusilirivvik Inuit Cultural School program, which "gives young Inuit an opportunity to learn how to hunt using both traditional and modern techniques. The group got two walruses, which they cleaned and dressed before heading back to a tent camp at Iglulik Point."[96] Kautuk manages media and creates photography for Ittaq Heritage and Research Centre—an organization changing land and culture research methods in Nunavut toward Inuit-centered values—and he is "the proud husband of Eema and father to seven children and can often be found out hunting on the land with either a rifle or a camera (or usually both)."[97]

Leah Rose Kolakowski (Keweenaw Bay Ojibwa) is a photographer whose work highlights the life and presence of her subjects. The knowledge that influences her work comes from a combination of traditional cultural practices and her exploration into various fields of photography, which creates images that live in modernity. Kolakowski's dedication to her craft has allowed her to be part of the first cohort of the Native Arts & Culture Foundation's Mentor Artist Fellowship program where her work developed into a practice of Indigenous survivance.

Nadya Kwandibens is an Anishinaabe (Ojibwe) photographer from Animakee Wa Zhing #37 First Nation in Sioux Narrows, ON. Kwandibens is known for her award-winning portrait and event photography and is the founder of Red Works Photography. Founded to uplift and empower Indigenous people, Red Works produces photo-based projects to document, and strengthen the cultures and life ways of communities. Kwandibens' series, *Concrete Indians,* is a collaboration between the photographer and subjects she meets through an open-call format. "I began thinking about photography as a means for others to express feelings of disconnection and/or to explore and reflect on what decolonization means and looks like."[98] The resulting images of Indigenous people in vibrant traditional dress juxtaposed against modern, urban, westernized public spaces is an impactful record of reclamation and resistance.[99] She currently lives and works in Tkarón:to (Toronto) on Wendat,

Haudenosaunee, Mississauga of the Credit River & Dish With One Spoon Territory.

Eve-Lauryn Little Shell LaFountain is a member of the Turtle Mountain Band of Chippewa Indians. LaFountain is also Jewish, and as an artist and educator she "investigates her mixed heritage, history, feminism, ghosts, and magic through lens-based media and installation art."[100] *NIIBIDOON (Weave)* is made from strips of found film that she scratched "You Are on Native Land" upon and wove together. The resulting work, in collaboration with Cody Edison, and Christine Wood, is one of a series of three images that were then printed as postcards and continue to sell as a fundraiser for the Black Hills Legal Defense Fund.

Shelby Lisk (born 1992) is a multidisciplinary Kanyen'kehá:ka artist and journalist who lives between Ottawa and Kenhtè:ke (Tyendinaga Mohawk Territory), ON. In her work, Lisk addresses the complexity of mixed-race Indigenous identity and the essential connection of First Nations people to the land and each other.[101] She is deeply committed to the Mohawk language and has a certificate in language and culture from Queen's University and Tsi Tyónnheht Onkwawén:na. Lisk's respect for artists and ongoing collaborative nature is evident in her 2022 podcast with fellow journalist Chris Beaver: *The Art of Sovereignty,* which "explores the lives of eight First Nations artists whose art reclaims Indigenous voices and identities in a country that tried to silence them."[102] At the beginning of the Covid 19 pandemic, two Métis artists—Nathalie Bertin and Lisa Shepherd—created the *Breathe Challenge* for Indigenous artists to create masks in their community's style of beadwork or sewing. Lisk traveled home to Kenhtè:ke to photograph the project in her community where women created Rotinonhsyón:ni (Haudenosaunee) style raised beadwork masks. Her subsequent images shed light on the seriousness of the global pandemic, while also proclaiming the strength and creative sovereignty of the makers.

Erica Lord (born 1978) is an Athabascan/Iñupiaq and Finnish-American artist living in Santa Fe, NM. Lord's work unpacks the complexities of home, identity, and belonging. She grew up between her hometown of Nenana, AK, and Michigan's Upper Peninsula. Education took her to Fairbanks, AK, Santa Fe, NM, and Northfield, MN, where she completed her BA in studio arts at Carleton College; she completed an MFA at The School of the Art Institute of Chicago where she focused on developing projects in film and video, photography, and sculpture.[103] "Constant moving and rootlessness are part of the American experience, but my near perpetual movement is an experience that lies within a larger history: the Native diaspora."[104] Her series of four nude self-portraits, *The Tanning Project (Indian Looking, Half-breed, Colonize Me, and I Tan to Look More Native),* highlight the settler-systematic gaze upon Native women, while depicting another common experience of the mixed-race Native diaspora: not looking Native enough.

James Luna (Payómkawichum Luiseño/Ipi/Mexican-American) was a installation, performance, and multi-disciplinary artist who was at one point dubbed, "America's most dangerous Indian." His work has been exhibited nationally and internationally, and it has been a major catalyst in educating the general public about the misrepresented depictions of Indigenous people in institutional settings. His contribution to Native art has been integral to creating space for Native people in contemporary art communities internationally. His work is still used today as a mechanism for challenging inaccurate and harmful institutional narratives exhibited in American museums.

Dakota Mace (Diné) is an interdisciplinary artist who highlights Diné culture and language by creating works that combine photography, weaving, and beadwork. Through her work she examines the concepts of relationship, identity, and community which engages viewers to delve into an exploration of Diné culture. She has been outspoken on topics such as cultural appropriation and has emphasized the use of Indigenous symbology in contemporary art. Her work has been exhibited in galleries and museums throughout the United States and internationally.

Lee Marmon (Laguna Pueblo) was a photographer whose images have remained timeless and engaging. Choosing to photograph his family, friends, and Pueblo community members have led to the heartwarming documentation of the spiritual and human element of Indigenous communities. From the moment he captured his first images as child he worked to share his community with the outside world and bring the outside world to his community. His honest and sincere approach allowed his sitters to look past the lens and become comforted creating natural and spiritual images. Through his photos the stories of his community will be celebrated for future generations.

Murray McKenzie (1927–2007) was a prolific Scots-Métis/Cree photographer and biographer born in Cumberland House, SK. McKenzie was sent to sanitarium in his teens due to a bout of tuberculosis. His parents visited him and as a balm to his healing, gave him a camera. He was immediately deeply engaged with the new technology and photographed his fellow patients. McKenzie went on to a life of photographing communities and was thrilled to capture on film the spirit and energy of Indigenous peoples. Primarily self-taught, he worked freelance and was noted as the most published photographer in the *Winnipeg Free Press*.[105] He was a founding board member of the Native Indian/Inuit Photographers' Association (NIIPA), and the father of seven children with his wife, Mary Kwandibens.[106]

Parker McKenzie (Kiowa) was most notably a linguist who worked for the United States government in several roles. Much of his work focused on the documentation of the Kiowa language. Along with his wife Nettie Odlety, they are known as the earliest known

Kiowa photographers whose works documented Native American students attending the Phoenix Indian Boarding School. He was noted to have been the oldest living Kiowa tribal member at the time of his death in 1981.

Kimowan Metchewais McLain (1963–2011) was a Cree photographer from Cold Lake First Nations. Metchewais McLain began his career as a political cartoonist for *Windspeaker*, Canada's most widely distributed Indigenous newspaper. He received his BFA from the University of Alberta in 1996. His work was politically engaged, concerned with Indigenous identity, the pursuit of sovereignty, and the plight of Indigenous artists being required to perform connections to their culture in order to get ahead. He was diagnosed with a brain tumor in 1993 but continued to work with Polaroids and make sculptures after surgery, including works on the experience of his treatment-related hair loss and its impact on him as an Indigenous person. He completed an MFA from the University of New Mexico in 1999, and began developing his method of mixed media, photo-based work that he is renowned for. Metchwais McLain experienced ongoing complications from the cancer but continued to work as an artist. In 2011, the tumor returned and he ultimately passed away at his mother's home in Alberta that summer.[107] His archive is held at the Smithsonian, and contains his artwork, sketches, and journals.[108]

Meryl McMaster (born 1988) is a nêhiyaw artist from Red Pheasant Cree Nation, a member of Siksika Nation, and is of English and Dutch descent.[109] Rich with her innate ability to thoughtfully merge landscape with mise en scène, garmenting, and performance, McMaster portrays the intricacies of life and lineage through elaborate, fantastical, photographic scenes. From her series of self-portraits, *As Immense As the Sky*, her work, *On the Edge of This Immensity* was created on Manitoulin Island in Gore Bay, ON.

"Travelling into unknown land.
Birds as companions and guides.
Retracing ancestral steps.
On paths walked many times.
Great migrations across land and water.
Connecting with kinfolk.
On journeys that lead here.
Time passes by in cycles.
On journeys leading to my being."[110]

McMaster's work has been broadly collected, exhibited, and published in Canada, the United States, and abroad. She is a recipient of many awards, including the Scotiabank New Generation Photography Award and the Eiteljorg Contemporary Art Fellowship. McMaster contemplates time, life cycles, and her western and Indigenous worldviews from her home in Ottawa, ON.

Larry McNeil (born 1955) is a Tlingit/Nisga'a photographer and printmaker from Dakl'aweidi K'eet Gooshi H'it, Killer Whale Fin

House in Klukwan, AK—one of the Northwest Coast's oldest Tlingit tribal houses.[111] McNeil's creative range is vast; beautiful traditional black and white portraits, humorous and satirical riffs on western depictions of Native people, and engaging combinations of both by way of digital collage and printing. All iterations are rooted in the duality of Native and American identity. "Art will always be about some kind of beauty, and some of the most meaningful art is nearly always about the struggles we face in life. What's captivating is how we're able to offer our interpretations of our encounters along the way and maybe share it with people who can identify with it, or even those who cannot."[112] McNeil is the recipient of numerous awards and served as a vice-president of the Native Indian/Inuit Photographer's Association (NIIPA). He is an associate professor of photography at Boise State University, ID.

Ossie Michelin (born 1983) is a Labrador Inuk photographer and freelance journalist from North West River, NL. At university, Michelin was disheartened to learn most people didn't know about Labrador or the Inuit, and this drove him to focus his work on Indigenous and Inuit communities and issues faced in the north. *Mi'kma'ki*—his iconic photo of Angela Polities confronting riot police—was captured on his mobile phone during an APTN (Aboriginal Peoples Television Network) assignment covering Elsipogtog First Nation's 2013 fracking protests in New Brunswick.[113] Amidst the chaos between the community and RCMP (Royal Canadian Mounted Police) officers, Michelin posted the photo on Twitter, where it quickly went viral. "I was so busy in the middle of the protest that I had no idea what was going on in the outside world whatsoever." The image has since become a beacon of Indigenous resistance. "It's not my picture anymore. It doesn't belong to me, it belongs to everyone, I guess. It's incredible and just goes to show the power of social media."[114]

Based in Dena'ina Ełnena (Anchorage, AK) Wiagañmiu **Jenny Irene Miller** (she/they, born 1988) is an Iñupiaq artist working with photography and video to explore the relationship of identity to queerness. Central to the process is Miller's connection to the storytelling of her family and community. "I am inspired by kinship, home, and our stories. This allows me to further understand my knowledge of self, place, and ways of knowing that have been instilled in me by my family, culture, and experiences. The work I make is quiet and intimate and explores notions of identity, place, Indigenous feminism, refusal, and access."[115] She has exhibited in Canada, the United States, and South Korea and holds a BFA in Photomedia, a BA in American Indian Studies, and completed the MFA Studio Art and Photography program at the University of New Mexico in 2022.

Michael Namingha (Tewa/Hopi) is a photographer that utilizes his work to document environmental changes and the impacts of industrial excavations. Through his work he's able to create dialogue between the ancestral landscapes of the Pueblo people and the oil industry. His non-confrontational approach invites audiences to engage with his works in ways that allow them to witness the true environmental effects of the oil and gas industries. He aims to bring attention and awareness to the treatment of Pueblo homelands.

Virgil Ortiz (Cochiti Pueblo) is a multidisciplinary artist who is most notable for his traditional and contemporary clay works. He follows in the footsteps of a long line of traditional Cochiti potters. Other mediums he works in include fashion, video, film, photography, and installations. His art comes from natural and ceremonial spaces that have him diversify his practice and evolve where his work will take him. His works have been exhibited nationally and internationally with notable pieces in the permanent collections of the Minneapolis Institute of Art and the Denver Art Museum. His is the true expression of identity and celebration of Pueblo culture and history.

Henry Payer (Ho-Chunk) is a mixed media artist primarily working in collage. Although he creates work focused on traditional Native narratives his work is developed in contemporary practice. Using traditional knowledge, he has developed contemporary methodologies for utilizing space and symbolism to support his narrative of contrasting histories and modernity. Through his works he also has versed audiences on Indigenous issues such as identity, consumerism, and the inaccuracies of history.

Aggeok Pitseolak (1906–1977) was an Inuk artist from Kinngait (Cape Dorset), NT. She married photographer Peter Pitseolak in 1941 and became a frequent collaborator on his photographic projects, a muse, and his main developer and printer. The Pitseolaks worked together in a hunting iglu, experimenting with photographic techniques and production methods, such as making a filter out of sunglasses and developing prints with a cloth-covered flashlight.[116] An esteemed artist in her own right, Aggeok Pitseolak created beautiful prints and graphite drawings that are held in collections across Canada.

Peter Pitseolak (1902–1973) was a prominent Inuk artist and writer born in Tujjaat, from Kinngait (Cape Dorset), NU. He acquired his first camera in 1939 while working at Baffin Trading Company, one of six cameras he would use to make over two thousand photographs throughout his life.[117] Pitseolak made works of drawing, painting, and sculpture, but his most prolific medium was photography, which he focused on the betterment of the Inuit people and recording the traditions of his community for future generations. He had seven children with his first wife Annie, who died from tuberculosis in 1939. He married Aggeok Pitseolak and together they experimented with the many opportunities of photography as a medium. Aggeok was his frequent collaborator and primary production person. The

Pitseolaks made many photographs together, documenting Peter in his studio and among patrons and communities. Peter Pitseolak High School in Kinngait bears his name, and an archive of negatives are held at the McCord Museum in Montreal, QC. A 1982 film, *Peter Pitseolak: The Man Who Made Pictures*, was produced by the National Film Board of Canada. The Canadian Museum of history holds over fifteen-hundred negatives and photographs, purchased from his estate after his death in 1973 at Cape Dorset, NT.

Horace Poolaw (Kiowa) was a photographer who produced images that depicted Native peoples as living thriving community members, which was in great contrast to other images being produced at the time. His photos told the story of Native peoples living and thriving in the contemporary world rather than posed photos of the "Dying Race" taken by non-Native photographers. Many of the images he captured were of his community, which included family, friends, and the tribal leaders of the Kiowa. Many of his photos were in postcard format and made available to his community. Though he mostly photographed his community he was able to share accounts of Native issues, such as forced assimilation and Indian relocation. His work has paved the road for photographers that have followed, and he made Native survivance applicable in modern times.

Inuk artist **Barry Pottle** (born 1961) is originally from Tikigâksuagusik (Rigolet) in Nunatsiavut, Labrador. He has lived in Ottawa, ON, for over thirty years,[118] where he works within the large Inuit communities of the region. "I try to capture what is taking place in and beyond the Ottawa Inuit community ... the camera allows me to explore space, connection and continuity with my heritage, culture, and realities, especially contemporary realities."[119] One of those realities is the mid-20th-century Canadian government's use of "Eskimo Identification Tags." The tags seemingly excused the callous disassociation of white government officials who, when distributing social services to Inuit communities, chose to refer to Inuk by their tag number instead of learning their Inuit names.[120] Pottle's *Awareness Series* (2009–11) developed from his time at university, where he learned about the history of the Eskimo Identification System and that some Inuit artworks were signed with a number in place of a name.[121] His straightforward yet warm images capture the legacy of this program through magnified photographs of ID tags, alongside portraits of his fellow Inuit, as he wanted to put a face to the Eskimo Identification System[122] to incite greater connection for the viewer.

Ryan RedCorn (Osage) is a writer, filmmaker, actor, and photographer whose work often uses aspects of Indigenous humor to create commentary on the various issues facing Native communities. He is a founder the Native American comedy troupe, the 1491's. His photography explores his community through images that honor their identity and vitality.

Currently he is a writer on the hit tv program *Reservation Dogs*. RedCorn also founded the ad agency, Buffalo Nickel Creative.

Wendy Red Star (Apsáalooke) is a multidisciplinary visual artist whose works are exhibited nationally and internationally and are housed in the permanent collections of museums throughout the United States and in Europe. Along with her art practice Red Star is an educator who has held multiple visiting faculty positions with universities and colleges throughout the US. Her work contrasts colonial constructs with Native American ideologies by utilizing contemporary art practices to create conceptual and pop art pieces that highlight Apsáalooke culture, tradition, and feminism. Her work also explores issues of identity, race, gender, and society.

Jolene Rickard (Tuscarora Nation Turtle Clan) is an educator, curator, and multidisciplinary artist whose work and talks have been exhibited nationally and internationally. Her work encompasses issues that affect Native people. Throughout her art she creates connections between spirit, space, and Hodinöhsö:ni cultural teachings. Her works are expressions of the shared knowledge gained through the study of indigeneity on a global scale. Her work is found in the permanent collections of museums internationally. She is the Associate Professor in the Department of Art History and American Indian and Indigenous Studies at Cornell University.

Cara Romero* (Chemehuevi Indian Tribe) is a contemporary fine art photographer who captures depictions of identity, history, and social issues that affect Native peoples and her community. Her narrative was developed by her experience in higher education and the realization that Indigenous identity is mis-portrayed and misrepresented in museums. She has since used the power of images to create a genuine and more authentic representation of Native people in museums and other institutions.

Alejandra Rubio (Yavapai/Apache) works in photography and mixed media. She is an artist that creates works grounded in her culture and experience. Rubio's upbringing in Camp Verde, Arizona, is rooted in her community, land, and culture. Her work is created as stories that share and engage her audiences through the unique lens of Indigenous experience. She immerses her viewers in a transference of knowledge utilizing the patience, teachings, and empathy procured through wisdom shared with her from her community. She works with Native communities on and off the reservation where she is able develop and become inspired by new relationships and new adventures of the human spirit.

Camille Seaman (Shinnecock, African American) is highly published photographer with an eye for catching the human spirit in its truest natural form. Her depictions of icebergs, storms, and the natural world have been incredible documentations of climate change that help bring awareness to her viewers. Her works have been featured in many international publications. Her photographs have received multiple international awards, such as the *National Geographic* Award in 2006. Her work was exhibited in a solo show in 2008, entitled, *The Last Iceberg*.

Sarah Sense (Chitimacha/Choctaw) is a multidisciplinary artist and photographer that draws inspiration from the traditional basketry practices of her Chitimacha and Choctaw heritage. Her work documents her travels and studies to create works that share the authentic narratives of Indigenous peoples around the globe. Her images tell the stories of her community and her family, with many of whom she collaborates in her various projects. Her works have been exhibited nationally and internationally and her works have been acquired in museum collections worldwide. Her most recent works explore topics such as historical maps and the historical impacts of colonization.

Louis V. Shotridge, Stoowukháa (Astute Man) (1883–1937) was born to a prominent family of the Kaagwaantaan clan Tlingit in Klukwan, AK. He attended Haines Presbyterian Mission School where he met his wife Florence (Lukaax.ádi, clan of Chilkoot), who went on to be a respected maker of weavings and Chilkat blankets. They had an arranged marriage in a traditional ceremony. The Shotridges went on to collect and sell Tlingit works from Klukwan in the United States and Canada. While on a visit to Philadelphia, they met anthropologists and scholars with whom they shared Tlingit cultural information and objects. Louis Shotridge traveled broadly to purchase and photograph Indigenous objects, and he mapped and photographed past and present Tlingit communities. Shotridge attended Wharton Business School for a time, and—despite his claim that he "trained himself for only one thing ... namely to help his people negotiate the complex forces of Western capitalism as they impacted the Indian communities of southeast Alaska"[123]—he was a controversial figure among the Tlingit due to his collection and distribution of cultural patrimony. He went on to work as a curator and was the first Northwest Coast Native person to be employed by a museum in the US. He returned to Alaska in 1932 after being laid off and worked at a salmon cannery. Shotridge died after a mysterious fall from a ladder in 1937.[124] His digital archive is held at the University of Pennsylvania, where he worked as a curator from 1912–32.

Bently Spang (Northern Cheyenne), is a mixed media artist creating sculptures and installation works that utilize an array of materials. He grew up on and off the reservation, which has been a component in his creative process. His work focuses on the contrasting aspects of European and Native American cultures. Drawing on aspects of cultural history he develops his works in the same manner his ancestors created art. His artwork is an example of Indigenous resilience and resourcefulness through his incorporation of materials and mediums to expand his creativity.

Kali Spitzer (born 1987) is Kaska Dena from Daylu (Lower Post), BC, on her father's side and Jewish from Transylvania, Romania, on her mother's.[125] Spitzer's father is a survivor of the Canadian residential school genocide of First Nations, Inuit, and Métis people. She is motivated by her heritage to uplift and preserve Indigenous culture and knowledge ways through artwork and documentation of her community and traditional practices through photography. She studied photography at the Institute of American Indian Arts, Santa Fe Community College, and with the renowned artist Will Wilson to learn alternative photography practices. Spitzer is an Indigenous, Femme, Queer artist living on the Traditional Unceded Lands of Musqueam, Squamish and Tsleil-Waututh in Vancouver, BC.[126]

Greg Staats (born 1963) is a Kanien'kehá:ka Six Nations Hodinǫhsǫ:ni artist living in Tkaronto (Toronto), ON. He has a degree in Applied Photography from Sheridan College and was a founding board member of the Native Indian/Inuit Photographers' Association (NIIPA).[127] Staats' work, *Auto-Mnemonic Six Nations,* is a multi-panel view of a particular person's history; a massive eroding tree, folding chair, planked up building, a clearing, and a stone monument. These segments are a visual story, directing the viewer to recall their own history within the quietness of landscape, the resilience of memory, and the nature of living beings to desire a place for peace.

Katherine Takpannie (born 1989) is a self-taught urban Inuk photographer originally from Montreal, QC, and based in Ottawa, ON. She works in respect of her Inuit worldview, celebrating the joys of tradition and community while reckoning the traumas, cultural and political life, and challenges of Indigenous Canadians. Her project, *Our Women and Girls are Sacred,* honors Indigenous people who are violently stolen from their relatives, cases often never solved or prosecuted. "We must examine the underlying social, economic, cultural, institutional, and historical causes that contribute to the ongoing violence and particular vulnerabilities of Indigenous women, girls, and two-spirit in Canada. The number of #MMIWG2S are disproportionately high."[128] Takpannie is a proud alumni of the Nunavut Sivuniksavut post-secondary program and a recipient of the 2020 New Generation Photography Award from the National Gallery of Canada.

Jeffrey M. Thomas (born 1956) is a self-taught Onondaga photographer living in Ottawa, ON. He was born in Buffalo, NY, where he also attended the American Studies program at State University, NJ. It was while living in Tkaronto (Toronto) in the mid-1980s that Thomas learned of and subsequently became a founding board member of the Native Indian/Inuit Photographers' Association (NIIPA). Toronto is also where Thomas created the iconic photograph of his son, Bear, *Culture Revolution Today.* He self-identifies as Urban-Iroquois: "My study of Indian-ness seeks to create an image bank of my Urban-Iroquois experience, as well as re-contextualize historical images of First Nations people for a contemporary audience."[129] "My elders taught me to be proud of being Iroquois, inspiring me with their stories and their caution to never forget where I came from. It was my challenge, and I was determined to ensure that the description "urban Iroquois" could not be used as a derogatory assessment of my Indian-ness."[130]

Richard Throssel (Nehiyawak Cree/Adopted Apsáalooke) was a photographer whose work documented the life of Native people on the Apsáalooke Reservation in the early twentieth century. He captured his adopted community in their natural element of day-to-day activities. Throssel wasn't known for posing his images, which added a grand sense of authenticity. Rather than focusing on capturing the romanticized images of the past, his works portrayed Native peoples as living and progressing in contemporary existence.

Hulleah J. Tsinhnahjinnie (Seminole/Muscogee/Diné) was born into the Bear Clan of the Taskigi Nation, born for Tsi'naajinii of the Diné Nation, adopted into the Eagle House of Metlakatla, and adopted into the Killer Whale Fin House of Klukwan. Tsinhnahjinnie's education includes the Institute of American Indian Arts (Santa Fe, NM), California College of Arts and Crafts (Oakland, CA), and the University of California Irvine (Irvine, CA). During her residency in the Bay Area (1978–1998), she worked with several Native American organizations, the San Francisco Indian Center, Intertribal Friendship House, and Gay American Indians. In 2004, Tsinhnahjinnie was appointed Director of the C.N. Gorman Museum and a professor within the Native American Studies Department at the University of California Davis. Tsinhnahjinnie is known nationally and internationally as a photographer and multimedia artist creating portraiture and social commentary art works. Tsinhnahjinnie's photographs respond to the perpetuating stereotypes of Native Americans caused by ubiquitous early Western photography of Native people fixed in a historical past. Tsinhnahjinnie's work is held in several collections including, NMAI, MoMA, The Eiteljorg Museum, and the Fred Jones Jr Museum of Art.

Zoë Marieh Urness (born 1984) is an award-winning Alaskan Tlingit photographer, whose work focuses on Indigenous communities living and thriving through traditions and in relationship with their lands. Her work, *Raven Tells His Story in the Fog,* is an atmospheric portrait of traditional Tlingit dancer Gene Tagaban dressed in his Raven clan regalia.[131] She is well-known for *No Spiritual Surrender,* her 2016 photograph from the pipeline protests at Standing Rock Indian Reservation. The image was widely published, included in Mia's exhibition *Hearts of Our People: Native*

Women Artists, and nominated for a Pulitzer Prize in Feature Photography. She attended the Brooks Institute of Photography in Santa Barbara, CA, and has presented work at Art Basel Miami Beach, Heard Market, and the Santa Fe Indian market. Urness is the recipient of the 2022 Sony Alpha Female+ grant, in support of her project, *Indigenous Motherhood*.[132]

Lehuanani C. Waipa Ah Nee (Kānaka Maoli) is a photographer who works to connect generational tradition and knowledge to her community and environment. Her art is reflective of her upbring on the Hawaiian Islands and conveys the culture of her ancestors in a way that allows her relationship with the earth to expand throughout her community. Her work acts as a protective measure to ensure that her culture and heritage are preserved for future generations.

Matika Wilbur (Swinomish/Tulalip) is a photographer whose works allow her viewers to engage in personal way with her sitters. Her images have been a way for her to connect over 300 Native communities across the US. Through her portraits she has been able to document the narratives of the contemporary lives of Native peoples. Her process creates a truly empathetic view into Indigenous identity and existence. Her work has been featured in exhibitions and campaigns that explore the topics of cultural appropriation and authentic representations of Native identity.

Will Wilson* (Citizen of the Navajo Nation) is a photographer, curator, multidisciplinary artist, and educator whose work is a transformative approach to the historical depictions of Native people. His practice of utilizing traditional photographic techniques and his use of technology have been integral to restoring identity and existence which was stolen from Native people in the past by photographers of historical works. His work brings attention to environmental changes and its impact on cultural practices and has been exhibited in museums nationally and internationally.

Ryan Young (Lac du Flambeau Ojibwe) is a multi-disciplinary Two Spirit artist whose work spans photography and performance. Their work explores the impacts of gender, sexual identity, and how it intersects with cultural and Indigenous identity. They have worked as a fashion photographer for *Native Max Magazine* and their works have been chosen to be featured as a blanket designer for Eighth Generation representing the two-spirit community.

** Denotes an author contributing to the publication.*

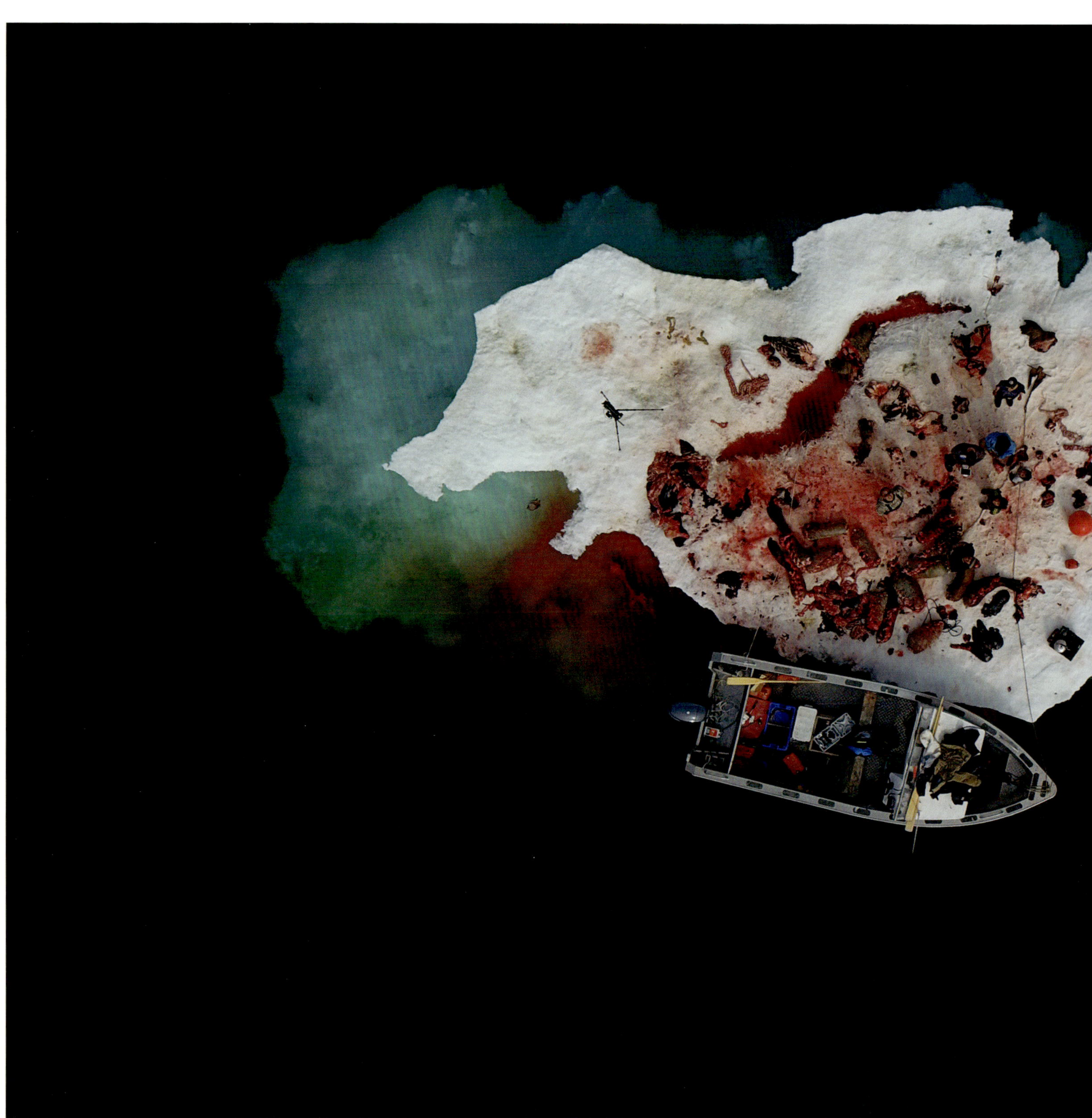

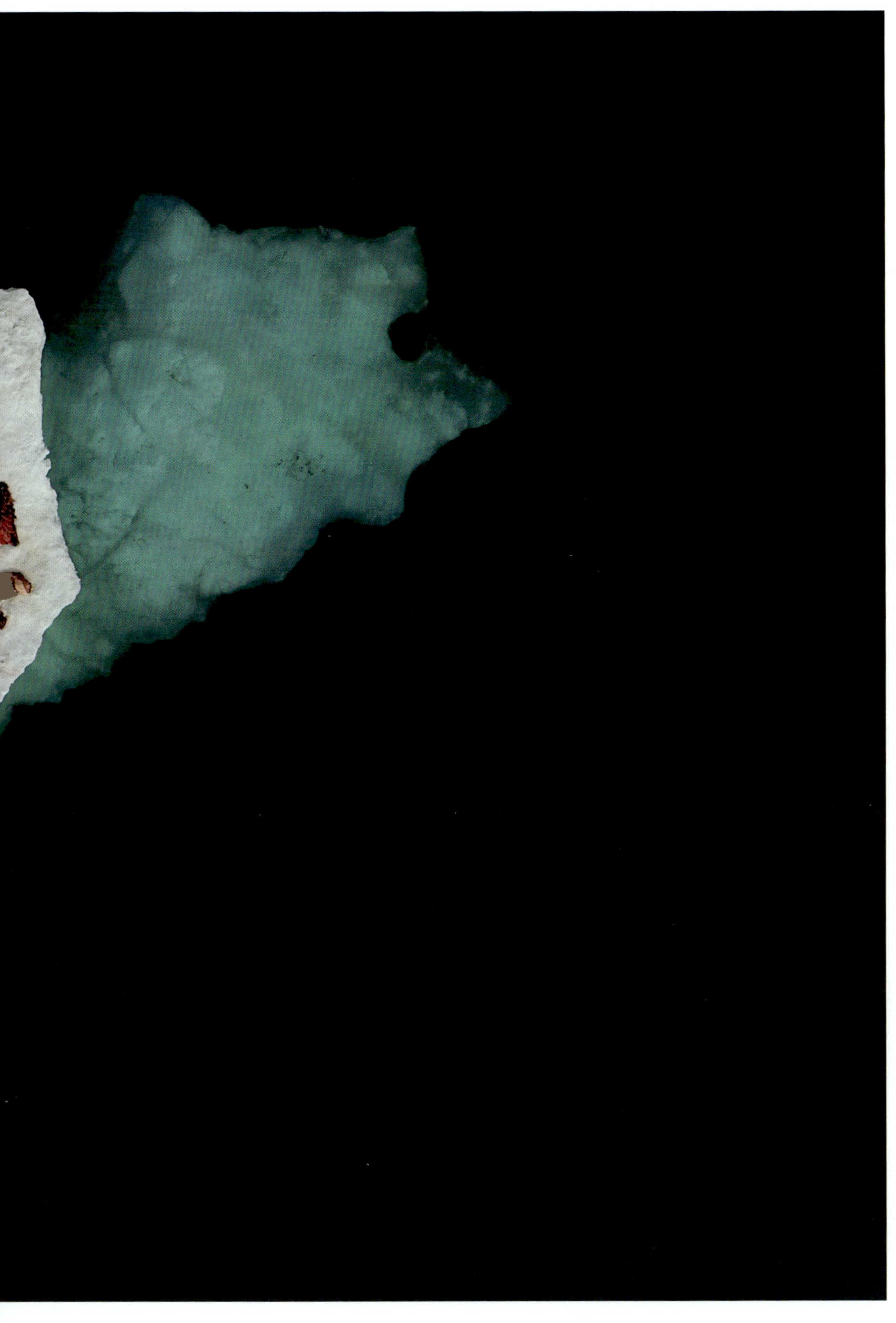

Robert Kautuk
Inuit, born 1984
After cutting up two walruses, Igulik, 2016
Inkjet print
Courtesy of the artist

NOTES

1 Shelley Niro. Interview, Brantford, August 22, 2003.

2 Shelly Niro. "Artist Statement." In *Transitions: Contemporary Canadian Indian and Inuit Art*, edited by Ministry of Indian Affairs and Northern Development. Ottawa, 1997.

3 Sogorea Te' Land Trust, https://sogoreate-landtrust.org/ (accessed Sep. 29, 2022).

4 Hulleah Tsinhnahjinnie, "Compensating Imbalances" in Exposure, vol.29, no. 2, 1993.

5 *Aperture*, "Strong Hearts: Native American Visions and Voices" (1995), Exposure, Vol. 29, no.2, 1993, and *The Journal of Photography of New England*, Views, vol.13–4/14-1, 1993, p.30.

6 Hulleah Tsinhnahjinnie, "Dragonfly's home" in *Visual Currencies: Reflections of Native American Photography*, National Museums of Scotland, edited by Henrietta Lidchi and Hulleah J. Tsinhnahjinnie, 2009: 3–18.

7 Hulleah Tsinhnahjinnie, Artist Statement: When Did Dreams of White Buffalo Turn to Dreams of White Women? 2022.

8 Tsinhnahjinnie, Artist Statement.

9 Jolene Rickard, "Indigenous and Iroquoian Art as Knowledge: In the Shadow of the Eagle." PhD diss., State University New York at Buffalo, 1996.

10 Corrine Reeve, personal communication, August 10, 2003.

11 Reeve, personal communication.

12 Mique'l Askren, "Memories of Fire and Glass: B.A. Haldane, Nineteenth-century Tsimshian Photographer," in Henrietta Lidchi and Hulleah J. Tsinhnahjinnie, eds, *Visual Currencies: The Native American Photograph in Museum and Galleries* (Museum of Scotland Publishing, Edinburgh, 2010), 90–107.

13 On the history of Metlakatla, Alaska, see: Mique'l Icesis Dangeli, "Bringing to Light a Counter-Narrative of Our History: B.A. Haldane, 19th Century Tsimshian Photographer," in *Sharing Our Knowledge: The Tlingit and their Coastal Neighbors*, ed. Sergei Kan, 265–297 (Lincoln: University of Nebraska Press, 2015).

14 B.A. Haldane to Elmer E. Brown, U.S. Commissioner of Education, May 22, 1909, "A-L File," Folder 329, Document 1, Box 112, Sir Henry S. Wellcome Collection, 1856, Group Record 200, National Archives—Pacific Alaska Region, Anchorage.

15 Benjamin Haldane, Native Statement, January 17, 1917, "A–L File," File 279, Box 108, Page 10, Sir Henry S. Wellcome Collection ,1856–1936, Record Group 200, National Archives–Pacific Alaska Region, Anchorage.

16 Viola Garfield, "1930 Survey of Benjamin Haldane: Notes—Tsimshian Marriage—Clan and Tribal Affiliation," Box 4, Folder 3, Viola Garfield Papers, Accession number 2027-72-25, University of Washington Libraries, 1.

17 The earliest dated portrait taken in his studio is an 1899 image of George McKay, a Tlingit from Saxman, Alaska. ARC# 29751, Sir Henry Wellcome Collection, 1856–1936; National Archives–Pacific Alaska Region.

18 George Davis, Metlakahtla: A True Narrative of the Red Man (Chicago: The Ram's Horm Company, 1904), 123.

19 Early residents of Metlakatla, Alaska, lived under eight regulations constructed by Duncan called the "Declaration of Residents." It was similar to the "Rules" that he used to govern Metlakatla, BC, Duncan outlawed attending or supporting "heathen festivals" (potlatches) and made it mandatory to observe the Sabbath, attend school, and to be clean, industrious, and honest, with additional rules regarding land ownership and loyalty to the United States government. These regulations were published in full in: Edward Delor Kohlstedt, *William Duncan, Founder and Developer of Alaska's Metlakatla Christian Mission* (Palo Alto: The National Press, 1957), 47–48

20 Garfield, "Change in the Marriage Customs of the Tsimshian," 10.

21 In her own words, Garfield said she utilized his knowledge to gather "much of the information concerning practices and traditions of the days before the influx of whites." Garfield, "Change in the Marriage Customs of the Tsimshian," 1–2.

22 Viola Garfield, "1930 Survey of Sidney Campbell: Notes—Tsimshian Marriage—Clan and Tribal Affiliation," Box 4, Folder 3, Viola Garfield Papers, Accession number 2027-72-25, University of Washington Libraries, 1.

23 Garfield, "1930 Survey of Sidney Campbell."

24 In her master thesis on Tsimshian marriage customs, anthropologist Viola Garfield notes that during his marriage ceremony, "Sidney received from his uncle the dancing blanket which had been the property of his father." Garfield, *Change in the Marriage Customs of the Tsimshian*, 39.

25 The 1880 portrait may have been a part of B.A.'s personal collection of images, as his photos were used to illustrate Archtander's book. It was published without Sidney's name, however, and was captioned "regalia of a Tsimshian Chief." John W. Archtander, *The Apostle of Alaska: The Story of William Duncan of Metlakahtla* (New York: Fleming H. Revel Company 1909), 76.

26 Peter Murray, *The Devil and Mr. Duncan: a History of the Two Metlakatlas*. (Victoria, BC: Sono Nis Press, 1985), 264; John W. Arctander, *The Apostle of Alaska: The Story*

of William Duncan of Metlakahtla. (New York: Fleming H. Revel Company, 1909), 388–389, Davis, George. *Metlakahtla: A True Narrative of the Red Man*. (Chicago: The Ram's Horn Company, 1904).

27 Patricia Roppel, *Southeast Alaska: A Pictorial History* (Norfolk: The Donning Company, 1983), 70.

28 Haldane, Native Statement, 9. Wilfred Walter was born January 30, 1897, and Anna Laura was born June 24, 1899. B.A. married Martha Calvert, daughter of Aldolphus and Matilda Calvert of Metlakatla, Alaska in 1896. In chronological order their children are: Wilfred Walter (b. Jan. 30, 1897), Anna Laura (b. June 24, 1899), Egbert Oscar (a.k.a. Oscar Egbert) (b. Dec. 30, 1901), Boyd Anthony (a.k.a. Anthony "Tony" Boyd) (b. Sept. 28, 1903), a baby girl who died in infancy (b. May 1905), Raymond Victor (b. Feb. 13, 1907), Francis Floyd (b. Sept. 22, 1908), Alexander Frederick (b. April 22, 1910), Sandy (died in infancy, Nov. 1911), Emma Louise (b. July 14, 1913), and Dennis Everett (b. Sept. 11, 1915). I am grateful to genealogist Chris Roth along with B.A.'s grandchildren Loretta Baines and Francis Haldane and his wife Kathy, for providing me with the names and birthdates of each of B.A.'s children.

29 R. Bruce Parham, "Benjamin Haldane and the Portraits of a People" Alaska History 11, no. 1 (Spring 1996), 37.

30 There are many examples of this type of arrangement in B.A.'s early family portrait that are held in the Sir Henry S. Wellcome Collection in the National Archives–Pacific Alaska Region, Anchorage including ARC #297465 and ARC # 297474.

31 Our community is grateful to the late Dennis Dunn (Tsimshian) for not only saving the negatives, but also for ensuring their preservation by placing them the archives of the Tongass Historical Museum in Ketchikan, Alaska. We are also thankful to Richard Van Cleave, Senior Curator of Collections for Ketchikan museums, for inventorying and scanning the negatives, and for the Tongass Historical Museum for housing them until we establish our own museum in Metlakatla.

32 See Mique'l Icesis Dangeli, "Bringing to Light a Counter-Narrative of Our History: B.A. Haldane, 19th Century Tsimshian Photographer," in *Sharing Our Knowledge: The Tlingit and their Coastal Neighbors*, ed. by Sergei Kan, 265–297, Lincoln: University of Nebraska Press, 2015) for my analysis of the photographs that he took of Nisga'a ceremonies during the Potlatch Ban.

33 Carol Williams, *Framing the West: Race, Gender, and the Photographic Frontier in the Pacific Northwest* (New York: Oxford University Press, 2003), 149.

34 Dan Savard, "Changing Images: Photographic Collections of First People of the Pacific Northwest Held in the Royal British Columbia Museum, 1860–1920," BC *Studies 145* (Spring 2005), 72.

35 See George Davis, *Metlakahtla*.; Philip Drucker, *Cultures of the North Pacific Coast* (San Francisco: Chandler Publishing Company, 1965), 199–204; William Beynon, "Tsimshian of Metlakatla, Alaska," *American Anthropologist* 43, no. 1 (1941): 83–88. Edward Delor Kohlstedt, *William Duncan, Founder and Developer of Alaska's Metlakatla Christian Mission*

(Palo Alto: The National Press, 1957); Phylis Bowman, *Metlakatla—The Holy City!* (Port Edward: Phylis Bowman Publishing, 1983); Peter Murray, *The Devil and Mr. Duncan: A History of the Metlakatlas* (Victoria, BC: Sono Nis Press, 1985); The Reader's Digest association, *Through Indian Eyes: The Untold Story of Native Americans Peoples* (Pleasantville: The Readers Digest Association Inc., 1995), 254–55; Time-Life Books, *Keepers of the Totem* (Alexandria: Time-Life Books, 1993), 160–67.

36 Pat Glascock and Michael D. Hall, *Carvings and Commerce: Model Totem Poles 1880–2010*. Seattle, WA. (University of Washington Press, 2011), 96.

37 Many of B.A.'s photos, including his self-portrait in his studio (Ketchikan Museum 89.2.14.21), are postcards.

38 I am grateful for their support and would like to thank the elders of the Haldane family for their participation in these forums and their support throughout my research: B.A.'s granddaughter, Loretta Baines (daughter of Wilfred and Fannie Haldane), and B.A.'s great grandchildren, who are the grandchildren of Wilfred and Fannie Haldane: Fran Majors (daughter of Clara [née Haldane] Chalmers–Dundas), Alice Ann Nelson (daughter of Pauline [née Haldane] Dundas) and Wayne Hewson (son of Mary [née Haldane] Hewson). I would also like to thank B.A.'s granddaughter, Lindarae Shearer (daughter of Raymond "Ray" Haldane) for inviting me into her home to discuss my research in 2005, and B.A.'s grandson, Francis Haldane (son of Boyd Anthony "Tony" Haldane) for his beautiful words of encouragement in *Sm'algyax* during our meetings in Anchorage, Alaska 2006. B.A.'s only surviving grandchild, Wilfred "Neddy" Haldane, who I met at the Killerwhale Clan Potlatch in Metlakatla in 2013. has also expressed his enthusiasm and support of my work. Neddy keeps in regular touch with me over Facebook and inspires me to do more research and publishing on his grandfather's photography.

39 Wayne Hewson, Personal Interview, Metlakatla, AK (February 28, 2006).

40 Stanford University's Charles Junkerman, then assistant dean of undergraduate studies, initiated the conservation and research of Horace Poolaw's archive. Linda Poolaw brought her father's archive to Stanford where she worked with undergraduates to print, research, and identify individuals within the photographs.

41 This work was accomplished through multiple UW-Madison faculty grants.

42 Conversation with the artist, February 14, 2022.

43 Conversation with the artist.

44 Rosalie Favell's portfolio, "Portraits in Blood," https://rosaliefavell.com/portfolio/portraits-in-blood/, accessed September 23, 2022. The Métis are one of three groups of legally recognized Indigenous peoples in Canada (the other two being First Nations and Inuit). Métis peoples maintain shared history and culture stemming from their mixed Indigenous and European (predominantly French) ancestry, developed over centuries through entanglements of colonization and the fur trade in North America. Although the Canadian government officially uses the term

Métis—which derives from the French word for "mixed" or "mixed-race"—Rosalie Favell prefers to use Metis without the accent aigu, as she is of English (rather than French) and Cree heritage. Her embrace of this spelling conveys the specificities of self-identification and family history in Indigenous communities, and I use it throughout.

45 See Nicole St-Onge, Carolyn Podruchny, and Brenda Macdougall, edited, *Countours of a People: Métis Family, Mobility, and History* (Norman: University of Oklahoma Press, 2012). Métis people lost their lands following the Red River (1869–70) and Batoche (1885) resistances and through scrip, in which ancestral land rights were terminated in exchange for a parcel of property to be farmed in government surveyed territory then being opened to settlement. Rosalie Favell has located the scrip certificates and scrip affidavits that her grandmother's grandparents signed resulting in their loss of land. She integrates both these materials into the piece, "Stealing Home" (2021), and the scrip affidavits into *Walking Through Time* (2021).

46 Rosalie Favell, "Holding Our Ground," *Rosalie Favell's Family Legacy* (Winnipeg: Winnipeg Art Gallery, 2021), 9.

47 Favell, "Holding Our Ground."

48 Rosalie Favell, tour of *Rosalie Favell's Family Legacy*, Winnipeg Art Gallery, https://youtu.be/VGm5ic1WJME, Accessed September 23, 2022.

49 Tina Campt, *Image Matters: Archive, Photography, and the African Diaspora in Europe* (Durham: Duke University Press, 2012).

50 Rosalie Favell, tour of *Rosalie Favell's Family Legacy*, Winnipeg Art Gallery, https://youtu.be/VGm5ic1WJME . Accessed September 23, 2022.

51 Conversation with the artist, February 14, 2022.

52 Favell, "Holding Our Ground," 11.

53 Favell, "Holding Our Ground," 10.

54 Rosalie Favell's portfolio, "Closer to Heaven," https://rosaliefavell.com/portfolio/closer-to-heaven/. Accessed September 23, 2022.

55 Favell, "Holding Our Ground," 29.

56 Conversation with the artist, February 20, 2022. Italics added for emphasis.

57 The devastating effects of Indian Residential Schools in Canada, as well as the horrendous physical and emotional abuses that students suffered continue to be reckoned with to the present day. For recent reportage regarding the human rights violations uncovered in this ongoing reckoning, see Ian Austen, "How Thousands of Indigenous Children Vanished in Canada," *The New York Times*, June 7, 2021, Ian Austen, "With Discovery of Unmarked Graves, Canada's Indigenous Seek Reckoning," *The New York Times*, June 26, 2021, and Ian Austen, "Canada's Residential Schools Were a System of 'Cultural Genocide,' a Commission Found," *The New York Times*, July 25, 2022.

58 For further discussion of mimicry in postcolonial theory see Homi K. Bhabha, *The Location of Culture* (London: Routledge, 1994).

59 Favell, "Holding Our Ground," 14, and Sherry Farrell Racette, "Returning Fire, Pointing the Canon: Aboriginal Photography as Resistance," *The Cultural Work of Photography in Canada*, edited by Carol Payne and Andrea Kunard (Montreal: McGill-Queen's University Press, 2011), 86.

60 Favell, "Holding Our Ground," 9.

61 On vernacular photographies as a tool for constructing and projecting both family relations and larger cultural belonging, see Marianne Hirsch, *Family Frames: Photography, Narrative, and Postmemory* (Cambridge: Harvard University Press, second edition, 2012) and Tina Campt, Brian Wallis, Marianne Hirsch, and Gil Hochberg, ed., *Imagining Everyday Life: Engagements with Vernacular Photography* (New York: Steidl and The Walther Collection, 2020).

62 Archaeologists and art historians have made a strong public case that Greco-Roman sculpture was not white, but polychromatic, historicizing and challenging the idea of a classical white city. See, recently, Astrid Nunn and Heinrich Plenning, eds., *Mesopotamian Sculpture in Color* (Gladbeck, Nordrhein-Westfalen Germany: Pewe-Verlag, 2020), and Jennifer Stager, *Seeing Color in Classical Art: Theory, Practice and Reception, from Antiquity to the Present* (Cambridge, Cambridge University Press, 2023).

* Ernest Amoroso, Cultural Resource Center, Smithsonian National Museum of the American Indian, telephone interview with the author, February 2023.

63 Marie Muracciole and Benjamin J. Young, eds., "Introduction to Allan Sekula, *The Traffic in Photographs*," in *Art Journal* 41, no. 1, *Photography and the Scholar/Critic* (Spring 1981), p. 6. See also, Daniell Cornell and Cheryl Finley, *Imaging African Art: Documentation and Transformation* (New Haven: Yale University Art Gallery, 2000).

64 Tina Campt, Marianne Hirsch, Gil Hochberg and Brian Wallis, eds., *Imagining Everyday Life: Engagements with Vernacular Photography* (New York: Steidl/The Walther Collection, 2020), 11.

65 Laura Wexler, Karintha Lowe, and Guigui Yao, "Urban Albums, Village Forms: Chinese Family Photographs and the Cold War," in Thy Phu, Andrea Noble, and Erina Duganne, *Cold War Camera* (Durham and London: Duke University Press, 2023), 292.

66 Vicentius, P.; Underhill, John; Gardener, Lion; and Mason, John, "Four English Histories of the Pequod War," 1637. https://digitalcommons.uni.edu/zeaamericanstudies/18.

67 John Underhill, The Figure of the Indians' Fort or Palizado in New England and the Maner of the Destroying It by Captayne Underhill and Captayne Mason, 1638. Engraving, 11 ¼ x 14 ½ in. (28.6 x 6.8 cm). Archives and Special Collections, Mashnuntucket Pequot Museum and Research Center, CT, MSS 52. The Underhill engraving represents the events of a massacre and is purposely excluded from this chapter's illustrations. The image in question may be accessed via www.loc.gov/item/2001695745/.

68 Ariella Aïsha Azoulay, "Unlearning the Decisive Moments of Photography," n.p., in *Unlearning the Origins of Photography*,

photomuseum.ch/en/2018/09/08/unlearning-the-origins-of-photography/

69 Azoulay, "Unlearning the Decisive Moments of Photography," n.p.

70 Azoulay, "Unlearning the Decisive Moments of Photography," n.p.

71 Edward S. Curtis, *The North American Indian*, Norwood, MA: The Plimpton Press, 1907–1930: 20 volumes, 20 portfolios.

72 See, for example, Jill Sweet and Ian Berry, *Staging the Indian: The Politics of Representation*, Saratoga Springs, NY: The Tang Teaching Museum at Skidmore College, 2001.

73 Jo-Ann Archibald Q'um Q'um Xiiem, Jenny Bol Jun Lee-Morgan, and Jason De Santolo, "Introduction: Decolonizing Research: Indigenous Storywork as Methodology," in *Decolonizing Research: Indigenous Storywork as Methodology*, ed. Jo-Ann Archibald Q'um Q'um Xiiem, Jenny Bol Jun Lee-Morgan, and Jason De Santolo, with a foreword by Linda Tuhiwai Smith (London: ZED Books Ltd, 2019), 11.

74 My discussion of the Mabel Mary Lonetree photograph is also featured in, Amy Lonetree, "A Heritage of Resilience: Ho-Chunk Family Photographs in the Visual Archive," *The Public Historian* 41, no. 1 (February 2019): 34–50.

75 Matthew Daniel Mason, "'Native in the Frame': Viewing the Ho-Chunk Nation in Black River Falls, Wisconsin, 1870–1930," (Paper presented at the Annual Meeting of the Association of American Geographers, Los Angeles, CA, 2002), 5.

76 I greatly appreciate the assistance of George Hushi Greendeer for locating Lucy Emerson Brown's Ho-Chunk name. I also thank John Greendeer Lee for his help with the spelling of the names.

77 James Clifford, "Looking Several Ways: Anthropology and Native Heritage in Alaska," *Current Anthropology* 45, no.1 (2004): 9.

78 This term was used by scholar Bill Anthes in his prepared remarks to a great paper by Lakota scholar, Claire Thomson, on historic images of her own tribal nation at the *Western History Association Conference*, online, October 17, 2020.

79 Benteli Books online (no date), *I Am Inui*t. www.benteli.ch/en/photography/i-am-inuit.html.

80 Citrawireja, M. (January 29, 2018) *New Sincerity*, " Q&A with Inupiaq Photographer Brian Adams."

81 Lodestar Studios (2019). Aakideh: *The Art and Legacy of Carl Beam* [Video]. YouTube. www.youtube.com/watch?v=5ExmLKxmT3k.

82 *The Canadian Encyclopedia* (n.d.). www.thecanadianencyclopedia.ca/en/article/jim-brady.

83 CBC Books (May 6, 2022). *Selina Boan, Tenille K. Campbell, and Brian Thomas Isaac among finalists for the 2022 Indigenous Voices Awards*. www.cbc.ca/books/selina-boan-tenille-k-campbell-and-brian-thomas-isaac-among-finalists-for-the-2022-indigenous-voices-awards-1.6443675.

84 Government of Canada NWT Archives. *Dorothy Carseen photo collection*. gnwttest.accesstomemory.org/n-2010-003.

85 Dana Claxton. www.danaclaxton.com/artwork/the-mustang-suite.

86 Never Apart (2020). *2Spirit Resurgence: Jade Konwataroni & Dayna Danger* [Video]. Vimeo. vimeo.com/461979610.

87 CBC Arts (2017). *Queer (Self) Portraits: Dayna Danger* [Video]. YouTube. www.youtube.com/watch?v=-McnlbcOE1w.

88 Lockyear, Jon (2015). *Sisters*. www.daynadanger.com.

89 National Gallery of Canada (n.d.). Rosalie Favell. www.gallery.ca/collection/artist/rosalie-favell.

90 Dangeli (Askren), M. (April 16, 2010). *Bringing our History into Focus: Re-Developing the work of B.A. Haldane, 19th Century Tsimshian Photographer*. notartomatic.wordpress.com/2010/04/16/bringing-our-history-into-focus/.

91 Martin, M.C. (November 16, 2016). *Photographic sovereignty in Metlakatla. Juneau Empire*. www.juneauempire.com/life/photographic-sovereignty-in-metlakatla/

92 Dangeli (Askren), M. (April 16, 2010) [website]. *Bringing our History into Focus: Re-Developing the work of B.A. Haldane, 19th Century Tsimshian Photographer*. notartomatic.wordpress.com/2010/04/16/bringing-our-history-into-focus/.

93 Thornton, T.F. (March 2000) "Picturing a People: George Johnston, Tlingit Photographer"in *American Anthropologist*.

94 Beside (n.d.). Through the lens of Pat Kane. beside.media/through-the-lens/pat-kane/.

95 Lenscrath (October 13, 2021). "Spirit: Focus on Indigenous Art, Artists, and Issues: Pat Kane." lenscratch.com/2021/10/spirit-focus-on-indigenous-art-artists-and-issues-pat-kane/.

96 "*Up Here*, The Voice of Canada's Far North" (April/May 2018). www.uphere.ca/articles/summer-school.

97 Ittaq Heritage and Research Centre (n.d.). ittaq.ca/about/.

98 Scott, C. (2017). "Concrete Indians—Nadya Kwandibens." *PhotoEd Magazine*.

99 Red Works (n.d.). www.redworks.ca/info.

100 Eve Lauryn Little Shell La Fountain. www.evelaurynlafountain.com.

101 400 Years Project (n.d.) [website]. *Shelby Lisk*. www.400yearsproject.org/photographers/shelby-lisk.

102 TVO Today (May 16, 2022). The *Art of Sovereignty*. www.tvo.org/article/the-art-of-sovereignty.

103 School of Advanced Research (2008). Erica Lord: 2008 Eric and Barbara Dobbin Fellowship. sarweb.org/iarc/native-american-artist-fellowships/2008-artists/erica-lord/.

104 Erica Lord. ericalord.com/home.html.

105 Rozyk, A. (n.d.). *Murray McKenzie* (1927–2007). Métis Museum. www.Métismuseum.ca/media/document.php/11395.Murray%20McKenzie.pdf.

106 Flanagan, R. (July 16, 2020). *Remembering Murray McKenzie. Thompson Citizen*. www.thompsoncitizen.net/nickel-belt-news/remembering-murray-mckenzie-4277889.43. Scott, C. (2017).

107 Green, C. (September 24, 2020). "Kimowan Metchewais's Search for Visual Sovereignty." *Aperture*. aperture.org/editorial/kimowan-metchewaiss-search-for-visual-sovereignty/.

108 Smithsonian Institution (n.d.) [website]. *Kimowan Metchewais* [McLain], 1991–2011. National Museum of the American Indian. sova.si.edu/record/NMAI.AC.084.

109 Stephen Bulger Gallery (n.d.) [website]. Meryl McMaster. www.bulgergallery.com/artists/122-meryl-mcmaster/overview/.

110 Pierre-François Ouellette Art Contemporain (n.d.). *Meryl McMaster*. www.pfoac.com/en/artists/32-meryl-mcmaster/works/2-oeuvres-phares-highlights/2071-meryl-mcmaster-on-the-edge-of-this-immensity-2019/.

111 Larry McNeil Photography (n.d). www.larrymcneil.com/about.

112 Larry McNeil Photography (n.d.)

113 Ossie Michelin (n.d.). osmich.ca/about/.

114 CBC News (January 20, 2014). "Ossie Michelin on his iconic fracking protest image." www.cbc.ca/news/canada/newfoundland-labrador/ossie-michelin-on-his-iconic-fracking-protest-image-1.2502891.

115 Jenny Irene Miller. www.jennyirenemiller.com/info.

116 Canadian Museum of History (n.d.) www.historymuseum.ca/cmc/exhibitions/tresors/ethno/etp0300e.html.

117 *Inuit Art Quarterly* (n.d.). "Peter Pitseolak." www.inuitartfoundation.org/profiles/artist/Peter-Pitseolak.

118 Saba, R. (October 23, 2018). "Through a different lens: Photographer Barry Pottle explores Ottawa's Inuit culture." www.ottawalife.com/article/through-a-different-lens-photographer-barry-pottle-explores-ottawas-inuit-culture?c=2.

119 *AGO Insider* (July 27, 2020), Artist Spotlight: Barry Pottle. http://ago.ca/agoinsider/barry-pottle

120 MacDonald-Dupuis, N. (December 16, 2015). "The Little-Known History of How the Canadian Government Made Inuit Wear 'Eskimo Tags". www.vice.com/en/article/xd7ka4/the-little-known-history-of-how-the-canadian-government-made-inuit-wear-eskimo-tags.

121 CBC Radio (July 28, 2017). "Beyond a number: Inuit photo exhibit brings controversial 'Eskimo' I.D. system to light." www.cbc.ca/radio/day6/episode-348-the week-in-trump-marketing-friendly-a-i-nasa-does-origami-inuit-photography-and-more-1.4222917/beyond-a-number-inuit-photo-exhibit-brings-controversial-eskimo-i-d-system-to-light-1.4222950.

122 B. Pottle, personal communication, September 12, 2022.

123 University of Pennsylvania Museum of Archaeology and Anthropology (n.d.) [website]. *The Louis Shotridge Digital Archive*. www.penn.museum/collections/shotridge/shotridgebio.html.

124 400 Years Project (n.d.) [website]. *Louis Shotridge (Stoowukáa).* www.400yearsproject.org/photographers/louis-shotridge.

125 400 Years Project (n.d.). [website]. *Kali Spitzer.* www.400yearsproject.org/photographers/kali-spitzer.

126 Kali Spitzer [website]. kalispitzer.photoshelter.com/about.

127 Greg Staats (n.d.) [website]. https://sites.google.com/view/gregstaats/home.

128 400 Years Project (n.d.) [website]. *Katherine Takpannie* www.400yearsproject.org/photographers/katherine-takpannie.

129 Washington State Arts Commission [website]. Jeffrey Thomas. www.arts.wa.gov/artist-collection/?request=record;id=4422;type=701.

130 National Gallery of Canada. *Jeffrey Thomas*. www.gallery.ca/collection/artist/jeffrey-thomas.

131 Rhoades, R. (2017, July) *The Keepers of Tradition*. Phoenix Home and Garden Magazine, 66-69

132 Sony (2022, March 14). *Fine Art Photographer Zoë Urness Wins Alpha Female+ Grant*. alphauniverse.com/stories/fine-art-photographer-zoe-urness-wins-alpha-femaleplus-grant/

INDEX

Note: Page numbers in **bold** indicate illustrations.

INDEX